ONTARIO

Pascale Couture
3rd edition

ULYSSES
TRAVEL PUBLICATIONS
Travel better... enjoy more

Author Pascale Couture	**Series Director** Claude Morneau	**Cover Photograph** Derek Trask, Superstock McFarland House, Niagara-on-the-Lake
Editing Tara Salman Stephanie Heidenreich	**Production Supervisor** Pascale Couture	**Interior Photographs** T. Beck (Megapress)
Translation Troy Davidson	**Layout** Christian Roy	J. Burke (Megapress) Emma (Megapress)
Danielle Gauthier Eric Hamovitch	**Cartography** André Duchesne	M. Grahame (Megapress) P. Quittemelle (Megapress)
Tracy Kendrick Sarah Kresh	*Assistants* Patrick Thivièrge	Oriane Lemaire Tibor Bognar
Janet Logan Suzanne Murray	Isabelle Lalonde	
Christina Poole	**Illustrations** Lorette Pierson Myriam Gagné	**Design** Patrick Farei (Atoll Direction)

Thanks to: Benoit Prieur, Lorette Pierson, Oriane Lemaire, Judy Hammond (Tourism Ontario).

DISTRIBUTORS

AUSTRALIA: Little Hills Press, 11/37-43 Alexander St., Crows Nest NSW 2065, ☎ (612) 437-6995, Fax: (612) 438-5762

BELGIUM AND LUXEMBOURG: Vander, Vrijwilligerlaan 321, B-1150 Brussel, ☎ (02) 762 98 04, Fax: (02) 762 06 62

CANADA: Ulysses Books & Maps, 4176 Saint-Denis, Montréal, Québec, H2W 2M5, ☎ (514) 843-9882, ext.2232, 800-748-9171, Fax: 514-843-9448, www.ulysses.ca

GERMANY AND AUSTRIA: Brettschneider, Fernreisebedarf, Feldfirchner Strasse 2, D-85551 Heimstetten, München, ☎ 89-99 02 03 30, Fax: 89-99 02 03 31, Brettschneider_Fernreisebedarf@t-online.de

GREAT BRITAIN AND IRELAND: World Leisure Marketing, Unit 11, Newmarket Court, Newmartket Drive, Derby DE24 8NW, ☎ 1 332 57 37 37, Fax: 1 332 57 33 99, E-mail: office@wlmsales.co.uk

ITALY: Centro Cartografico del Riccio, Via di Soffiano 164/A, 50143 Firenze, ☎ (055) 71 33 33, Fax: (055) 71 63 50

NETHERLANDS: Nilsson & Lamm, Pampuslaan 212-214, 1380 AD Weesp (NL), ☎ 0294-494949, Fax: 0294-494455, E-mail: nilam@euronet.nl

PORTUGAL: Dinapress, Lg. Dr. Antonio de Sousa de Macedo, 2, Lisboa 1200, ☎ (1) 395 52 70, Fax: (1) 395 03 90

SCANDINAVIA: Scanvik, Esplanaden 8B, 1263 Copenhagen K, DK, ☎ (45) 33.12.77.66, Fax: (45) 33.91.28.82

SPAIN: Altaïr, Balmes 69, E-08007 Barcelona, ☎ 454 29 66, Fax: 451 25 59, altair@globalcom.es

SWITZERLAND: OLF, P.O. Box 1061, CH-1701 Fribourg, ☎ (026) 467.51.11, Fax: (026) 467.54.66

U.S.A.: The Globe Pequot Press, 6 Business Park Road, P.O. Box 833, Old Saybrook, CT 06475, ☎ 1-800-243-0495, Fax: 800-820-2329, sales@globe-pequot.com

Other countries, contact Ulysses Books & Maps (Montréal), Fax: (514) 843-9448

«*Out on the lake the last thin threads of the mist are clearing away like flecks of cotton wool.*

The long call of the loon echoes over the lake. The air is cool and fresh. There is in it all the new life of land of the silent pine and the moving waters.»

Stephen Leacock
Sunshines Sketches of a Little Town

TABLE OF CONTENTS

WRITE TO US

The information contained in this guide was correct at press time. However, mistakes can slip in, omissions are always possible, places can disappear, etc. The authors and publisher hereby disclaim any liability for loss or damage resulting from omissions or errors.

We value your comments, corrections and suggestions, as they allow us to keep each guide up to date. The best contributions will be rewarded with a free book from Ulysses Travel Publications. All you have to do is write us at the following address and indicate which title you would be interested in receiving (see the list at the end of guide).

Ulysses Travel Publications
4176 Rue Saint-Denis
Montréal, Québec
Canada H2W 2M5
www.ulysses.ca
E-mail: guiduly@ulysses.ca

CATALOGUING

Couture, Pascale, 1966 -

        Ontario 3rd ed. (Ulysses travel guide)
        Translation of; Ontario.
        Includes index.

ISBN 2-89464-119-2

1. Ontario - Guidebooks. 2. Ontario - Tours. I. Title II. Series.

FC3057.C6813 1999   917.1304'4   C98-941533-3   F1057.7.C6813 1999

"We acknowledge the financial support of the Government of Canada through the Book Publishing Industry Development Program (BPIDP) for our publishing activities." We would also like to thank SODEC for their financial support.

Canada

LIST OF MAPS

MAP SYMBOLS

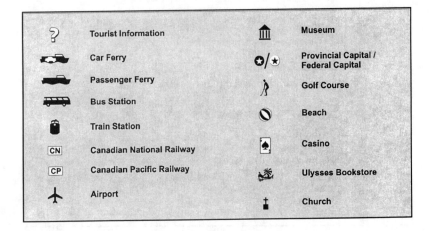

⁇	Tourist Information	🏛	Museum
🚗	Car Ferry	⊕/★	Provincial Capital / Federal Capital
🚢	Passenger Ferry	🏌	Golf Course
🚌	Bus Station	◓	Beach
🚉	Train Station	♠	Casino
CN	Canadian National Railway		Ulysses Bookstore
CP	Canadian Pacific Railway		
✈	Airport	✝	Church

SYMBOLS

🌴	Ulysses' favourite
☎	Telephone number
⊨	Fax number
=	Air conditioning
⊗	Ceiling fan
≈	Pool
ℜ	Restaurant
⊛	Whirlpool
ℝ	Refrigerator
K	Kitchenette
△	Sauna
⊘	Exercise room
tv	Colour television
pb	Private bathroom
sb	Shared bathroom
bkfst	Breakfast
✕	Pets allowed
♿	Wheelchair access
fb	Full board (lodging + 3 meals)
½b	Half-board (lodging + 2 meals)

ATTRACTION CLASSIFICATION

★	Interesting
★★	Worth a visit
★★★	Not to be missed

Admission prices in this guide are for one adult.

HOTEL CLASSIFICATION

Prices in the guide are for one room, double occupancy in high season.

RESTAURANT CLASSIFICATION

$	$10 or less
$$	$10 to $20
$$$	$20 to $30
$$$$	$30 or more

Prices in the guide are for a meal for one person, excluding drinks and tip.

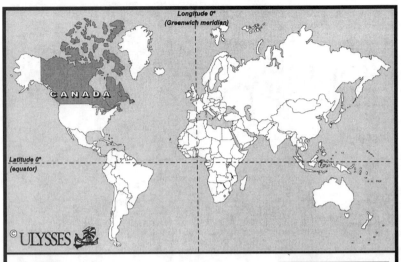

 Where is Ontario?

Ontario
Capital: Toronto
Population: 9,105,000 inhab.
Currency: Canadian dollar
Area: 1,068,630 km²

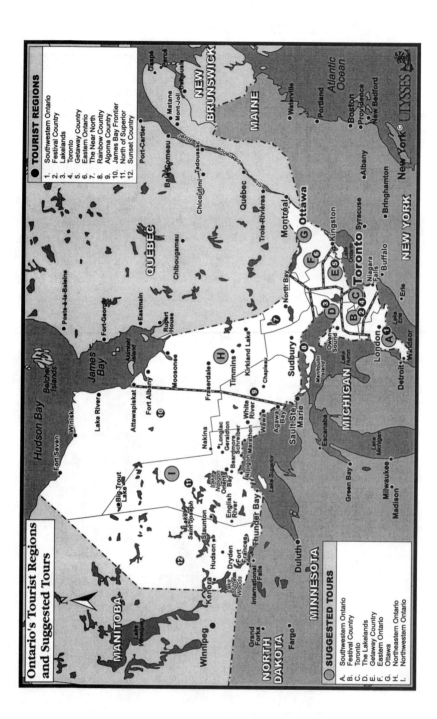

Ontario's Tourist Regions and Suggested Tours

PORTRAIT

Often the first image that comes to mind when thinking of Ontario is the Great Lakes, those tremendous expanses of fresh water surrounded by the untamed abundance of nature. Another obvious image invokes vast, fertile fields dotted with farmhouses charmingly adorned with balconies, shutters and flowers. Finally, there are those tiny hamlets with their splendid dwellings that in many cases have reigned over their surroundings for more than a century-and-a-half. And those towns with a priceless architectural heritage, silent witnesses to the prosperity of Canada's richest province. Rural Ontario certainly has plenty to delight romantic souls looking for tranquillity and a glimpse of the past, but this province also has an eminently modern, urban face. After all, it encompasses Toronto, Canada's biggest city, and Ottawa, its federal capital.

With a land mass of 1,068,000 km² (412,400 mi²), Ontario is the second biggest Canadian province in terms of surface area, behind only Québec. It is bordered to the east by Québec, to the west by Manitoba, to the north by Hudson Bay, and to the south by the United States. Part of its southern boundary is delineated by the 49th parallel, with the rest formed by lakes Superior, Huron, Erie and Ontario, and, furthest east, by the St. Lawrence River. These waterways allow easy access to much of Ontario and in the past set the basis for settlement of the province.

GEOGRAPHY

Tom Thomson and members of the Group of Seven were able to capture Ontario's natural beauty in paintings such as *The Jack Pine*, revealing wild landscapes that create a feeling of solitude and serenity. These typical scenes of the Canadian Shield are among the many faces of this province you will discover in the course of your travels.

The Canadian Shield

The Canadian Shield stretches in a semi-circle around Hudson Bay from Québec right into the Northwest Territories and covers a big chunk of Ontario. Formed in the pre-Cambrian period, this vast expanse of rock has endured the ravages of time, scraped bare by glaciers, which gave way to river and lake beds as well as to hills that are almost never more than 100 metres high. While the forests covering these lands have spurred prosperous industries, it is the subsoil that holds much of the wealth, with impressive deposits of gold, silver, nickel and other minerals.

The Forest

Very sparsely populated, the Canadian Shield is mostly covered by forest, which changes according to latitude. Southwestern Ontario, in the area around Hamilton well to the south of the Canadian Shield, is covered with **deciduous forest**, largely maple, beech, elm, oak and ash.

Deciduous forest yields quickly to **mixed forest** where broad-leaved trees such as maple and aspen are mixed with coniferous trees such as balsamic fir, larch and Banks pine. This extends along the St. Lawrence Valley and up to the boundaries of Ontario's middle north (including the areas around Sudbury and Thunder Bay).

Further north, deciduous trees become ever rarer, with the boreal forest dominated instead by conifers (mostly species of pine, larch, spruce and fir). This evergreen forest begins in Ontario's middle north and gives way in turn to transitional boreal forest containing smaller forms of vegetation that are better adapted to the rigours of the northern climate.

The harsh climate in the province's far north is characterized by long and very cold winters, short summers with fewer than 120 frost-free days, and low rainfall. This allows only stunted forms of vegetation to develop. Tundra dominates a small parcel of territory, where only miniature trees, lichens and moss can grow.

Agriculture

The St. Lawrence plain and the far southwest of the province form the breadbasket of Ontario. Wheat, corn, tobacco, vegetables and other crops are grown on these fertile plains, which are well suited to agriculture. A special microclimate favours the Niagara region, with its peach and cherry orchards and its vineyards.

The Lakes

Ontario prides itself on having four of the five Great Lakes (Ontario, Erie, Huron and Superior) form its southern and southwestern boundaries. (Lake Michigan, the fifth of the Great Lakes, lies entirely within the United States.) These expanses of fresh water are truly enormous: the smallest of them, Lake Ontario, covers area of 19,529 km² (7,540 mi²), while Lake Superior, the biggest fresh-water lake in the world, covers 82,414 km² (31,820 mi²). They were formed during the retreat of the glaciers in the Quaternary period. These lakes are the main source of the St. Lawrence, a majestic river crossing the southeastern part of the province and through Québec before emptying into the Atlantic Ocean.

Besides the Great Lakes and St. Lawrence River, Ontario has about 400,000 other lakes and rivers. These have played a defining role in the history of the province. They were a source of essential food to indigenous nations and provided the main access into the territory.

FAUNA

Moose, deer, foxes and beavers are among the animal species inhabiting Ontario forests. To help you recognize them, here is a brief description of some of them. We shall not even attempt to give a thorough description of bird-life, for many hundreds of species can be observed year-round. You will, however, find bird-watching information in the "Outdoor Activities" sections of some chapters in this guide, with descriptions of good birding spots.

The Deer Family

The **moose** is the biggest of the *Cervidae,* nearly two metres high and weighing up to 600 kilograms (more than 1,300 pounds). It is easily distinguished by its long head, round nose, the hump on its back and its brown coat. Males have enormous antlers. Moose are found near streams in the north of the province. There are many in Algonquin Park.

The **white-tailed deer** is noted for its reddish-brown coat and its white tail. This deer is scarcely a metre high. It is found in forests in the southern part of the province, where it is relatively easy to observe. With few natural enemies apart from wolves and bears, it often forms oversized herds. Pinery and Ron-

deau parks are good places to observe this species.

Predators

The **wolf** lives in packs. It resembles a grey German-shepherd-type dog, is between 67 and 95 centimetres long, and weighs at most about 50 kilograms. It attacks its prey (often deer) in packs, making it unpopular with some animal-lovers. There have even been efforts in the past to eliminate it completely. These efforts failed, but they did reduce the numbers living in the wild. It is fairly common for campers in provincial parks to hear wolves howling, but they rarely approach human beings.

Wolf

The **coyote** is another canine predator. Smaller than the wolf, it is about 40 centimetres long and weighs about 15 kilograms. Its coat is grey and reddish-brown. This is another predator that, at one time, was slated for extermination. There remain a good number today despite trappers and hunters. They are found mostly in the bush.

The **fox** is a cute little reddish-brown animal with magnificent fur. It is found throughout the Ontario forest, but this cunning animal often avoids inhabited areas and visitors, and thus is rarely seen. It hunts alone and also feeds on berries and nuts.

The **black bear** is the most dangerous animal in the southern Ontario forest. Accidents are rare, but each year some visitors are mauled by this beautiful black animal. It is sometimes seen in parks, particularly in places where food can be found (campers: don't leave out any bait!). It is mostly nocturnal. This is the smallest bear in Canada, about 1.5 metres long and about 220 kilograms in weight.

The **raccoon** is easily identifiable. This little grey animal, scarcely bigger than a cat, has a black mask around its eyes and a black-and-grey-striped tail. It is seen frequently and does not hesitate to rummage through garbage or through campers' food. Beware: it is best not to feed it. It is omnivorous and seems to like everything, and is often found in cities. To compensate for its weak salivary glands, it wets its food before eating, which has lead some to believe it is a fastidious creature, this trait is at the origin of its name in French, *raton-laveur*, which translates literally as "little washing rat."

The **skunk** is a little black animal distinguished by white stripes on its back and its bushy tail. But it is identified most of all by the very unpleasant odour it can give off. It defends itself by spraying its enemies with a foul-smelling liquid.

Rodents

Canada's emblem, the **beaver**, is found near bodies of water, where it builds its lodge. The technique is simple: it cuts down several trees to form a dam that controls the water level, and then it builds its lodge! It is an excellent swimmer. This small brown animal, found mostly in the water, has a flat, spiky tail. With few means of defence, it has been heavily hunted, although there remain many in Ontario.

The **prairie dog** is also known as the dormouse. This small, pale brown animal is often found in the fields, where it lives in groups of about 20. It feeds on roots and herbs, and can quickly destroy crops. This explains the concern of farmers who find this animal in their fields. It is often hunted down.

The **porcupine** is a small rodent that abounds in coniferous forests and also in deciduous forests. It is well known for its unusual way of defending itself. In case of danger, it curls up, extends its bristles, and forms a sort of unassailable pin cushion.

HISTORY

When Europeans discovered the New World, a mosaic of indigenous peoples had already occupied this vast continent for thousands of years. The ancestors of these native groups crossed the Bering Strait toward the end of the last Ice Age, more than 12,000 years ago, and gradually occupied the entire continent. It was during the following millennia, encouraged by the retreat of the

Skunk

PORTRAIT

glaciers, that some of them began to migrate toward the most northerly lands of Eastern Canada.

When Europeans launched their first intensive explorations of North America, several nations grouped according to two linguistic families (Iroquoian and Algonquian) shared the territory that would later be known as Ontario. Living in bands, the native societies had to adapt themselves to the characteristics of the territory they occupied. The Algonquian nations who, in most cases lived in the middle north and the north of Ontario, developed a way of life suited to a rigorous climate that was too cold for agriculture. They were nomads, living in small bands and subsisting mostly from hunting. In contrast, the Iroquoian nations in the south were much more sedentary. The land they lived on enabled them to prosper from agriculture, which provided most of their food. The Iroquois lived in big villages, often protected by wooden palisades, some of them with populations over 1,000.

Efficient systems of communication and trading became established over the centuries between these Amerindian bands and nations. Using a barter system, the natives of southern Ontario traded their farming produce for furs from their more northerly neighbours, the Algonquians. The use of canoes along the many rivers and lakes lay at the heart of this system. Although they succeeded in making good use of the resources and the special characteristics of the lands they lived on, these societies would face unprecedented challenges with the arrival of Europeans beginning in the 16th century.

Iroquois – Senea
– Mohawk
– Huron

The Meeting of Two Civilizations

Toward the year 1000, Viking explorers had taken advantage of a climatic warming to sail along the eastern coast of what is now Canada. They also fished and built settlements there. It was not until several centuries later, however, with the first voyage of Christopher Columbus in 1492, that Europeans really began their intensive exploration and colonization of the American continent. In Canada, the first European expeditions that would have long-lasting results were led by John Cabot and, later, by Jacques Cartier.

John Cabot, born Giovanni Caboto, obtained financial and political support in England and set sail from the port of Bristol in 1497 and headed west. Cabot was looking for a route that would lead him to the much coveted riches of the Orient. His explorations ended instead in Newfoundland. Nonetheless, Cabot's expedition would have important consequences. Back in England, he spoke of the great riches he had discovered, the seemingly inexhaustible cod banks off the northern shores of the New World. From then on, English, French, Basque and Spanish fishermen left European ports in ever greater numbers in search of this marine wealth off Newfoundland.

In 1534, the Breton navigator Jacques Cartier launched the first of his three North American expeditions. Cartier was mandated by King François I to find gold and a passage to Asia. Cartier did not find either of these, although his expeditions did lead him up the St. Lawrence River as far as the site of the present-day city of Montréal. Disappointed by Cartier's discoveries, the French authorities soon abandoned any further exploration of this territory, which they considered inhospitable.

S. de Champlain

Even so, the expeditions of Cabot and Cartier were the prelude to colonization efforts in the following centuries.

A few decades later, the growing fashion among Europeans for fur hats and clothing, and the huge profits expected from this trade, rekindled the French authorities' interest in North America. The fur trade required constant contact with native suppliers, and a permanent presence thus became necessary. It was mostly for purposes of trade that posts were created at Québec in 1608 and at Montréal in 1642. In the following decades, these two posts along the St. Lawrence River would become the heart of New France.

Located deeper in the interior, far from the Atlantic coast and from the easily navigable portion of the St. Lawrence River, the Ontario territory was not considered suitable for colonization by French authorities. Its lands were surveyed nevertheless by French explorers. In 1610, only two years after the founding of Québec, the explorer Étienne Brûlé set out to discover the interior of the continent. Like several of his predecessors, Brûlé was seeking a route that could lead him quickly across the continent to the fabulous riches of the Orient. Travelling alone, he was the first European to reach Lake Ontario and Lake Huron.

A few years later, in 1615, Étienne Brûlé launched a new westward expedition, accompanied this time by the great explorer Samuel de Champlain, founder of the post at Québec. Champlain and Brûlé got as far as the shores of Georgian Bay, where an agreement was concluded between the French and the Huron Indians who inhabited the area. The Hurons agreed to trade exclusively with the French who, in return, offered them protection against their traditional Iroquois enemies who lived further south.

Even though the fur trade continued to lie at the origin of colonization efforts during this period, the New World also held great interest for French religious orders. The Récollets arrived first, in 1615, before being replaced by the Jesuits starting in 1632. They saw the evangelization of the natives as an unprecedented opportunity to extend Christianity. In 1639, deep in the Ontario hinterland on the shores of Georgian Bay explored earlier by Brûlé and Champlain, a small group of Jesuits founded the mission of Sainte-Marie Among the Hurons, near the present-day town of Midland. The agreement allying them with the French was probably the main reason the Hurons accepted this religious presence. The mission was abandoned a few years later, however, after five Jesuits perished during the military defeats that the Hurons suffered at Iroquois hands in 1648 and 1649.

This war was part of an extensive offensive campaign launched by the powerful Iroquois Five Nations confederacy between 1645 and 1655 intended to wipe out all rival nations. The Hurons, the Petuns, the Eries and the Neutrals each at least 10,000 strong, were almost completely annihilated within the space of ten years. These Iroquoian-speaking nations of southern Ontario were essentially victims of the war for the monopoly of the fur trade conducted by the European powers through intermediaries. Allied with the English, the Five Nations confederacy, whose traditional territories lay further south in what is now the United States, wanted to appropriate this lucrative trade for itself. The Iroquois military offensive even threatened the existence of the French colony. During 1660 and 1661, Iroquois warriors struck everywhere in New France, bringing a halt to the fur trade and ruining crops. French King Louis XIV reacted by sending in troops that succeeded in "pacifying" these natives.

The following years were marked by heavy growth in the fur trade, with Montréal at its centre. This period in the history of New France is also that which coincides with the glorious era of the *coureurs des bois*, literally the "runners of the woods." Leaving their lands behind, these intrepid young men headed deep into the back country, crisscrossing the territory of what is now Ontario, to trade directly with native fur suppliers.

Helped by the expeditions of these trappers and also by missionaries and explorers, French claims in North America grew rapidly. New France reached its zenith at the dawn of the 18th century, with a strong hold over the North American fur trade, control over the St. Lawrence River and the Great Lakes, and plans to further exploit its lands in Louisiana. These strategic positions enabled it to limit the expansion of the far more populous English colonies, wedged in the territory between the Atlantic Ocean and the Appalachian mountains. But France, after being conquered in Europe, agreed under the terms of the Treaty of Utrecht of 1713 to turn over official control of Hudson Bay, Newfoundland and Acadia to the English. This treaty led to New France's loss of strategic military positions, weakening it severely and presaging its downfall.

In the following years, the noose kept tightening around New France. When the Seven Years' War (1756-63) broke out in Europe, the North American colonies quickly became one of the key stakes. On the territory of present-day Ontario, French troops managed in the early years to contain the British thrust and to remain masters of navigation on the Great Lakes. The French forces were small in numbers, but they held strategic positions: Fort Frontenac, at the mouth of Lake Ontario; Niagara, an important link between Lake Ontario and Lake Erie; Detroit, situated at the point of Lake Erie; Michilimackinac, where lakes Michigan and Huron meet; and Fort Rouillé, built in the excellent port at the site that is now called Toronto. One after another, however, each of these fortifications would fall into British hands. Although Montréal was the last city to fall, in 1760, the fate of New France had already been sealed the previous year in Québec in the famous battle of the Plains of Abraham. By the Treaty of Paris, in 1763, France officially gave up all its North American possessions to England.

British North America

In the early years after the British conquest of Canada, little changed in Ontario, which remained a vast and largely unoccupied territory, apart from Amerindian bands and fur traders. The British Crown did not decree any colonization or development plans during this period apart from the fur trade. Ironically, it was the American War of Independence (1775-83) that would give birth to Ontario, radically changing the history of Canada.

In the early years of the conflict that pitted England against insurgents in its 13 southern colonies, British forces established strategic positions in Ontario from which they launched attacks against the American rebels. Overall, however, the war went against the British troops and their allies, and they finally had to concede defeat. The American Revolution, at least in the beginning, had been a genuine civil war between two factions: the supporters of independence and the Loyalists who wished to maintain colonial ties with the British. More than 350,000 of these loyalists played an active part, fighting on the British side.

The signing of the Treaty of Versailles in 1783, which recognized the British defeat at the hands of the American Revolutionaries, pushed tens of thousands of these Loyalists to seek refuge in Canada. Between 5,000 and 6,000 of them settled on the virgin western lands of what is now Ontario and developed the first permanent colonies in this territory. Most of them settled along the northern shore of the St. Lawrence River and Lake Ontario in the area around what are now Prince Edward County and the city of Kingston, as well as in the Niagara region. Some Indian bands that had fought alongside the British were granted lands in the Grand River Valley.

Until the arrival of the Loyalists, few citizens of British descent had emigrated to Canada, apart from some merchants who took the place of the French in the fur trade. Thus, two decades after the British conquest, the backgrounds of the vast majority of the Canadian population remained French and Catholic. With the rise of pro-independence feelings in the 13 southern colonies, the British Crown gave them the right to maintain their religion and customs to ensure the loyalty of these former subjects of the King of France.

To keep the Loyalists from being in a minority, while at the same time upholding the rights of French Catholics, London promulgated the Constitutional Act of 1791 dividing Canada into two provinces, Lower Canada and Upper Canada. Lower Canada, with its large French majority, remained subject to French civil law, while Upper Canada, located west of the Ottawa River, was inhabited mostly by Loyalists of British stock and was subject to English common law. The Constitutional Act also introduced to Canada the beginnings of a parliamentary system, with the creation of a House of Assembly in each of the provinces.

Upper Canada at first chose Newark, in the Niagara region, as its capital. But this did not last long, for the site was poorly protected and could easily fall if the Americans decided to invade Canada. In August 1793, Toronto, an easily defended port a good distance from the American border, was chosen to be capital of the new province. This site was strategic, but it remained virtually uninhabited. That same year, a little colony was set up along the Don River. Known as York until 1834, the capital of Upper Canada had only 800 inhabitants in 1810, and it would have been difficult then to predict its brilliant future.

The Upper Canadian settlers certainly had reason to mistrust their southern neighbours, who soon justified these fears. In 1812, allegedly fed up with excessive British control over the Great Lakes, the Americans declared war on Britain and, thus, on Canada. Loyalists and their descendants still formed the majority of Upper Canada's population, lending a rather emotional aspect to this conflict. Britain, tied down in Europe by the Napoleonic Wars, could not provide significant aid to its colony. The settlers managed nonetheless to repulse the American attacks and to inflict on the United States of America the first military defeat in its young history.

Even though its downfall had been narrowly avoided, Upper Canada's geographic isolation became evident in the War of 1812. Quite apart from rendering the colony vulnerable in wartime, the various sets of rapids that blocked navigation along the St. Lawrence River and between the Great Lakes limited commercial trade with the colony even in peacetime. To open the route to Upper Canada, canals were built in several places, notably at Lachine, in 1814, and at Welland, in 1824. The fear of a new American invasion even led colonial authorities to approve the building of the Rideau Canal (1828-32), a difficult project that provided a direct link between Fort Henry (now Kingston) and the Ottawa River that bypassed the St. Lawrence River, whose southern shore forms the border with the United States. Where this canal meets the Ottawa River, a small colony was born and given the name Bytown; later in 1855, it was renamed Ottawa and became the federal capital of Canada.

Immigrants began arriving, mostly from the British Isles, and joined the Loyalist inhabitants who had been settling in Upper Canada since 1783, slowly occupying the province's agricultural lands. With a population made up mostly of Loyalist descendants and new immigrants from the British Isles, the British colonial status created few arguments, and allegiance to the Crown was never seriously questioned. In Lower Canada, however, with its French Catholic majority, colonial authority was more difficult to tolerate. Starting in the mid-1830s, there were growing demands for reforms, inspired by the liberal revolutions that had already shaken several countries in Europe. In 1837, after London refused any compromise with the people of Lower Canada, rebellions broke out in Montréal and in several rural communities.

Many people in Upper Canada looked askance at this challenge to British authority in mostly French-speaking Lower Canada. But political strife was brewing in Upper Canada as well, with calls for a more representative form of government than London was willing to concede and for an end to the power wielded by the Family Compact, a small clique that controlled much of the col-

ony's economic and political life. William Lyon Mackenzie, a radical journalist and politician, led an armed rebellion in Toronto in 1837 that was quickly put down. Mackenzie himself fled to the United States.

In response to these rebellions, London sent an emissary, Lord Durham, to study the situation and to seek solutions to the colonies' problems. Expecting to find a people united against colonial authority, Durham noted that it was more the French-speaking inhabitants of Lower Canada who rejected British rule. In his famous report, Durham proposed a radical solution to settle the Canadian problem once and for all: assimilate the French-speaking colonists. Inspired by the Durham report, London promulgated the Act of Union of 1840, unifying the two colonies into one, with English as the sole official language.

The following year, Kingston, a small military garrison that had become an active little town because of the Rideau Canal, was chosen as the seat of Parliament. But this choice failed to please everyone. Toronto, Montréal and Québec City all felt cheated. Two years later, the seat of Parliament was moved to Montréal before being moved back to Kingston in 1849. Queen Victoria finally decided in favour of Ottawa in 1855, an astonishing choice given Ottawa's small size and its distance from the main communication routes, but it did have the advantage of being on the border between Canada West (formerly Upper Canada) and Canada East (formerly Lower Canada).

If the period preceding the Act of Union was characterized by great canal-building projects, it was the construction of the railways that took over starting in the 1850s. Railways were regarded as a new panacea for Canada West's communication challenges. Big projects were undertaken, among them the building of what was then called the Grand Trunk Railway linking Montréal with Sarnia. Several other lines connected with the American railway networks.

These immense undertakings burdened the public finances with debt. At the same time, the Canadian economy suffered a blow when Britain abandoned its policies of mercantilism and preferential tariffs toward its colonies. To absorb the shocks of this sweeping change in British colonial policy, Canada signed a treaty in 1854 with the United States allowing the free entry of certain goods, among them wood and wheat, Canada's main exports at the time. The Canadian economy had barely begun to recover when the treaty was repudiated in 1866 under pressure from American business interests. The abandonment of the colonial preference and then of the treaty of reciprocity hit the Canadian economy hard. It was in this climate of economic gloom, and partly because of it, that the Canadian Confederation was born.

Confederation

Upper Canada was reshaped under the 1867 Confederation, adopting the name Province of Ontario, from an Iroquoian word probably meaning beautiful lakes or beautiful waters, an obvious reference to the province's hydrographic wealth. Three other provinces, Québec (formerly Lower Canada), New Brunswick and Nova Scotia joined this pact, which was soon to unite a vast territory reaching from the Atlantic to the Pacific. The confederation pact established a division of powers between two layers of government, the federal government, based in Ottawa, and the provincial governments, with

Ontario choosing Toronto as its capital. This capital of the former Upper Canada had become an important commercial city over the decades and the province's biggest population centre, with about 45,000 inhabitants.

From a political standpoint, the establishment of the federal system turned to Ontario's advantage. In the new Parliament in Ottawa, the number of members representing each province was proportionate to its population. Ontario, which has remained the most populous of the Canadian provinces since that time, had much to gain from this new deal. In the preceding decades, the availability of excellent lands had drawn a growing number of new arrivals, mostly from the British Isles, leading to strong population growth.

From an economic standpoint, Confederation failed initially to provide the expected results. It was not until three decades had passed, characterized by sharp fluctuations, that Ontario really experienced its first great period of rapid economic growth. The foundations for this growth were laid several years after Confederation by Sir John A. Macdonald, the federal Conservative prime minister re-elected in 1878 after five years out of office. His electoral campaign had centred around his National Policy, a series of measures aimed at protecting and promoting Canada's nascent industries by means of protective tariffs, the creation of a big internal market unified by a transcontinental railway, and the growth of this internal market by a policy of populating the Prairies through massive immigration.

The settlement of southern Ontario's remaining lands, population growth, urbanization, industrialization and development of natural resources were matters of pride to residents of European descent, but they marked painful setbacks for most of the native people living in Ontario as the century drew to a close, threatening their traditional way of life. Before the century ended, the federal government stepped in and created reserves, territories granted to natives under state control. For those who accepted the reserve system, the lands put at their disposal represented the lesser of evils but also put an end to the autonomy and freedom essential to their traditions and way of life. Ultimately, the meeting of the two cultures could not take place without one of them virtually disappearing.

Growth and Internationalization

The beginning of the 20th century coincided with the start of a period of prodigious economic growth for Ontario, lasting until the Great Depression of the 1930s. Euphoric and optimistic, like so many other Canadians, Sir Wilfrid Laurier, federal Prime Minister from 1896 to 1911, predicted that the 20th century would be Canada's. Laurier perhaps ought to have predicted that the century would be Ontario's. Macdonald's National Policy had borne fruit and launched Ontario into a process of speedy industrialization. Ontario's geographic location benefited its industries with the proximity of the growing new markets of Western Canada, where rapid population growth created a strong demand for various manufactured goods, now made in Canada instead of Britain. In the decades to come and long after that, heavy industry would form the backbone of the province's industrial structure, with rich iron ore deposits in the north providing some of the raw material.

Ontario's industrial growth was part of a continental movement in both Canada and the United States that favoured the Great Lakes region to the disadvantage of the older industrial centres further east. Naturally, this industrialization brought about a massive population exodus toward places such as Toronto and other cities around the Great Lakes. Although increasingly deserted, the countryside managed to increase and diversify its farm production with the introduction of new techniques. This unprecedented growth of the Ontario economy certainly did not benefit the whole population equally. Industrialization led to often insalubrious new residential districts where poorly paid workers clustered.

When the First World War broke out in Europe, the Canadian government joined at Britain's side without hesitation. It quickly set itself the goal of mobilizing 500,000 men, a colossal effort for a country of about eight million people. Since there were not enough volunteers, the government considered imposing conscription, knowing well that the country was divided on this question, with the majority of English-speaking Canadians, mostly Ontarians, remaining strongly attached to Britain and highly favourable to conscription, while on the other hand a majority of French Canadians were vehemently opposed. French Canadian feelings of ambiguity toward the British were reinforced when loyalist Ontario promulgated a regulation in 1912 aimed at forbidding the teaching of French in the schools that were to serve those who had settled recently in Ontario's middle north as farmers, woodcutters or miners. Ontario's political weight carried the day, and conscription was adopted in 1917, not without violent demonstrations in Québec.

The war years had considerable repercussions on Canada's social life. Lacking male workers, factories turned to a female workforce, giving women a

PORTRAIT

social role they had not known previously. Even though most women returned to their traditional place in society after the war, their demands were no less ambitious than before. In 1917, even before the war ended, the federal and Ontario governments had already decided to accord voting rights to women, a plea that had long gone unanswered. In another matter, the prohibition on the sale and consumption of alcohol in Ontario, a measure adopted only for the duration of the war, now seemed to have many supporters. Even as the province lay on the verge of entering the Roaring Twenties, a majority of Ontario voters decided in a 1919 referendum to maintain the prohibition on alcohol.

The Ontario economy emerged from the First World War stronger than ever, and the following decade was marked by continual economic growth. But between 1929 and 1945 two big world events, the Great Depression and the Second World War, shook Canada's political, economic and social life severely. The Depression, perceived at first as a cyclical and temporary phenomenon, endured in a decade-long nightmare. The Canadian economy, very dependent on foreign markets, collapsed with the slowing of international trade. Faced with the growing misery that was spreading everywhere, governments finally decided to intervene. A system of family allowances was set up, a prelude to the post-war welfare state. In 1935 the federal government created the Bank of Canada, thereby seeking to increase its control over the monetary and financial systems. In late summer of 1939, the Second World War broke out in Europe, and Canada became involved officially on September 10 of that year. After ten years of economic crisis, Canadians entered the war in a spirit of gloom. The war would have the effect of reviving the Canadian economy, however.

Canada's total commitment during the war rose to 600,000 soldiers.

The Contemporary Era

The end of the Second World War began an exciting period of economic growth, with the Depression-induced collapse in consumption and the rationing of wartime finally laid to rest. In the decades following the war, the Ontario economy moved ahead at full throttle, and subsequent economic crises, up to the 1980s, were short and inconsequential. Ontario's domination of the Canadian economy became symbolized by Toronto surpassing long-time rival Montréal during the 1970s to become the biggest city in Canada. The remarkable performance of the Ontario economy was largely due to the proximity of the United States, which absorbed three-quarters of its international exports and whose big corporations set up branch plants in Ontario. For example, in the automobile industry, the big American companies agreed in the 1960s to guarantee that a certain portion of their vehicles would be built in Canada under the terms of what was called the Auto Pact. Southern Ontario became home to most of these automobile plants.

Economic growth lead to an increase in immigration to Ontario after interruptions during the Depression and war years. In the quarter-century following the war, Ontario received nearly two million immigrants, almost two-thirds of the Canadian total during that period. No longer did the majority of immigrants come from the British Isles, as had been the case before. At first immigrants came mostly from southern and eastern Europe, and later from all parts of the world. In the space of only a few decades, Ontario's cultural face was changed radically.

Economic growth also lead to a remarkable degree of political stability in Ontario. The Conservative party, which led the provincial government at the end of the war, held onto power without interruption until 1985. Even in the 1985 election, the Conservatives managed to elect more members than any other party, though the New Democratic Party's support of the Liberals lead to an alliance that was able to replace the Conservatives. The Liberal reign of five years saw the adoption of several progressive laws by the Ontario legislative assembly. The 1990 election led to a surprising sweep of Ontario by the New Democratic Party. Coinciding with a long economic recession, however, the NDP's period in power was also limited to five years. The Conservatives were brought back in 1995, elected on a platform of drastic measures aimed at cutting the provincial deficit.

POLITICS

The British North America Act, the constitutional document that forms the basis of Canada's 1867 Confederation, divides power between two levels of government. Besides the federal government in Ottawa, each of the ten Canadian provinces, including Ontario, elect their own governments with the power to legislate in certain areas. Based on the British model, the political systems in Canada and Ontario give legislative power to parliaments elected by universal suffrage. The political party with the greatest number of elected members forms the government except in very rare cases where very close results allow the government to be formed by a coalition between the second-place and third-place parties. This is what happened after the 1985 Ontario election when the Liberal Party obtained the support of the New Democratic Party to prevent the Conservatives from forming the government even though the Conservatives had won more seats than either of the other two parties on their own.

Elections are usually held every four years, but a government can prolong its mandate for up to five years. Unlike the systems in the United States, the party in power decides on the timing of elections, which are based on a simple plurality in single-member constituencies. As in Britain, this usually leads to battles between only two strong parties.

On the federal scene, two political parties, the Liberal Party and the Progressive Conservative Party, have traditionally taken turns governing Canada ever since Confederation in 1867. The current Canadian prime minister, Jean Chrétien, was elected under the Liberal banner in 1993 and again in 1997. He succeeded Conservative Prime Minister Brian Mulroney, who had won the 1984 and 1988 federal elections before giving up his post to the party's new leader Kim Campbell near the end of his second mandate.

In Canadian political history, the 1993 federal election was doubtless a watershed, for it led to an unprecedented realignment of the political spectrum, with the Conservatives and New Democrats nearly wiped out. After nine years in power, the Conservatives fell victim to a general feeling of discontent among the Canadian people. The New Democrats, the eternal third-place finishers on the federal scene, saw a decline in popular support for their left-leaning program, especially after the difficult time in power for the Ontario Provincial Conservatives under Bob Rae, who had been elected in 1990.

At the same time, the 1993 federal election results showed the growing popularity of two new regional political parties, the Bloc Québécois and the Reform Party, whose respective programs address some of Canada's current political concerns in very different ways. Born following the collapse of the Meech Lake Accord which sought to offer Québec special status within Canada, the Bloc Québécois set its sights on Québec's departure from the Canadian federal system.

The 1997 elections, however, saw another Liberal Victory but also brought the NDPs under Alexa McDonough and the Conservatives under Jean Charest (now leader of the Québec Liberal Party) back to life.

The current Canadian Prime Minister, Jean Chrétien, has often been portrayed as the less talented spiritual heir to Pierre Elliott Trudeau, who was Prime Minister from 1968 to 1979 and 1980 to 1984. Trudeau, fiercely opposed to Québec nationalism, self-assured, recalcitrant, but with a charm that led to a real Trudeau-mania, personified a pan-Canadian nationalism for an entire era. His vision of the country found a receptive response in Ontario, and even today it is probably Ontarians who have the most Trudeau-esque view of Canada. Support from Ontario is nearly always pivotal at election time, for this one province accounts for about one-third of the seats in the federal Parliament.

As for provincial politics, the Conservative party has traditionally held sway in Ontario. In fact, between 1943 and 1985, the province was governed without interruption by Conservative premiers. Although they have had to make compromises, especially at times of minority governments, the Conservatives have never been very warm to the idea of promoting the interests of women, the poor or minorities such as the numerous French-speaking people in the northern part of the province. The 1985 election put an end to the long Conservative reign in Ontario, though the results still favoured the Conservatives, who won 52 seats against 48 for the Liberals and 25 for the New Democrats. It took a coalition between David Peterson's Liberals and Bob Rae's New Democrats to end nearly a half-century of Conservative rule in Ontario.

Peterson became premier of the province and enacted a proactive law on equal wages for women. Two important matters greatly reduced his popularity with the electorate, however. One was the Free Trade Agreement with the United States. The other was the Meech Lake Accord, which sought to offer Québec a special status within the Canadian Confederation but which two provinces failed to ratify. Peterson was opposed to the Free Trade Agreement but could not persuade the federal government to back off on this deal, which a majority of Ontarians saw as negative for their province's economic development. As for Meech Lake, which eventually fell through, Peterson gave it his support despite opposition from many people in Ontario.

Peterson was beaten in the 1990 provincial election but, to almost everyone's surprise, he was replaced by the New Democrats, lead by a brilliant intellectual, Bob Rae. During their years in coalition with the Liberals, Rae and his party had succeeded in ridding the party of its left-wing image, thereby winning the confidence of many Ontarians. Rae's five years as premier turned out to be very difficult, however, because of a harsh economic recession which lead to an increase in the province's debt. Like his predecessor, Rae was to hold power for only five years. In 1995, he was replaced by Mike Harris of the Conservative party, the essence of whose platform was to

PORTRAIT

fight tooth and nail against the deficit through radical cuts in government services.

ECONOMY

Very early in the colonial period, the province's economy was centred mainly around the fur trade. With the arrival of numerous settlers starting in the 18th century in southern Ontario, endowed with some of Canada's best farmland, agriculture began to develop and became the province's main economic activity. Two centuries later, farming is still a major activity, mainly producing wheat, corn and vegetables. Ontario also ranks second, just behind Québec, in Canadian milk production. The vast forests in the north of the province have also been put to use. The Ontario paper industry supplied England at first, early in the 19th century, and later found excellent markets in the United States with the development of newspapers there.

The beginning of the 20th century gave rise to the discovery of substantial mineral deposits in the north of the province, especially cobalt, nickel, silver, iron and zinc. In the 1950s, the world's richest uranium deposit was discovered near Elliot Lake. These discoveries, together with development of the railway network, spurred settlement in the north of the province and contributed substantially to the province's economic prosperity for a good part of the 20th century.

The Ontario economy has also counted on a very solid industrial sector, the most dynamic in Canada, which developed rapidly starting in the late 19th century. Although the service sector is playing an increasing role, just as elsewhere in the industrialized world, Ontario's very diversified heavy industry is still one of the jewels of the province's economy and has long benefited from its strategic location in the centre of Canada and close to the United States. This is one of the main reasons for the economic success of Ontario, the wealthiest of Canadian provinces, with nearly 40 per cent of the gross national product.

ARCHITECTURE

When the first European colonists arrived here, what is now Ontario was already populated with Native people who belonged to two linguistic groups: the Algonquians who inhabited the northern part of Ontario and the Iroquois who lived in the southern part, in the St. Lawrence Valley and on the shores of the Great Lakes. Their wood and bark dwellings were the first architectural forms to be built on this land. The Amerindians of the Iroquois Nation built "long houses" covered with bark in which all the members of a clan or family group would live. A village was comprised of several long houses, the average size being 24 m by 8 m, and was enclosed by a wooden fence. No authentic villages remain today because of the materials used, but some very beautiful reconstructions have been made such as in Midland where a Huron village (Sainte-Marie Among the Hurons, see p 217) has been reproduced. The Algonquians, who were nomadic people, developed the *wigwam*, a living space that was easy to dismantle and transport. Made of tree trunks driven into the ground and tied together at the top, the *wigwam* was covered with bark and could shelter one or two families.

The French founded New France in 1608 and travelled all over the vast hinterland that is today's Ontario from as early as 1615. Military and commercial demands soon prompted them to construct wooden forts at strategic spots where they could keep watch over the waterways, their main lines of communication. The first forts were erected at the end of the 17th century in Kingston (Fort Frontenac) and in Windsor, on the shores of Lake Ontario and Lake Erie respectively. Several trading posts were also built for the lucrative fur trade. The French did not control this territory for long however, because in 1763 it passed into the hands of the British. New forts were then erected by the British, often on the sites of the former French forts.

The real colonization of the Ontario territory began only when the American War of Independence (1775-1783) ended. Some 6,000 Loyalists left the United States and came to Ontario where they settled mainly on the banks of the St. Lawrence River and Lake Ontario. They were American settlers who wanted to remain faithful to the British Crown. Towards the end of the 18th century, three fairly large towns had developed on Lake Ontario: Kingston, York (today Toronto) and Newark (Niagara-on-the-Lake). Several towns in the Ottawa River Valley were also founded. In near-virgin land, the newcomers had to quickly make themselves a place to live; their dwellings were constructed very simply just to give them a roof over their heads.

From the beginning of the 19th century, impressive buildings began to appear. The new settlers kept their architectural traditions, favouring the Georgian style of building construction. Made of cut stone and in a strict, symmetrical manner, their houses towered up on the horizon. Perth (see p 107) has the most elegant residences built in this architectural style. Toronto also has a few impressive examples such as The Grange (see p 176), a magnificent former residence.

Nevertheless, most settlers were not able to build themselves such lavish homes and had to make do with log cabins. They were easy to build, inexpensive and served their occupants' basic needs. However, as their material conditions improved over the years, the colonists were able to build more permanent and architecturally elaborate homes.

With the development of the colony, the construction of public buildings was needed in the territory. Various towns expressed their political aspirations by constructing sumptuous public buildings. The first ones were built in the Georgian style. Over the years, the rigour of Georgian architecture diminished and made way for a number of styles inspired by older forms of architecture. This era coincided with the succession of Queen Victoria (1837-1901) to the throne, which is why all these different styles are grouped together under the one term "Victorian Architecture." This was a significant time for Ontario because the province was experiencing a rapid expansion. In numerous cities a great many Victorian public buildings were erected such as the Kingston City Hall (see p 111) with its combination of Georgian and neo-classical architecture and the Parliament Buildings in Ottawa (see p 66) built in the Gothic Revival style. These styles also dominated the religious architecture of the period, especially Gothic Revival: Our Lady of the Immaculate Conception Cathedral in Guelph (see p 244) is a good example.

In the 20th century, Victorian architecture remained fashionable but became more restrained. Two handsome buildings constructed in this style are Hart House at the University of Toronto (see p 177) and the central building of the Ottawa Parliament Buildings (see p 68).

Another style gradually appeared that would in turn create an architectural identity for the country, in particular for the capital city of Ottawa. This was the Château style influenced by the French châteaux of the 14th and 15th centuries, especially those of the Loire Valley. The Château Laurier was the first building constructed in this style in Ontario. It was erected in 1912 on the banks of the Ottawa River. According to the then Federal Government, this architecture presented a good image for a National Capital and so quickly drew favour. Several government buildings were constructed and to blend in well with the buildings already in place, the novel combination of Château and Gothic Revival architecture was used and now gives Ottawa its unique appearance.

Acting as a counterbalance to the exuberance of Château and Gothic Revival architecture, Art Deco experienced a certain popularity with its sleek geometric forms. Banks and buildings in this style slowly sprang up in the urban landscape between the two wars.

Throughout the 20th century, urbanization accelerated and cities continually increased in size. By the 1950s, cities had become huge metropolises and there was a need to set up major public infrastructures: road networks were reorganized, and schools and hospitals were built. Today the urban landscape has been transformed by towering modern architectural steel and glass constructions and by the emergence of sprawling suburbs which are the preferred habitat of the middle class.

THE ARTS

Whether in painting, literature, music or film, Ontario artists have sought over the years to create Canadian-accented works and have managed to differentiate themselves from the undeniably influential English and American artistic movements. This quest has not been easy, although it has been helped by government bodies such as the Canada Council and the Ontario Arts Council, whose role is to subsidize artistic endeavours.

Painting

It was not until the 19th century that it became possible to speak of Ontario art movements. Starting in the early days of settlement, talented painters emerged and found a source of inspiration in the European masters. Their main clients at first were the Church and the bourgeoisie, who encouraged them to produce religious works such as altars and silver carvings or to paint family portraits.

At the turn of the 1840s, a few artists began to stand out, producing paintings that extolled the land, portraying the immensity of a scarcely inhabited territory, with pastoral scenes and typical landscapes. Encouraged by local collectors, a few artists began gradually to develop personal styles. This was true, for instance, of **Cornelius Krieghoff**, a painter of Dutch descent whose canvases evoke the rustic lives of the new settlers, and of **Robert R. Whale**, a landscape painter.

At the beginning of the 20th century, the creation of the Canadian Art Club set out to promote painting in Canada and to raise the profile of Canadian artists, some of whom had emigrated to Europe, through a series of exhibitions held between 1907 and 1915. Among Ontario-born painters who spent much of their lives in Europe, **James Wilson Morrice** is no doubt the most famous, creating works that show the mark of European masters, especially of the impressionists and of Matisse.

In the early years of the 20th century, some of the great Ontario landscape painters became known by creating genuinely Canadian art. **Tom Thomson**, whose paintings provide a distinctive portrayal of landscapes unique to the Canadian Shield, was an originator of this movement. He died prematurely in 1917 at the age of 40 though his work had an indisputable effect over one of the most notable groups of painters in Ontario, the **Group of Seven**, whose first exhibition was held in Toronto in 1920. These artists, **Franklin Carmichael, Lawren S. Harris, Frank H. Johnson, Arthur Lismer, J.E.H. MacDonald, Alexander Young Jackson** and **Frederick Varley**, were all landscape painters. Although they worked together closely, each developed his own pictorial language. They were distinguished by their use of bright colours in their portrayal of typical Canadian landscapes. Their influence over Ontario painting is substantial, and only a handful of contemporary artists distinguished themselves from the movement, among them **David Milne Brown** developed a technique inspired by Fauvism and impressionism.

Painters began gradually to put landscapes aside and to exploit social themes instead. This was true of **Peraskeva Clark**, whose canvasses evoke the difficult years of the Great Depression, and of **Carl Schaefer**, who chose to reproduce rural scenes from his home region of Hanover, Ontario, using them to portray the Depression's harsh consequences.

Abstract art, which flourished in Québec around the 1940s with painters such as Alfred Pellan, Paul-Émile Borduas and Jean-Paul Riopelle, also had its disciples in Ontario, among

them **Lawren Harris**, a former member of the Group of Seven, and also the **Painters Eleven**, Ontario's second great pictorial movement, created in 1954.

This brief retrospective would not be complete without mentioning native art, whose beginnings are manifested in the petroglyphs that can be seen in Petroglyph Provincial Park (see p 142) and Lake Superior Provincial Park (see p 334). Later, more advanced art forms were developed. The Inuit, among the groups dominating certain currents in the art world, have included great masters of sculpture and engraving. In the 20th century, Ontario native communities have also produced an artistic heritage. Among the top artists are **Benjamin Chee-Chee**, of Ojibwa descent, who has produced works with abstract lines and geometric motifs, and **Norval Morrisseau**, who developed a style dubbed "pictographic," with themes drawn from native legends.

Literature

Although trading posts were set up at points across Ontario and there was a small population of settlers in the 17th century, it was not until the end of the 18th century that colonization began in earnest, with towns and villages developing along the St. Lawrence and the Great Lakes. One cannot really speak of Canadian literature in English until the 1820s.

The first writers, mostly poets, set out to describe the geographic reality that surrounded them, with its wild, untamed nature. This movement can well be described as realist literature and is representative of the concerns of Canadian society of that era, with a vast space to occupy. Several works mark these early moments in English-Canadian literature, such as those of **William**

Kirby and **Alexander McLachlan**. There gradually developed a desire to create a romantic literature with Canadian accents. Literary works reflecting urban realities and their harmonization with nature also began to evolve, giving a foretaste of important urban developments in the 20th century and issuing warnings of their dangers. These themes are brought out in the works of **Archibald Lampman, Duncan Campbell Scott** and **Isabella Valancy Crawford.**

The beginning of the 20th century was marked by a tragic world event, the outbreak of the First World War with its profound influence on English-Canadian thinking. Some people began to feel a need to face up to the British Empire and seek a more equal position for Canada. Writers were hardly exempt from this movement, and the first demands for the development of Canadian culture began to be heard. Writers felt a need to break away from the omnipresent British cultural domination. In the United States, many authors had established themselves not merely as writers of English but as American writers. This emancipation drew envy from several English-speaking Canadian authors and spurred them to create a style of their own. But this movement was not unanimous in its support, and some authors, such as **Mazo de la Roche** in her chronicles, still called for solid links with the British Empire.

This movement would grow all the same, allowing modern Canadian literature in English to define itself more clearly. **Hugh McLennan**, in his novel *Two Solitudes*, speaks of relations between English- and French-speakers, creating a work with distinctly Canadian themes. The 20th century was also the era of industrialization and of the deep social upheavals that came in its wake, bringing on a more active social engagement and the denunciation of injustice and social evils. This led to a protest movement reflecting a need the build a more just Canadian society. Many voices were heard, including those of authors such as **Morley Callaghan**, who depicted the hard life of city-dwellers and promoted a stronger social engagement, **Stephen Leacock**, whose works offer humorous criticisms of Canadian society, and **Raymond Souster**, a Toronto writer known for his political engagement.

The theatre world has also blossomed thanks, among others, to the works of playwright and novelist **Robertson Davies**. Summer theatre festivals have become an important element in Ontario cultural life, in particular the Shakespeare festival held every year in Stratford since 1953, and the Shaw festival in Niagara-on-the-Lake.

Margaret Atwood, a feminist and nationalist, carried modernism into the seventies. Her literary and critical writings have contributed much to an attempt at defining Canadian culture and literature. The 1970s saw the appearance of modern movements such as Open Letter in Toronto, seeking to bring new contributions to old ideas. Several authors have also distinguished themselves, notably **John Ralston Saul** for his essay *Voltaire's Bastards*, **Michael Ondaatje**, the Sri Lankan-born Toronto author who won Britain's prestigious Booker Prize in 1993 for his novel *The English Patient* (made into an Academy-Award-winning movie in 1997), and, more recently, Toronto writer **Timothy Findley**, upon whom the French government conferred the title of *chevalier des arts et lettres* for his work as a whole.

Over the years, Canadian literature has sought to create its own space among English-language literatures. Although Britain and the United States have had a commanding influence in defining this identity, English-speaking Canadian authors have gradually given shape to a literary thinking they can call their own.

Film

The weak sister of the arts scene, the Canadian film industry has developed only slowly, financially unable to match the big-budget films produced by the major American studios. As a result, it has not achieved much recognition among the Canadian public. During the 1950s, the creation of the National Film Board paved the way for the emergence of many documentaries and other quality films, as well as bringing fame to Canadian film-makers.

The 1970s were important for the Canadian film industry, with the production of certain films that finally found favour with the public. Some producers, such as **Don Shebib** with his film *Goin' Down the Road*, even achieved commercial success.

Despite difficult beginnings, Canadian cinema has recently achieved greater recognition thanks to talented producers such as **David Cronenberg**, with his films *Rabid*, *The Fly*, *Naked Lunch*, *M. Butterfly*, and *Crash*, which won the jury prize at Cannes in 1996. His latest film is *Existence*. Others include **Robin Spry**, with *Flowers on a One-Way Street* and *Obsessed*, and **Atom Egoyan**, with *The Adjuster*, *Family Viewing*, *Exotica* and *The Sweet Hereafter*. Several avant-garde film-makers have also stood out, notably **Bruce MacDonald**, with *Road Kill* and *Highway 61*.

Animated films from the early days of the National Film Board achieved great success on the international scene. **Norman McLaren**, who developed various techniques that revolutionized this art such as painting directly onto the film, won an Oscar for his 1952 film *Neighbours*. Other contributions to this field include **J. Hoedman** with *Sand Castle* and **John Weldon** and **Eunice Macaumay** with *Special Delivery*.

Music

Many musical artists from Ontario have become known on the international scene. Here is a brief retrospective of some of the better known ones.

Born in Toronto on September 25, 1932, **Glen Gould** was raised in musical surroundings from a very early age. His mother, who was related to Norwegian composer Edvard Grieg, taught him the basics of piano and organ until the age of 10. The young Glen Gould stood out very quickly as an exceptionally gifted pupil who learned musical composition starting at age 5. His virtuosity was recognized unanimously during his first public concert, in 1945. Scarcely a year later, he set out as a soloist in a concert at the Royal Academy in London, where he interpreted Beethoven's fourth piano concerto, and he joined the Toronto Symphony at age 14.

Working with the greatest musicians, including Herbert von Karajan, musical director of the Berlin Philharmonic Orchestra, and Leonard Bernstein of the New York Philharmonic Orchestra, Gould stood out on the world scene as one of the most talented musicians of his period. Drawn more by composition and studio recording than by public concerts, Gould decided prematurely to leave the stage after a recital in Los Angeles on April 10, 1964. He devoted the rest of his career to composition and to the recording of numerous works. He died in Toronto on October 4, 1982.

Neil Young was born in Toronto on November 12, 1945. He spent only part of his youth there before moving with his mother to Winnipeg, Manitoba, where he began his career as a musician in California. At first he was a member of various groups, including The Squires, Buffalo Springfield and, most notably, Crosby, Stills, Nash and Young. He began his solo career in 1969, and in 1972 he recorded *Harvest*, his most popular and best known album.

Bruce Cockburn was born in Ottawa on May 27, 1945, and spent much of his childhood on a farm nearby. The impressions and feelings that came from this rural experience would appear later in the words of his first albums. Influenced by the great pop music stars such as Elvis Presley, Bob Dylan and John Lennon, Cockburn took courses at the Berkeley Music School in Boston to study composition and harmony. Later he made a detour to Paris, where he performed in the streets, before returning to his home town, Ottawa. In the late 1960s, Cockburn's music took a much more acoustic turn, which he never abandoned. Up to now, this musical star has recorded 19 albums and has been showered with countless tributes to his talent.

Widely recognized in the United States and Europe, especially in Britain, as well as in Canada, Cockburn sits atop many lists of pop music writers, composers and singers. His words, often poetic, sometimes present thoughts on rural life, as in his early albums, sometimes offer more mystical connotations, or sometimes display political and environmental commitment, as in his album *Humans*. Among his recordings, some that stand out are *High Winds, White Sky* (his second album), *Dancing in the Dragon's Jaws* (nominated for various awards), *Stealing Fire*, *Humans* and *Big Circumstance*. He also wrote musical scores for famous films such as *Goin' Down the Road*, which won him a BMI Award as well as a Juno Award for Canadian popular singer of the year.

The popular singer ans songwriter **Paul Anka** (1941-) has recorded a number of hit songs himself, such as *You Are My Destiny*, and composed many others for such renowned fellow artists as Frank Sinatra (*My Way*). With more than 400 songs to his name, he was one of the most famous Canadian singers and songwriters in the world in his heyday.

Born in Ottawa to a French Canadian father and a Hungarian mother, **Alanis Nadine Morissette** (1974-) is one of the most successful Canadian singers of the 1990s. Her first album, recorded when she was just 17, won the Juno Award for most promising female singer. Though she was already off to a good start, she attained true celebrity status in 1995, at the age of 21, with her album *Little Jagged Pill* which won all sorts of awards, including the coveted Grammy for album of the year.

Among other Ontario musicians who have become noted on the international scene are the hard-rock group **Rush**, and, more recently, the Toronto-based group **Barenaked Ladies**, whose music moves between rock, jazz and folk. Country singer **Shania Twain**, from Timmins, has gained renown and has contributed to country's move into the mainstream.

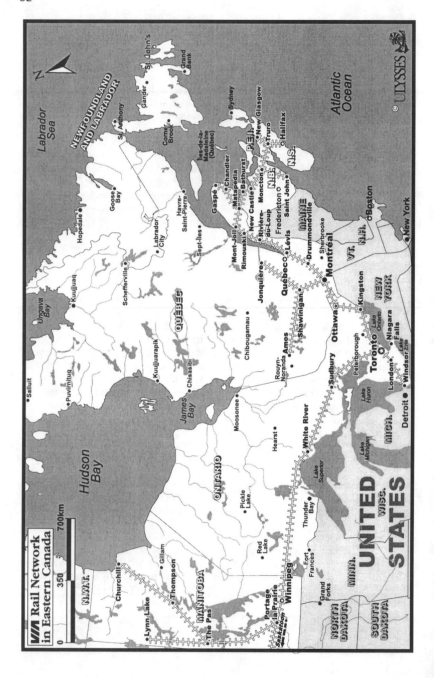

PRACTICAL INFORMATION

Information in this section will help visitors better plan their trip to Ontario.

Entrance Formalities

Passport

For a stay of less than three months in Canada, a valid passport is usually sufficient for most visitors from Western Europe and a visa is not required. American residents do not need a passport, though it is the best form of identification. A three-month extension is possible, but a return ticket and proof of sufficient funds to cover this extension may be required.

Caution: most countries do not have an agreement with Canada concerning health and accident insurance, so it is advisable to have the appropriate coverage. For more information, see the section entitled "Health" on page 47.

While visiting certain regions you may want to enter the United States; Canadian citizens who wish to enter the United States do not need a visa, nor do citizens from most of Western European countries. A valid passport is all that is needed for a stay of less than three months. A return ticket and proof of sufficient funds to cover your stay may be required.

Extended Visits

Visitors must submit a request to extend their stay **in writing** and **before** the expiration of their visa (the date is usually written in your passport) to an Immigration Canada office. To make a request you must have a valid passport, a return ticket, proof of sufficient funds to cover the stay, as well as a

$65 non-refundable administrative fee. In some cases (work, study), however, the request must be made **before** arriving in Canada.

CUSTOMS

If you are bringing gifts into Canada, remember that certain restrictions apply:

Smokers (minimum age is 16) can bring in a maximum of 200 cigarettes, 50 cigars, 400 g of tobacco, or 400 tobacco sticks.

For wine and alcohol the limit is 1.1 litres; in practice, however, two bottles per person are usually allowed. The limit for beer is 24 355-ml size cans or bottles.

Plants, vegetation, and food: there are very strict rules regarding the importation of plants, flowers, and other vegetation; it is therefore not advisable to bring any of these types of products into the country. If it is absolutely necessary, contact the Customs-Agriculture service of the Canadian embassy **before** leaving.

Pets: if you are travelling with your pet, you will need a health certificate (available from your veterinarian) as well as a rabies vaccination certificate. It is important to remember that the vaccination must have been administered **at least** 30 days and not more than one year **before** your departure and should not be more than a year old.

Tax reimbursements for visitors: it is possible to be reimbursed for certain taxes paid on purchases made while in Ontario (see p 50).

EMBASSIES AND CONSULATES

Abroad

Australia
Canadian Consulate General: Level 5, Quay West, 111 Harrington Road, Sydney, N.S.W. 2000, ☎(612) 9-364-3000, ✻(612) 9-364-3098.

Belgium
Canadian Embassy: 2 Avenue de Tervueren, 1040 Brussels, ☎(02) 741.06.11, ✻(02) 741.06.43.

Denmark
Canadian Embassy: Kr. Bernikowsgade 1, DK=1105 Copenhagen K, ☎(33) 12.22.99, ✻(33) 14.05.85.

Finland
Canadian Embassy: Pohjos Esplanadi 25 B, 00100 Helsinki, ☎(9) 171-141, ✻(9) 601-060.

Germany
Canadian Consulate General: Internationales Handelzentrum, Friedrichstrasse 95, 23rd Floor, 10117 Berlin, ☎(30) 203.120 ✻(30) 203.12590.

Great Britain
Canada High Commission: Macdonald House, One Grosvenor Square, London W1X 0AB, ☎(171) 258-6600, ✻(171) 258-6333.

Italy
Canadian Embassy, Via G.B. de Rossi 27, 00161 Roma, ☎(06) 44.59.81, ✻(06) 44.59.87.50.

Netherlands
Canadian Embassy: Sophialaan 7, 2514 JP The Hague, ☎(70) 311-1600, ✻(70) 311-1620.

Norway
Canadian Embassy: Wergelandsverein, Oslo 7, 0244 Norway, ☎(70) 361-4111, ✆(70) 365-6283.

Spain
Canadian Embassy: Edificio Goya, Calle Nunez de Balboa 35, 28001 Madrid, ☎(91) 431.43.00, ✆(91) 431.23.67.

Sweden
Canadian Embassy: Tegelbacken 4, 7th Floor, Stockholm, ☎(8) 613-9900, ✆(8) 24.24.91.

Switzerland
Canadian Embassy: Kirchenfeldstrasse 88, 3000 Berne 6, ☎(31) 357.32.00, ✆(31) 352.32.10.

United States
Canadian Embassy: 501 Pennsylvania Avenue NW, Washington, DC, 20001, ☎(202) 682-1740, ✆(202) 682-7726.

Canadian Consulate General: 1175 Peachtree Street NE, 100 Colony Square, Suite 1700, Atlanta, Georgia, 30361-6205, ☎(404) 532-2050, ✆(404) 532-2050.

Canadian Consulate General: Three Copley Place, Suite 400, Boston, Massachusetts, 02116, ☎(617) 262-3760, ✆(617) 262-3415.

Canadian Consulate General: Two Prudential Plaza, 180 North Stetson Avenue, Suite 2400, Chicago, Illinois, 60601, ☎(312) 616-1860, ✆(312) 616-1877.

Canadian Consulate General: St. Paul Place, Suite 1700, 750 North St. Paul Street, Dallas, Texas, 75201, ☎(214) 922-9806, ✆(214) 922-9815.

Canadian Consulate General: 600 Renaissance Center, Suite 1100, Detroit, Michigan, 48234-1798, ☎(313) 567-2340, ✆(313) 567-2164.

Canadian Consulate General: 550 South Hope Street, 9th Floor, Los Angeles, California, 90071, ☎(213) 346-2700, ✆(213) 620-8827.

Canadian Consulate General: 701 Fourth Avenue South, Suite 900, Minneapolis, Minnesota, 55415-1899, ☎(612) 332-7486, ✆(612) 332-4061.

Canadian Consulate General: 1251 Avenue of the Americas, New York, New York, 10020-1175, ☎(212) 596-1683, ✆(212) 596-1790.

Canadian Consulate General: One Marine Midland Center, Suite 3000, Buffalo, New York, 14203-2884, ☎(716) 858-9500, ✆(716) 852-4340.

Canadian Consulate General: 412 Plaza 600, Sixth and Stewart Streets, Seattle, Washington, 98101-1286, ☎(206) 443-1777, ✆(206) 443-9662.

PRACTICAL INFORMATION

In Ontario

Australia
Australian High Commssion: 50 O'Connor Street, Suite 710, Ottawa, K1P 6L2, ☎(613) 236-0841, ✆(613) 236-4376.

Australian Consulate General 175 Bloor Street East, Suite 316, Toronto, M4W 3R8, ☎(416) 323-1155, ✆(416) 323-3910.

Belgium
Belgian Embassy: 80 Elgin Street, 4th Floor, Ottawa, K1P 1B7, ☎(613) 236-7267, ✆(613) 236-7882.

Belgian Consulate: 2 Bloor Street West, Suite 2006, Box 88, Toronto, N4W 3E2, ☎(416) 944-1422, ✆(416) 944-1421.

Denmark
Embassy of Denmark: 47 Clarence, Ottawa, K1N 9K1, ☎(613) 562-1811.

Consulate General of Denmark: 151 Bloor Street West, Suite 310, Toronto, M5S 1S4, ☎(416) 962-5661, ⌨(416) 962-3668.

Finland
Embassy of Finland: 55 Metcalfe, Suite 850, Ottawa, K1P 6L5, ☎(613) 236-2389.

Consulate General of Finland: 1200 Bay Street, Toronto, M5R 2A5, ☎(416) 964-0066, ⌨(416) 964-1524.

Germany
German Embassy; 1 Waverley, Ottawa, K2P 0T8, ☎(613) 232-1101, ⌨(613) 594-9330.

German Consulate: 77 Admiral Road, Toronto, M5R 2L4, ☎(416) 925-2813, ⌨(416) 925-2818.

Great Britain
British Embassy: 80 Elgin Street, Ottawa, K1P 5K7, ☎(613) 237-1303, ⌨(613) 237-6537.

British Consulate: 777 Bay Street, Suite 2800, Toronto, M5G 2G2, ☎(416) 593-1290, ⌨(416) 593-1229.

Italy
Italian Embassy: 275 Slater Street, 21st Floor, Ottawa, K1P 5H9, ☎(613) 234-8424, ⌨(613) 233-1484.

Italian Consulate General: 136 Beverly Street, Toronto, M5T 1Y5, ☎(416) 977-1566, ⌨(416) 977-1119.

Netherlands
Embassy of the Netherlands: 350 Albert Street, Suite 2020, Ottawa, K1R 1A4, ☎(613) 237-5030, ⌨(613) 237-6471.

Consulate of the Netherlands: 1 Dundas Street West, Suite 2106, Toronto, M5G 1Z3, ☎(416) 598-2520, ⌨(416) 598-8064.

Norway
Norwegian Embassy: 90 Sparks Street Ottawa, K1P 5B4, ☎(613) 238-6571.

Honorary Consulate of Norway: 2600 South Sheridan Way, Clarkson, L5J 2M4, ☎(905) 822-2339, ⌨(905) 855-1450.

Spain
Spanish Embassy: 74 Stanley Avenue, K1M 1P4, ☎(613) 747-2252, ⌨(613) 744-1224.

Spanish Consulate General: Simcoe Place, 200 Front Street West, Suite 2401, Toronto, M4W 3R8, ☎(416) 977-1661, ⌨(416) 593-4949.

Sweden
Swedish Embassy: 377 Dalhousie, Ottawa, K1N 9N8, ☎(613) 241-8553, ⌨(613) 241-2277.

Swedish Consulate General: 2 Bloor Street West, Suite 1504, Toronto, M4W 3E2, ☎(416) 963-8768.

Switzerland
Swiss Embassy: 5 Marlborough Avenue, Ottawa, K1N 8E6, ☎(613) 235-1837, ⌨(613) 563-1394.

Swiss Consulate: 154 University Avenue, Suite 601, Toronto, M5H 3Y9, ☎(416) 593-5371, ⌨(416) 593-5083.

TOURIST INFORMATION

Ontario is divided into 12 travel regions, and each one has its own Travel Association. The complete addresses of these offices are located at the beginning of each chapter in the "Practical

Information" section. You can also obtain all sorts of information on the province by visiting Ontario's official tourist information website:

www.travelinx.com

or by phoning:

From Canada and the United States
☎800-ONTARIO (668-2746)

From elsewhere
☎(416) 314-0956

GETTING TO AND AROUND
ONTARIO

By Plane

Toronto's Lester B. Pearson International Airport

Lester B. Pearson International Airport *(☎247-7678)* welcomes international flights from Europe, the United States, Africa and Asia, as well national flights from the other Canadian provinces. It is the biggest and busiest airport in Canada.

Besides the regular airport services like duty-free shops, cafeteria and restaurants, you will also find an exchange office. Several car rental companies also have offices at the airport. Shuttle buses run regularly between the three terminals of the airport.

For information concerning a flight:
Terminal 1 ☎(905) 676-3506
Terminal 2 ☎(905) 676-3506
Terminal 3 ☎(905) 612-5100

The airport lies 27 km from downtown Toronto. By car take Highway 427 south to Queen Elizabeth Way (QEW), take this heading east until it joins the Gardiner Expressway. Get off at the York, Yonge or Bay exits for downtown.

Car rentals at the airport:

Avis ☎(905) 676-3844
Budget T1 ☎(905) 676-0311;
T2 ☎(905) 676-1500;
T3 ☎(905) 676-0522
Hertz ☎(905) 676-3241
Thrifty ☎(905) 673-9308
National T1 ☎(905) 676-2647;
T2 ☎(905) 676-2648;
T3 ☎(905) 676-4000.

If you are not renting a car, expect to pay about $40 for a taxi.

There is also a shuttle bus service, called the **Airporter** *(☎798-2424 or 798-2425)* that links the airport with various points throughout downtown, including some of the major hotels. This is an economical way of getting into town ($12.50) even if you aren't staying at one of the hotels it serves, since anyone can take the bus.

Ottawa's Macdonald-Cartier Airport

Ottawa's international airport *(50 Airport Dr., ☎998-5213, ≈954-2136)* is small, but welcomes several fights a day from other Canadian cities and different countries. It is located about twenty minutes from downtown and easily reached by car (there are a number of car-rental companies here), by taxi or by bus (OC Transpo 96).

By car, you can reach downtown Ottawa via Airport Drive.

To rent a car:

Avis
☎(613) 739-3334

Budget
☎(613) 729-6666

Hertz
☎(613) 521-3332

From Europe

Toronto is an air traffic hub in Eastern Canada. Air Canada, Canadian Airlines, Air France, British Airways, KLM, Lufthansa, TAP Air Portugal and SwissAir are among the major airlines that offer direct flights to Toronto (Lester B. Pearson International Airport) from major European cities.

From the United States

Air Canada and Canadian Airlines both offer direct flights out of Toronto to major US cities. The following American airline companies fly into Toronto's Pearson International Airport: Delta Airlines, Northwest Airlines, USAir, American Airlines and United Airlines.

From Elsewhere

Pearson International Airport is also served by flights on the following airlines: Air Europe, Air Ukraine, Air India, Air Jamaica, Royal Jordanian, Cubana, El Al, Finnair, Guyana, Iberia, Lot Polish Airlines, Pakistan Air, Alitalia and Vasp, among others.

Within Ontario

Air Ontario, NorOntario and Bradley FirstAir offer flights within the province.

By Train

Via Rail Canada is the only company that offers train travel between the Canadian provinces, and serves many destinations in northern and southern Ontario. This is one of the fastest and most efficient ways to travel, with several trains running to Montréal, Ottawa, Toronto and Windsor every day. (See box on p 40)

By Car

By car is the best way to see Ontario at your own pace, especially when you consider the excellent road conditions and the price of gas, which is three times cheaper than in Europe. An extensive network of roads links the United States and Canada as well as the eastern provinces with the rest of the country. The most famous of these is surely the impressive TransCanada Highway which links Saint John's, Newfoundland with Victoria, British Columbia.

Driver's licenses from Western European countries are valid in Canada and the United States. While North American travellers won't have any trouble adapting to the rules of the road in Ontario, European travellers may need a bit more time to get used to things. Here are a few hints:

Pedestrians: Drivers in Ontario are particularly courteous when it comes to pedestrians, and willingly stop to give them the right of way even in the big cities, so be careful when and where you step off the curb. Pedestrian crosswalks are usually indicated by a yellow sign. When driving pay special attention that there is no one about to cross near these signs.

Turning **right on a red light** when the way is clear is permitted in Ontario.

When a **school bus** (usually yellow in colour) has stopped and has its signals flashing, you must come to a complete

© ULYSSES

Table of distances (km)

Via the shortest route

Example: the distance between Ottawa and Toronto is 410 km.

	Collingwood	Hamilton	Kenora	Kingston	Kitchener-Waterloo	London	Montréal (Qué.)	Niagara Falls	Ottawa	Peterborough	Sault Ste. Marie	Sudbury	Timmins	Toronto	Thunder Bay
Hamilton	210														
Kenora	1851	1957													
Kingston	410	338	2011												
Kitchener-Waterloo	162	69	1980	369											
London	238	140	1908	451	110										
Montréal (Qué.)	698	621	2122	299	650	738									
Niagara Falls	276	77	2019	408	156	227	689								
Ottawa	499	480	1985	203	511	600	202	544							
Peterborough	207	207	1914	189	242	323	482	280	280						
Sault Ste. Marie	643	748	1210	894	777	699	1003	814	806	714					
Sudbury	349	460	1520	609	490	572	700	529	508	424	302				
Timmins	708	759	1341	888	784	868	879	824	740	716	573	308			
Toronto	162	75	1918	263	123	198	547	144	410	137	696	411	711		
Thunder Bay	1364	1469	501	1623	1496	1414	1638	1534	1516	1431	723	1019	856	1421	
Windsor	424	318	1789	626	306	191	912	413	773	500	584	751	1049	386	1310

VIA Rail: Discover Canada By Train!

In this part of North America where the highway is king, the train is often overlooked as a different and enjoyable way of exploring Canada. What better way to contemplate the spectacular and unique Canadian scenery than through huge picture windows while comfortably seated in your wide reclining chair?

The Routes

Modern and rapid (reaching up to 150 km/h), **VIA Rail** trains connect eastern Canadian cities in no time.

Preferred by businesspeople, the Québec-Windsor corridor, one of the busiest routes, connects the downtown metropolis's of Québec, Montréal, Ottawa, Toronto, Windsor and other towns quickly and comfortably.

VIA Rail also provides a regular service to New Brunswick and Nova Scotia. Particularly interesting is the transcontinental *Chaleur*, leaving from Montreal, which follows the river, taking passengers to Gaspé via Carleton, New Carlisle and Percé, among other cities. The *Abitibi* train, acquaints passengers with the Lanaudière, Mauricie and Abitibi-Témiscamingue regions. There is also the *Saguenay*, which travels to Saguenay—Lac-Saint-Jean, the land of Marie Chapdelaine. And of course, the train also links Montréal and Québec City, travelling though Montérégie and Bois-Francs.

An exciting way of seeing the country is aboard the *Canadian*, which departs from Toronto and travels all the way to Vancouver running through Ontario's forests, the central Prairies and the mountains of the West. The *Skeena* offers just as spectacular a route, departing from Jasper in the Rockies and travelling through the mountains and along the magnificent Skeena River all the way to Prince Rupert. Finally, the *Malahat* makes daily trips on Vancouver Island, between Victoria and Courtenay, serving up magnificent views along the way.

Economy or First Class?

Economy class carriages are equipped with comfortable seats and wide aisles and, for a slight surcharge, passengers can have something to eat as well. If you enjoy being waited on hand and foot, opt for first class, where the price of your ticket includes access to a waiting room, priority boarding and meals served with wine and spirits at your seat, in warmly decorated carriages.

Some trains have a Skyline carriage with a café and saloon car where you can enjoy yourselves in the company of other passengers. These carriages have large panoramic windows whence you can admire the passing landscape.

Save with *VIA*!

VIA offers several types of savings:

Up to 40% off on travel outside peak periods and tourist season, on certain days of the week and on advance bookings (five days), depending on the destination;

Student rebates (24 years and under, 40% year-round on advance booking except during Christmas period);

A 10% discount for people aged 60 and over, on certain days during off-peak travel times up to 50%, depending on the destination;

Special rates for children (2 to 11 years, half-price; free for 2 years and under, accompanied by an adult).

Special Tickets

With the **CANRAILPASS**, you can travel throughout Canada on one ticket. The ticket allows 12 days of unlimited travel in a 30-day period for $569 in high season and $369 in low season (Jan 1 to May 31 and Oct 16 to Dec 31).

The **North America Rail Pass**, valid on all *VIA* and *Amtrak* trains, is available in economy class for a 30-day period for $643 during off-peak periods and $919 during peak periods.

For further information, call your travel agent or closest *VIA* office, or visit the website at: www.viarail.ca

In Australia: Asia Pacific/Walshes World, ☎(02) 9319 2664, ⌨(02) 9319 4151.

In Canada: ☎(800) 561-8630 or contact your travel agent.

In Italy: Gastaldi Tours, ☎(10) 24 511, ⌨(10) 28 0354.

In the Netherlands: Incento B.V., ☎(035) 69 55111, ⌨(035) 69 55155.

In New Zealand: Walshes World, ☎(09) 379-3708, ⌨(09) 309-0725.

In Sweden: Tour Canada of Sweden, ☎(46) 54 53 23 65, ⌨(46) 54 53 23 00

In Switzerland: Western Tours, ☎(1) 455 4417, ⌨(1) 455 4470

In the United Kingdom: Leisurail, ☎01733-335-599, ⌨01733-412853.

In the United States: ☎(800) 561-3949 or contact your travel agent.

PRACTICAL INFORMATION

stop, no matter what direction you are travelling in. Failing to stop at the flashing signals is considered a serious offense, and carries a heavy penalty.

Wearing of **seatbelts** in the front and back seats is mandatory at all times.

All highways in Ontario are toll-free, and there are no toll bridges. The **speed limit** on highways is 100 km/h. The speed limit on secondary highways is 90 km/h, and 50 km/h in urban areas.

Gas Stations: Like in the rest of Canada, Ontario's gasoline prices are much less expensive than in Europe, and only slightly more than in the United States. Some gas stations (especially in the downtown areas) might ask for payment in advance as a security measure, especially after 11pm.

Winter driving: Though roads are generally well plowed, particular caution is recommended. Watch for slippery surfaces and reduced visibility. In some regions gravel is used to increase traction, so drive carefully.

Always remember that wildlife abounds near roads and highways in Ontario. It is not unheard of to come face to face with a deer even close to a city or town. Pay attention and drive slowly especially at nightfall and in the early morning. If you do hit any large animal, try to contact the Royal Canadian Mounted Police (RCMP). Dial 0 or 911 to reach the police.

Car Rentals

Packages including air travel, hotel and car rental or just hotel and car rental are often less expensive than car rental alone. It is best to shop around. Remember also that some companies offer corporate rates and discounts to auto-club members. Some travel agencies work with major car rental companies (Avis, Budget, Hertz, etc.) and offer good values; contracts often include added bonuses (reduced ticket prices for shows, etc.).

When renting a car, find out if the contract includes unlimited kilometres, and if the insurance provides full coverage (accident, property damage, hospital costs for you and passengers, theft).

Certain credit cards, gold cards for example, cover the collision and theft insurance. Check with your credit card company before renting.

To rent a car, you must be at least 21 years of age and have had a driver's license for **at least** one year. If you are between 21 and 25, certain companies will ask for a $500 deposit, and in some cases they will also charge an extra sum for each day you rent the car. These conditions do not apply for those over 25 years of age.

A credit card is extremely useful for the deposit to avoid tying up large sums of money.

Most rental cars come with an automatic transmission, however you can request a car with a manual shift.

Child safety seats cost extra.

Accidents and Emergencies

In case of serious accident, fire or other emergency dial ☎**911** or **0**.

If you run into trouble on the highway, pull onto the shoulder of the road and turn the hazard lights on. If it is a rental car, contact the rental company as soon as possible. Always file an accident report. If a disagreement arises over who was at fault in an accident, ask for police help.

By Ferry

Only one of the regions can be reached by ferry: Manitoulin Island. If you are coming from the southern part of the province, you can reach Manitoulin Island aboard the ferry *Chi-Cheemaun (car $24.50, adults $11.20; ☎800-461-2621)*, which links Tobermory (at the northern tip of the Bruce Peninsula) to South Baymouth from spring to fall. The crossing takes 1 hour 45 minutes. Reservations are accepted, but to keep them you must arrive one hour before boarding.

Summer Schedule:

Tobermory-South Baymouth
7am, 11:20am, 3:40pm, 8pm

South Naymouth-Tobermory
9:10am, 1:30pm, 5:50pm, 10pm

Spring and Autumn Schedule:

Tobermory-South Baymouth
8:50am, 1:30pm, 6:10pm (Fri only)

South Naymouth-Tobermory
11:10am, 3:50pm, 8:15pm (Fri only)

By Bus

Extensive and inexpensive, buses cover most of Canada. Except for public transportation, there is no government-run service. Gray Coach, Greyhound and Voyageur Colonial all service the country. Here are the phone numbers of the principal stations:

Toronto
610 Bay Street, ☎(416) 393-7911

Ottawa
265 Catherine Street,
☎(613) 238-5900

The addresses of the main bus stations in the major cities are listed in the "Finding Your Way Around" section of each chapter.

Smoking is forbidden on almost all lines and pets are not allowed. Generally children five years old or younger travel for free and people aged 60 or over are eligible for discounts.

The RoutPass

The various bus companies offer what is called a RoutPass; it is a single ticket that allows unlimited travel throughout most of Ontario and all of Québec. The ticket costs $199 and is valid for 14 days from May 1 to October 29. The ticket can be extended for up to six days for $19.37 a day. The extension must be purchased at the same time as the RoutPass, however. The RoutPass is less expensive if it is purchased in the pre-sale period from March 1 to April 22. Children under 12 get a 50% reduction, and children under 5 travel for free. The RoutPass is available at the above-mentioned stations.

Hitchhiking

There are two kinds: unorganized (illegal on highways) and organized with a car-pooling company called Allo Stop. The first kind is more common and easier to do outside large urban centres.

Allo Stop offers rides all year round with drivers who are willing to take other passengers for a small remuneration (mandatory membership card:

passenger $6 per year, driver $7 per year). The driver receives a percentage of the fare (about 60%). Allo Stop mainly operates in Ontario and Québec.

Here's a sample price:

Montréal - Toronto: $26

N.B.: Children under 5 years cannot travel with Allo Stop because of a regulation stipulating the mandatory use of child safety seats. Also, call ahead to find out whether your lift is smoking or not.

For information and reservations:

Allo-Stop Montréal
4317 Rue Saint-Denis, Montréal, H2J 2K9, ☎(514) 985-3032 or 985-3044.

Allo-Stop Québec
467 Rue Saint-Jean, Québec, G1R 1P3, ☎(418) 522-3430.

Allo-Stop Ottawa
238 Dalhousie Street, Ottawa, K1N 7E3, ☎(613) 562-8248.

Allo-Stop Toronto
398 Bloor Street West, Toronto, M5S 1X4, ☎(416) 975-9305.

TIME DIFFERENCE

Almost all of Ontario is in the same time zone (Eastern Time). The part of the province to the west of Thunder Bay falls in another time zone (Central Time) which is one hour behind the rest of the province. The majority of the province is therefore six hours behind continental Europe and five hours behind the United Kingdom. Daylight Savings Time (add one hour) begins the first Sunday in April and ends the last Sunday in October. Furthermore, do not forget that there are several time zones in Canada, for example when in it noon in Toronto, it is 9am in Vancouver.

BUSINESS HOURS AND PUBLIC HOLIDAYS

Business Hours

Stores

Generally stores remain open the following hours:

Mon to Fri10am to 6pm;
Thu and Fri10am to 9pm;
Sat 9am or 10am to 5pm;
Sun noon to 5pm

Well-stocked stores that sell food, sometimes called convenience stores or variety stores, are found throughout Ontario and are open later, sometimes 24 hours a day.

Banks

Banks are open Monday to Friday from 10am to 3pm. Most are open on Thursdays and Fridays, until 6pm or even 8pm. Automatic teller machines are widely available and are open night and day.

Post Offices

Large post offices are open Monday to Friday from 9am to 5pm. There are also several smaller post offices located in shopping malls, convenience stores, and even pharmacies; these post offices are open much later than the larger ones.

Holidays and Public Holidays

The following is a list of public holidays in the Ontario. Most administrative offices and banks are closed on these days.

January 1 and 2 (New Years)
Good Friday or Easter Monday
Victoria Day: 3rd Monday in May
Canada Day: July 1st
Civic holiday: 1st Monday in August
Labour Day: 1st Monday in September
Thanksgiving: 2nd Monday in October
Remembrance Day: November 1 (only banks and federal government services are closed)
Christmas Day: December 25

MAIL AND TELECOMMUNICATIONS

Mail

Canada Post provides efficient mail service (depending on who you ask) across the country. At press time, it cost 46¢ to send a letter elsewhere in Canada, 55¢ to the United States and 95¢ overseas. Stamps can be purchased at post offices and in many pharmacies and convenience stores.

Telecommunications

There are six telephone area codes in Ontario. The area code is **613** for the easternmost part of the province up to and including Kingston, **416** for Metropolitan Toronto, **905** for Greater Toronto (not including Metro) and the Golden Horseshoe, **519** for the area south and west of Georgian Bay to the American border, **705** for northeastern Ontario, and **807** for northwestern Ontario. The area codes are given in the "Practical Information" section of each chapter in this guide.

Long distance charges are cheaper than in Europe, but more expensive than in the US. Pay phones can be found everywhere, often in the entrance of larger department stores, and in restaurants. They are easy to use and most accept credit cards. Local calls to the surrounding areas cost 25¢ for unlimited time. Have plenty of change on hand or use a credit card or calling card if you want to make a long distance call from a public phone. It is less expensive to call from a private residence. All numbers beginning with **800** and **888** are toll free.

MONEY AND BANKING

Currency

The monetary unit is the dollar ($), which is divided into cents (¢). One dollar = 100 cents.

Bills come in 5, 10, 20, 50, 100, 500 and 1000 dollar denominations, and coins come in 1 (pennies), 5 (nickels), 10 (dimes) and 25 (quarters) cent pieces, and in 1 (loonies) dollar and 2 (twoonies) dollar coins. The new 2 dollar coin will eventually replace the 2 dollar bill, though the bill will remain legal tender.

Exchange

Most banks readily exchange American and European currencies but almost all will charge **commission**. There are, however, exchange offices that do not charge commissions and have longer hours, though their rates aren't as good. Just remember to **ask about fees** and **to compare rates**.

Exchange Rates

$1 US	=	$1.52 CAN	$1 CAN	=	$0.66 US
1 Euro	=	$1.67 CAN	$1 CAN	=	0.60 Euro
1 £	=	$2.47 CAN	$1 CAN	=	£0.40
$1 Aust	=	$0.96 CAN	$1 CAN	=	$1.04 Aust
$1 NZ	=	$0.81 CAN	$1 CAN	=	$1.24 NZ
1 fl	=	$0.76 CAN	$1 CAN	=	1.32 fl
1 SF	=	$1.04 CAN	$1 CAN	=	0.96 SF
10 BF	=	$0.41 CAN	$1 CAN	=	24.13 BF
1 DM	=	$0.85 CAN	$1 CAN	=	1.51 DM
10 pesetas	=	$0.10 CAN	$1 CAN	=	99 pesetas
1000 lire	=	$0.86 CAN	$1 CAN	=	1158 lire

Traveller's Cheques

Traveller's cheques are accepted in most large stores and hotels, however it is easier and to your advantage to change your cheques at an exchange office. For a better exchange rate buy your traveller's cheques in Canadian dollars before leaving.

Credit Cards

Most major credit cards are accepted at stores, restaurants and hotels. While the main advantage of credit cards is that they allow visitors to avoid carrying large sums of money, using a credit card also makes leaving a deposit for car rental much easier and some cards, gold cards for example, automatically insure you when you rent a car (check with your credit card company to see what coverage it provides). In addition, the exchange rate with a credit card is generally better. The most commonly accepted credit cards are Visa, MasterCard, and American Express.

Credit cards offer a chance to avoid service charges when exchanging money. By overpaying your credit card (to avoid interest charges) you can then withdraw against it. You can thus avoid carrying large amounts of money or traveller's cheques. Withdrawals can be made directly from an automatic teller if you have a personal identification number for your card.

Banks

Banks can be found almost everywhere and most offer the standard services to tourists. Visitors who choose to stay in Canada for a long period of time should note that **non-residents** cannot open bank accounts. If this is the case, the best way to have money readily available is to use traveller's cheques, a credit card or an automatic banking card. People who have residence status, permanent or not (such as landed-immigrants, students), can open a bank account. A passport and proof of residence status are required.

CLIMATE AND CLOTHING

Ontario has a continental climate, with very defined season. In summer the temperature can reach 30°C, while in the winter it can drop to -25°C and snow is common and often very abundant. In spring and fall, the sun is often hidden behind rain clouds.

Winter

December to March is the ideal season for winter-sports enthusiasts (skiing, skating, etc.). Warm clothing is essential during this season (coat, scarf, hat, gloves, wool sweaters and boots). Toronto and the southwestern part of the province generally benefit from slightly milder conditions than the rest of southern Ontario.

Spring and Fall

Spring is short (end of March to end of May) and is characterized by a general thaw leading to wet and muddy conditions. Fall is often cool. A sweater, scarf, gloves, windbreaker and umbrella will therefore come in handy.

Summer

Summer lasts from the end of May to the end of August and can be very hot. Bring along t-shirts, lightweight shirts and pants, shorts and sunglasses; a sweater or light jacket is a good idea for evenings. If you plan on doing any hiking, remember that temperatures are cooler in the forest.

HEALTH

General Information

Vaccinations are not necessary for people coming from Europe, the United States, Australia and New Zealand. On the other hand, it is strongly suggested, particularly for medium or long-term stays, that visitors take out health and accident insurance. There are different types so it is best to shop around. Bring along all medication, especially prescription medicine. Unless otherwise stated, the water is drinkable throughout Ontario.

In the winter, moisturizing lotion and lip balm are useful for people with sensitive skin, since the air in many buildings is very dry.

During the summer, always protect yourself against sunburn. It is often hard to feel your skin getting burned by the sun on windy days. Do not forget to bring sun screen!

Canadians from outside Ontario should take note that in general your province's health care system will only reimburse you for the cost of any hospital fees or procedures at the going rate in your province. For this reason, it is a good idea to get extra private insurance. In case of accident or illness make sure to keep your receipts in order to be reimbursed by your province's health care system.

Emergencies

The ☎911 emergency number is in operation throughout most of Ontario. If it does not work dial **0** and tell the operator that this is an emergency.

INSURANCE

Cancellation Insurance

Your travel agent will usually offer you cancellation insurance when you buy your airline ticket or vacation package. This insurance allows you to be reimbursed for the ticket or package deal if your trip must be cancelled due to serious illness or death. Healthy people are unlikely to need this protection, which is therefore only of relative use.

Theft Insurance

Most residential insurance policies protect some of your goods from theft, even if the theft occurs in a foreign country. To make a claim, you must fill out a police report. It may not be necessary to take out further insurance, depending on the amount covered by your current home policy. As policies vary considerably, you are advised to check with your insurance company. European visitors should take out baggage insurance.

Life Insurance

Several airline companies offer a life insurance plan included in the price of the airplane ticket. However, many travellers already have this type of insurance and do not require additional coverage.

Health Insurance

This is the most useful kind of insurance for travellers, and should be purchased before your departure. Your insurance plan should be as complete as possible because health care costs add up quickly. When buying insurance, make sure it covers all types of medical costs, such as hospitalization, nursing services and doctor's fees. Make sure your limit is high enough, as these expenses can be costly. A repatriation clause is also vital in case the required care is not available on site. Furthermore, since you may have to pay immediately, check your policy to see what provisions it includes for such situations. To avoid any problems during your vacation, always keep proof of your insurance policy on your person.

EXPLORING

Each chapter in this guide covers a different city or region of Ontario. The main tourist attractions are given along with a historical and cultural description of them, and they are classified according to a star-rating system so you will know which ones to visit if you don't have much time.

★   Interesting
★★   Worth a visit
★★★   Not to be missed

The name of each attraction is followed by the price of admission (for one adult), the hours of operation, and the location and contact information in brackets. Many places offer discounts for children, students, seniors and families; call or visit to find out. Some sites are only open during the tourist season, this is also specified in the parentheses. However, in off-tourist season, some of these places offer visits upon request, especially for groups.

SHOPPING

What to Buy

Local crafts: needlepoint, paintings, wood carving, ceramics, copper-based enamels, weaving, etc.

Native Arts & Crafts: beautiful native sculptures made from different types of stone, wood and even animal bone are available, though they are generally quite expensive. Make sure the sculpture is authentic by asking for a certificate of authenticity issued by the Canadian government.

ACCOMMODATIONS

A wide choice of types of accommodation to fit every budget is available in most regions of Ontario. Most places are very comfortable and offer a number of extra services. Prices vary according to the type of accommodation and the quality-to-price ratio is generally good, but remember to add the 7% G.S.T (federal Goods and Services Tax) and the provincial sales tax of 8%. The Goods and Services Tax is refundable for non-residents in certain cases (see p 50). A credit card will make reserving a room much easier, since in many cases payment for the first night is required.

Many hotels and inns offer considerable discounts to employees of corporations or members of automobile clubs (CAA, AAA). Be sure to ask about corporate and other discounts as they are often very easy to obtain. You'll also find many coupons in the brochures given out for free by the Travel Associations.

Hotels

Hotels rooms abound, and range from modest to luxurious. Most hotel rooms come equipped with a private bathroom. Internationally reputed hotels can be found throughout Ontario, including several beauties that belong to the Canadian Pacific chain.

Inns

Often set up in beautiful historic houses, inns offer quality lodging. There are a lot of these establishments which are more charming and usually more picturesque than hotels. Many are furnished with beautiful period pieces. Breakfast is often included.

Bed & Breakfasts

Unlike hotels or inns, rooms in private homes are not always equipped with a bathroom. Bed and breakfasts are well distributed throughout Ontario, in the country as well as the city. Besides the obvious price advantage, is the unique family atmosphere. Credit cards are not always accepted in bed and breakfasts. The term "Bed and Breakfast" is often used loosely and does not necessarily mean lodging in a private home. A homey atmosphere and congenial hosts are generally guaranteed, however.

Motels

There are many motels throughout the province, and though they tend to be cheaper, they also lack atmosphere. These are particularly useful when pressed for time.

Youth Hostels

Youth hostel addresses are listed in the "Accommodations" section for the cities in which they are located.

University Residences

Due to certain restrictions, this can be a complicated alternative. Residences are generally only available during the summer (mid-May to mid-August); reservations must be made in advance, usually by paying the first night with a credit card.

This type of accommodation, however, is less costly than the "traditional" alternatives, and making the effort to reserve early can be worthwhile. Visitors with valid student cards can ex-

PRACTICAL INFORMATION

pect to pay approximately $25 plus tax. Bedding is included in the price, and there is usually a cafeteria in the building (meals are not included in the price).

Camping

Next to being put up by friends, camping is the least expensive form of accommodation. Unfortunately, unless you have winter-camping gear, camping is limited to a short period of the year, from about June to August. Services provided at the campsites vary considerably; the prettiest sites are usually in the provincial or national parks. The price vary from $8 to $20 or more per night.

TAXES

The ticket price on items usually **does not include tax**. There are two taxes, the G.S.T., or federal Goods and Services Tax of 7% and the P.S.T., or Provincial Sales Tax of 8%. They are cumulative and must be added to the price of most items and to restaurant and hotel bills.

There are some exceptions to this taxation system, such as books, which are only taxed with the G.S.T. and food (except for ready made meals), which is not taxed at all.

Tax Refunds for Non-Residents

Non-residents can obtain refunds for the G.S.T. paid on purchases if they spend $200 or more. To obtain a refund, it is important to keep your receipts. Refunds are made at the border or by returning a special filled-out form. For further information contact:

Revenue Canada
Summerside Tax Centre
Summerside, P.E.I.
C1N 6C6
☎800-668-4748 or (902) 432-5608
www.rc.gc.ca

You can also get a refund on the provincial sales tax if the total value of goods purchased is $625 or more, before taxes. This refund is not valid for car rentals, hotel rooms or transportation costs. For more information, contact:

Ontario Ministry of Finance
Retail Sales Tax Branch Refund
1600 Champlain Avenue, 4th Floor
Whitby, ON
☎(905) 432-3431 or 800-263-7965
≈(905) 435-3543

TIPPING

In general, tipping applies to all table service: restaurants, bars and nightclubs (therefore no tipping in fast-food restaurants). Tips are also given in taxis and in hair salons.

The tip is usually about 15% of the bill before taxes, but varies of course depending on the quality of service.

RESTAURANTS AND BARS

Restaurants

There are several excellent restaurants throughout Ontario. Every city has a wide range of choices for all budgets, from fast food to fine dining.

Bars and Nightclubs

In most cases there is no cover charge, aside from the occasional mandatory coat-check. However, expect to pay a few dollars to get into discos on weekends. The legal drinking age is 19; if you're close to that age, expect to be asked for proof. Bars close at 2am and it is illegal to sell alcohol after that time.

WINE, BEER AND LIQUOR

The legal drinking age is 19. Beer, liquor and wine can only be purchased at the provincially run "Beer Store," "Liquor Store" and "Wine Store," respectively. These places are open quite late, until 10pm during the week and 11pm on Saturdays. Keep in mind that they are all closed on Sundays.

ADVICE FOR SMOKERS

As in the United States, cigarette smoking is considered taboo, and is being prohibited in more and more public places:

- most shopping centres;
- buses;
- government offices.

Most public places (restaurants, cafes) have smoking and non-smoking sections. Cigarettes are sold in bars, grocery stores, newspaper and magazine shops.

SAFETY

By taking the normal precautions, there is no need to worry about your personal security. In fact, Toronto is considered one of the safest cities in North America. If trouble should arise, remember to dial the emergency telephone number ☎911 or 0.

CHILDREN

As in the rest of Canada, facilities exist in Ontario that make travelling with children quite easy, whether it be for getting around or when enjoying the sights. Generally children under five travel for free, and those under 12 are eligible for fare reductions. The same applies for various leisure activities and shows. Find out before you purchase tickets. High chairs and children's menus are available in most restaurants, while a few of the larger stores provide a babysitting service while parents shop.

DISABLED TRAVELLERS

Though considerable efforts have been made to make things more accessible to handicapped individuals, there is still a lot of work to be done.

PETS

Ontario is generally quite tolerant of pets, which are permitted in all provincial parks as long as they are on a leash. Several hotels even permit them. Remember that animals are not allowed in grocery stores, restaurants or buses.

MISCELLANEOUS

Drugs

Recreational drugs are against the law and not tolerated (even "soft" drugs).

PRACTICAL INFORMATION

Anyone caught with drugs in their possession risks severe consequences.

Electricity

Voltage is 110 volts throughout Canada, the same as in the US. Electric plugs have two parallel flat pins, and adaptors are available here.

Laundry

Laundromats are found almost everywhere in urban areas. In most cases, detergent is sold on site. Although change machines are sometimes provided, it is best to bring plenty of quarters (25¢) with you.

Museums

Most museums charge admission. Reduced prices are available for people over 60, for children, and for students. Call the museum for further details.

Newspapers

Each big city has its own major newspaper:

Toronto
The Globe and Mail
Toronto Star
Toronto Sun
National Post
Now (free weekly cultural paper)
Eye (free weekly cultural paper)
Xtra! (gay paper)

Ottawa
Ottawa Citizen
Le Droit (French paper)
X Press (free weekly cultural paper)
Xtra! (Gay paper)

Pharmacies

In addition to the smaller drug stores, there are large pharmacy chains which sell everything from chocolate to laundry detergent, as well as the more traditional items like cough drops and headache medications.

Restrooms

Public restrooms can be found in most shopping centres.

Weights and Measures

Although the metric system has been in use in Canada for several years, some people continue to use the Imperial system in casual conversation. Here are some equivalents:

Weights
1 pound (lb) = 454 grams (g)
1 kilogram (kg) = 2.2 pounds (lbs)

Linear Measure
1 inch = 2.54 centimetres (cm)
1 foot (ft) = 30 centimetres (cm)
1 mile = 1.6 kilometres (km)
1 kilometre (km) = 0.63 miles

Land Measure
1 acre = 0.4 hectare
1 hectare = 2.471 acres

Volume Measure
1 US gallon (gal) = 3.79 litres
1 US gallon (gal) = 0.83 imperial gallon

Temperature
To convert °F into °C: subtract 32, divide by 9, multiply by 5
To convert °C into °F: multiply by 9, divide by 5, add 32.

OUTDOORS

Bound by the largest bodies of fresh water in the world and blessed with a beautiful but untamed wilderness, Ontario has everything a nature-lover could want: trails leading deep into the Algonquin forest for hikers to trample, the opportunity to spot rare migrating birds, some of the highest rock faces for daring climbers to conquer and in the winter vast expanses of fresh white show for cross-country skiers to traverse. This chapter offers some helpful hints about various activities to helps you get the most of Ontario's great outdoors.

 PARKS

In Ontario, like elsewhere in Canada, there are national parks, run by the federal government, and provincial parks, administered by the Ontario government.

These parks offer facilities and services such as information centres, park maps, nature interpretation programs, guides, accommodation (equipped and back-country camping sites) and restaurants. Not all of these services are available in every park (and some vary depending on the season), so it is best to contact park authorities before setting off on a trip.

National Parks

There are six national parks in Ontario: St. Lawrence Island National Park (Mallorytown), Point Pelee National Park (Leamington), Bruce Peninsula National Park (Tobermory), Fathom Five National Marine Park (Tobermory), Georgian Bay Islands National Park (Georgian Bay) and Pukaskwa National Park (Marathon). Besides these parks, Parks Canada also runs several national historic sites, which are described in the "Exploring" sections of each chapter.

Information on the parks is available by calling toll free ☎(800)-839-8221 or by writing to:

Parks Canada
111 Water Street East,
Cornwall, Ont.,
K6H 6S3,
☎(613) 938-5866 or 800-839-8221,
☞(613) 938-5785,
www.parkscanada.pch.gl.ca

Provincial Parks

Ontario runs some 270 parks, which cover only 6% of its territory. Some are very small and are only open during the day, while others are much bigger and offer visitors the chance to explore wild expanses for several days on end. Beaches, campsites, canoe routes and hiking trails are maintained in many of these parks. Descriptions of the major parks are found throughout the guide in the "Outdoors" sections of each chapter. If you would like more information on the provincial parks contact the tourist office of the region where the park is located or call ☎(800)-667-1940 (toll free) or fax your request to ☞(416) 314-1593.

Camping

Some parks have a reservation service for campsites; these are listed throughout the guide. A free brochure that lists all the provincial parks is available as well. The parks that do not offer a reservation service are those that are not as busy and that work on a first come first served basis.

As far as reservations are concerned:

- full payment by credit card is recommended to guarantee the reservation;

- sites are reserved until 8am the day following the reservation;

- a maximum of two nights can be reserved;

- you can reserve by sending a cheque which the park must receive a minimum of 21 days prior to the reservation date and which should be made out to the Minister of Finances. Reservations by fax are accepted for Algonquin Provincial Park at ☞705-633-5581;

- certain parks accept reservations for back-country camp sites, but be sure you know the canoe routes and access points. A map of the park will indicate this.

Safety Considerations

Various safety regulations should be followed when heading off on an excursion in Ontario's parks.

A number of parks are crisscrossed by marked trails stretching several kilometres, perfect for hiking, cycling, cross-country skiing and snowmobiling. Useful maps that indicate the trails and camp sites are available for most parks. They can be obtained from the park administration offices. Always tell someone your itinerary before heading off.

Primitive camping sites or shelters can be found in some parks, usually right in the middle of the forest. Some of the camping sites are very rudimentary,

Respect the forest!

As a hiker, it is important to realize your role in preserving and respecting the fragility of the ecosystem, and to comprehend your impact on your surroundings. Here are a few guidelines:

First of all, stay on the trails even if they are covered in snow or mud in order to protect the ground vegetation and avoid widening of the trail.

Unless you're heading off on a long trek, wear lightweight hiking boots, they do less damage to the vegetation.

It is just as important to protect waterways, bodies of water and the ground water when in forest regions. When digging back-country latrines, place them at least 30 m from all water sources, and cover everything (paper included) with earth.

Never clean yourself in lakes or streams.

At campsites, dispose of waste water only in designated areas.

The water in forest regions is not always potable and therefore should be boiled for at least 10 min before drinking it.

Never leave any garbage behind. Bags for this are provided at Parks Canada offices.

Certain types of flowers are endangered, so do not pick anything.

Leave everything as you find it, that way those that follow can enjoy the beauties of nature as you did.

For safety reasons, always keep your dog on a leash if you take it along on a hike or a walk. Dogs that roam free have a tendency to wander off and chase after wild animals. They have even been known to chase down a bear and then take refuge with their master.

OUTDOORS

and a few don't even have water; it is therefore essential to be well equipped.

Always store your food far from your tent and out of reach of animals. Before leaving your site, douse your fire well to ensure it is extinguished. Take all your garbage with you.

It is important to be well aware of the potential dangers before heading off into these parks. Each individual is ultimately responsible for his or her own safety. Dangers to watch out for include hypothermia or sunstroke, rapid changes in temperature, wild animals and non-potable water.

Hypothermia

Hypothermia begins when the internal body temperature falls below 36°C, at which point the body loses heat faster than it can produce it. Shivering is the first sign that your body is not able to warm itself. It is easy to discount the cold when hiking in the summer. However, in the mountains, rain and wind can lower the temperature considerably. Imagine sitting above the tree line in a downpour, with the wind blowing at 50 km/h. You are tired and have no raincoat. In such conditions, your body temperature drops rapidly and you run the risk of hypothermia. It is thus important to carry a change of warm clothes and a good wind-breaker with you at all times. When hiking, it is preferable to wear several layers instead of a big jacket that will be too warm once you are exercising, but too light when you stop to rest. Avoid wet clothes at all costs.

Potable Water

Water can be found in most Canadian parks, but it is not always clean enough

to drink. For this reason, be sure to bring along enough water for the duration of your hike, or boil any water you find for about 10 minutes.

Wild Animals

Visitors who enter Ontario's parks run the risk of encountering wild, unpredictable and dangerous animals. It is irresponsible and illegal to feed, trap or bother any wild animals. Large mammals like bears, moose and deer may feel threatened and become dangerous if you try to approach them. Stay at least 30 m from large mammals and at least 50 m from bears.

 SUMMER ACTIVITIES

Warm weather means the opportunity to enjoy a variety of activities. Anyone intending to spend more than a day in the park should remember that the nights are cool (even in July and August) and that long-sleeved shirts or sweaters will be very practical in some regions. In June, and throughout the summer in northern regions, an effective insect repellent is indispensable for an outing in the woods

 Hiking

Hiking is an activity open to everyone, and it can be enjoyed in all national and most provincial parks. Before setting out, plan your excursion well by checking the length and level of difficulty of each trail. Some parks have long trails that require more than a day of hiking and lead deep into the wild. When taking one of these trails, which can stretch tens of kilometres, it is crucial to respect all signs and trail markers.

To make the most of an excursion, it is important to bring along the right equipment. You'll need a good pair of walking shoes, a windbreaker, appropriate maps, sufficient food and water and a small first-aid kit containing a pocket knife and bandages.

Besides those trails that crisscross Ontario's national and provincial parks, there are also several trails that traverse the whole province. The most renowned of these is the Bruce Trail which stretches 736 km from Niagara to Tobermory. The Hike Ontario association is responsible for the maintenance of 11 of these trails, some of which are described in this guide. For more information contact:

Hike Ontario
1185 Eglinton Avenue East,
Suite 411,
North York, Ontario,
M3C 3C6
☎/≈(416) 426-7362,
ww3.sympatico.ca/hikers.net/hikeont.
htm

 Climbing

Climbing fans can practise their favourite sport in winter and summer. There are a few ice walls especially for climbers in the Thunder Bay region as well as along the Niagara Escarpment (see p 259). Proper equipment (sometimes rented on site) and experience are musts with this sport. Some centres offer introductory courses.

 Bicycling

Bicycling is a wonderful way to discover Ontario, either along the usually quiet secondary roads or the trails crisscrossing the parks. The roads offer prudent cyclists one of the most enjoyable means possible of touring these picturesque regions. Keep in mind, however, that distances in this vast province can be very long.

If you want to embark on a cycling tour of one or more days, you can procure the Green Escapes *Cycling in Ontario* guide by Ulysses Travel Publications.

If you are travelling with your own bicycle, you are allowed to bring it on any bus; just be sure it is properly protected in an appropriate box. Another option is to rent one on site. For bike rental locations, look under the heading "Bicycling" in the "Outdoor Activities" section of the chapters, contact a tourist information centre or check under the "Bicycles-Rentals" heading in the *Yellow Pages*. Adequate insurance is a good idea when renting a bicycle. Some places include insurance against theft in the cost of the rental. Inquire before renting.

 Beaches

Whether you decide to stretch out on the sand dunes of Sandbanks Provincial Park or Quinte's Isle, or prefer the long crescent of beach on Providence Bay on Manitoulin Island, or perhaps the tranquil and wild beaches of the numerous lakes and rivers of Algonquin Park or one of the magnificent beaches on Lake Huron, Erie or Superior, you are sure to find something that strikes your fancy in Ontario.

 Canoeing

Many parks are strewn with lakes and rivers on which canoeists can spend a day or more exploring. Back-country camp sites have been laid out to accommodate canoeists during long excursions. Canoe rentals and maps of possible routes are usually available at the park's information centre. It is always best to have a map that indicates the length of the portages in order to determine how physically demanding the trip will be. Carrying a canoe, baggage and food on your back is not always a pleasant experience. A one-kilometre portage is generally considered long, and will be more or less difficult depending on the terrain.

For more information contact:

Canoe Ontario
1185 Eglinton Avenue East,
North York, Ont.,
M3C 3C6,
☎(416) 426-7170,
≈(416) 426-7363,
www.canoeontario.on.ca

 Pleasure Boating

The waters of Ontario are a joy to explore, and the opportunities to do so are endless. Some of these are listed throughout the guide.

Besides the open waters of the lakes and rivers, the province is also crisscrossed by canals that are open to pleasure-boaters. The Rideau Canal links Ottawa and Kingston, and once in Kingston, Georgian Bay is accessible along the Trent-Severn Canal.

These fascinating routes lead visitors along a series of canals and locks and offer a new perspective of Ontario. A certain amount of preparation is required, and to take these canals you will need a lock permit. Permit prices vary depending on the size of your boat and how long the permit is valid for. Rather strict regulations govern the use of the locks; for a complete list of

these and any other information concerning Ontario's historic canals, write to:

Rideau Canal
12 Maple Avenue North,
Smith Falls,
K7A 1Z5,
☎(613) 283-5170.

Trent-Severn Canal
P.O. Box 567,
Peterborough,
K9J 6Z6,
☎(705) 742-9267.

 Bird-watching

The Ontario Wilderness attracts all sorts of birds, which can easily be observed with the help of binoculars. Some of the more noteworthy species that you might spot include the mallard, the black duck, the Canada goose, the loon, the merganser, the kingfisher, the great heron, the white pelican (northern Ontario), the tundra swan (migratory), the osprey, bald eagle, the common raven, the ruffed grouse, the goldfinch, the black-capped chickadee, the cedar waxwing, the red-winged blackbird, the European starling, the sparrow, the mourning dove, the blue jay and the grey jay, an audacious little bird that will gladly help itself to your picnic lunch if you aren't careful. Some areas, like Point Pelee National Park, are exceptional refuges for a profusion of winged creatures, and during the migratory season it is possible to spot close to 350 different species. For help identifying them, purchase a copy of *Peterson's Field Guide: All the Birds of Eastern and Central North America*, published by Houghton Mifflin.

Hunting and Fishing

In Ontario, anglers can cast their lines in the many rivers and lakes and hunt in various parks. Don't forget, however, that hunting and fishing are regulated activities. The laws are complicated, so it is wise to request information from the Ontario Ministry of Natural Resources and obtain the brochure stating key hunting and fishing regulations.

For information contact:

Ontario Ministry of Natural Resources
Information Centre,
McDonald Building,
Office M1-73,
900 Bay Street,
Toronto, Ontario,
M7A 2C1,
☎(416) 314-1177 for fishing.
☎(416) 314-2225 for hunting.

As a general rule, keep in mind that:

- you must obtain a permit from the provincial government before going fishing or hunting;

- a special permit is usually required for salmon fishing, and for bear and moose hunting;

- fishing and hunting seasons are established by the ministry and must be respected; the seasons differ for the various species;

- fishing and hunting is permitted in some national parks, but you must obtain a permit from park officials beforehand.

 ## WINTER ACTIVITIES

In winter, Ontario is covered with a blanket of snow creating ideal condi-

tions for a slew of outdoor activities. Most parks with summer hiking trails adapt to the climate, welcoming cross-country skiers and dog teams.

 ## Cross-country Skiing

Some parks in the central and northern parts of the province are renowned for their long cross-country ski trails, in particular Algonquin, Frontenac and Kiilarney provincial parks. Some parks even have winter camping sites, recommended only for those who are well equipped.

 ## Downhill Skiing

Ontario does not have any huge mountains like the Rockies in Western Canada or the Chic-Chocs in Québec. There are, however, a few downhill skiing centres on the hills spread here and there throughout the province. The most well known being those on Blue Mountain, in the Collingwood area and those around Thunder Bay.

 ## Snowmobiling

Snowmobiling has made many fans in Ontario in recent years, and to satisfy these new snow adventurers, Ontario has developed a vast network of trails stretching some 43,200 kilometres across the northern part of the province.

To make the most of your excursion, keep the following safety regulations in mind: follow the signs; get a permit; get personal liability insurance; stay on the snowmobile trails; drive on the right side of the trail; wear a helmet; keep the snowmobile's headlights lit at all times.

OUTDOORS

Dog-sledding

 ## Ice-fishing

Who hasn't dreamed of leading a dog-team across snowy plains just like the Inuit used to do? Well it is now possible to participate in one of these thrilling excursions, a f#ew outfits offers such adventures, mostly around Algonquin Park and North Bay.

This sport has become more and more popular in recent years. The basic idea, as the name suggests, is to fish through the ice. A small wooden shackbuilt on the ice keeps you warm during the long hours of waiting for the big one. The main regions for this activity are around Quinte's Isle. Various good spots are mentioned throughout the guide.

OTTAWA

Who would have thought, less than 200 years ago, that at the confluence of the Ottawa and Rideau rivers, in the heart of a dense forest, a city would develop one day that would become the capital of Canada?

The history of Ottawa goes back to the days after the War of 1812, in which British forces in Canada were pitted against American troops. The war proved beneficial to the development of the Ottawa region, for it was during these difficult years that the English authorities recognized the importance of protecting the navigable waters of the St. Lawrence between the newly built towns along the river, in particular between Montréal and Kingston. The St. Lawrence had become essential to the transporting of troops; defending the boats that used the river, however, was not a simple matter since, over a sizable distance, one shore lay on the Canadian side and the other on the American side. A canal between the Ottawa River and Kingston that would bypass the St. Lawrence between the present-day cities of Ottawa and Kingston was proposed as a solution. In 1825, General By was charged with carrying out the project.

An early agricultural settlement had begun on the site of what is today Hull, on the Québec side of the border, at the beginning of the 19th century. The first settlers in the Ottawa region, on the Ontario side, were mostly Irish workers who built the canal. It took seven years to complete the canal; in 1832, a little village was built at the confluence of the Ottawa River and the Rideau Canal. It was named Bytown, in honour of General By. In 1855, Bytown was renamed Ottawa after a native tribe, who had been decimated by the Iroquois in the 17th century. This same name was given to the river that forms much of the boundary between Québec and Ontario.

The town flourished, mostly because of the dense forest surrounding it; woodcutting gave work to many people. Two very distinct areas developed on each side of the canal: the upper town, on the west side, where the more affluent inhabitants had sumptuous dwellings built, and the lower town, on the east side, which became home to the town's poorer residents, mostly French and Irish, both groups being predominantly Catholic. After the War of 1812, the threat of an American attack ended, and contrary to the original plans for the canal, it never served in wartime. The waterway was instead used by pleasure-boaters out enjoying fine summer days.

In the middle of the 19th century, Kingston was named capital of Upper and Lower Canada, but its proximity to the United States worried the authorities who feared eventual attacks on this important, yet vulnerable colonial administrative centre. They sought another site for the capital, with Toronto, Québec City, Montréal and Ottawa all vying for the title. It was Queen Victoria who decided in favour of Ottawa in 1857 because of its location at the boundary between Upper and Lower Canada. Some observers at the time derided this choice, for they judged the site, set deep in the woods, to be inappropriate for a capital. But Ottawa remained capital, nevertheless; the British North America Act was signed in 1867, and the city has kept its title ever since.

Forestry allowed the town and the surrounding region to prosper, but this industry went into decline during the 20th century. At the same time, however, its status as national capital enabled it to attract the burgeoning federal civil service, which became the principal local employer. A city plan was adopted at the turn of the 20th century to beautify the area. Though it

wasn't until 1937, when French architect and town planner Jacques Greber was appointed to develop a new layout for the city centre, that Ottawa was transformed and took on the grand appearance it has today. Today, the elegant buildings of Parliament Hill and the broad avenues lined with splendid Victorian dwellings bear witness to the success of this plan that brought Ottawa among the ranks of Canada's most beautiful cities.

FINDING YOUR WAY AROUND

By Car

An excellent system of highways and expressways makes Ottawa easy to reach from many points in Ontario and Quebec.

From Toronto, follow Highway 7, which runs through Peterborough and goes directly to Ottawa. It is also possible to drive along the St. Lawrence, taking Highway 401 to Prescott and, from there, Highway 16 to Ottawa.

From Montréal, take Highway 40 and then the 417, and get off at the Nicholas St. exit to reach the downtown area.

By Bus

Extensive and inexpensive, buses cover most of Canada. Except for public transportation, there is no government-run service; several companies service the country. Gray Coach, Greyhound and Voyageur Colonial all serve the Ontario region.

Moreover, bus service, from Montreal and Toronto, is both rapid and punctual, and departures are frequent.

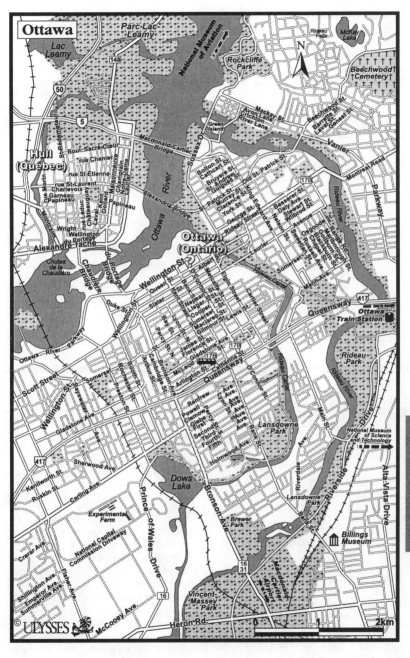

Ottawa Bus Station:
265 Catherine Street, ☎238-5900.

From the bus station, you can get to the downtown area by bus (OC Transpo no. 4) or by car via Kent or Bank Streets.

By Train

VIA Rail transports passengers between the various Canadian provinces and serves several cities in southern and northern Ontario. This is without a doubt the most pleasant way of travelling from Montreal or Toronto to the capital. You will thus be treated to a comfortable ride while being waited on hand and foot.

The Ottawa train station is located a dozen minutes by car from the downtown area and is served by a good road network and public transport.

Ottawa Train Station
200 Tremblay Road, ☎244-1660.

To get there by car, take the eastbound 417. The station is located a short distance past Riverside Drive.

If you want to take public transportation, the OC Transpo bus no. 95, which runs from the station to downtown, stopping right near Parliament Hill. A ticket costs $1.85.

By Plane

Macdonald-Cartier Airport

Ottawa's international airport *(50 Airport Dr., ☎998-5213, ≈954-2136)* is small, but welcomes several fights a day from other Canadian cities and different countries. It is located about twenty minutes from downtown and

easily reached by car (there are a number of car-rental companies here), by taxi or by bus (OC Transpo no. 96).

 PRACTICAL INFORMATION

Tourist Information

A brand new tourist information office has just opened its doors a stone's throw from Parliament Hill. Brochures, information, hotel-room reservation centre... all the services you could possibly need are available here.

Capital Call Centre
90 Wellington Street, ☎239-5000 or (800) 465-1867.
Late May to early Sep, everyday, 8:30am to 9pm; rest of the year, everyday, 9am to 5pm.

You can also obtain a great deal of additional tourist-related information by checking out various websites. Here are a few:

www.capcan.ca
www.ottawakiosk.com
www.tourottawa.org

 EXPLORING

The Rideau Canal is the heart of Ottawa in two senses. The very foundation of the city was spurred by the construction of the canal, and, geographically, the canal is the dividing line between the eastern part of the city, called Lower Town, and the western part, known as Upper Town. The first tour described in this chapter runs the length of this crucial waterway and presents the main attractions along its shores. The next two tours, Upper Town and Lower Town, reveal the

The Odawa

Ottawa was named after the Algonquian tribe that used to live in the Ottawa Valley. The name apparently means "to trade." These First Nation people lived on farming, hunting, fishing and trade, and used the Ottawa River as a route inland. Their economy, closely linked to those of other tribes such as the Huron, who lived on the shores of Georgian Bay, was greatly disrupted by the arrival of the first Europeans. When the Iroquois destroyed Huronia in 1649, the Odawa were forced to flee westward. They didn't return to Ontario until about 20 years later, when they settled on Manitoulin Island and around the Great Lakes.

beautiful architectural achievements that transformed Ottawa's image at the turn of the century. Along Sussex Drive tour explores the city's pretty residential neighbourhoods. Finally, a visit to Canada's national capital would not be complete without a jaunt across the Ottawa River to Hull, Québec, Ottawa's sister city.

Tour A: The Rideau Canal ★

Ottawa's existence is in part a result of the British-American War of 1812, in which British authorities realized the extent of the vulnerability of the St. Lawrence River, the vital link between Montreal and the Great Lakes. Once the conflict ended, the British began to devise plans to defend the waterway, and they concluded that a canal linking the village of Wrightown on the south bank of the Ottawa River to the city of Kingston would provide the security they desired.

The canal's impressive entrance, created by Scottish mason Thomas McKay, is still visible from the city. It is made up of eight stone locks that permit boats to descend the first 24.4 metres of the channel. Two mountains overlook the canal, one on either bank. The summit of the eastern

hill is now the site of Major's Hill Park (see p 74), but it once bore the stone house of Colonel By, which was destroyed by fire in 1849. The barracks and hospital for the soldiers that built the canal occupied the top of Barrack Hill, on the western shore, until the Parliament Buildings (see p 66) were erected there.

The **Bytown Museum ★** *($2.50; mid-May to late Nov, Mon to Sat 10am to 5pm, Sun 1pm to 5pm; next to the locks, ☎234-4570)* was built at the foot of Barrack Hill, just next to the locks, in 1827. This stone house is the oldest edifice in the city and it still encloses the Intendance, in which various exhibitions are mounted.

From very early on beautifying the canal was one of the central preoccupations of developers, so starting at the beginning of the 20th century, measures were taken to landscape its shores. Its banks were cleared of debris and a panoramic highway was opened on its western shore.

The **Rideau Canal** snakes through the city, to the great delight of people who come for a breath of fresh air in the urban mêlé. In the summer, its banks boast parkland dotted with picnic tables, and there are paths alongside the canal for pedestrians and cyclists. In

OTTAWA

the winter, once the canal is frozen over, it is transformed into a vast skating rink that crosses the city. There is a small lodge facing the National Arts Centre, where skaters can don their blades and warm up.

The **National Arts Centre** *(between Confederation Square and the Rideau Canal, 53 Elgin St., ☎996-5051)* on the west bank of the canal, occupies the former location of Ottawa's 19th-century city hall, which was destroyed by fire. It was built between 1964 and 1967 by Montreal architects Affleck, Desbarats, Dimakopoulos, Lebensol and Sise. Excellent concerts and plays are presented here throughout the year (see p 96), and the advantages of the centre's canal-side location are amplified in summertime by pleasant patios.

Continue along the canal, either on the Queen Elizabeth Highway on the west bank or on Colonel By Drive on the east bank. If you choose the latter option and want to reach Dow's Lake Park, take Bronson Avenue, which crosses the canal.

Dow's Lake is in a location that was once nothing but swampland. It was artificially created by a dyke and a dam erected during construction of the Rideau Canal. Today this beautiful body of water, situated not too far from downtown Ottawa, is the perfect spot for weekend unwinding: pedal boats, canoes and skates are all available for rent (see p 84), and the lake shore is bordered by a rambling garden that is ideal for picnics and strolls.

Tour B: Upper Town ★★★

From Bytown's very beginnings, the beautiful west bank of the Rideau Canal was a magnet for the well-to-do English Protestant families who were migrating to the fledgling city. Upper Town, the city's upper-class neighbourhood (if the nascent community could be called a city in those days), became ever more attractive over the years as new houses sprang up to accommodate newly arriving families. The area entered its heyday around the 1860s when Ottawa was chosen as the national capital and the magnificent federal Parliament Buildings were erected on the summit of Barrack Hill, which belonged to the British Crown at the time and which, of course, is still capped by the impressive sight of these government buildings. Within about fifty years, the broad avenues of Upper Town were trimmed with exquisite Victorian buildings by a construction boom in part triggered by the neighbourhood's new prominence.

The half-day tour of this neighbourhood begins at the Parliament Buildings and visits some of the most beautiful buildings in the city.

The **Parliament Buildings** ★★★ *(information on activities, ☎239-5000 or 800-465-1867)* truly dominate Ottawa. The summit of the hill is topped by three buildings spread over a 200-square-metre garden. Centre Block contains the House of Commons and the Senate, the two chambers of the federal government (see p 68). The two other buildings, East Block and West Block, enclose various administrative offices.

In 1857, when Ottawa was designated the capital of the Province of Canada, city authorities realized that these splendid buildings would have to be built, as there was no appropriate edifice in which to accommodate parliament. A contest was held, and Thomas Fuller and Chilion Jones's plans for a neo-Gothic building won the contract. The deadlines imposed on the designers were very tight and construction began before all of the inevitable kinks in a

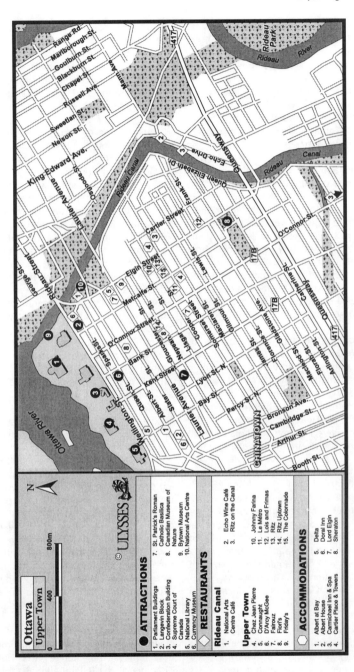

Ottawa
Upper Town

0 400 800m

N

© ULYSSES

ATTRACTIONS

1. Parliament Buildings
2. Langevin Block
3. Confederation Building
4. Supreme Court of Canada
5. National Library
6. Currency Museum
7. St. Patrick's Roman Catholic Basilica
8. Canadian Museum of Nature
9. Bytown Museum
10. National Arts Centre

RESTAURANTS

Rideau Canal

1. National Arts Centre Café
2. Echo Wine Café
3. Ritz on the Canal

Upper Town

4. Chez Jean Pierre
5. Connaught
6. D'Arcy McGee
7. Fairouz
8. Fiori's
9. Friday's
10. Johnny Farina
11. Le Métro
12. Lois and Frimas
13. Ritz
14. Ritz Uptown
15. The Colonnade

ACCOMMODATIONS

1. Albert at Bay
2. Albert House
3. Carmichael Inn & Spa
4. Cartier Place & Towers
5. Delta
6. Doral Inn
7. Lord Elgin
8. Sheraton

OTTAWA

project of this scale could be worked out. The impressive budget of 250,000 pounds sterling that had been allotted for the project was surpassed barely one year later. Authorities were accused of mismanaging public funds, and work on the building was interrupted. Three years passed before a Royal Commission of Inquiry into the affair recommended that construction resume. In 1866, the first session of Parliament was held in the building, which was still unfinished.

Although construction of Centre Block was riddled with problems, the overall project's final result is justifiably the pride of the Ottawa's citizens: three splendid neo-Gothic buildings dominate the horizon of the city, which, up until the erection of the Parliament Buildings, had been a conglomeration of modest wood houses.

At first, Centre Block was comprised of a semi-basement, a ground floor, and only one story. It was topped by a copper mansard roof. At its centre stood Victoria Tower, at a height of 77 metres, which sheltered the entrance. The House of Commons and the Senate were situated in rooms of equal dimensions in either wing of the building. Construction work was finally completed in 1876.

Just 40 years later, on February 3, 1916, a terrible fire broke out in Centre Block, destroying the rooms of the west wing before spreading to those of the east wing. The magnificent edifice was entirely consumed by flame, with the exception of the Library of Parliament, which was spared thanks to the quick wittedness of a clerk who closed the thick iron doors that separated it from the rest of the building. The library, a splendid, 16-sided neo-Gothic building covered by a lantern-shaped roof, may still be visited today. Its interior is richly decorated in white-pine woodwork and comprises a large reading room lit by lancet windows on each of its sides and small alcoves that enclose part of the library collection. In its centre is a white-marble statue of Queen Victoria that was sculpted by Marshall Wood in 1871.

Reconstruction of Centre Block began some time later and lasted nine years. The architects, John A. Pearson and J. Omer Marchand, designed the new building to be consistent with the East and West Blocks, opting once again for the neo-Gothic style and reproducing the aspect of the original main building. Financial reasons figured in the decision to construct the new building in a style similar to that of its predecessor with like materials. As well, the size of the building had to be reduced; it was later expanded. Its façade is pared by the 90-metre-high Peace Tower which encloses, among other features, a carillon of 53 bells. Nothing, however, was omitted in the decoration of the interior of this splendid building, which incorporates especially magnificent sculptures and woodwork.

Guided tours of **Centre Block** *(free; late May to early Sep, Mon to Fri 9am to 7:40pm, Sat and Sun 9am to 4:40pm; Sep to May, every day 9am to 4:40pm)* visit the interior of the building, including the west wing where visitors are treated to an up-close look at the House of Commons, in which members of parliament elected through universal suffrage hold debates and adopt federal laws. This vast, rectangular, green-toned room is decorated in white pine, limestone and stained-glass windows depicting the floral emblems of the provinces and territories of Canada.

In the east wing of the building, these guided tours pause at the large room that houses the Senate, the Upper Chamber of the federal administration, whose government-appointed members are responsible for studying and approving laws adopted by the House of Commons. This distinctive room is set apart by carpeting and red armchairs, a coffered ceiling adorned with gold maple leaves and two magnificent and imposing bronze chandeliers.

In addition to these two rooms, the guided tours visit the Library of Parliament as well as the Peace Tower, where you can see the white-marble Memorial Chamber.

Beautiful views of the Ottawa river can be had from the **summer pavilion** on the grounds of Centre Block, behind the building on the west side.

Since the earliest days of its construction, Centre Block has been flanked on either side by East Block and West Block, the work of Thomas Stent and Augustus Laver. East Block, a beautiful composition of asymmetrical elevations, is made of cut stone in shades that range from cream to ochre and is embellished by towers, chimneys, pinnacles, lancet windows, gargoyles and various sculptures. Originally, it was built to house the Canadian civil service; now it encloses the offices of senators and members of Parliament. A guided tour is offered and highlights a few rooms that have been restored to their 19th-century appearances. The Office of the Governor General and the Chamber of the Privy Council are also located here. West Block is used exclusively for the offices of Members of Parliament and is not open to the public.

Parliament is also the scene of numerous events, notably the **changing of the guard**, which takes place every day from late June to late August at 10am, when you can see soldiers parading in their ceremonial garb. A **sound and light show** *(free admission; mid-May to*

mid-Jun, 9:30pm and 10:30pm) presents the history of Canada.

On the vast lawn graced with beautiful flowers stretching in front of the parliament buildings, is the centennial flame, inaugurated in 1967 to commemorate the 100th anniversary of Canadian confederation.

The large bay windows of the Ottawa tourist information centre, the **Infocentre** *(90 Wellington St.)*, are located two steps away from Langevin Block. A stop here provides a wealth of additional information on accommodations and restaurants in the city, as well as a hotel reservation service.

Ottawa's aesthetic face began to take shape at the beginning of the 20th century, as government buildings went up to meet the needs of a growing bureaucracy, most of these influenced by the adoption of a Public Works Department mandate that endorsed the neo-Gothic and Château styles. Wellington Street was the result of the infatuation with these styles and was embellished by cut-stone buildings with pointed roofs, turrets, balconies and dormers. The **Confederation Building ★**, for example, was built next to West Block in about 1928. In the shape of an "L," with an asymmetrical entrance surmounted by a turret with a pointed roof, this building was one of the first projects to combine both of the architectural styles of the day.

Continuing along Wellington Street, another Canadian institution comes into view: the **Supreme Court of Canada ★** *(guided tours: ☎995-5361; corner of Wellington St. and Kent St.).* This Art Deco building was conceived by architect Ernest Cormier, who began its construction in 1939. Only one modification was brought to its original plans, which called for a flat roof. The Public

OTTAWA

Supreme Court of Canada

Works Department, which still favoured the Château style, required that the roof be altered to give it its current appearance (or it may have been requested by Prime Minister Mackenzie King). The tremendous interior space created by this peaked roof is now occupied by the court's library.

At the end of Wellington Street stand the buildings of the **National Library and Archives of Canada** *(395 Wellington St.)*, which contain an impressive collection of documents dealing with Canada, as well as Canadian publications. Temporary exhibitions are presented here.

Queen Street offers little else of interest. A series of high-rises sprouted up in the years around 1965, when the law that proscribed buildings taller than the Parliament was revoked. Businessman Jean Campeau took advantage of this relaxation of restrictions to erect **Place de Ville**, a tall black monolith. Following this lead, many office towers were built in this part of the city. As these are of no particular charm, continue along Sparks Street.

The considerable changes that Ottawa underwent in the second half of the 19th century had repercussions on the development of its commercial arteries. From the town's very beginnings, two sections of it have vied for the status of business centre: the surroundings of the Byward Market, in Lower Town, and **Sparks Street**, in Upper Town. Great effort was expended by local residents and shopkeepers to embellish Sparks Street and, thanks to them, this elegant road of five- and six-story buildings was one of the very first to be paved with asphalt, to have streetcar service and to be illuminated by street lamps. In those days it was known as the "Broadway" of Ottawa. Its commercial role never ebbed, and today it offers a beautiful pedestrian mall between Kent and Elgin Streets that is especially pleasant in the summertime when its concentration of pretty shops attracts crowds of patrons and browsers.

The first stop on Sparks Street is a visit to the **Currency Museum** ★ *($2; Tue to Sat 10:30am to 5pm, Sun 1pm to 5pm; 245 Sparks St., ☎782-8914)*, which is located inside the Bank of Canada, by the rear entrance. The exhibition is spread over eight rooms and retraces the history of the creation of currency. The first room deals with the first objects that served as trading tender: natives used wampum "belts" adorned with shell beads. From there the exhibition traces the evolution of the coin from China, where it had its earliest use, to Florence, where coins were made out of precious metals for the first time (the florin). Rooms three through six cover the development of Canadian currency from the exchange of glassware for beaver pelts to the French colonists' use of playing cards as bills of exchange while they waited for money to arrive from France, to the creation of Canadian paper currency. Numismatists will be interested in room eight, which displays a beautiful collection of antique coins and bills. Finally, there is a short educational film about the role of the Bank of Canada.

Either continue along Elgin Street – explore its pretty shops or take a break at one of its many restaurants – or, for a longer tour, turn right on McLoed Street to visit the Canadian Nature Museum.

The **Canadian Museum of Nature** ★ *($5; May to Sep, every day 9:30am to 5pm, Thu to 8pm; Sep to May, every day 10am to 5pm, Thu to 8pm; corner of McLoed St. and Metcalfe St., ☎566-4700)*, in a huge, recently renovated three-story building, houses many small exhibitions on various facets of nature. Myriad themes, including geology, the formation of the planet, animals of prehistoric Canada, indigenous mammals and birds of Canada, and the fantastic world of insects and of vegetation, are presented in an interesting manner.

Tour C: Lower Town ★★★

In the early days of Bytown, the poorly irrigated land on the east bank of the canal was unappealing to newcomers. Irrigation work was carried out in 1827, making it more attractive, and gradually it was populated, but not by the well-to-do. Labourers looking for affordable housing established themselves here, and French and Irish workers, most of them Catholic, made up the majority in this neighbourhood. Conditions were difficult; skirmishes between the Irish and the French, who were often competing for the same jobs, were frequent; and life in the neighbourhood was not always rosy. Few traces remain of these first difficult years in Lower Town, as the buildings of the era, most of which were made of wood, rarely resisted the wear of the years. A few of these scattered here and there mostly reflect the French origins of neighbourhood residents. Left by the wayside in the second half of the 19th century, the neighbourhood was left out of the building boom that overtook Upper Town. Here, there are very few of the neo-Gothic constructions that were so popular in that period. At the beginning of the 20th century, Sussex Drive, which marks the western edge of the neighbourhood, was embellished by the construction of magnificent Château-style buildings. Then, over the course of this century, other buildings, including the very beautiful National Gallery of Canada, perfected the image of this elegant artery.

Wellington Street spans the canal, becoming Rideau Street on this bank, where it is lined with a multitude of shops that are fun to browse through.

The first building on the tour is the unmistakable and imposing **Château Laurier** ★★ *(1 Rideau St.)*, on

OTTAWA

Château Laurier

the shore of the Rideau Canal, and has been one of the most prestigious hotels in the city since the day it opened its doors (see p 87).

The Château Laurier's origins are intrinsically linked to the construction of the cross-Canada Grand Trunk Railroad. Cornelius Van Horne, then the head of the Canadian Pacific Railway Company, realized that he needed to increase the number of passengers on this track to make it turn a profit, so he decided to establish a coast-to-coast chain of prestigious hotels along the route. The first of these establishments to be erected was the Château Frontenac in Quebec City, but the nation's capital would not be outdone: about 15 years later, the company contracted Bradford Lee Gilbert to design Ottawa's luxury hotel. Gilbert was let go before construction could begin, so architects

Ross and MacFarland were hired in 1908 to complete the blueprints. They favoured the Château style, to keep with the look of the other Canadian Pacific hotels, and built an elegant, romantically alluring hotel of relatively bare stone façades topped by pointed copper roofs, turrets and dormers. No detail was overlooked in making this a hotel of the highest quality, and the interior decoration, which can be admired in the lobby, is sumptuous. The very first guest to register, in 1912, was none other than Sir Wilfrid Laurier, who had strongly supported the creation of the railroad and in whose honour the hotel was named.

Next to this is the **Canadian Museum of Contemporary Photography** *(free admission; May to Sep, Mon and Tue, Fri and Sun 11am to 5pm, Wed 4pm to 8pm, Thu 11am to 8pm; Sep to Apr, Wed*

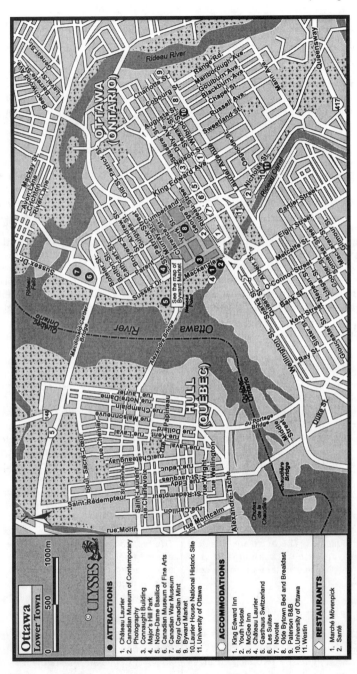

Ottawa
Lower Town

0   500   1000m

© ULYSSES

● **ATTRACTIONS**

1. Château Laurier
2. Canadian Museum of Contemporary Photography
3. Connaught Building
4. Major's Hill Park
5. Notre-Dame Basilica
6. Canadian Museum of Fine Arts
7. Canadian War Museum
8. Royal Canadian Mint
9. Byward Market
10. Laurier House National Historic Site
11. University of Ottawa

◇ **ACCOMMODATIONS**

1. King Edward Inn
2. Youth Hostel
3. McGee Inn
4. Château Laurier
5. Gasthaus Switzerland
6. Les Suites
7. Novotel
8. Olde Bytown Bed and Breakfast
9. Paterson B&B
10. University of Ottawa
11. Westin

◇ **RESTAURANTS**

1. Marché Mövenpick
2. Santé

OTTAWA

and Thu 11am to 8pm, Fri to Sun 11am to 5pm; 1 Rideau Canal, ☎993-4497), with a collection containing more than 158,000 images created from the photographic resources of the National Film Board of Canada.

Continue on Mackenzie Avenue.

Faithful to the architectural tradition that prevailed in the capital at the beginning of the century, the **Connaught Building** ★, erected in 1913-1914, is pure neo-Gothic. Architect David Ewart was inspired by many English buildings of the Tudor era, particularly Hampton Court and Windsor Castle, in the conception of these plans. The building boasts crenellated turrets at each end and at its centre.

Major's Hill rises at the mouth of the Rideau Canal, on the east bank. This land which borders the entrance to the canal and the Ottawa River, belonged for a long time to the British Crown, which, when Bytown was founded, had decided to keep it in order to ensure the protection of the canal. The only building erected on its summit was the residence of Colonel By, but it was destroyed by fire in 1849. In 1864, in a project to beautify the city, the land was transformed into a huge park – the city's very first – **Major's Hill Park**. Sprawled along the Ottawa River, it remains one of the city's most beautiful green spaces. It envelops **Nepean Point**, which juts into the river and which offers a lovely view of the Parliament Buildings. The Astrolabe Theatre, where various events are organized in summer, is also within the park confines.

Turn right onto St. Patrick Street.

In 1841, **Notre Dame Basilica** ★★ *(Sussex Dr. at the corner of Saint Patrick St.)*, topped by two elegant steeples, was built to serve Catholics in Lower Town, French-speakers as well as the English-speaking Irish. In the choir stall, you will notice the presence of Saint John the Baptist and of Saint Patrick. This is the oldest church in the city. Its magnificent choir stall of finely worked wood and statues of the prophets and evangelists by Louis-Philippe Hébert are still in perfect condition.

Continue along Sussex Drive.

The **National Gallery of Canada** ★★★ *(free admission to the permanent collection; Jun to early Oct, every day 10am to 6pm; Oct to late May, Wed to Sun 10am to 5pm, Tue 10am to 8pm; 380 Sussex Dr., ☎990-1985)*, with its collection of 45,000 works of art, 1,200 of which are on display, offers a fabulous trip through the art history of Canada and elsewhere. Rising above the Ottawa River, this modern glass, granite and concrete building, a masterpiece by architect Moshe Safdie, is easily identified by its harmonious tower, covered with glass triangles, recalling the shape of the parliamentary library visible in the distance.

Once inside, the museum seems to draw you. You'll first walk up the Colonnnade, stopping for a minute to contemplate the Boreal Garden outside, inspired by the work of the Group of Seven. Once in the Grand Hall, the spectacular view of the Parliament Buildings and the Ottawa River unfolds before you.

The first rooms of the museum, on the ground floor, are devoted to the works of Canadian and American artists. Fifteen of these rooms trace the evolution of Canadian artistic movements. Some of the finest canvasses from the 19th century are exhibited there, notably *Sister Saint Alphonse* by Antoine Plamondon, recognized as one of the earliest Canadian masterpieces. You can also see works by Cornelius

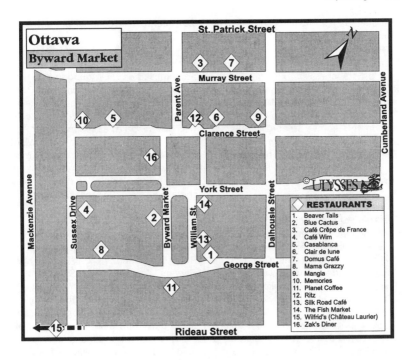

Ottawa
Byward Market

St. Patrick Street
Murray Street
Clarence Street
York Street
George Street
Rideau Street

Parent Ave.
Cumberland Avenue
Mackenzie Avenue
Sussex Drive
Byward Market
William St.
Dalhousie Street

© ULYSSES

RESTAURANTS

1. Beaver Tails
2. Blue Cactus
3. Café Crêpe de France
4. Café Wim
5. Casablanca
6. Clair de lune
7. Domus Café
8. Mama Grazzy
9. Mangia
10. Memories
11. Planet Coffee
12. Ritz
13. Silk Road Café
14. The Fish Market
15. Wilfrid's (Château Laurier)
16. Zak's Diner

Krieghoff, an artist of Dutch descent who portrayed the lives of ordinary people in the early days of colonization with great brio.

The following rooms present important works by artists who made their mark in the early 20th century. Among them, are canvasses by the Ontario painter Tom Thomson (*The Jack Pine*) and by members of the Group of Seven (including *The Red Maple* by A.Y. Jackson), who created unique works in the modern interpretation of natural scenes from the Canadian Shield. Space is also given to artists who gained renown by creating painting techniques and exploiting themes that were particular to them, including British Columbian artist Emily Carr (*Indian Hut, Queen Charlotte Islands*). You can also contemplate canvasses by great 20th-century Québecois painters, notably Alfred Pellan (*On the Beach*), Jean-Paul

Riopelle (*Pavane*), Jean-Paul Lemieux (*The Visit*), and Paul-Émile Borduas (*Leeward of the Island*).

The ground floor also includes Inuit art galleries, which merit special attention. With about 160 sculptures and 200 prints, they provide an occasion to admire several masterpieces of Inuit art, including *The Enchanted Owl* by Kenojuak and the beautiful sculpture *Man and Woman Seated with a Child*.

The museum also houses an impressive collection of American and European works. Works of the great masters are presented in chronological order, and in the course of your visit you can contemplate creations by famous painters such as the Pierre-Paul Rubens work *The Entombment*. The rooms containing 19th-century canvasses present several surprises, including *Mercury and Argus* by Turner, *Woman and Umbrella* by Edgar Degas, *Waterloo Bridge: The Sun in the Fog* by Claude Monet, *Forest* by Paul Cézanne, and *Hope I* by Gustav Klimt. The achievements of 20th-century artists are also highlighted; the museum exhibits canvasses including *Nude on Yellow Sofa* by Matisse, *The Small Table* by Picasso, *The Glass of Absinth* by Georges Braque, *Number 29* by Jackson Pollock, and *In the Line of Fire* by Barnett Newman. The collection of American art includes several lithographies by Roy Lichtenstein and Andy Warhol.

The string of rooms on the ground floor surrounds a very unique gallery that houses an under-appreciated work: the beautiful interior of the **Chapelle du Couvent Notre-Dame-du-Sacré-Coeur**, designed by Georges Bouillon in 1887-1888. When the convent was demolished in 1972, the structure of the chapel was taken apart piece by piece and preserved. A few years later, a room was specially laid out in the National Gallery to accommodate it. Its splendid choir and its wooden, fan-shaped vaults and cast-iron columns may still be admired here.

Museum lovers can continue along Sussex Drive to the Canadian War Museum and the Royal Canadian Mint.

The entrance to the **Canadian War Museum** ★ *($3.50; May to mid-Oct, every day 9:30am to 5pm, Thu to 8pm; mid-Oct to May, closed Mon; 330 Sussex Dr., ☎776-8600)* is impossible to miss, what with a tank sitting on the lawn in front of it. The museum was laid out in a beautiful building designed at the beginning of the century by David Ewart to house the National Archives. The exhibitions are spread over three stories and retrace the history of the Canadian Army from its very first battles in the early days of colonization to its participation in the great world events that have marked the

20th century. Weapons, uniforms and medals of the French military, from the very earliest stages of colonization, and of the British army, which came next, are exposed on the ground floor. These various objects, in addition to the interest they arouse, are used to relate some of the major events of the colonial wars. On the second floor, the Canadian army's involvement in WW II is recounted through short films, models, weapons of all sorts, uniforms and other objects. Finally, on the top story, there is an exhibition that highlights the role of peacekeepers.

Just next door to the Canadian War Museum is the building that houses the **Royal Canadian Mint** ★ *($2; Mon to Fri 9am to 4pm, Sat and Sun 10am to 5pm; 320 Sussex Dr., ☎993-8990)*, the plans of which were conceived by Ewart in 1905-1908. Common Canadian coins were once struck here, but today the mint produces only silver, gold and platinum collector's pieces. The entire process may be seen here: the selection and cutting of precious metals, the striking of the coins and the quality control procedure. It is best to visit during the week when it is possible to see the coins being made through large bay windows; tours are offered on the weekend, but in the absence of workers the whole process has to be imagined.

Backtrack to Clarence Street and turn left. Turn right onto Byward and proceed to the Byward Market.

One of Ottawa's liveliest places, the **Byward Market** ★★ *(around York and George Streets)* is a pleasant open-air market where various merchants gather to sell fruits, vegetables, flowers and all sorts of other treasures. All around, and on the neighbouring streets, there are many shops, restaurants, bars and cafés, some of them with pretty outdoor terraces. On fine summer days, the area is at its liveliest, with crowds of people out for a stroll or a little shopping.

Laurier House ★ *($2.25; Apr to Sep, Tue to Sat 9am to 5pm, Sun 2pm to 5pm; Oct to Mar, Tue to Sat 10am to 5pm, Sun 2pm to 5pm; 335 Laurier Ave. E., ☎692-2581)*, a delightful residence built in 1878, belonged to Sir Wilfrid Laurier. He was elected Prime Minister of Canada in 1896, and that year his party, the Liberal Party of Canada, offered him this house. Laurier was the first French Canadian Prime Minister, a post he held until 1911; he lived in this house until his death in 1919. Later, Lady Laurier gave it to William Lyon Mackenzie King, who succeeded her husband as Liberal leader. When King died in 1950, the house was bequeathed to the government as part of Canada's heritage. Visiting it today, you can explore several rooms decorated according to King's tastes and a few others decorated with the Laurier family's furniture.

Ottawa University, previously known as Ottawa College, was originally run by a religious order and served the Catholic communities of Ottawa. Now the university is a renowned educational institution. Its campus is bordered by Laurier Avenue, Nicholas Street and King Edward Avenue.

The end of Laurier Avenue abuts the Rideau Canal.

The **Ottawa Congress Centre**, located on the shore of the canal, hosts various events throughout the year.

Tour D: Along Sussex Drive ★★

Past the Royal Canadian Mint, Sussex Drive runs along the eastern bank of the Ottawa River to a posh section of the city. This tour is best explored by car or by bicycle since the attractions are rather spread out.

First stop is **Earnscliffe**, a superb neo-Gothic residence overlooking the Ottawa River that dates from 1856-1857. It was originally home to the family of John MacKinnon, son-in-law of Thomas McKay, who designed the entrance to the Rideau Canal. A few years after MacKinnon's death in 1870, Prime Minister John A. Macdonald was a tenant here. He bought the house about 10 years later and lived out the rest of his years in it. Today Earnscliffe is home to the British High Commission.

At Green Island the Rideau River empties into the Ottawa in two pretty waterfalls that form a curtain (hence the river's name; *rideau* is French for "curtain"). Take a moment to stop at the belvedere at the top of the falls; it offers a magnificent **view** ★ of the river and of the city in the distance.

Ottawa City Hall ★ stands on Green Island, and its modern look was the pride of the city in 1958 when it was inaugurated. Over the years the city administration outgrew this stone, aluminum and glass building, and, to preserve it, it was expanded rather than replaced. Moshe Safdie, the architect of the National Gallery of Canada (see p 74), was commissioned to oversee the work.

The **Canada and the World** interpretive centre *(free; early Jun to early Sep, every day; rest of the year, weekends only)* is also located on the island. It presents an exhibition that explains Canada's role in other countries.

A series of magnificent homes appears next, but number 24 should catch your eye. It is an immense stone house surrounded by a beautiful garden – the **Official Residence of the Prime Minister**

OTTAWA

of Canada. Built in 1867 for business-man Joseph Currier, it became the home of Canadian prime ministers in 1949. For obvious reasons it is not open to the public.

Not far from 24 Sussex Drive another splendid residence crops up, sur-rounded by a pleasant and huge garden that covers 40 hectares: **Rideau Hall** ★★ *(free; schedule varies; 1 Sus-sex Dr., 998-7113)*. This is the offi-cial residence of Canada's Governor General, the representative of the Queen of England, Elizabeth II. It is a sumptuous Regency-style home that was built in 1838 for Thomas McKay, the designer of the entrance to the Rideau Canal (see p 65). In 1865, the government rented the building to ac-commodate the governor general of the day, Lord Monck, and then bought the property in 1868. Since then, many modifications have been made to the original building, which has been in continual use as an official residence.

A vast and pleasant garden surrounds the house, where you can linger about. Guided tours are offered during the summer of the five rooms open to the public.

Facing Rideau Hall is a lovely green space, **Rockliffe Park**, with lookouts offering fine views of Hull and the Gatineau River.

Past the park, Sussex Drive becomes Rockliffe Drive.

Visitors are immediately impressed upon entering the **National Aviation Museum** ★★★ *($5; May to Sep, every day 9am to 5pm, Thu to 8pm; Sep to May, Tue to Sun 10am to 5pm; Rockliffe Airport, 993-2010)* by the unique atmosphere of this huge, won-derfully laid-out building. The fascinat-ing exhibition housed here and culled from the museum's beautiful collection

of airplanes thoroughly brings to light the dazzling, rapid-fire evolution that so far is just one-hundred-years long. Eight themes are explored: the era of pio-neers, the First World War, bush pilot-ing, airlines, the British Commonwealth training plan, the Second World War, air and sea forces, and the era of jet planes. Among the 45 planes displayed in the interior of the museum (seven planes are exhibited outside and there are even more in a storage area that sometimes figures on the guided tour), some are particularly captivating. An exhibit features models of wood and canvas planes that were the first ever to take to the air, and a short film re-lates the exploits of the first brave pilots to ride these flying engines. The Curtiss HS-2L and the sturdy Beaver are used to illustrate the importance of commercial flying in the exploration of Canada's immense territory. Planes that became famous in the Second World War, such as the Avro Lancaster bomber, the Hawker Hurricane fighter and the Messerschmitt, a German-de-signed jet, are highlighted. Finally, a few jets are displayed, including the Lockheed F-104A Starfighter. The appeal of this museum, aside from the airplanes, lies in the great story of aviation that it retells through recon-structions and consistently clear expla-nations of both technical and historical aspects. Interactive exhibitions – partic-ularly "Full Flight," which uses games to explain the basic principals of aero-dynamics – along with films and dem-onstrations, including the very popular "Lighter than Air," aim to familiarize young people and the young-at-heart with the aeronautical world. An audio tour may be rented *($2)*.

Tour E: Other Attractions

Ottawa has a few other sights worth visiting that, although not far, are lo-

Three Ottawa Neighbourhoods

Somerset Street is a long thoroughfare lined with charming shops and restaurants that crosses the southern part of Upper Town from east to west. The first little nexus of businesses is in the vicinity of Bank Street. Going west, strollers come upon another facet of the capital: **Chinatown**. Although it is not as large as those of Montreal or Toronto, Ottawa's Chinatown does cover a few blocks between Bronson and Booth. It has a flurry of storefronts filled with a thousand and one Chinese products, shops fragranced by Oriental spices and restaurants with menus of Dim Sum and Cantonese specialties.

East of Bank Street, Somerset intersects Preston Avenue, a north-south artery that fostered the development of another very pleasant ethnic neighbourhood, **Little Italy**. Although to some this neighbourhood might seem less exotic than Chinatown, it does conceal a few gratifying finds, including fine grocery stores and family restaurants that serve incomparable cuisine.

Finally, **The Glebe**, which extends out from Bank Street south of Queensway, is a lively, stylish neighbourhood of chic boutiques and fine restaurants where the urge to wander about, eye's wide at the sight of pretty houses, is very compelling. This peaceful residential area is ideal for sunny-day strolls.

cated outside the city centre and not within the confines of any tour described above.

From downtown take Rideau Street, which becomes Montreal Road past Cummings Bridge, to St. Laurent Boulevard, which leads to the National Museum of Science and Technology.

The **National Museum of Science and Technology** ★★ *($6; May to Sep, every day 9am to 6pm, Fri to 9pm; Sep to Apr, Tue to Sun 9am to 5pm; 1867 St. Laurent Blvd., ☎991-3044)* offers a pleasant opportunity to enter the world of science and technology – a universe that may seem too complex at first glance to some. The appeal of this museum is not based on any particular exhibition but rather on its panoply of interactive presentations on various subjects. For example, computer science is tackled in an exhibition entitled "Connexions": about 500 computers are displayed, illustrating the

extraordinary technological leaps and bounds that the field has made in just 50 years. Another exhibition, "Love, Leisure and Laundry," recounts the evolution of the multitude of little tools used in our daily lives – like lamps, toilets and iceboxes – that have greatly contributed to our improved standard of living. Other fascinating topics are also dealt with, such as transportation and printing. Through games, explanatory panels and models of all sorts, visitors to the museum gain a better understanding of how the world works and have fun at the same time.

From downtown, take Queen Elizabeth Drive, then Bank Street to Riverside Drive, then Pleasant Park Road to the intersection of Cabot Street.

The Billings family were among the first colonists to settle in Bytown. In 1827-1828, a beautiful neoclassical home was built for them; it has survived all

OTTAWA

Canadian Museum of Civilization

these years and now houses the **Billings Estate Museum** *($2.50; May to Oct, Sun to Thu noon to 5pm; 2100 Cabot St., ☎247-4830)*. Furniture, photographs and various curios are exhibited, illustrating daily life in the early days of the city, and guides make the museum even more pleasant. A large garden of flowers and trees surrounds the building.

From downtown take Queen Elizabeth Drive, which becomes Prince of Wales Drive.

The **Central Experimental Farm** *(Prince of Wales Drive, ☎995-5222)* is surrounded by a vast garden adorned with lovely flowers in the summer. It includes an arboretum where nearly 2,000 species of trees are grown. You can also see animals, including dairy cows, beef cattle, horses and sheep. As well, an agriculture museum presents different types of farm machinery used throughout the 20th century.

Tour F: Hull (Québec) ★

The Du Portage Bridge crosses the Ottawa River over Victoria Island, leading from Ottawa to Hull. The area at the foot of the bridge on the Ottawa side of the river was once known as Lebreton Flats, and an industrial district developed there in proximity to the sawmills. Until the decline of the lumber industry in the 20th century, piles of wood cluttered the banks of the river, but today the only traces of this era that remain are the defunct mills on Victoria Island.

Although the road leading into Hull is named after an important post-war town planner, the city is certainly not a model of enlightened urban development. Its architecture is very unlike that of Ottawa, just across the river. The town was founded in 1800 by American Loyalist Philemon Wright who was involved in agriculture and the exploitation of the Ottawa valley's rich virgin forests. In 1850, Hull became an important wood-processing centre. For many generations the Eddy Company, which is based in the area, has been supplying matches to the entire world.

The modest wood-frame houses that line the streets of Hull are nicknamed "matchboxes" because they once housed many employees of the Eddy match factory, and because they have had more than their fair share of fires.

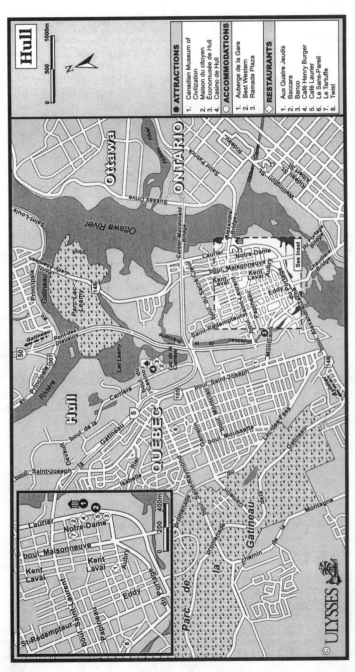

Hull

0 500 1000m

N

● **ATTRACTIONS**
1. Canadian Museum of Civilization
2. Maison du citoyen
3. Economusée de Hull
4. Casino de Hull

○ **ACCOMMODATIONS**
1. Auberge de la Gare
2. Best Western
3. Ramada Plaza

◇ **RESTAURANTS**
1. Aux Quatre Jeudis
2. Baccara
3. Banco
4. Café Henry Burger
5. Café Laurier
6. Le Sans-Pareil
7. Le Tartuffe
8. Twist

© ULYSSES

In fact, Hull has burned so many times throughout its history that few of the town's historical buildings remain. The former town hall and beautiful Catholic church burned down in 1971 and 1972, respectively. Ottawa has the reputation of being a quiet city, while Hull is considered more of a fun town, essentially because Québec laws are more lenient.

Turn left onto Rue Papineau. The parking lot of the Canadian Museum of Civilization is at the end of this street.

The **Canadian Museum of Civilization** ★★★ *($5, free admission on Sun 9am to noon; May to mid-Oct, every day 9am to 6pm; mid-Oct to late Apr, every day 9am to 5pm; Jul to Sep, Fri to 9pm; Thu until 9pm all year; 100 Rue Laurier, ☎776-7000)* or the Musée Canadien des Civilisations. Many parks and museums were established along this section of the Québec-Ontario border as part of a large redevelopment program in the National Capital Region between 1983 and 1989. Hull became the site of the magnificent Canadian Museum of Civilization, dedicated to the history of Canada's various cultural groups. If there is one museum that must be seen in Canada it is this one. Douglas Cardinal of Alberta designed the museum's two striking curved buildings, one housing the administrative offices and restoration laboratories, and the other the museum's collections. Their undulating design brings to mind rock formations of the Canadian Shield, shaped by wind and glaciers. There is a beautiful view of the Ottawa River and Parliament Hill from the grounds behind the museum.

The Grande Gallerie (Great Hall) houses the most extensive collection of native totem poles in the world. Another collection brilliantly recreates different periods in Canadian history, from the arrival of the Vikings around AD 1000

to life in rural Ontario in the 19th century and French Acadia in the 17th century. Contemporary native art, as well as popular arts and traditional crafts are also on display. In the Musée des Enfants (Children's Museum), young visitors choose a theme before being led through an extraordinary adventure. Screening rooms are equipped with OMNIMAX technology, a new system developed by the creators of the large-screen IMAX. Most of the movies shown here deal with Canadian geography.

Continue south on Rue Laurier. At Rue Montcalm, turn right.

The mission of the **Écomusée de Hull** *($5; Apr to Oct 10am to 6pm, Nov to Mar 10am to 4pm; Rue Montcalm, ☎595-7790)* is to make people more aware of ecological issues, and to achieve this goal, it presents various exhibits on themes such as the origin of the solar system and the evolution of planet Earth. This institution, however, goes beyond tracing the origins of life on earth, because it is also home to an insectarium with no less than 4,000 different species of insects. Finally, you can also take a look at a small exhibit on the industrial history of the city.

Take Highway 50, then Highway 5 north to the Boulevard du Casino exit. Then take Rue Saint-Raymond, which becomes Boulevard du Casino.

The **Casino de Hull** ★★ *(11am to 3am; 1 Boulevard du Casino, ☎800-665-2274 or 772-2100)* has an impressive location between two lakes; Leamy Lake, in the park of the same name, and Lac de la Carrière, which is in the basin of an old limestone quarry. The theme of water is omnipresent all around the superb building, inaugurated in 1996. The magnificent walkway leading to the main entrance is dotted with towering fountains, and the harbour has 20 slips for boaters. The gambling area, which is 2,741 square metres in size, includes 1,300 slot machines and 58 playing tables spread around a simulated tropical forest. Quebec painter Jean-Paul Riopelle's famous 40-metre-long painting, *Hommage à Rosa Luxembourg*, dominates the room. The artist created this immense triptych in honour of Joan Mitchell, his partner of many years. The opening of the casino also marked the first annual fireworks festival, **Les Grands Feux du Casino** *(☎771-FEUX or 800-771-FEUX)*, which takes place every year in August. The casino has excellent restaurants, including Baccara (see p 94), and two bars. The casino opened a heliport in 1997.

Continue driving south of the Ottawa River. Take Boulevard de la Carrière to Rue Deveault.

Imagine contemplating the magnificent landscape of Parc de la Gatineau, while comfortably seated aboard a steam train dating back to 1907: **Hull-Chelsea-Wakefield Steam Train** ★ *($26; late May to late Oct, departures Sat to Thu 1:30pm; Fri 10am; 165 Rue Deveault, ☎778-7246, ⇌778-5007)*. As well as giving you a chance to see beautiful natural sites, this half-day excursion takes you to Wakefield, a charming little English town, where you have two hours to explore and shop. If you're interested in the trip but don't want to take the train both ways, you can cross Gatineau park on bicycle and return by train. Packages including a meal are also available.

Parc de la Gatineau ★ *(6$; visitor centre is located in Chelsea, also accessible via Boulevard Taché in Hull; ☎827-2020)* is not far from downtown Hull. The 35,000-hectare park was founded during the Depression in 1934 in order to protect the forests from people looking for firewood. It is crossed by a 34-kilometre-long road dotted with panoramic lookout points, including **Belvédère Champlain**, which offer superb views of the lakes, rivers and hills of the region. Outdoor activities can be enjoyed here throughout the year. Hiking and mountain biking trails are open during the summer. There are many lakes in the park, including Lac Meech, which also was the name of a Canadian constitutional agreement drawn up nearby but never ratified. Watersports such as windsurfing, canoeing and swimming are also very popular and the park rents small boats and camp sites. **Lusk Cave**, formed some 12,500 years ago by water flowing from melting glaciers can be explored. During the winter, approximately 190 kilometres of cross-country skiing trails are maintained *(approx. $7 per day)*. **Camp Fortune** *(☎827-1717)* has 19 downhill-ski runs, 14 are open at night. It costs $24 during the day and $20 at night.

The **Domaine Mackenzie-King** ★★ *($6 for parking; mid-May to mid-Jun, Wed to Sun 11am to 5pm; mid-Jun to mid-Oct, 11am to 5pm; Rue Barnes in Kingsmere, Parc de la Gatineau, ☎613-239-5000 and 827-2020)*. William Lyon Mackenzie King was Prime Minister of Canada from 1921 to 1930, and again from 1935 to 1948. His love of art and horticulture rivalled his interest in politics and he was always happy to get away to his summer residence near Lac Kingsmere, which today is part of Parc de la Gatineau. The estate consists of two houses (one of which is now a charming tea room), a landscaped garden and follies, false ruins that were popular at the time. However, unlike most follies, which were designed to imitate ruins, those on the Mackenzie-King estate are authentic building fragments. For the most part, they were taken from the original Canadian House of Parliament, destroyed by fire in 1916, and from Westminister

OTTAWA

Abbey, damaged by German bombs in 1941.

OUTDOOR ACTIVITIES

Bicycling

The Ottawa region is crisscrossed by no fewer than 150 kilometres of pathways that are very pleasant to meander on foot or by bicycle. Whether you opt for an outing along the Rideau Canal, on the Rockliffe promenade or along the Ottawa River, you will benefit from pleasant landscapes, from peace and quiet and, above all, from trails that are very well laid out for cycling. On Sunday mornings from late May to early September, cyclists are in seventh heaven as these routes are closed to automobile traffic. Maps of Ottawa's bicycle and walking paths are available at the capital Infocentre.

Bicycle Rental

Cyco's: 5 Hawthorne Ave., ☎567-8180.
Dow's Lake Pavilion: ☎232-1001.

Cruises

As soon as the fine weather arrives, cruises are operated along the waterways surrounding Ottawa. You can see the city from a different angle while drifting quietly on the waves. Several companies offer such excursions, notably:

Ottawa Riverboat
30 Murray St., Ottawa, Ontario, K1N 5M4, ☎562-4888.

Skating

Imagine lacing on a pair of skates and gliding uninterrupted over 8 kilometres of ice. Every winter, as soon as the **Rideau Canal** has frozen over, in late December or early January, the canal is transformed into a vast skating rink, one of the longest in the world. The ice surface is cleared and maintained for the pleasure of skaters of all ages. There is a heated cabin just a few steps from the National Arts Centre where skaters can lace up away from the cold.

Dow's Lake also has a heated lodge in which you can don your skates, warm up and have a bite to eat.

Ice Conditions: ☎239-5234.

ACCOMMODATIONS

A wide choice of types of accommodation to fit every budget is available in Ottawa. Most places are very comfortable and offer a number of extra services. Prices vary according to the type of accommodation and the quality-to-price ratio is generally good, but remember to add the 7% G.S.T (federal Goods and Services Tax) and the provincial sales tax of 5%. The Goods and Services Tax is refundable for non-residents in certain cases (see p 50).

Tour B: Upper Town

Right in the city, on the Lebreton flats, travellers will find a small, friendly **campground** *(free for children under 12; Jun to early Sep; tents only; ☎236-1251)* easily reached by a bicycle path as well as by car or bus. It is run by the National Capital Commission and has 200 places. Toilets, showers and picnic tables. Reservations are not accepted.

Visitors can stay in proximity of the Parliament Buildings on Albert Street, which changes in this part of Ottawa – the shops and the hubbub of downtown giving way to a quiet residential district (some may even fault it for being virtually devoid of shops). This area boasts two charming inns. The first of these, the **Doral Inn** *($69 bkfst incl.; K, tv; 468 Albert St., K1R 5B5, ☎230-8055)* is set up in a lovely Victorian house and contains about forty rooms. Alongside the hall are two small lounges appointed with secondhand furniture, giving them an antiquated look that will appeal to some. The rooms are simply furnished and offer decent comfort for the price. All are equipped with private bathrooms and some also have kitchenettes. Rooms can be rented for the day, the week, or the month.

Next door, the **Albert House** *($80 bkfst incl.; tv; 478 Albert St., K1R 5B5, ☎236-4479)* is also located in an appealing residence. There are only 17 rooms, giving it a pleasant family atmosphere. Each of the rooms is perfectly maintained and decorated with care.

As you enter the **Delta** *($105; ≈, ℜ, △, ℗; 361 Queen St., K1R 7S9, ☎238-6000, ⇝238-2290)* you will straightaway notice the efforts made to create a more intimate atmosphere than at the standard downtown chain hotel. The glass ceiling allows plenty of light to penetrate the vast lobby. It also boasts ficuses, mahogany chairs and a warm fireplace to cosy up to during the winter. The rooms are of a good size and are furnished with comfortable mahogany pieces. Finally, children will be thrilled with the pool's long waterslide.

At first glance, the **Albert at Bay** *($110; K, ℗; 435 Albert St., K1R 7X4, ☎238-8858 or 800-267-6644, ⇝238-1433)*, a banal building, looks more like a high-rise apartment complex that has seen better days than a hotel. This place, however, is a good choice for practical reasons rather than charm. Every suite boasts a bedroom, a living room, a dining area and a fully equipped kitchenette (microwave oven, coffee-maker). Also, over and above the comfort of a real apartment, guests benefit from the perks of a hotel, such as a daily cleaning service and a fitness centre.

The **Lord Elgin Hotel** *($115; ℜ, ⅄; 100 Elgin St., K1P 5K8, ☎235-3333 or 800-267-4298, ⇝235-3223)* is among those untimely Ottawan institutions. Very few pieces of furniture, however, have managed to conserve any traces of its past, save for the lobby, which still has a pretty centre light and an antique mobile hanging from the ceiling. The rooms are large and decorated with modern furnishings that may fail to lend the charm of yesteryear but make for a pleasant stay nonetheless.

Some prefer older establishments filled with antiques and an elegant decor, still others opt for modern styling and the utmost in service. Those who fit into the latter category will appreciate the very modern **Sheraton** *($119; ≈, ℜ, △, ℗, ⅄; 150 Albert St., K1P 5G2, ☎238-1500 or 800-489-8333, ⇝235-2723)*, with its conference halls, large rooms with offices, telephones with voice-mail, hair dryers and fitness centre with a pool, sauna and whirlpool.

Inside an imposing old house, the **Carmichael Inn & Spa** *($134 bkfst incl.; ℜ; 46 Cartier St., K2P 1J3, ☎236-4667, ⇝563-7529)* is part of Ottawa's heritage. This non-smoking

OTTAWA

establishment has 11 rooms, decorated with antiques and fitted with queen-size beds.

Tour C: Lower Town

For low-priced accommodations during the summer **Ottawa University** *(85 University St., ☎562-5771, ⊷562-5157)* and **Carleton University** *(1125 Colonel By Promenade, ☎520-5611, ⊷520-3952)* rent basic but decent rooms in their residences.

Right next to the Rideau Centre, in the middle of everything, you will see an imposing building that once housed the city's prison. Entirely remodeled, it now houses a **youth hostel** *($17 - $21 for dormitories, $37 for a room; K; 75 Nicholas St., K1N 7B9, ☎235-2595)*. In addition to dormitories and three rooms, the hostel has a fully-equipped communal kitchen.

The Sandy Hill district is full of charming Victorian style houses. If you would like to stay in one but cannot afford the luxury, the **McGee Inn** *($68 bkfst incl. and sb, $78 bkfst incl. and pb; ◈, ☰; 185 Daly Ave., K1N 6E8, ☎237-6089)* is a good choice. This red-brick house, erected in 1886 has maintained its original character. Admittedly, the rooms are simply decorated, but they are tasteful nonetheless. Moreover, the place is well-kept and all the rooms are air conditioned.

Located in a quiet neighbourhood and affording a superb view of Strathcona Park, the **Olde Bytown Bed and Breakfast** *($75 bkfst incl.; pb, sb; 459 Laurier Ave. E., K1N 6R4, ☎565-7939, ⊷565-7981)* is a choice place for those who appreciate the cachet of turn-of-the-century Victorian houses. Every room in the B & B is meticulously kept and graced with beautiful antiques, flowered wallpaper and old artifacts. There are seven wonderfully cosy rooms in which guests could easily spend hours daydreaming.

The impeccably kept **Gasthaus Switzerland** *($78; 89 Daly Ave., K1N 6E6, ☎237-0335, ⊷594-3327)* is a small, unpretentious hotel whose Swiss-chalet-style decor may be a little too colourful for some tastes. You will have a restful stay, however, for the owners are friendly, breakfasts are plentiful, and the atmosphere is pleasant.

The **Auberge King Edward** *($80; 525 King Edward Ave., K1N 7N3, ☎565-6700)* is inside a very beautiful house dating from the beginning of the century and, in keeping with the period of the building, all the rooms are graced with antiques and myriad old curios. This somewhat cluttered decor has undeniable charm and imparts an atmosphere of calm and well-being to the establishment. The inn boasts two charming living rooms, as well as three exceedingly well-kept bedrooms (one with a private bathroom).

With its dark blue foyer trimmed with steel and wood, the **Novotel** *($105; ℜ, ≈, ◯, ⊘; 33 Nicholas St., K1N 9M7, ☎230-3033 or 800-NOVOTEL, ⊷230-7865)* stands apart from the city's Victorian hotels. This modernity is not without refinement, despite the fact that some will describe it as cold. The rooms are somewhat warmer, with, their dark colours pleasantly adorning the spacious quarters, and all boast a rather large bathroom.

If you prefer the comfort of a suite at a reasonable price, **Les Suites** *($109; ≈, ℜ, ◯, ◈, ♿, ✗; 130 Besserer St., Ottawa K1N 9M9, ☎232-2000, ⊷232-1242)* welcomes you. Just a few steps from the Rideau Centre, you will enjoy a one- or two-bedroom apartment with full kitchen, dining room and lounge. Children under 18 stay free. The hotel also has an indoor pool.

At the very end of Wilbrod Street stands the magnificent stone building housing the **Paterson B&B** *($115-$175 bkfst incl.; 500 Wilbrod St., K1N 6N2, ☎565-8996, ≈565- 6546)*, one of the district's gems. This monumental Queen Anne house was entirely renovated in 1992 leaving in place its treasures of yesteryear. Its cut-stone façade proudly heralds the splendours awaiting inside. The first room guests enter displays panelled walls and ceilings, finely-wrought wainscotting, beautiful antique furniture, carpets and a grand wooden staircase leading to the rooms upstairs. The Victorian decor of the four rooms combines antique furnishings, floral prints, frames and curios of all kinds. The establishment's good taste extends to the private bathrooms, all exceedingly charming and impeccably clean. Some rooms have small boudoirs, where guests can watch TV. Breakfast is served in a spacious and elegant dining room. A very gracious welcome completes this idyllic scene.

The **Westin Hotel** *($135; ≈, ℜ, △, ⊛, ⊘, ᕖ, ✕; 11 Colonel By Dr., ☎560-7000, ≈569-2013)* has what may be the most enviable location in Ottawa, facing the Rideau Canal, opposite the National Arts Centre and right in the heart of Ottawa's bustle. It is part of the complex that includes the Rideau Centre shopping mall and the Ottawa Convention Centre. Rooms are very spacious and extremely comfortable, offering magnificent views of the canal. The hotel has a very good restaurant, Daly's (excellent atmosphere, interesting and refined cuisine), and even a happening night club. Very good weekend packages are usually available.

The opulence and luxury of the **Château Laurier** *($169; ≈; △; ᕖ; 1 Rideau St., Ottawa K1N 8S7, ☎241-1414 or 800-441-1414, ≈562-7030)* (see p 71), part of the Canadian Pacific hotel chain, will appeal to those who like to rave about beautiful things. Upon entering the hotel, visitors will be swept away by the decor: wainscotted walls, cornices, bas reliefs and antiques. The lobby itself gives an idea of the comfort and elegance of the rooms, all stocked with wooden furnishings, plush couches and comfortable beds. Undeniably pleasant, the rooms combine onetime elegance with today's comforts. Two very good restaurants (see p 91) and a sports centre with a lovely Art-Deco swimming pool add to the place's overall appeal.

Ottawa Neighbourhoods

The Glebe

Located on a quiet street in the pleasant Glebe district, the **Blue Spruces Bed & Breakfast** *($85 bkfst incl.; 187 Glebe Ave., K1S 2C6, ☎236-8521, ≈231-3730)* is enchanting. This elegant Edwardian house welcomes only non-smokers and is furnished with 19th-century Victorian and Canadian antiques. The luxury of the decor is rivalled only by that of the bedding. And if that is not enough, the breakfasts and the hospitality of the owner will round out the enchantment.

Tour F: Hull (Québec)

The **Auberge de la Gare** *($74 bkfst incl.; 205 Boulevard St-Joseph, J8Y 3X3, ☎778-8085 or 773-4273, ≈595-2021)* is a simple, conventional hotel that offers good value for your money. The service is both courteous

OTTAWA

and friendly, and the rooms are clean and well kept, albeit nondescript.

The small, austere lobby of the **Hôtel Best Western** *($79; ≈, ℜ; 131 Rue Laurier, J8X 3W3, ☎770-8550 or 800-265-8550)* is hardly inviting. The rooms, decorated with modern furniture, are neither cozy nor luxurious but are nonetheless comfortable.

The **Hôtel Ramada Plaza** *($95; ℜ, ≈, ♿; 35 Rue Laurier, J9Y 4E9, ☎778-6111 or 800-567-9607, ≈778-8548)* is located opposite the Canadian Museum of Civilization. It is a simple-looking building in the typical chain-hotel style, and the rooms are stocked with nondescript, functional furnishings. During the low season, you can take advantage of the hotel's economical package rates.

✕ RESTAURANTS

The city of Ottawa has many different kinds of restaurants of all kinds. Whether you like steak or roast beef, fish or French, Italian, Asian or other specialties, the city's restaurants are sure to meet your culinary expectations. A number of them are open for both lunch and dinner; keep in mind, however, that satisfying your hunger after 11pm can prove difficult.

This chapter offers you a selection of the best restaurants in the city. If you would like more information on Ottawa's restaurants, consult the www.dine.net web site.

Tour A: The Rideau Canal

The menu at the **Ritz on the Canal** *($$; 375 Queen Elizabeth Dr., at Fifth Ave., ☎238-8998)* differs somewhat from those of its sister establishments (see p 89, 91) in that it also features "gourmet" pizzas baked in a wood-burning oven. This restaurant is particularly appreciated in summer, on account of its outstanding setting and huge terrace facing a part of the canal that resembles a bay. No smoking.

 The **Café of the National Arts Centre** *($$$; 53 Elgin St., ☎594-5127)* offers an unbeatable view of the teeming activity on the Rideau Canal, with boats in the summer and skaters in the winter. During the summer months, meals are served on a comfortable, well-designed terrace. Beyond a doubt, this is one of the most pleasant outdoor terraces in town. Refined Canadian cooking is offered; the chef makes inventive use of quality products from various regions of Canada. Grilled Atlantic salmon is a specialty. Not to be missed are the wonderful desserts. Prices are on the high side, however, unless a fixed-price menu is offered, which is unfortunately rare.

Tour B: Upper Town

If there is one place in Ottawa in which to enjoy a good meal in an unparalleled ambiance, it is definitely the **D'Arcy McGee** *($$; 44 Sparks St., ☎230-4433)*. This typical Irish pub, located a stone's throw from Parliament Hill, is the haunt par excellence of the capital's civil cervants. Extremely warm and frequented by a clientele of all ages, it has become one of the city's absolute musts.

A little further west, the **Fairouz** restaurant *($$; 343 Somerset St. W., ☎233-1536)* occupies another of these fine, renovated Victorian houses. If you like Lebanese specialties, go no further: the food here will delight you.

In terms of decor, **Johnny Farina** *($$; 216 Elgin St., ☎565-5155)* has no cause to be envious of other very trendy restaurants on Elgin Street. Its vast dining room, graced with very high coffered ceilings, is adorned with a ceramic-tile floor, brick walls and a lovely black staircase. It is ideal for dining with friends, as you can have a good time and eat well without spending a fortune. The menu features dishes prepared with a modicum of originality, such as tortellini with goat cheese sauce and pizzas baked in a wood-burning oven. Moreover, while waiting for your meal, you can watch the cooks in action, for the open kitchen looks directly onto the dining room. The only thing to find fault with here is the TV, always on (though at low volume) in the corner.

Elgin Street is home to an institution known to just about everyone in town : the **Ritz** *($$; 274 Elgin St., ☎235-7027)*. Waiting is almost obligatory at this Italian restaurant, which does not accept reservations. Its pasta dishes are deservedly renowned. Fortunately, this restaurant now has younger siblings. The **Ritz Uptown** *(226 Nepean, ☎238-8752)* is in an old house, and reservations are accepted.

At the very end of the lobby of the Lord Elgin hotel, the **Connaught** *($$-$$$; 100 Elgin St., ☎235-3333)* is bathed in sunlight pouring in through its large glass veranda. The restaurant opens at the crack of dawn, when you can enjoy a good breakfast. The dinner menu features various dishes, including filet mignon and prime ribs.

A little to the east, toward Elgin Street, **Chez Jean-Pierre** *($$$; 210 Somerset St. West, ☎235-9711)* does not have the most inviting of façades, and the interior decor is not its strong point, but these are things you can live with, for the fine French cuisine and the service are solid. This is a restaurant where quality is a long-time tradition.

Not far from the Ritz Uptown (see further above), in another pretty little house, is **Fiori's** *($$$; 239 Nepean St., ☎232-1377)*, an Italian restaurant with excellent food. The veal dishes are especially delectable. The restaurant is small, friendly and full of charm. Service is warm and attentive. This comes at a price, of course, but it is worth it.

A feeling of well-being will sweep over you as soon as you walk into **Friday's** *($$$; 150 Elgin St., ☎237-5353)*, which occupies a magnificent Victorian house built in 1875. With its large antique-decorated rooms, its big wooden tables and its high-backed chairs, which exude old-fashioned charm, the place is irresistible. Its rooms have been transformed into dining rooms where a relaxing atmosphere prevails. If the decor doesn't win you over, the succulent roast surely will. Of course, with all this going for it, Friday's has a devout following, so reservations are recommended.

Le Métro *($$$; 315 Somerset St. West, ☎230-8123)* is undoubtedly one of the best eating spots in town. The *escargots* with roquefort in pastry are a true joy, as are the steak tartare or simple beef fillet with *béarnaise* sauce. The opulent, harmonious decor, the quiet atmosphere and the big, comfortable leather chairs assure you a relaxing and delicious evening.

OTTAWA

Tour C: Lower Town

Rideau Street

Having a good meal in a shopping centre may seem illusory... And yet, **Marche Mövenpick** *($; Rideau St., at Sussex Dr.)*, in the Rideau Centre, attracts crowds of happy diners. The restaurant's recipe for success is simple: a large dining-room, attractively decorated with plants and wooden tables, and delicious, quickly prepared dishes from fresh, quality ingredients. In this lively place, everyone is free to stroll about, choosing their dishes from one of the various stations where sushi, salads, pasta, quiches and all sorts of other dishes sure to please the most demanding palates are prepared before your eyes.

Located on the second floor of a building facing the Rideau Centre, **Santé** *($$$; 45 Rideau St., ☎241-7113)* is easy to miss, so keep your eyes peeled; its Californian, Thai and Caribbean specialties are true delights, especially the Bangkok noodles. This spot is an oasis of quiet repose with big bay windows opening onto some of the city's main attractions. Save room for something from the tempting dessert list. Attentive service.

Around the Byward Market

Although the surroundings of the Byward Market form the area most visited by tourists and locals alike, there are disappointingly few worthwhile restaurants. On the other hand, if you have sudden pangs of hunger or thirst, this is the place to be, especially in the summer. There are a number of friendly outdoor cafés and plenty of pedestrian traffic. In short, it is lively and very pleasant.

Your sweet tooth will want to sample **Beaver Tails** *(at George St. and William St.)*. Do not be alarmed : these are merely delicious treats made from sugared deep-fried dough, something of a cross between a doughnut and a cookie.

Rickety tables, mismatched chairs and all kinds of old-fashioned knick-knacks make up the somewhat ill-assorted but oddly charming decor at **Café Wim** *($; 537 Sussex Dr., ☎241-1771)*. Early in the morning, you can enjoy a good breakfast here (pancakes, eggs, sausages and fresh fruit salad). The place is also pleasant at lunch time, the sun pouring in through the large picture windows and the menu featuring simple dishes, including salads and sandwiches.

Memories *($; 7 Clarence St., ☎232-1882)* is almost always packed. Why? Because almost everyone in Ottawa comes to try the many desserts that have made its reputation. The selection of cakes and pies of all sorts is so impressive that it can be hard to choose. But the greatest temptation may fall on the delicious, oversized portions of apple pie. Light meals (good soups, sandwiches, salads) are also available. The coffee is good.

A delightful little café looking out on Byward Market, **Planet Coffee** *($; George St.)* offers a good selection of coffees and pastries.

Some spots draw attention more for their decor than for their food. This is the case of **Zak's Diner** *($; 89 Clarence St., ☎238-7182)*, whose bright lights and Coca-Cola signs are meant to make it look like a 1950s American diner. The menu seems not to have evolved since that time, with the usual hamburgers, milkshakes and fries, served in large portions. This is a pleasant spot for breakfast.

Blue Cactus *($-$$; 2 Byward Market, ☎241-7061)* is a Tex-Mex restaurant with the usual megacocktails, *nachos* (try the very filling Blue Cactus *nachos*), *fajitas* and so on. The atmosphere at this spot, which is popular with young people, may be a little too lively for some.

For years now, **Clair de lune** *($-$$; 81B Clarence St.)* has been delighting diners, with its laid-back ambiance as well as its menu, which features good, simple dishes.

What will undoubtedly catch your eye at **Mangia** *($-$$; 121 Clarence St., ☎562-4725)* are the large picture windows, for the menu offers no surprises: pasta and good pizzas. This place is ideal for having a bite to eat on a sunny day, without spending a fortune.

If, by any chance, you are looking for something a little different, head to the **Silk Road Café** *($-$$; 47 William St., ☎241-4254)*, which serves Afghan food. Though very simple, this little restaurant, whose decor essentially consists of salmon-pink and black walls as well as a few works of art for sale, has a certain charm. The lunch menu features less exotic dishes, such as quiches, chicken salads and burgers.

The **Café Crêpe de France** *($$; 76 Murray St., ☎241-1220)* is worth a visit for its Breton-style crepes, its salads or for its weekend brunch. The setting is congenial, with exposed brick, red-and-white-checked table-cloths, and subdued lighting. Big bay windows let in plenty of daylight. In the summer, you can dine on the pretty little outdoor terrace. Besides crepes, different full-course meals are offered each day, but they aren't as good. This

is an ideal spot for a light lunch or for a dessert crepe in the evening.

If you want to discover the flavours of Morrocco appeals to you, head to **Casablanca** *($$; 41 Clarence St., ☎789-7855)*, the restaurant, whose tasty dishes offer a wonderful opportunity to sample unique flavours and aromas.

Set in a small, pleasant space, where you will feel at ease almost immediately, the **Mama Grazzy** restaurant *($$; 25 George St., ☎241-8656)* also boasts original, delicious and delightful Italian cooking.

If you like the cuisine at the **Ritz** *($$; 89 Clarence St., ☎789-9797)* there is a second one near Byward Market.

Would a jaunt to the Château Laurier strike your fancy? If you go in for this kind of treat but do not wish to squander a fortune on a single meal, head to **Wilfrid's** *($$; 1 Rideau St., ☎241-1414)* come lunch time. You will thus be regaled with a warm dining room, comfortable armchairs, an unobstructed view of the Rideau Canal and a delicious but affordable lunch (*à-la-carte* dishes are around $10). The dinner menu is more refined and more expensive *($$$-$$$$)*. Breakfast is also very pleasant, but will cost you at least $10. On Sundays, **Zoe's** is the place to go for a delicious brunch *($22.95)* served in a quiet and elegant ambiance.

An Ottawa institution since 1979, **The Fish Market** restaurant *($$-$$$; 54 York St., ☎241-3474)* is, on the approaches to the Byward Market.. The dining-room is decorated with nets, buoys and other objects related to fishing, as is only right and proper in an establishment specializing in fish, shellfish and seafood, always impeccably fresh. Downstairs, two other dining

OTTAWA

rooms meet other culinary needs. **Coasters**, whose large picture windows look out on the bustling market, is just as pleasant. Dishes here are less sophisticated (fish n' chips) and more moderately priced, but quite good. The other room, **Vineyards**, is the place to go if all you want is a drink (good selection of wine by the glass) and a bite to eat. Shows are sometimes featured here.

Domus Café *($$$; 85 Murray St., ☎241-6007)* is undoubtedly one of the best restaurants in Ottawa. The food is refined and innovative, made with the freshest of ingredients; its success is derived from original combinations of international flavours. Recipes are drawn from the many cookbooks sold at the adjacent store. The menu changes every day, but some of the most popular items keep reappearing. The choice is never exhaustive, but the selection is interesting enough to make it difficult to decide. The desserts, limited to a choice of four or five, are the best in Ottawa. The wine list includes excellent Californian wines, some of them available by the glass. And finally, try the Sunday brunch. It is divine and well worth the wait (reservations are not accepted for brunch).

Ottawa's Neighbourhoods

Heading west along Somerset Street West, you first cross **Chinatown**, between Bronson and Booth streets, which does not have any outstanding restaurants, though the more popular ones always seem to be filled to capacity. **Little Italy** is next, along Preston Avenue and stretching south, and finally the **Wellington Street** area, which harbours plenty of good little eateries.

Chinatown

Scores of restaurants with enticing menus succeed each other along Somerset Street in Chinatown. **Yangtze** *($$; 700 Somerset St., ☎236-0555)* is one with a more solid reputation. Indeed, the place is always full to capacity. Its very spacious dining room is equipped with large round tables and thus is ideal for Sunday family dinners. Though somewhat impersonal, it is nonetheless pleasant. The menu features delectable Cantonese specialties.

Ottawa West

At the beginning of Wellington Street, in its least inviting and most forgotten part, is hidden an exotic little gem called **Addis Café** *($$; closed Mon; 1093 Wellington St., ☎725-5127)*. This is a real discovery. Solomon, the friendly owner, will guide you cheerfully through the wonders of Ethiopian cuisine, whose secret lies in combinations of different spices and seasonings. The setting is congenial, a small room with high ceilings and, on the walls, modern works of art that change every five or six weeks. The cooking will seduce you, especially if you like garlic, ginger and lentils. The base is a flat, pancake-shaped bread called *injera* on top of which other food is served. Small portions of this bread are used to scoop up the puréed lentils or the long-simmering meat stews. Solomon will be pleased to show you how to eat without utensils. Food can also be taken out. Definitely worth trying!

This little-known part of town harbours a few boutiques and some good restaurants. Though **Juniper** *($$-$$$; 1293 Wellington St., ☎728-0220)* only recently opened its doors here, it soon left its mark. This bistro sparse decor, consisting merely of small, coloured frames and parchment lamps, turns out to be both soothing and elegant. The two perfectly lovely dining rooms are delightful; but what will catch your attention above all is the menu, featuring always toothsome and originally prepared dishes.

🦞 Almost next door, **Opus Bistro** *($$$; closed Sun and Mon; 1331 Wellington St., ☎722-9549)* is worth the trip. This small bistro, with dark, simple, tasteful decor, serves tasty and impeccably presented dishes, some of them marrying eclectic ingredients. Save room for the tempting desserts. The wine selection is enticing, by the glass or by the bottle, with some excellent South African, Australian or Californian wines at relatively inexpensive prices compared to better known vintages. Service is outstanding and friendly, with helpful advice on the best choices.

The Glebe

A number of boutiques with enticing window displays line Bank Street, near Glebe Street. These arrays are dazzling in the winter, especially in December, though you will have to dawdle along in order to truly contemplate them. Fortunately, you can then warm up and have something to eat at one of the pleasant **Starbucks**, **Guabbajabba** or **Second Cup** cafés located in the area. You will not be alone, however, for all three, with their selections of coffees and teas and mouthwatering goodies, are always full in the afternoons.

Fratelli *($$-$$$; 749 Bank St., ☎237-1658)* is one of those restaurants one chances upon with delight. The sober decor, essentially composed of splendid hardwood floors, wall lights and a few mirrors, makes the place inviting at first glance. The menu, which features Italian dishes tastefully

prepared in an innovative way, is equally attractive. A good place to keep in mind in the Glebe.

Tour F: Hull (Québec)

A pleasant café-restaurant-bar-gallery-movie theatre-terrace with a very laid-back atmosphere, **Aux Quatre Jeudis** *($; 44 Rue Laval, ☎771-9557)* is patronized by a young, slightly bohemian clientele. It shows movies, and its pretty terrace is very popular in the summertime.

The **Cafe Laurier** *($-$$; 35 Rue Laurier)*, located in the lobby of the Ramada Plaza hotel, offers a good breakfast buffet, as well as a reasonably priced table d'hote in the evening. The laid-back atmosphere and courteous service make this a good place to keep in mind.

🦞 **Le Twist** *($$; 88 Rue Montcalm, ☎777-8886)* is known for its burgers, mussels and home-made fries, among the best in town, which are savoured in a charming setting and relaxed ambiance. In summer, you can dine on a large, completely private terrace. It is best to make reservations for lunch, as the place is often jam-packed.

Le Tartuffe *($$$; closed Sun; 133 Rue Notre Dame, ☎776-6424)* is a marvelous little gourmet French restaurant located just steps from the Canadian Museum of Civilization. With its friendly, courteous service and delightful, intimate ambiance, this place is sure to win you over.

🦞 **Le Sans-Pareil** *($$$-$$$$; closed Sun and Mon; 71 Boulevard St-Raymond, ☎771-1471)* is located 5 minutes from Hull's new casino, and right near the shopping centres. This is a Belgian restaurant, so it's only normal that chef Luc Gielen offers a two-for-one special on mussels (prepared in twelve different ways) on Tuesday nights. The sinfully good menu usually changes every three weeks, and the focus is on fresh products from various parts of Québec. The chef has a flair for combining ingredients in innovative ways, so don't hesitate to opt for the *menu gourmand*, which includes several courses, complete with the appropriate wines to wash them down. This place may be small, but it's truly charming. Check it out!

The Casino has all the facilities for your gambling pleasures – two restaurants that serve excellent meals away from all the betting: **Banco** (*$$*) offers a reasonably priced, quality buffet and various menu items; the more chic and expensive **Baccara** (*$$$$; closed for lunch; 1 Boulevard du Casino, ☎772-6210*) has won itself a place among the best restaurants of the region. The set menu always consists of superb dishes that you can enjoy along with spectacular views of the lake. The well-stocked wine cellar and impeccable service round out this memorable culinary experience.

The stylish **Café Henry Burger** (*$$$$; 69 Laurier, ☎777-5646*) specializes in fine French cuisine. The menu changes according to what is available, and always offers dishes made of the freshest ingredients that will please the most discerning palate. The restaurant has a long-standing excellent reputation.

  ## ENTERTAINMENT

Ottawa has never been famous for its nightlife. Though its streets are often deserted after 11pm, you can enjoy the rest of your nights by knowing a few of its secrets. In addition to the warm pubs and lively bars, mostly set up along Elgin Street and around Byward Market, the city has a flourishing cultural life. Excellent shows are presented at the National Arts Centre, where the city's various theatre companies perform. Finally, entertaining festivals are organized throughout the year.

Bars and Nightclubs

Up until a few years ago, many Ottawans would finish off the night in Hull, where bars in that city were open until 3am. Since April 1996, however, the two cities have adopted the same closing hours, so that bars in both Ottawa and Hull now close at 2am. Whatever your preference, you will find enjoyable bars on either side of the Ottawa River.

Near downtown Ottawa, there are several bars and pubs along Elgin Street, which is quite lively in the evening.

Maxwell's (*340 Elgin St., ☎232-5771*), upstairs from a restaurant, is popular with trendy youth. In the summer, there are tables on a large balcony facing the lively street.

If you are put off by flashy bars, you may appreciate the youthful and unpretentious atmosphere of the **Fox and Feather** (*Elgin St., at MacLaren St.*). A bar and large picture windows are all that decorate this noisy, smoky room, but the place boasts a fairly pleasant ambiance nonetheless.

Right next door, the **MacLaren** (*Elgin St., at MacLaren St.*) boasts a huge room in which several pool tables are set up. Those waiting for their turn can kill time by watching videos on the big-screen television.

The **D'Arcy McGee** *(44 Sparks St.)* can pride itself on being the only real Irish Pub in Ottawa, because the interior was completely built in Ireland, then transported to Ottawa where it was reconstructed piece by piece. Extremely warm, decorated with woodwork and stained-glass windows and decorated with scores of marvellous knick-knacks, the place is always full. Concerts are presented here on certain evenings. Good selection of beers on tap.

Yuk Yuk's *(Wed to Sat; 88 Albert St., ☎236-5233)* is part of a chain offering comedy shows, some of them actually quite funny. This is an interesting alternative to a conventional bar. No smoking on Thursdays.

The area around the Byward Market is home to several bars, many of them clustered along George and York streets.

Stoney's *(62 York St., ☎241-8858)* is probably the oldest nightclub in Ottawa. Young people have been coming here forever to have a drink and dance on a small dance floor. In the summer, it is open in back. The music generally tends towards rock and roll.

Vineyard's Wine Bar Bistro *(54 York St., ☎241-4270)* is a friendly, congenial little bar where you can enjoy wine, beer and cheese. Musicians often perform here, with jazz at the top of the list.

Part of the well-known chain, Ottawa's **Hard Rock Café** *(73 York St.)* is a carbon copy of its sister establishments: blaring rock music and electric guitars adorning the walls.

Though lacking the character of the D'Arcy McGee, the **Heart and Crown** *(67 Clarence St.)* is another fashionable Irish pub in the capital. Relaxed ambiance and good selection of beers.

Ottawa just wouldn't be right whitout an English pub: so the **Earl of Sussex** *(431 Sussex Dr.)* was thus set up here. Warm decor, beer on tap and fish 'n chips on the menu as is only fitting in this type of establishment.

If spending hours in a smoky nightclub playing deafening music is not your thing, the chic **Zoe's** *(1 Rideau St.)*, at the Château Laurier might instead. Everything here is calm and comfy, from the delightfully soft music to the cosy armchairs.

Hull (Québec)

For many years now, **Aux Quatre Jeudis** *(44 Laval)* has been *the* place for the café crowd. It has lots of ambiance, and there's a big, attractive terrace to hang out on in the summer.

Le Bop *(5 Aubry)* is a pleasant little place in old Hull. You can kick off your evening with a reasonably priced, decent meal. The music ranges from techno and disco to soft rock and even a little hard rock.

Le Fou du Roi *(253 Boulevard St-Joseph)* is where the thirty-something crowd hangs out. There's a dance floor, and the windows open onto a little terrace in the summertime. This place is also a popular after-work gathering place.

Gay Bar

Le Club *(77 Wellington St., ☎777-1411)* is a gay meeting spot that has been around for several years. Set on two stories, it has a crowded dance floor.

OTTAWA

Cultural Activities

The **National Arts Centre** *(53 Elgin St., ☎996-5051, ⌐996-9578)* is Ottawa's cultural headquarters, with an opera house and two theatres where top-notch performances are offered year-round.

Festivals

February

Winterlude no longer needs an introduction: its reputation is well established in Canada. For 10 days in early February all sorts of winter festivities are held on what is billed as the world's longest skating rink.

May

The **Tulip Festival** is held in May, during the Victoria Day long weekend. The city is then abloom with thousands of tulips, bestowed by the Netherlands by way of thanks to Canada for taking in Queen Wilhemina during the Second World War. Shows and activities of all kinds take place in various parts of the city, including Confederation Park and Dow's Lake.

June

The **Festival Franco-Ontarien** is held at the end of June. This is a celebration of French culture in Ontario. There are activities of all sorts, handicrafts stalls, and an important series of shows presenting many of the greats of French song from here and elsewhere.

July

The **Festival Canada** *(☎996-5051)* takes place in July. Culture holds pride of place for four weeks as 70 dance, jazz and opera performances are presented at the National Arts Centre.

August

The casino's opening was the origin of an annual fireworks festival, **Les Grands Feux du Casino** *(☎819-771-FEUX or 800-771-FEUX)*, held every year during the month of August.

 SHOPPING

Ottawa has plenty to offer those who consider prowling along main thoroughfares bordered by enticing shop windows among the pleasures of travelling. Indeed, the city boasts four areas ideal for abandoning yourselves entirely to shopping: Sparks Street, Bank Street, Elgin Street and the area surrounding Byward Market. In summer, Byward Market, with its flower, fruit and vegetable vendors, is unquestionably the liveliest. During the holiday season, Bank Street is dazzling as the city is festooned with an abundance of lights. One thing is sure, whatever the time of year, you will be able to unearth a thousand and one finds as you walk the streets of the capital.

Tour B: Upper Town

Sparks Street, a long pedestrianized thouroughfare lined with trees, benches and lovely shops, makes for a very pleasant little stroll. On rainy days, you can browse around inside at the **240 Sparks** shopping centre, which comprises several attractive boutiques. Among these is **Holt Renfrew**, which

The bastion of Canadian democracy, Ottawa's
parliament buildings overlook the Rideau Canal.
– *P. Quittemelle*

The monument to Canadian peace-keeping forces
in front of the Notre Dame Basilica in Ottawa.
– *Tibor Bognar*

offers a wide choice of high-quality items, including men and women's clothing by great European, American and Canadian designers, beauty products and accessories.

Handicrafts

Sparks Street, between Elgin and O'Connor Streets, is a good place to shop for Canadian-made handicrafts. The first among many such shops is the **Snow Goose** *(83 Sparks St.)*, which boasts a wide selection of creations by Inuit and Native-American artisans, including sculptures and engravings. The shop also carries an abundance of leather and fur accessories, notably mocassins, gloves and hats.

A stone's throw away, **Canada's Four Corners** *(93 Sparks St.)* also sells Native-American handicrafts; however, you'll have to rummage through all the assorted junk and plastic objects just to find a good-quality item. Plastic place mats, T-shirts bearing Canada's colours, Inuit sculptures and leather mocassins are all jumbled together here. At the very back of the store are reproductions of engravings by native artists (Norval Morisseau, Benjamin Chee-Chee, Doris Cyrette, etc.), perhaps the greatest find in the place.

Books

Canada Books *(Sparks St.)* has a fine selection of Canadian books, whether it be literature, arts, photography or other topics.

If you couldn't find anything at Canada Books, you can check out the incredible selection at **Smithbooks**, across the street. In addition to a wide selection on Canada, there are books on many other subjects, as well as novels and travel guidebooks.

For newspapers, books and magazines from all over, try the **Place Bell Books** *(175 Metcalfe St., ☎233-3821)* or the **Maison de la Presse Internationale** *(100 Bank St., ☎230-9774)*.

Tour C: Lower Town

The shopping mall par excellence in the capital, the **Rideau Centre** *(50 Rideau St.)*, with some 200 shops including Eatons, is where you'll find it all. Noteworthy among these are HMV (music store), the Disney store, Oh Yes Ottawa (for souvenirs of the city), Mrs. Tiggy Winkles (toys), The Gap (clothing for all) and Roots (leather garments). The centre also houses two pharmacies, banks (Royal, Nova Scotia, TD), as well as several fast-food restaurants and Marché Mövenpick (see p 90).

For window shopping and some interesting finds, nothing beats a stroll around the **Byward Market**. All year round, there are handicrafts stalls on the two floors of the central pavillion; in summer, fruit and vegetable producer set up shop here. You can buy all sorts of items: jewellery, leather goods, scarves, paintings, and so on. The vegetable market lies at the heart of the action in the summer. It is a pleasant spot to shop or merely to linger.

Kitchen Supplies

Domus is not only the name of a very good restaurant (see p 92), but also the name of a top-of-the-line kitchenware store. **Domus Housewares** *(85 Murray St., ☎241-6410)* is big and bright. Besides selling almost every kitchen accessory imaginable, it offers cookbooks for every taste, from which the recipes for dishes prepared at the restaurant are derived.

OTTAWA

Sporting Goods

Backpacks, top-quality camping material at good prices, and sportswear are part of the assortment you will find at **Mountain Equipment Co-op** *(5B Beechwood St., ☎745-1094)*. This is the place to go to equip yourself for an outdoor excursion.

Jewellery

Those who appreciate unusual jewels should pop round to **Striking** *(531A Sussex Dr.)*, whose gold or silver earrings, necklaces, brooches and bracelets are sure to prove irresistible.

Gift Ideas

The museum shop at the **National Gallery of Canada** *(380 Sussex Dr.)* is just the place for those who like to rummage for hours through a mind-boggling amount of reproductions, be they posters, jewellery or decorative objects. In addition to these quality copies, the boutique boasts an amazing collection of art books as well as works by Native-American and Canadian artisans and sculptors.

Fans of Tintin or Asterix should pop round to **Planet BD** *(493 Sussex Dr., ☎789-6307)*, where several figurines and effigies of these comic-book heroes are displayed. The cost of some of these items may seem exorbitant, but, after having admired the finely detailed hand-made objects, they will seem more like them to small works of art rather than mere paraphernalia.

Finding the appropriate words to describe **Cow's** *(43 Clarence St., ☎789-COWS)* can prove rather difficult. The shop mostly carries T-shirts and other cotton apparel, coffee mugs and other kitchen items, all adorned with stylized cows and short, amusing captions. Delicious ice-cream is also served here.

Books, Newspapers and Magazines

Part of the huge chain of bookshops, Ottawa's **Chapters** *(Rideau St., at Sussex Dr.)* boasts an incredible selection of books for all tastes, in both English and French.

Ottawa's Neighbourhoods

The Glebe

In fine weather, after exploring Sparks Street turn onto Bank Street, another one of Ottawa's pleasant main thoroughfares. As you walk along, some parts of the street are duller than others, but it will not fail to charm you. It boasts two distinct commercial sections: one around Somerset Street and a second one south of Queensway.

Toys

The very beautiful high-quality toys at **Mrs. Tiggy Winkles** *(809 Bank St., ☎234-3836)* have been delighting children since time immemorial.

Stationery

The Papery *(11A William St., ☎241-1212)* is the top spot for paper supplies: magnificent greeting cards, agendas, calendars, wrapping paper, filing boxes in various sizes, and so forth. There is another branch in The Glebe *(850 Bank St., ☎230-1313)*.

Clothing

At **La Cache**, you are sure to find a little something to please you *(763 Bank St.)*, for the boutique overflows with a profusion of goods: cotton and wool garments, scarves and hats of all kinds, beauty products, bedding, dishes and other items.

For leather bags, shoes and coats, both casual and durable, head to **Roots** *(787 Bank St.)*, whose reputation is long-standing. Other items, such as wool sweaters, are also worth the trip.

Piles and piles and sweaters in every colour of the rainbow hang on the walls of **Penelope's Haberdashery** *(81 Bank St., ☎232-9565)*. Finding something here therefore entails taking the time to rummage through the countless, often classically cut, but always high-quality wool sweaters.

Tour F: Hull (Québec)

The **boutique of the Canadian Museum of Civilization** *(100 Rue Laurier)* is, in a way, part of the exhibit. Although the Canadian and native craft pieces aren't of the same quality as those exhibited at the museum, you'll find all sorts of reasonably priced treasures.

The museum also has a **bookstore** with a wonderful collection on the history of crafts in many different cultures.

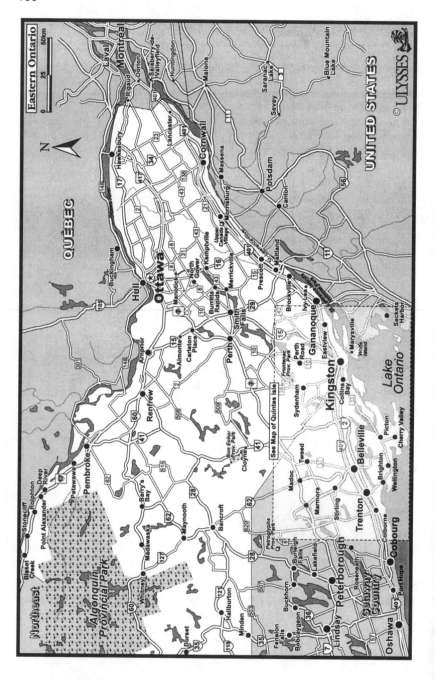

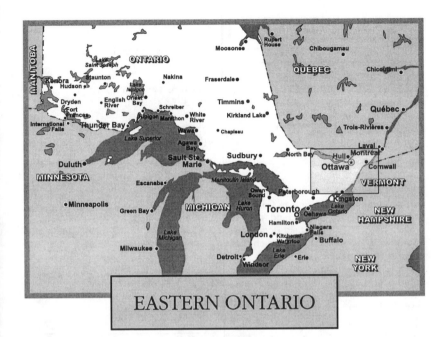

EASTERN ONTARIO

Eastern Ontario, a rich plain between the St. Lawrence River and the Canadian Shield, has always been a favourable place for human habitation. Natives were drawn here by the fertile land and abundant supply of fresh water; French colonists, by the region's strategic location along the lucrative fur route. Later, Loyalists arriving from the newly independent United States chose to establish their new villages in these vast spaces. This hospitable region has been welcoming new inhabitants ever since, and some villages have since developed into lovely cities, like Kingston, while others, having preserved their old-fashioned character, have become popular vacation spots.

Vast, rolling fields greet visitors who explore this magnificent region. Splendid old houses that seem to have been there since the earliest days of colonization, pop up around every other bend in the road. The region's first hamlets, now cities like Brockville, remain virtually unchanged and are still graced with lovely Victorian buildings. In some places, where the human presence is less obvious, the landscape consists largely of a forest of hardwoods and conifers strewn with lakes and rivers.

Three tours cross this region. "Tour A: Following the Rideau Canal" lets you discover a very pretty rural area dotted with charming small hamlets; "Tour B: Following the St. Lawrence" goes along by the river and passes through a few of Ontario's oldest towns such as Kingston and Cornwall; "Tour C: From Pembroke to the Haliburton Highlands" takes you to the heart of a still undeveloped area, Algonquin Park, one of the province's natural gems.

FINDING YOUR WAY AROUND

Tour A: Following the Rideau Canal

This tour follows the Rideau Canal through Ontario's countryside.

By Car

From Ottawa, take Colonel By Drive, which runs along the Rideau Canal for quite a distance. At the end of this road, turn left on Brookfield Road then right on Riverside Drive, which becomes Route 19.

Tour B: Following the St. Lawrence

This first tour follows the St. Lawrence River through part of southeastern Ontario. It includes the industrial city of Cornwall, the charming towns of Prescott and Brockville, and historic Kingston.

By Car

From the Quebec border, Highway 401 runs all the way to Oshawa, in the Toronto area. If you have more time, however, we recommend Route 2, which runs alongside the St. Lawrence, leading through lovely pastoral scenery and offering some magnificent views. It runs through or near all the stops on this tour (Cornwall, Morrisburg, Prescott, Brockville, Gananoque and Kingston).

From Ottawa, Route 2 can be reached via Highway 417 and Route 138.

Bus Stations

There is bus service to every little town along this tour.

Kingston: 175 Counter St.,
☎(613) 547-4916.

Cornwall: 120 Tolgate Rd. W.,
☎(613) 932-9511.

Train Stations

The train through the Montreal-Windsor corridor runs alongside part of the area covered by this tour, so visitors can easily reach Cornwall, Kingston and Oshawa by train.

Kingston: 800 Counter St.

Cornwall: Station St.

Tour C: From Pembroke to the Haliburton Highlands

Starting in Ottawa, this tour runs along the Québec border to Pembroke and then Petawawa. From Pembroke it branches to the magnificent Algonquin Provincial Park after passing through several small villages in the back country.

Bus Stations:

Pembroke: 213 Lake St.,
☎(613) 732-2866.

PRACTICAL INFORMATION

The area code is **613**, except for the tour of Pembroke and the Haliburton Highlands, where it is either **613** or **705**. Only the **705** area code is indicated for this chapter; if no area code is given, it is 613.

Tour A: Following the Rideau Canal

Tourist Information

Eastern Ontario Travel Association
R.R. 1, Lansdowne, K0E 1L0, ☎(613) 659-4300, ☎(800) 567-EAST (toll-free from Canada and the Eastern United States), ≈659-4306.

Tour B: Following the St. Lawrence

Tourist Information

Central Ontario Association
Getaway Country, 1040 Gardiners Rd., Office B, Kingston, K7P 1R7, ☎(613) 384-3682 or (800) 461-1912.

Kingston's Visitors Welcome Centre
209 Ontario Street, Kingston, K7L 2Z1, ☎(613) 548-4415, ☎(888) 855-4555.

Eastern Ontario Travel Association
R.R. 1, Lansdowne, K0E 1L0, ☎(613) 659-4300, ☎(800) 567-EAST (toll-free from Canada and the Eastern United States), ≈659-4306.

Tour C: From Pembroke to the Haliburton Highlands

Tourist Information

Bancroft & District Chamber of Commerce
P.O. Box 539, Bancroft, K0L 1C0, ☎(613) 1513 or (800) 461-1912, ≈(613) 332-8089.

EXPLORING

Tour A: Following the Rideau Canal

The settlement of eastern Ontario began at the turn of the 19th century when the Empire Loyalists fled the newly independent United States and began to settle on land bordering the St. Lawrence River. A few of them continued their journey a little further north choosing the fertile hinterland where water was abundant. Facing almost untouched territory, these new arrivals brought their architectural traditions with them; severe, symmetrical Georgian-style buildings constructed of cut stone slowly began to appear in the landscape, and villages were founded, notably Merrickville (1793) and Perth (1816). However, it was a few years before settlers came in great numbers to make their homes here. The construction of the Rideau Canal really marked the beginning of the settlement of eastern Ontario.

The War of 1812 between the British and the Americans showed the government how vulnerable the St. Lawrence River was. The construction of a 202-kilometre-long canal was envisaged to allow boats to travel to Kingston (Fort Henry) without laying themselves open to American cannons on the south shore of the St. Lawrence. Work began in 1826.

During the construction of the Rideau Canal, small communities began to develop in this region as people took advantage of the rich agricultural soil. Villages were established here and there, but in this immense territory they still remained fairly far apart; these new arrivals often had to be self-sufficient to survive. The mill was one of the key elements of survival because each

Dickinson Mill

community had to be able to process the fruit of its harvest. The first mills were modest, a kind of central point in each village, but they became great and architectural creations and feats of engineering as the population grew. They even made some communities wealthy. Certain villages still pride themselves on their handsome buildings constructed during the period of prosperity in the 19th century, and they have conserved their former style quite beautifully over the years.

Starting from Ottawa, follow the Rideau Canal and take Route 19 south.

Manotick

The village of Manotick is composed of a few small wooden houses and a main street. At first glance there is nothing exceptional, without could easily pass through and miss seeing its finest creation: the **Dickinson Mill** ★, a magnificently built and carefully restored mill on the banks of the Rideau River. It was built between 1859 and 1860 when Joseph Currier and Moss Kent Dickinson decided to set up a mill capable of grinding large quantities of grain. To assure the success of this project, nothing was left to chance: it was constructed of cut stone so there would be less risk of fire, and was built large enough to meet all the needs. People settled around the mill and some quite elegant houses were built, especially the one belonging to Dickinson who soon became the sole owner of the mill (when Currier's wife died he sold his share to Dickinson). Today, it has been beautifully renovated and landscaped. The place is especially pleasant on Saturday mornings when there is a market. Beside the mill is a wooden bridge connecting the two

Scottish and Irish Stone Masons

Construction of the Rideau Canal required a certain expertise for the time because it was necessary to dig down through sheer rock in certain sections. Master Scottish and Irish stone masons were called in. When the canal was finished, these new arrivals remained in the area and marked the landscape with their constructions. They built their homes with the materials they found in the area; familiar with limestone and sandstone, they developed a style of architecture very particular to this part of the province.

sides of the river: cross it and have a picnic in the park which has a superb view of the mill.

Leave Manotick and continue south on Route 19. When you arrive at Route 6, take it west to North Gower.

North Gower

In this area, farming has beautified the countryside; old farmhouses of cut stone or wood follow one after the other and are surrounded by far-reaching fields. Handfuls of houses form quaint little villages with an air of the past, giving this corner of Ontario a particular charm. North Gower has a few lovely Victorian homes that almost seem to be frozen in time. There is even an antique shop at the entrance of town as if to emphasize its historic character.

Continue along on Route 5m then turn right onto Route 2.

Burritts Rapids

As you continue along the route, another group of small houses signals your arrival in the village of Burritts Rapids, which you might have passed through unnoticed were it not for **Christ Church**. Built in 1831, this little clapboard Gothic Revival church reminds us

that settlers have been in this region for more than 150 years.

Route 2 continues along the Rideau Canal. Cross the Rideau River to Merrickville: the village is easy to spot.

Merrickville

A surprising number of splendid stone buildings line the streets of this small village. Dating back to the 19th century, they bear witness to the former wealth of this hamlet. In 1793, William Mirick undertook the construction of mills next to the waterfalls located at this point on the Rideau River, and this led to the village's prosperity. During the 19th century, development gained pace with the building of the Rideau Canal. The advent of the railways, however, curtailed Merrickville's prosperity, when the town was bypassed by railway builders. One positive repurcussion of this decline, however, is that the village was spared from modernization, and its distinct character seems frozen in time.

Walking alongside the Rideau Canal, the first building you come to is the **Merrickville Public Library ★** *(Main St.)*, built around the 1890s by William Pearson. This elegant brick building has a gable and a veranda. It was Pearson's daughter Mary who bequeathed this superb dwelling to the town to house its library.

In front, the **Sam Jakes Inn**, now converted to a stylish and comfortable inn, is the former residence of Samuel Jakes, who had it built in 1861.

Next to the inn at the corner of Main Street and Lawrence stands **Jakes Block**, an imposing stone building dating back to 1860. The main floor used to be occupied by a store, one of the largest in the area. Today it houses a restaurant, the Baldachin (see p 126), as well as shops.

Continue along Main Street until Saint Lawrence Street.

The **Blockhouse** *($1; mid-May to mid-Oct, every day; ☎692-2581)* is the biggest military building erected along the Rideau Canal to protect the boats using this waterway. It could accommodate up to 50 soldiers, and today houses a small museum.

Turn left on Saint Lawrence Street.

At the edge of the Rideau River is the Merrickville **industrial zone ★**, with the ruins of the mills that once assured the village's prosperity. Among these buildings, the oldest of them built in 1793 by William Mirick, you will see a sawmill, a weaving mill, a flour mill and an oat-processing mill. Not far from this area, on Mill Street, is William Mirick's last residence.

Return along Street Lawrence Street.

Saint Lawrence Street is lined with a cluster of shops, each more charming than the last, where you can linger for hours in front of the tempting display windows. For those who wish to explore the other treasures in this delightful village, a small brochure entitled

Merrickville Walking Tour is also available.

Follow Route 43 to Smith Falls.

Smiths Falls

As you enter Smiths Falls, you will immediately feel that it is different from the quaint little towns you have just travelled through: this is an industrial town, with a slightly dreary atmosphere in some places. Its history goes back to 1823 when Thomas Smyth took advantage of the waterfalls at this point in the Rideau River to construct a sawmill. Although it is very rustic, this wooden mill was the start of the this city's development. Hardly a few years had passed when a new entrepreneur, Able Russel Ward, bought the mill and in turn constructed more mills, most notably for flour and to card fibers, as well as another sawmill. These buildings were more modern and resistant, so that the city would be sure to stay competitive and keep its industry. Nevertheless, at the turn of the 20th century, despite the efforts of Alexander Wood, the third owner of the mills, Smiths Falls's mills could not compete with the higher productivity of the steam mills found in large Canadian cities. Little by little they closed down. Restored in the 1980s, they still stand on the river bank and house the **Rideau Canal Museum ★** *(34 Beckwith St. South, ☎284-0505)* which has an interesting exhibition about the canal, the history of its construction and explanations about its workings.

Smith Falls' location along the Rideau Canal also has several advantages in the summer when you can watch the comings and goings of boats travelling the waterway.

In the town, you may perhaps notice the wonderful smell of chocolate wafting through the air. **Hershey** *(free admission; Hershey Dr., ☎283-3300)* has a factory here which you can visit.

From Smith Falls, you have two options. Depending how much time you have, you can either take the shorter Route 43 which goes to Perth, or continue your tour of the countryside and take Route 15 to Carleton Place.

Carleton Place

Carleton Place developed at the northern tip of Mississippi Lake. It is a pretty village whose buildings are of red brick and whose main street has several businesses with large display windows.

Route 15 goes north to Almonte.

Almonte

Like Carleton Place, Almonte is one of the most charming villages in Ontario. Although it is a quiet town today, it was one of the principal centres of wool production in Canada in the last century. This town also developed because of its mill; the **Victoria Woollen Mill**, built in 1857. At the end of the 19th century, the Rosamond Company, which ran this carding mill, employed about 500 people. The mill remains one of the town's attractions because it now houses a charming restaurant.

Return to Carleton Place and follow Route 7 to Perth.

Perth ★

Just after the War of 1812 against the Americans, the British government decided to avoid another conflict with this imposing neighbour by improving the organization of Upper Canada's defence. The construction of the Rideau Canal was one of the strategies adopted, but it was also necessary to position battalions throughout the territory so they would be able to act swiftly in case of an attack. The authorities decided to post soldiers in the hinterland. This is how Perth was founded in 1816 by half-retired soldiers and Scottish settlers who had been promised fertile land and tools to go with it. This hamlet grew quickly and soon became the capital of Bathurst district, attracting new and affluent inhabitants. Splendid homes were built around the Tay River, transforming the little settlement into an elegant town which can still can take pride in its inhabitants today.

We suggest a short tour through the streets of Perth which will give you a chance to see some of the most beautiful homes and will take you back in the history of this "country town."

The centre of town is situated around Gore Street where you will find many pretty little shops and restaurants. In addition to enticing stores, this street is lined with magnificent stone houses revealing the dexterity and art of the stone masons at the end of the last century. It is a perfect place to take a stroll and window shop on a beautiful sunny day.

On Gore Street, the first house that should catch your attention is **Matheson House Museum** *($3; Mon to Sat 10am to 5pm, Sun 1pm to 4pm; 11 Gore St. E., ☎267-1947)*, a beautiful Georgian style residence built by Roderick Matheson in 1840. It now houses a small museum which relates the history of the town and its inhabitants. You can view four rooms decorated with furniture of the time as well as a kitchen with a fireplace where meals were prepared. Various objects belonging to the native people of the region are also on display.

The **Perth Town Hall** was erected in 1863, not far from the Tay River. This is more or less the centre of town. **Tay Basin** opens out a few feet from the river's edge. There is a very pleasant garden on the riverbank where you can rest a bit. On Saturday mornings, however, the place is very animated as a Farmer's Market is held here.

Turn right on Drummond Street.

Perth's architectural heritage cannot be summed up as a few stone residences, but is rather a cohesive ensemble of houses that are among the finest examples of Georgian style architecture in this region. In 1823, James Boulton, a lawyer, had one of these elegant brick houses built. It is called **Summit House** *(on the corner of Drummond St. and Harvey St.)* today, and is the model that inspired The Grange (see p 176), the magnificent house his brother, D'Arcy Boulton Jr., built in York (Toronto).

Turn left on Harvey Street.

Less than a dozen years later, another influential lawyer, Daniel McMartin constructed another of the town's elegant homes. **McMartin House** *(corner of Harvey St. and Gore St.)* is also made of brick and shows the influence of slightly different styles. Certain elements are borrowed from the Adam style (Great Britain) and the Federal style (United States).

The third interesting house is built in the Georgian style, and is one of Perth's most beautiful architectural heritage sites. **Inge-Va** *(66 Craig St.)* was built in 1823 by Michael Harris, an Anglican minister. This magnificent stone house, with a gabled roof and splendid windows embellishing the façade, was sold to another lawyer, Thomas Radenhurst, in 1832.

Perth was a small town in those days, and these three rival lawyers maintained what could be called a strained relationship. In 1833, these tensions came to a head when two law students, Robert Lyon a student of Radenhurst, and John Wilson, who lived at Boulton's house, fought for the affections of Elizabeth Hughes. Their hatred was so vicious that the two students challenged each other to a duel. At the end of the duel, Lyon lost his life. This duel, the last one to take place in Canada, was held on the banks of the Tay River where **Last Duel Park** *(corner of Cole Rd. and Brock St.)* is situated today. The court pardoned Wilson's act but blamed Boulton for having witnessed the duel and for not having tried to stop the two young men. Rumours spread quickly in this small town, and as Boulton's reputation was now marred, his career faltered. He was forced to leave Perth and to settle in Newark.

Take Route 43 to Smith Falls. You can then go to Kingston following Route 15 south.

Tour B: Following the St. Lawrence ★★★

The shores of the St. Lawrence River were among the very first parts of Ontario to be colonized on the Great Lakes route. As early as the 17th century, a number of French forts were built here, most notably Fort Frontenac (1673), on the site now occupied by Kingston. Long before any forts were erected, however, Iroquoian tribes (Hurons and Iroquois) fought over the borders of this vast territory, delimited by the southern part of the St. Lawrence River and the shores of the Great Lakes. This tour will guide you alongside the majestic St. Lawrence, which meets Lake Ontario at Kingston. In addition to picturesque towns like

Kingston

● ATTRACTIONS

1. Royal Military College and the National Defense College
2. Fort Henry
3. Kingston City Hall
4. Confederation Park
5. Prince George Hotel
6. St. George's Cathedral
7. St. Mary's Roman Catholic Cathedral
8. Marine Museum of the Great Lakes
9. Pump House Steam Museum
10. Murney
11. Tower Museum
12. Frontenac County Court House
13. Queen's University
14. Miller Museum of Geology and Mineralogy
15. Villa Bellevue
16. Kingston Archeological Centre
17. Correctional Service of Canada Museum
18. International Hockey Hall of Fame and Museum
19. Kingston Haunted Walk

◇ ACCOMMODATIONS

1. Alexander Henry
2. Belvedere
3. Best Western Fireside Inn
4. Conway
5. Hochelaga Inn
6. Holiday Inn
7. Kingston International Hostel
8. Painted Ladies
9. Queen University
10. Queen's Inn
11. Rosemount
12. Secret Garden

◇ RESTAURANTS

1. Café Max
2. Caveau
3. Chez Piggy
4. Curry Village
5. Darbar
6. Kingston Brewery Co.
7. River Mill
8. Sleepless Goat Cafe
9. Stoney's
10. Windmill Café

EASTERN ONTARIO

Kingston, this tour features a visit to Upper Canada Village, a reconstructed pioneer village which will transport you 100 years back in time, and outstanding natural sites like the Thousand Islands.

Kingston ★★

In 1673, the Comte de Frontenac sent René-Robert Cavelier de La Salle up the St. Lawrence River to scout out the perfect location for a trading post. La Salle chose to erect a fort, Fort Frontenac, at the point where the river met Lake Ontario. The site was a strategic one, since it was located along the route taken by both explorers and *coureurs des bois* (trappers). From that point on, the French began to develop lucrative commercial ties with the natives. They remained in the region for nearly a century, until 1758, when the fort was captured by the English under Colonel Bradstreet, putting an end to French colonization in the area.

After the English conquest, the area was abandoned until 1783, when Loyalists arriving from the United States founded Kingston here. As a stopping point on the Great Lakes Route, the town enjoyed renewed prosperity, and Fort Henry was built to protect the area during the War of 1812. Kingston gradually became bigger and bigger, and was even the capital of Upper and Lower Canada for a few years (1841-1844). Due to its proximity to the U.S. border and the fear of an American invasion, however, it lost the title to Montréal, which only held it itself until 1849, when Ottawa was finally named capital.

A number of magnificent Victorian buildings bear witness to the city's glorious past, as do several large military schools, most importantly the Royal Military College and the National Defense College. Furthermore, Kingston lies on the shores of Lake Ontario and has an extremely attractive downtown area, which is bustling with life when the weather is fine. We have outlined a walking tour to help you explore this town, one of Eastern Ontario's jewels.

Fort Henry ★★ *($9.50; May to Sep, every day 10am to 5pm; Rte 2, ☎542-7388)* was built between 1832 and 1837 on a promontory overlooking Lake Ontario, in order to protect Upper Canada in the event of an American invasion. This large military post was never attacked, however, and was abandoned after the 1870's, when an invasion no longer seemed likely. Later, in the 1930s, the building underwent renovations.

Upon entering, you will be greeted by guides in period costume, who will tell you about life at the fort in the 19th century. You will also have a chance to attend shooting drills performed by the Fort Henry Guard, whose uniforms are similar to those worn by English soldiers in 1867. This is definitely the most memorable part of the visit. After watching these demonstrations, you can tour the barracks, whose rooms still contain 19th-century furnishings and tools, offering a good idea of what daily life was like here back then. Finally, you can spend some time admiring the museum's fine collection of 19th-century English military equipment.

The Royal Military College is visible on nearby Point Frederick. Not far from there, Frederick Tower, a Martello tower dating from 1846, houses the **Royal Military College of Canada Museum** *(free admission; late Jun to early Sep, every day 10am to 5pm, ☎541-6000, ext. 6664)*, where you can learn about the history of the college and the first military conflicts to take place in this region. This stone tower

Kingston City Hall

with thick walls (the section facing Lake Ontario is 15 m wide) is the largest of the six Martello towers built in the 19th century to protect Kingston.

Head down to the centre of town on the Lasalle Causeway. Go as far as Brock Street, where you'll find some of the most attractive shops in town, then retrace your steps and walk along Ontario Street.

Kingston's era of prosperity during the 1840s and 1850s corresponds to the apogee of neoclassicism in Canada. It is therefore not surprising to find a significant collection of buildings in this style, the majority of which are of grey limestone extracted from local quarries. This is the case with the Kingston's **City Hall ★** *(216 Ontario St.).* This vast building was constructed between 1842 and 1844 when the town was the seat of government for United Canada. Following the decision to move the colonial capital to Montréal, the town councillors graciously, though unsuccessfully, offered the government this city hall in the hopes that it might change its mind. City Hall overlooks the water and is reminiscent of the grand public buildings of Dublin, Ireland. The Council Room and Ontario Hall on the second floor have what are considered the most beautiful interior neoclassical decors in Canada.

Just opposite City Hall, on the banks of the Cataraqui River, lies **Confederation Park**. This vast stretch of greenery is a perfect place for a stroll. Right beside the park, you'll find the tourist office, where you can catch the **Confederation Tour Train** *($8; mid-May to Sep, 10am to 7pm),* a small train that runs through the old parts of Kingston.

Cruises to the Thousand Islands set out from the marina by the park (see p 121).

Keep walking on **Ontario Street**, Kingston's major downtown artery, which is lined with all sorts of little shops and restaurants with pretty terraces. You'll come first to the **Prince George Hotel** whose original section was built in 1809. Two additions were added later and the building as it stands now was completed in 1867. It was further renovated and transformed into a hotel in 1978.

EASTERN ONTARIO

Continuing to the corner of Johnson and King streets, you'll pass the lovely St. George's Cathedral.

St. George's Cathedral is the seat of the Anglican bishopric of Kingston. This lovely neoclassical building was completed in 1825 and designed by Thomas Rogers. The portico, tower and clock were added in 1846, while the cupola dates from 1891. On the same block, the former **post office** and **customs house** are reminiscent of the 17th-century England of Inigo Jones. These two edifices were built in 1856 by Montreal architects Hopkins, Lawford and Nelson.

Continue along Johnson Street to Clergy Street.

At the beginning of the 19th century, the Catholic bishopric of Kingston covered all of Upper Canada (Ontario). In 1843, **St. Mary's Roman Catholic Cathedral ★** *(corner of Johnson and Clergy Streets)* was built so that the bishopric would have a worthy house of worship. The 60-m-high neo-Gothic tower was added in 1887.

Retrace your steps and continue west on Ontario Street.

You will eventually come to two little museums located almost side by side. The first, the **Marine Museum of the Great Lakes** *($3.95; Mon to Fri 10am to 5pm, Jun to Sep every day; at the corner of Ontario and Union, ☎542-2261)*, deals with the history of navigation on the Great Lakes, from 1678 on. Moored in front of the museum is the *Alexander Henry*, an icebreaker that has been converted into an inn (see p 123).

The second museum, the **Pump House Steam Museum** *(55 Ontario St., ☎546-4696)* is a fully restored pumping station containing different models of

steam pumps, as well as other machinery dating from 1849. These huge pumps were one of the most important sources of energy in the 19th century.

At the end of Ontario Street, continue your tour on King Street.

Martello Towers, invented by the engineer of the same name, were a common part of the British defence system in the early 19th century. The Murney Tower, located in **Macdonald Park**, was erected in 1846 to defend the port. This squat stone tower now houses the **Murney Tower Museum** *($2; May to Sep every day 10am to 5pm; at the corner of King and Barrie, ☎544-9925)*, which displays an assortment of 19th-century military articles.

Take Barrie Street to the Frontenac County Court House.

Built entirely of local sandstone, the **Frontenac County Court House ★**, designed by Edward Horsey, is a fine example of the neoclassical architecture of the mid-19th century. It was originally supposed to be the Parliament building, but was never used for that purpose. The huge fountain in front of it was erected in 1903.

The Court House looks out onto a pleasant park, which is flanked by a few magnificent Victorian houses.

The handsome stone buildings of Queen's University lie to the west. There are two museums on campus, the most noteworthy being the **Agnes Etherington Arts Centre ★** *(free admission; Tue to Fri 10am to 5pm, Sat and Sun 1pm to 5pm; temporarily located at 218 Berry St. due to renovations, but plans to return to its former location on campus in the spring of the year 2000; ☎545-2190)*, located in its namesake's former home, which was built in the 19th century. It contains all

Villa Bellevue

sorts of lovely objects, including beautiful collections of African and Inuit art, making it a delightful place to visit.

The second museum, the **Miller Museum of Geology and Mineralogy** *(free admission; Mon to Fri 9am to 5pm; at the corner of Union St. and Division St., ☎545-6767)* displays a collection of minerals, rocks and fossils.

Follow Union Street to Centre Street.

When it was built back in the 1840s, **Bellevue House ★** *($2.50; Jun to Sep, every day 9am to 6pm; Apr to May and Sep to Oct, every day 10am to 5pm; 35 Centre St., ☎545-8666)* was the subject of much discussion. Its Tuscan-style architecture, being somewhat novel at the time, earned it a variety of nicknames, including "the pagoda." In 1848 and 1849, it was the family residence of John A. Macdonald, Canada's first prime minister (1867-1873). Upon entering the house, you will discover a splendid interior adorned with furniture dating from the time when Macdonald lived here. You can visit the elegant dining room and the bedroom where Macdonald's spent her final days, and

enjoy a stroll in the pretty garden surrounding the house.

Return to King Street and go west.

Situated on the banks of Lake Ontario, **Kingston Archeological Centre** *(free admission; Mon to Fri 9am to 4pm; 370 King St. W., ☎542-3483)*, presents archaeological findings which reveal that there has been a human presence in this area for more than 8,000 years. Various objects and maps explain and illustrate the different cultural periods.

Continue west along King Street.

We inevitably approach the **Correctional Service of Canada Museum ★** *(free admission; late May to early Sep, Wed to Fri 9am to 4pm, Sat to Sun 10am to 4pm; 555 King St. W., ☎530-3122)* with a bit of scepticism: what could such a museum contain? However, the museum achieves its objective of providing an insight into several aspects of incarceration. In order to demystify a world that too remains obscure in the minds of the general population, several aspects of prison life are addressed, including the work carried out by some inmates who can do small jobs while living in prison, and a display of some of the various weapons that prisoners have managed to create. The museum also shows changes in attitudes towards correctional services, and presents the different kinds of corporal punishment to which prisoners could be subjected up until 1968. Perhaps the most captivating section is the one that displays the evolution of the prisoner's cell from a tiny dungeon that was used in the last century to the small room of today that is arranged more "ergonomically." The visit also encourages reflection on the role of correctional services in our society.

Hockey fans won't want to miss the **International Hockey Hall of Fame** *($2; Jul to early Sep, Mon to Sat 10am to 5pm, Sun noon to 5pm; at the corner of York and Alfred, ☎544-2355)*, which displays photographs and equipment, thus showing how the sport has evolved over the years. It is located a short distance from downtown Kingston.

This visit through the streets of Kingston has introduced you to the walls and history of the town. If you are curious and want to know about its more obscure side, go on one of the tours organized by **Kingston Haunted Walk** *(departure from the Visitor's Centre opposite Kingston City Hall, ☎549-6366)*. These walking tours will familiarize you with the different ghosts that still discreetly haunt the city.

Wolfe Island

South of Kingston, you can take a free ferry to Wolfe Island, an undeveloped stretch of land with a single hamlet, Marysville. Route 95 runs across the island, and another ferry carries passengers to the United States.

From Kingston, you can either get back on Route 2 and continue the tour or start Tour B in "Getaway Country", which covers Quinte's Isle (see p 136).

Frontenac Provincial Park

Frontenac Provincial Park *(P.O. Box 11, Sydenham, K0H 2T0, ☎376-3489)*, a stretch of wilderness just 50 km from Kingston, has 160 km of hiking trails, as well as rivers that are excellent for canoeing and camping in the wild. The park is open during daytime in the winter and has great cross-country ski trails.

Bon Echo Provincial Park

Bon Echo Provincial Park *(R.R. 1, Cloyne, K0H 1K0, ☎336-2228)* has a number of canoe routes, as well as hiking trails up to 24 km long. Visitors can also marvel at the 250-year-old pictograms on the cliffs alongside Mazinaw Lake, ancient reminders of a bygone era.

Gananoque

Upon entering Gananoque, you will be greeted by a long commercial artery lined with scores of fast-food restaurants and motels. The place is not especially inviting, but it does serve as a departure point for cruises in the Thousand Islands region, and several lovely houses from the last century line its waterfront.

Ivy Lea

The Ivy Lea Bridge crosses over the Thousand Islands into New York State, allowing you to stop at Hill Island, if you like. The island is home to the **Skydeck** *($3.95; Jun to Aug, 8:30am* to sunset, May, Sep and Oct every day 9am to 6pm; ☎659-2335), a 120-metre-high observation tower which commands an outstanding view ★★ of the region's myriad islands.

The Thousand Islands ★★

Islands, islands and still more islands... the Thousand Islands, which actually number 1,865, boast some remarkably beautiful scenery. The Cataraquis Indians, who inhabited this region before the colonists arrived, called it "The Garden of the Great Spirit." While exploring the area, you will discover all sorts of islands, ranging from tiny islets (two trees and 2.5 m² of land are the minimum requirements for an island to be categorized as such) to big islands adorned with opulent houses.

A cruise on the St. Lawrence is an extremely pleasant way to enjoy a close look at this veritable maze of islands, some of which are particularly interesting. In addition to taking in the fascinating scenery, you can actually visit some of the islands, such as Gordon Island, the smallest national park in Canada, and Heart Island, home of Boldt Castle; don't forget, however, that the latter is in American territory, so European passengers must show their passport before disembarking there. Visitors can choose from a number of Thousand Islands cruises, all of which set out from the Gananoque and Kingston marinas (see p 121).

Brockville ★

Brockville boasts a number of splendid buildings, which bear witness to the golden era of the Loyalists. From the late 18th century, when it was founded, up until the beginning of the 20th, Brockville, like many other towns

along the St. Lawrence, enjoyed a long period of opulence, which is reflected in its magnificent residences.

Several attractive buildings testify to the affluence of times gone by. In the middle of the town is the magnificent **Court House Square**, surrounded by several stone buildings, including the former **Johnston District Courthouse** (now the United Counties of Leeds and Grenville). One of the best examples of the Palladian style, this courthouse was built in 1841-45.

If you are interested in old stone buildings, you will appreciate **Fulford Place National Historic Site** (*$4; summer Wed to Sun 11am to 3:15pm; winter Sat-Sun 11am to 3:15pm; 287 King St. E., ☎498-3003*). You can admire this splendid Edwardian-style manor from all angles, and guided tours are available. With its period furnishings, it recreates the atmosphere of past times.

Maitland

Many of the Loyalists who came to Canada, chose to settle in Ontario on the advice of Dr. Solomon Jones, who had **Homewood ★** built in 1801. The stone house boasts sash windows with 24 panes each, and has belonged to the Ontario Heritage Foundation since 1974.

The Parks of the St. Lawrence ★★

The **Parks of the St. Lawrence** (*R.R. 1, Morrisburg, K0C 1X0, ☎543-3704*) are a group of tourist attractions, including historic sites such as Upper Canada Village (see p 117), Fort Henry (see p 110) and the Upper Canada Migratory Bird Sanctuary (see p 121) and the beautiful **St. Lawrence Islands National Park ★★**, whose 23 islands and countless islets lie strewn across a distance of 80 km, from Gananoque to Lancaster. These islands are actually the crests of mountains that were submerged when the glaciers receded and the St. Lawrence River was formed. Their vegetation is very distinctive, featuring species usually found either much farther north or south. As you go from one island to the next, you might be surprised by the diversity of the plant-life, which makes for a patchwork of remarkable settings.

Great Heron

Most of the islands have been adapted with tourists in mind. Some, like those along the **Long Sault** Parkway, are accessible by car, others only by boat. Picnic areas, beaches (Crysler Beach) and campgrounds (Ivy Lea and Mallorytown) are scattered here and there, enabling visitors to enjoy a variety of outdoor activities while exploring the fascinating natural surroundings. For further information, stop by at the **park headquarters** in Mallorytown.

Route 2 and the Thousand Islands Parkway run alongside the river, offering some magnificent views of the St. Lawrence and the islands. Some of the islands have hiking trails, which are very pleasant to walk along. If you are pressed for time and don't want to go

onto the islands, you can explore the banks of the St. Lawrence by taking the Mainland Nature Trail, which starts at the park headquarters in Mallorytown. Finally, if you prefer cycling to canoeing, go for a ride on the beautiful bike path that runs alongside the Thousand Islands Promenade.

Prescott

For many years, Prescott occupied a key location on the St. Lawrence Seaway because the rapids at this point on the river prevented boats from going any farther, forcing them to unload their merchandise here. A fort was thus built to defend the area. Today, this charming little town still has an active port, since it has the only deep-water harbour between Montreal and Kingston. Most people come here to see the fort, however.

In 1838-1839, **Fort Wellington** ★ *($3; May to Sep, every day 10am to 5pm; head east on Route 2, ☎925-2896)* was erected on the site of an earlier military structure built during the Canadian-American War of 1812. The fort, with its massive stone walls and blockhouse, was designed to protect the seaway. It remained in use until the 1920s, and has since been restored and opened to the public, complete with guides to liven up the atmosphere.

Morrisburg

Morrisburg would be just another little town if it weren't for the proximity Upper Canada Village, a remarkable tourist attraction consisting of houses from eight little villages that were flooded when the water level of the river was raised during the construction of the St. Lawrence Seaway. The houses were moved to Crysler Farm Battlefield Park, where they now make up a fascinating historical reproduction of a 19th-century community. The park also has a small monument commemorating the Canadian victory over American troops in the War of 1812.

Upper Canada Village ★★★

With 35 buildings, **Upper Canada Village** *($12.75; May to Oct, every day 9:30am to 5pm; Crysler Farm Battlefield Park, 11 km east of Morrisburg, on Route 2, ☎543-3704)* is an outstanding reconstruction of the type of village found in this part of Canada back in the 1860s. The place has a remarkably authentic feel about it, and you will be continually surprised by the extraordinary attention to detail that went into building it. A sawmill, a general store, a farm, a doctor's house... nothing is missing in this village, which you can explore on foot or by horse-drawn cart. To top off this almost idyllic tableau, the "villagers" are costumed guides able to answer all your questions. Their carefully designed outfits reflect both their trade and social class. You can spend several hours exploring Upper Canada Village and watching the various inhabitants go about their business (running the sawmill, working on the farm, using the flour mill, etc.).

Upper Canada Birds Sanctuary (see p 121).

Cornwall

In 1784, in the wake of the American Revolution, a number of Scots left the United States and settled on the shores of the St. Lawrence River, where they founded Cornwall. This industrial city is now the largest Ontarian town on the St. Lawrence. Located on the Quebec border, it is populated by both English- and French-speakers. The pulp and paper industry, hydroelectric dams and the cotton industry form the backbone of the local economy, but have never brought the town any real prosperity. Some particularly gloomy sectors and an uninteresting industrial zone ring the nondescript downtown area made up of uninspiring buildings. A bridge links Cornwall to New York State, and for many, Cornwall is just a place to pass through on their way somewhere else.

If you do decide to spend some time in Cornwall, however, there are a few interesting tourist attractions, including the **Inverarden Regency Cottage Museum** *(free admission; Apr to Nov, Tue to Sat 11am to 5pm, Sun 2pm to 5pm; Montreal Rd., east of Boundary, ☎938-9585)*. This magnificent house, erected in 1816 for fur merchant John McDonald, is one of the finest examples of Regency architecture in Ontario. It has no fewer than 14 rooms, all decorated with lovely period furniture. The museum's splendid garden, which looks out onto the St. Lawrence, is an exquisite place to stroll about on a fine summer day.

The little **United Counties Museum in the Wood House** *(free admission; Apr to Nov, Tue to Sat 11am to 5pm, Sun 1pm to 5pm; 731 Second St. W., ☎932-2381)*, better known locally as the Wood House Museum, displays a number of paintings by Canadian artists, as well as various everyday objects from the early days of colonization, including toys and tools.

Just outside of Cornwall, **Cornwall Island** is home to the Saint-Régis Indian Reserve.

Tour C: From Pembroke to the Haliburton Highlands

East of the Kawartha Lakes, the verdant plains of the St. Lawrence gradually give way to a dense forest, and

Loon

then hills and rocky escarpments, offering a glimpse of the landscape that characterizes the Canadian Shield to the north. Some 600 lakes and rivers lie strewn across this territory, which attracts fans of outdoor activities like canoeing in the summer and skiing in the winter. The region is also scattered with a handful of peaceful hamlets like **Minden** and **Haliburton**, each of which has restaurants and hotels.

Departing from Ottawa, the tour runs along the Ottawa River and passes through Pembroke before leaving the river and turning inland to the edge of the Canadian Shield.

Pembroke

Pembroke is a rather nondescript town located on the banks of the Ottawa River. Its main attraction is the river flowing alongside it, especially the rapids, which are popular with rafting buffs (see p 121).

Petawawa

A few kilometres after Pembroke, you will come to the little town of Petawawa. Local activity is centred around a large military base, the headquarters of the Canada's Air Force. Two museums, the **Museum of the History of the Canadian Forces** and the **Canadian Airborne Museum** *(free admission; every day, on the military base)*, provide an historical overview of the base and display models of various types of aircraft and other military vehicles.

Algonquin Provincial Park ★★★

In 1893, **Algonquin Provincial Park** *(PO Box 219, Whitney, K0J 2M0, ☎705-633-5572, ≈705-633-5581, www.algonquinpark.on.ca)* was created, thus protecting 7,700 square kilometres of Ontario's territory from the forest industry. This vast stretch of wilderness boasts some fantastic scenery, which has charmed many a visitor. Back in 1912, it was a source of inspiration for Canadian painter Tom Thomson, whose presence will linger here forever, since he not only created his most beautiful works in the park, but also died here mysteriously in 1917. Shortly after, following in Thomson's footsteps, the Canadian landscape painters known as the Group of Seven came here in search of subject matter.

For over a century, Algonquin Park has been captivating outdoor enthusiasts, who are drawn here by the shimmering lakes with their small population of loons, the rivers that wind around the bases of rocky cliffs, the forest of maples, birches and conifers, the clearings covered with blueberry bushes, and the varied animal life that includes beavers, racoons, deer, moose, black bears and more. As you set out by foot or by canoe into the heart of this untamed wilderness, you will be embarking on one of the most enchanting journeys imaginable.

Only one road (Route 60, which is 56 kilometres long), starting in Pembroke and leading as far as Huntsville, runs through the southern part of the park. The information office is located along the way. You can only go deeper into the wilderness by foot, on skis or by canoe. The park obviously attracts a lot of visitors, and a limited number of people are allowed access to certain sites. It is therefore advisable to make reservations.

The **Algonquin Visitor Centre** *(at Kilometre 43)* was opened in 1993 as a reception area for visitors to the park. It encompasses a bookstore where you can find many brochures on the park's flora and fauna, as well as maps of hiking trails and canoeing routes crissing the park; a small exhibition presenting the history of this region's people and animals. There is also a restaurant.

A few kilometres from the East Gate, the old Visitor Centre has been transformed into the **Algonquin Logging Museum** which relates the history of logging in this region. As well as looking at the exhibition, you can follow a 1.5-kilometre path that leads into the forest. This hike is interspersed with 19 points of interest including a woodcutter's cabin and a dam, both made of logs.

Bancroft

Bancroft, with its modest streets and simple little houses, is not one of those picture postcard towns. Its subsoil, however, is rich in semi-precious stones, so it attracts large numbers of collectors and amateur geologists, especially during the mineral and gem show known as the Rockhound Gemboree.

The **Bancroft Mineral Museum** *(free admission; Jul and Aug every day 8:30am to 6pm; mid-Sep to Jun, Mon to Fri 9am to 5pm, Sat 10am to 4pm, closed Sun; Station St.,* ☎*332-1513)* displays a fine collection of stones and minerals from this region and elsewhere.

From Bancroft take Route 28 to Peterborough to return to the tour of the Kawartha Lakes (see p 140), or Route 62 which goes as far as Belleville (see p 134).

OUTDOOR ACTIVITIES

 Hiking

Tour A: Following the Rideau Canal

A lovely boardwalk runs along the Rideau Canal and marks the beginning of the 300-km *Rideau Trail*, which runs through the forests and valleys of Eastern Ontario until the Canadian Shield to the north and from Kingston to Ottawa. In some areas, parallel trail are accessible. For more information and a map of this trail, write to the association below:

Rideau Trail Association
P.O. Box 14, Kingston, K7L 4V6.

Tour B: Following the St. Lawrence

Short hiking trails have been cleared on a number of islands in the **St. Lawrence Islands National Park**. Another trail, the **Mainland Nature Trail ★**, starts at the park headquarters in Mallorytown and leads hikers on an easy, half-hour walk along the banks of the St. Lawrence.

Tour C: From Pembroke to the Haliburton Highlands

Hikers are sure to find a trail that suits them in **Algonquin Provincial Park**. Some relatively short trails require little effort, and can easily be covered in a day. Most of these 16 trails begin along Highway 60. Each path is a small loop of about 0.8 to 11 kilometres and takes no more than a day to cover. Each hike has a different theme: for example, Peck Lake Trail looks at the ecology of the Algonquin Lakes, Booth's Rock Trail presents the impact of human beings on the park and Beaver Pond Trail

shows the importance of a beaver dam on the forest's equilibrium.

Other trails call for more preparation and lead hikers deep into the park over a period of several days. They can vary in length from 6 to 88 kilometres winding through the park and revealing the grandeur of the landscape. However, you must be well organized before disappearing into the depths of nature; an almost indispensable map, *Backpacking Trails of Algonquin Provincial Park ($1.95)* is available in the park bookstores.

 Canoeing

Tour B: Following the St. Lawrence

Eastern Ontario only has a few parks where you can take long canoe trips. Among these, **Frontenac Park** and **Bon Echo Park**, north of Kingston, both have pleasant stretches of water offering beautiful panoramas.

For equipment rentals, contact:

Frontenac Outfitters
Salmon Lake Rd., (at the entrance to Frontenac Park), ☎(613) 376-6220.

Tour C: From Pembroke to the Haliburton Highlands

Algonquin Provincial Park has about 1,000 lakes and rivers, with a total of 1,500 km of canoeing waters. Visitors can take in the majestic scenery on canoe trips lasting a day (N.B.: limited number of canoeists permitted on the water on some weekends; reservations recommended) or more. Before setting out, make sure to check the distance you will be covering by water and on land, when portaging. Always bring along all necessary equipment, sufficient supplies of food and potable water and a map of the park's canoe routes *($4.95)* which will show you where to find natural campsites.

The 60 is the only road that runs through the park, and is the starting point of a number of excursions. Canoes and other equipment can be rented at several outfits along this road, including:

Portage Algonquin
R.R. 6 K8A 6W7.

Portage Store
Route 60, ☎(705) 633 5622.

Algonquin Outfitter
Route 60, ☎(705) 635-2243.

If you don't know how to paddle and would like to learn the basics, contact:

Algonquin Paddling School
Ostongue Lake, Dwight,
☎(705) 635-1167

 Rafting

Tour C: From Pembroke to the Haliburton Highlands

In the **Pembroke** area, thrill-seekers can brave the turbulent waters of the Ottawa and Petawawa Rivers aboard a rubber raft. The ride is especially exciting during the spring thaw, when the waters are at their highest. Rafting excursions are organized by a number of different outfits, including:

Esprit Rafting Adventures
P.O. Box 463, Pembroke, K8A 6X7,
☎(819) 683-3241, ⚞(819) 683-3641.

River Run
P.O. Box 179, Beachburg, K0J 1C0,
☎646-2501 or (800) 267-8504.

Wilderness Tour
P.O. Box 89, Beachburg, K0J 1C0,
☎646-2291 or (800) 267-9166.

 Cruises

Tour B: Following the St. Lawrence

The **Thousand Islands** region is the perfect place for a pleasant trip on the St. Lawrence. Cruises from **Gananoque** and **Kingston** offer a chance to take in some lovely scenery. Boats also leave from **Brockville**.

From Gananoque:
Gananoque Boat Line
☎382-2144
☎382-2146
3-hour cruise: $16

From Kingston:
Island Queen
☎549-5544
3-hour cruise: $18
90-min cruise: $12.50

Sea Fox II
☎542-4271
Catamaran cruise
2 hours: $12

 Bird-watching

Tour B: Following the St. Lawrence

In spring and fall, various species of migratory birds stop along the St. Lawrence River, especially along the stretch protected by the **Upper Canada Migratory. Bird Sanctuary** *(14 km east of Morrisburg, ☎613-543-3704)*, where you can observe them. A variety of other species can also be spotted here all summer long.

Cross-country Skiing

Tour B: Following the St. Lawrence

Frontenac Provincial Park has cross-country ski trails, where hardy souls can venture into the forest to ski and camp.

Tour C: From Pembroke to the Haliburton Highlands

Algonquin Provincial Park welcomes outdoor enthusiasts in winter as well, especially for cross-country skiing, and has well-maintained trails. There are even winter campsites for visitors wishing to stay the night.

Dog-sledding

Tour C: From Pembroke to the Haliburton Highlands

The second to last weekend of January is the occasion of some thrilling dog-sled races in **Minden**.

ACCOMMODATIONS

Tour A: Following the Rideau Canal

Merrickville

In town, **Milliste Bed & Breakfast** *($68 bfkst incl.; ≡; 205 Mill St., K0G 1N0, ☎269-3627, ⇝269-4735)* is a very charming place if you want to relax in a peaceful setting. Situated in an attractive brick house and surrounded by a pretty garden, it is beautifully decorated with antique furniture, curios and paintings that give it an inviting atmosphere. On the main floor, a sitting room and dining room welcome guests, and upstairs five comfortable, individually decorated rooms also assure a pleasant stay. Packages that include meals at the Baldachin restaurant (see p 126) are also available.

🌴 You might just as easily be swayed in favour of the delightful **Sam Jakes Inn** *($80 bfkst incl.; ℛ, △, ⊘, 118 Main St. E., K0G 1N0, ☎269-3711 or 800-567-4667, ⇝269-3713, www.samjakesinn.com)*, a very well renovated stone building that was constructed in the last century. The rooms are furnished with antiques and decorated with wallpaper. The soft eiderdowns on all the beds are part of the management's efforts to create a cozy environment. The old-fashioned style blends perfectly with the modern comforts. Most of the main floor is occupied by an immense restaurant where very good food is prepared (see p 126). This is a non-smoking establishment.

Smiths Falls

The Rideau Canal area has a number of charming places that are very popular. If by chance they are all full, you can always go to the **Colonel By Inn** *($82; ≈, ≡, ℛ; 88 Lombard St., K7A G5, ☎284-0694)*, part of the Best Western chain in Smith Falls. Although it lacks the charm of the historic inns, its 40 rooms are comfortable.

Perth

One of Perth's beautiful and charming stone houses has been converted into a Bed and Breakfast. **Drummond House** *($65 bfkst incl.; 30 Drummond St. E., K7H 1E9, ☎264-9175)* was built on top of a little hill overlooking the river and is a pleasant place. A lovely terrace with a view has been built at the back of the house, and there are three pretty rooms decorated with antique furniture. Each room has its own bathroom.

If you are planning to stay in Perth, you may have difficulty making a choice, since there is another beautiful inn, **Perth Manor** *($99 bkfst incl.; 23 Drummond St. W., K7H 2J6, ☎264-0050, www.pert.igs.net)*. This magnificent residence was built in 1878 and has been meticulously renovated, giving the place an atmosphere of elegance and warmth. In addition to the comfortable and beautifully decorated rooms, there is a splendid garden.

Tour B: Following the St. Lawrence

You will have no trouble at all finding places to stay on this tour, since the road is lined with lovely inns, campgrounds and comfortable hotels, many of which have the advantage of being located on the banks of the St. Lawrence, thus offering a magnificent view and a peaceful setting.

Kingston

The **Kingston International Hostel** *($; 323 William, K7L 5C8)*, located close to the downtown area, welcomes visitors in both summer and winter. Fewer beds are available during winter.

You can also find inexpensive accommodation at the residence halls of **Queen's University** *($47 bkfst incl.; Jean Royce Hall, K7M 2B9, ☎545-2550)*, which rents out a few rooms during summer.

The *Alexander Henry ($42 sb, $65 pb; 55 Ontario St., K7L 2Y2, ☎542-2261)*, which you are sure to have noticed on your way past the Maritime Museum, is

a restored icebreaker that has been converted into a very unusual inn (you can only stay here between May and October). Don't expect a luxurious room; people stay here for the experience, not the comfort.

A series of hotels and motels line Princess Street, including the **Conway** *($55; 1155 Princess St., ☎546-4285)* which is very plain-looking, but has decent rooms for the price.

Continuing down Princess Street, you'll also notice the **Best Western Fireside Inn** *($126; ≡, ≈, ℜ, ☺; 1217 Princess St., K7M 3E1, ☎549-2211 or 800-567-8800, ≈549-4523)*. Its main building, made of logs, has a rustic appearance that is somewhat unusual for this type of establishment. In keeping with the rural theme, the interior is decorated with flowered wallpaper and pine furniture. To top it all off, there is a switch-operated (!) fireplace in every room. The result is an altogether inviting ambiance. Not surprisingly, the place is often full during the cold winter months.

Downtown, the **Queen's Inn** *($89 to $126; 125 Brock, K7L 1S1, ☎546-0429)*, a 19th-century stone house with a restaurant on the ground floor offers pleasant accommodations. Although well-kept, the rooms are decorated with imitation wood furniture, and therefore don't have the old-fashioned charm visitors might hope to find.

Kingston boasts some magnificent 19th-century houses, which have been carefully restored over the years. A number of these have been converted into inns, which manage to combine charm and comfort. You will have little trouble tracking down a few of these masterpieces of Victorian architecture in the area around downtown Kingston.

🦑 Among these establishments is the **Painted Ladies** *($95, bkfst incl.; =; 181 William St., K7L 2E1, ☎545-0422)*, where the thoughtful owner will greet you when you arrive and do all she can to make sure your visit is a success. She is very helpful and can give you a wealth of information about the city. The place also has attractive rooms decorated with antiques, paintings and lots of little curios. Some rooms even have fireplaces and others have whirlpool baths. The beautiful terrace and fine home cooked breakfasts made with wholesome ingredients are just two more features that make this bed and breakfast special.

Another magnificent historic house has been converted into a bed and breakfast nearby. **The Secret Garden** *($95, bkfst incl.; =; 73 Sydenham St., K7l 3H3 ☎531-9884, www.the-secret-garden.com)* has beautiful stained glass windows and attractive flower arrangements inside, and the charming decorative objects placed here and there create a welcoming atmosphere. There are only four rooms but each one is furnished with antiques and is decorated differently to keep the feeling of a family setting.

🦑 The nearby **Rosemount** *($109 bkfst incl.; 46 Sydenham St. S., K7L 3H1, ☎531-8844)* is a delightful B&B with only eight rooms, all well-kept and attractively decorated with antiques. This splendid stone house, built in the 1850s, was renovated in order to satisfy modern standards of comfort, but did not lose its old-time charm in the process.

🦑 The **Belvedere** *($125 bkfst incl.; 141 King St. E., K7L 2Z9, ☎548-1565)* is another converted Victorian house, which is both as beautiful and as successfully renovated as the Hochelaga

Inn. A bright and sunny sitting room adorns the front of the house. Inside, the mouldings on the ceiling and the antique furniture create an atmosphere that is both elegant and inviting.

🦑 The beautifully maintained **Hochelaga Inn** *($135 bkfst incl.; 25 Sydenham St. S., K7L 3G9, ☎549-5534)* is a fine example of the city's establishments. Built in the 1880's, this superb red-brick house has an ornately decorated green and white façade with a pretty turret and a large balcony. It offers a peaceful atmosphere and 23 tastefully decorated rooms furnished with lovely antiques.

The **Holiday Inn** *($160; =, ≈, ℜ, ○, ®, &, ✕; 1 Princess St., K7L 1A1, ☎549-8400 or 800-465-4329, ⇀549-3508)* is a large, rather uninspiring modern building, but boasts an outstanding location right at the edge of Lake Ontario. The comfortable rooms offer a lovely view of the water and all the comings and goings at the Kingston marina.

Gananoque

When entering Gananoque by the highway, you'll find yourself on the main street lined with mundane fast-food restaurants. Press on however, towards the river and you'll discover two delightful inns. The **Victoria Rose Inn** *($95; 279 King St. W., K7G 2G7, ☎382-3368)*, located in a magnificent Victorian residence, has nine spacious and inviting rooms.

🦑 Another option is the **Trinity House Inn** *($90 bkfst incl.; 90 Stone St. S., K7G 1Z8, ☎382-8383, ⇀382-1599)*, in an elegant brick house built in 1859. Its historic charm has not been lost because it has been renovated with great care; the rooms blend the elegance of another era (antique furniture decorate the rooms) with the comforts of today. An attractive terrace, a pleasant sitting room and a pretty garden also make for an enjoyable stay.

Morrisburg

At the **Upper Canada Migratory Bird Sanctuary Nature Awareness Campsite** *($21.25; ☎543-3704 or 537-2024, ≈543-2847)*, which is part of the **Parks of the St. Lawrence**, has fifty campsites laid out in a lovely natural setting.

You can also camp at one of the other campgrounds in the **Parks of the St. Lawrence** *(☎800-437-2233)*, which are beautifully situated on the banks of the river.

Reservations:

Glengarry ☎347-2595
Mille Roches, Woodlands and McLaren ☎534-8202
Riversite/Cedar ☎543-3287
Ivy Lea ☎659-3507

Cornwall

Vincent Massey Street and Brookdale Avenue, both of which are lined with hotels and small motels, are located close to the entrance to town. The local inns have sacrificed old-fashion charm for modern comfort, but it is easy to find decent accommodation. The **Ramada Inn** *($73; ≡, ≈, △, ⊛, ✕; 805 Brookdale, K6J 4P3, ☎933-8000 or 800-272-6232 ≈933-3392)*, **Best Western** *($99; ≡, ≈, ℛ, △, ⊛, ✕; 1515 Massey, K6H 5R6, ☎932-0451 or 800-528-1234, ≈938-5479)* and the **Comfort Inn** *($78; ≡; 1755 Massey, K6H 5R6, ☎932-7786 or 800-4CHOICE, ≈938-3476)* are noteworthy for their wide range of amenities.

Tour C: From Pembroke to the Haliburton Highlands

Haliburton

🏊 If you dream of a peaceful getaway on the lake, surrounded by nature, **Domaine of Killien** *($335 ½b; from Haliburton, take Hwy. 118 west to Country Rd. 19, which you follow 10 km to Carrol Rd., PO Box 810, Haliburton, K0M 1S0, ☎705-457-1100, ≈705-457-3853, www.domainofkillien. on.ca)* is the place. This establishment has 12 large rooms, in a large house, or in charming cabins. All are attractively decorated with wood. The tranquil atmosphere is perfect for leaving the worries and stresses of city life far behind, and the exquisite garden of over 2,000 hectares has a vast array of well-maintained hiking and cross-country skiing trails. There is also a delicious French restaurant on the premises.

Pembroke

The highway runs through this town and a good part of main street is occupied by rather uninteresting businesses. It is a good place to stop and relax before continuing on further north as there are several respected establishments here. Among them is the **Pembroke Heritage Inn** *($77 or $99, bkfst incl.; 900 Pembroke St., K8A 3M2, ☎735-6868, ≈735-7171)*, which is a decent choice if you are looking for a place with modern conveniences.

Algonquin Park

Highway 60 crosses the southern part of the park for 56 kilometres where there are no less than eight camping areas. They are set up for visitors who want to discover the beauty of nature

EASTERN ONTARIO

without having to travel far into the park for several days. This is a great place for family excursions; some of the areas have more than 250 sites with electricity, while other smaller ones have camping in the wild. Whatever your preference, you will definitely be thrilled. You can make reservations (☎705-633-5538, ≈705-633-5581, www.algonquinpark.on.ca).

 Imagine spending the night in the heart of Algonquin Park's forest, far from the crush of the city at the **Arowhon Pines** *($175/person fb; POA 1B0, ☎705-633-5661, ≈633-5795)* hotel. You will slip into sweet slumber in a rustic decor that is just as inviting as the big city luxury hotels. Destined to become one of those special memories you will cherish long after returning to the bustle of the regular day-to-day.

✖ RESTAURANTS

Tour A: Following the Rideau Canal

Merrickville

The dining room of the **Country Corner Tea room** *($; Mill St.)* is very appealing with its antique furniture and pretty wallpaper with little geese. Everything is in place in this haven of tranquility. The menu offers simple, reasonably priced dishes like quiche.

Jakes Block, built in 1862, stands at the corner of Main and Lawrence and now houses the **Baldachin Restaurant** *($$-$$$; ☎269-4223)*. Large picture windows look out onto the street and antique furniture give it the feeling of another era. The place is an absolute delight! The menu has several specialities that are always well prepared.

Right next door and also decorated with an air of the past is the restaurant of **Sam Jakes Inn** *($$$; 118 Main St. E., ☎269-3711)*. The huge dining room has country-style furniture and pretty flowered wallpaper. The atmosphere is comfortable and the menu has a good selection of dishes that are tasty and hearty, though not the most innovative. The lamb chops, steak and trout all come with ample sauces and will satisfy any appetite.

Carleton Place

On the main street in town, **The Mississippi Café** *($)* is the perfect place if you feel like having a bite to eat particularly on a fine day because it has a very attractive terrace.

Almonte

This town's beautiful stone mill, the **Victoria Woollen Mill** *($$-$$$; beside the river)*, has been converted into a huge restaurant. The layout of the place is enough to leave you breathless; the ceiling is very high, light floods into the room through large windows, the walls are of stone and the tables are made of wood and wrought iron. In this superb dining room you can have brunch, lunch or dinner: the menu offers delicious meals all day long. In one corner there is a small gift shop.

Perth

Both a souvenir shop and a café, the **Passiflora** *($; 43 Gore St. E., ☎267-7994)* has only a few tables but it is the best place in town if you feel like sipping a café au lait or savouring a dessert.

Just seeing the large terrace is enough to understand why the **Courtyard Tea Room** *($; 91 Gore St. E., ☎276-5094)* is usually jam-packed on a lovely sunny day, especially at noon. Its popularity is also due to the meals it serves: the soups, quiches and salads are always prepared with fresh ingredients.

Tour B: Following the St. Lawrence

Kingston

The **Sleepless Goat Café** *($; 91 Princess)* is an altogether charming place to take a break from bustling Ontario Street while savouring a delicious cup of coffee and a slice of cheesecake.

If you like vegetarian food, visit the **Windmill Café** *($; 184 Princess St., ☎544-3948)*. This restaurant has a warm atmosphere and offers a good selection of vegetarian dishes prepared with wholesome ingredients that are always fresh.

Ontario Street runs alongside the lake, and a number of restaurants have set up terraces here to take advantage of the lovely view. **Stoney's** *($$; 189 Ontario St., ☎545-9424)* has probably one of the prettiest terraces of all; at lunchtime, it is a highly coveted spot from which to observe the nonstop activity on the street while enjoying a slice of quiche or a salad.

The **Kingston Brewery Co.** *($$; 34 Clarence St., ☎543-4978)* is well known by fans of micro breweries because it is the brewer of Dragon's Breath. The atmosphere is friendly and you can have a good meal with a choice of dishes such as chicken or rib steak while savouring a beer (other micro brewery beers are also served).

The **Café Max** *($$; Brock St., at the corner of King)* offers an inexpensive nightly *table d'hote*, with a choice of soup or Caesar salad, a main course such as Tandoori chicken served with pasta, and coffee. The food is honest and always served in generous portions, making the place extremely popular with the local residents, who willingly line up for a table on Saturday nights.

To enter **Chez Piggy** *($$; 68 Princess St., ☎549-7673)*, you must first pass through a small inner courtyard, where you will see the terrace and the lovely 19th century stone buildings that house the restaurant. These superb buildings have been tastefully renovated, and Chez Piggy has long been a favourite of Kingston residents, who readily line up for a delicious meal, both at lunchtime, when the restaurant serves simple fare like quiche and salads, and at dinnertime, when the menu is more sophisticated, listing a variety of dishes, notably chicken and lamb.

Although its nondescript façade makes it easy to overlook, **Darbar** *($$; 478 Princess St., ☎548-7053)* serves succulent Indian cuisine. The Tandoori dishes and curries are consistently delicious.

Kingston has everything to please Indian food lovers; if Darbar doesn't appeal to you, give the **Curry Village** *($$; 169A Princess St., ☎542-5010)* a try. Their curry and tandoori dishes have won over more than one fan, and some say it is the best Indian restaurant in town. It is up to you to decide.

Le Caveau *($$-$$$; 354 King St. E., ☎547-1617)* occupies the main floor and the basement, both with a limited number of tables. The brick walls and woodwork create a warm and cozy atmosphere in which you can savour delicious meals prepared with a dash of originality. Standard items such as filet mignon with cognac sauce and tuna fish steak with pink pepper sauce are always on the menu, and will not leave you disappointed. The restaurant also has good selection of wines sold by the glass.

If you aren't worried about breaking your budget and want to spend a memorable evening out, go to the **River Mill** *($$$; 2 Cataraqui St., ☎549-5759)*. Upon entering the elegant dining room, you will be greeted by the enchanting view over the lake through the big picture windows. The menu, whose delicious offerings change with the seasons, is sure to whet and satisfy your appetite.

Gananoque

At first glance, Gananoque seems to have only fast food restaurants, but as you go further into town you will discover charming establishments serving good food. There are two inns where visitors can eat well and enjoy themselves. The restaurant of the **Victoria Rose Inn** *($$-$$$; 279 King St. W., ☎382-3368)* is open all day long and serves delightful meals. If you want to eat in a very beautiful environment, **Trinity House Inn** *($$$; 90 Stone St. S., ☎382-8383)* has a mouth-watering dinner menu.

Cornwall

There are a number of fast-food restaurants on Vincent-Massey Street, including a Saint-Hubert for barbecue chicken.

If you are staying in town for a while, you can opt for something a little more interesting than fast food. The **Gemini Café** *($; 241 Pitt St., ☎936-9440)* has

a daily menu listing a variety of tasty dishes.

Tour C: From Pembroke to the Haliburton Highlands

Pembroke

The choice of restaurants in Pembroke is rather limited, but you can get a decent meal at **East Side Mario's** *($-$$; 100 Pembroke St. E., ☎732-9955)*. Good pasta dishes are served and the atmosphere is friendly.

Algonquin Provincial Park

The **Arowhon Pines** *($$$$; you can bring your own wine; ☎705-633-5661)* restaurant boasts an exceptional setting next to one of Algonquin Park's many lakes. The only thing that might interrupt your meal as you contemplate the enchanting surroundings, is the echo of the forest. Besides the cosy fireplace in the centre of the dining room, you will savour an excellent cuisine prepared with the freshest of ingredients.

 ENTERTAINMENT

Tour A: Following the Rideau Canal

Merrickville

It is difficult to think of a more charming place than the **Dicken's Den Pub** *($; Lawrence St.)* where the setting is sure to strike your fancy: high-backed armchairs, cozy sofas, paintings, bookcases full of books, antique curios, woodwork – you could spend hours here, nestled comfortably in an armchair sipping a beer or savouring a meal.

Tour B: Following the St. Lawrence

Kingston

The **Grand Theatre** *(218 Princess St., ☎613-530-2050)* is the hub of cultural activity in Kingston, presenting plays and concerts of classical music.

At the end of the day, the terrace of the **Kingston Brewery Co.** *(34 Clarence St.)* is the perfect place to drink a cold beer and chat with friends.

The Oak *(331 King E., ☎542-3339)*, a British-style pub, is very popular with university students. It has a good selection of imported beer on tap.

Toucan-Kirkpatricks *(76 Princess St., ☎544-1966)*, located right nearby, has a similar clientele and sometimes hosts live music.

If you are in a festive mood and feel like getting down to the latest tunes, there are a few options. These include **Stages** *(390 Princess St., ☎547-3657)* which has several dance floors on different levels.

Bancroft

The Rockhound Gemboree, Canada's largest mineral and gem show is held at the beginning of August and attracts crowds of collectors.

 SHOPPING

Tour A: Following the Rideau Canal

Manotick

In fine weather, a **Farmer's Market** is held every Saturday morning at the Dickinson Mill. It is an opportunity to buy fresh fruit and vegetables grown in the area, as well as homemade products such as maple syrup, jam or fudge.

North Gower

The Antique Shoppe is overflowing with curios and charms, tables and chairs, chests and cabinets, all the antiques you would need to transform any interior into a trip down memory lane. There is a large choice of quality pieces.

Merrickville

Mirick's handing *(Lawrence St.)* sells fine variety of items, including sopas, candles, tablecloths and napkins, and various trinkets.

The enticing selection of candies, fruit preserves, vinegars and other irresistible products at **Mrs. McGarrigle's** *(St. Lawrence St.)* is enough to make your mouth water.

Perth

The **Farmer's Market** *(late May to mid Oct, Sat 8am to 1pm; Crystal Palace, ☎264-9234)* is the meeting place of the region's farmers and small-market producers. You can buy fresh fruit and vegetables along with delicious wholesome products.

Tour B: Following the St. Lawrence

Kingston

Downtown Kingston centres around Ontario Street, with Brock and Princess as secondary arteries. If you hunt around a little, you're sure to find a few little treasures here.

The **Dansk Factory Outlet** *(166 Princess St., ☎531-9999)* has a good selection of kitchenware, vases and other articles for the home.

If it's books you're looking for, head straight to Princess Street, where you'll find an outlet of **Coles the Book People** *(101 Princess St.)*, among other places.

Outdoor enthusiasts can purchase sporting goods or get their equipment repaired at **Frontenac Cycle & Sport** or **Cycle Path**, both located on Princess Street.

Olden Green *(78 Princess St., ☎546-6423)* and the **Corner Store** *(corner of Princess and Ontario St.)* are good places to go for small gifts or handicrafts.

As you walk down King Street, keep an eye out for the pretty storefronts of **Metalwork**, which has a fantastic selection of jewellery, and **La Cache** *(208 Princess St., ☎544-0905)*, one of a chain of charming shops found all over Canada, which sells clothing, bed linens and other articles.

Brock Street boasts some of Kingston's prettiest storefronts, many seemingly right out of another era. **Cooke's**, a typical turn-of-the-century general store, is perfectly charming. It sells specialty foods like Rogers chocolates from Victoria (British Columbia) and delicious preserves.

On the other side of the street, relive some happy childhood memories at **Doll Attic** *(Brock St.)*, which sells some of the most beautiful dolls imaginable.

Finally, you should stop in at **Birds 'n Paws** *(79 Brock St.)*, which has a lovely collection of birdhouses as well as accessories for cats and dogs.

Kingston now has a great bookstore, **Indigo Books, Music & Café** *(259 Princess St., ☎546-7650)*, where you can browse and read in a comfortable environment. There is also a café.

Gananoque

Newly built on the shores of Lake Ontario, the **Historic 1000 Islands Village** *(Water St.)* has the most beautiful setting. A great place for a bit of shopping because there are several stores selling a range of articles such as souvenirs, mementos and books.

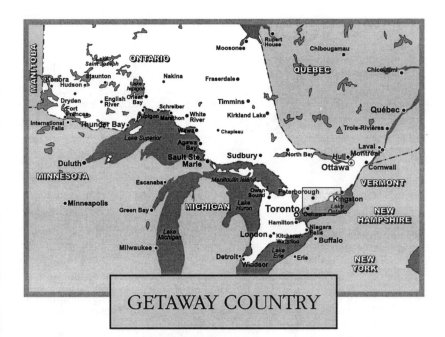

GETAWAY COUNTRY

The still relatively unpopulated stretch from Kingston to Toronto has some wonderful rural scenery, with charming little hamlets tucked away in the countryside and some spectacular views of Lake Ontario. The end of the 18th century was a significant period in Canadian history. After the American War of Independence, a surge of loyalists crossed the border to settle in this vast territory still under the British crown. Many of them established themselves around the Bay of Quinte, founding a string of villages that grew rapidly thanks to their proximity to the St. Lawrence Seaway and the rich agricultural land in the region, especially on Quinte's Isle. The back country was settled in the 19th century by new arrivals lured here by the lovely countryside surrounding the Kawartha Lakes, which quickly became a popular vacation spot.

This area is also where you'll find the Trent-Severn Seaway, which links Trenton to Georgian Bay.

 FINDING YOUR
WAY AROUND

Tour A: Along the Shores of Lake Ontario

By Car

The tour starts in Kingston and runs along Lake Ontario until Oshawa, the main city before Toronto. This tour can be combined with Tour B: Following the St. Lawrence (see p 127) in the Eastern Ontario chapter.

Bus Stations

Belleville: 45 Dundas St. E., at the corner of Pinnacle St.,
☎(613) 962-9544.

Oshawa: 47 Brown St. W.,
☎(905) 723-2241.

Train Station

Oshawa: On Thornton St. S.

Tour B: Quinte's Isle

By Car

On this tour, you can admire some truly charming rural scenery while exploring the little roads of Quinte's Isle.

Take the 33 from Kingston to Picton, and then around Quinte's Isle (the road goes all the way to Trenton).

Tour C: The Kawartha Lakes

By Car

Starting at Peterborough, the tour winds around the Kawartha Lakes through the towns of Lakefield, Bobcaygeon, Lindsay and Fenelon Falls.

The tour starts at Peterborough, which is easily accessible, located midway between Ottawa and Toronto.

From Ottawa: Take Route 7.
From Toronto: Take Route 2 to the 115, which leads to Peterborough.

Bus Stations

Peterborough: Simcoe St., corner of George St., ☎(705) 743-1590.

PRACTICAL INFORMATION

The **area code** is **613**, except for Cobourg, Port Hope and Oshawa where it is **905** and Tour C: The Kawartha Lakes where it is **705**. Where no area code is given, it is **613**.

Tour B: Quinte's Isle

Prince Edward County Chamber of Tourism and Commerce: P.O. Box 50, Picton, ON, K0K 2T0, ☎476-2421, ≈476-7461, www.pec.on.ca.

Tour C: The Kawartha Lakes

Peterborough Kawartha Tourism: 175 George St. N. Peterborough, ON, K9J 3G6, ☎(705) 742-2201, ☎(800) 461-6424.

EXPLORING

Tour A: Along the Shores of Lake Ontario

Travellers heading from Kingston to Toronto can hardly avoid taking this route. This section of the highway is often crowded with people in a hurry to get someplace or other. Just a few kilometres further south, however, life is tranquil in the small communities clustered on the shores of Lake Ontario. These towns were built about 100 years ago, and have retained their old-fashioned charm. If you have a little extra time or want to stay overnight in one of these lovely villages, make a brief detour. This is a wonderful place to leave all your worries behind.

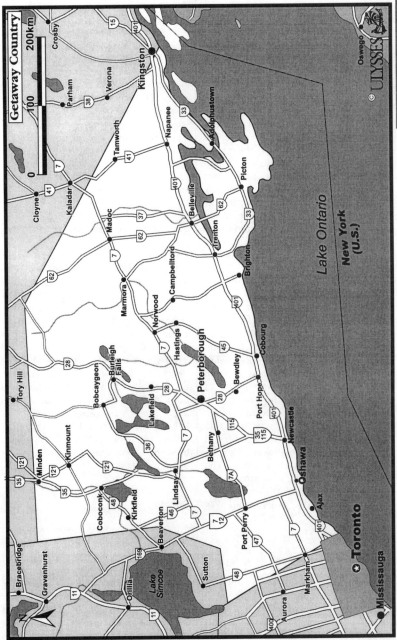

Belleville

Pleasantly situated at the mouth of the Moira river on the Bay of Quinte, Belleville was founded by Loyalists who fled from the United States in 1784. It has grown steadily throughout the 19th century, gradually transforming itself into the pretty city with attractive homes we know today. Its lovely residential areas are perfect for strolls. The main attraction, however, is the marina on the bay where there are many summertime activities, the most important of which is the Waterfront Festival, which turns the marina into a veritable fairground of outdoor activities. There is a picturesque promenade from which you can see the pretty little boats bobbing on the waves. Quinte's Isle is easily reached from Belleville.

The city has preserved many of its heritage buildings, most notably the **Glanmore Historic Site** *($3; Jun to Aug, Tue to Sun 10am to 4:30pm, Sep to May, Tue to Sun 1pm to 4:30pm; 257 Bridge St. E., ☎962-2329)*. Located in an elegant building, built in 1883 in the Second Empire style, all of its rooms have been renovated and adorned with lovely Victorian furnishings. The walls and ceilings have also been richly decorated. On the second floor, you will find several small exhibits, including a collection of lamps. The basement contains a reconstructed general store and servant's room, offering a glimpse of what everyday life was like in 19th-century Belleville.

Trenton

The Trent-Severn Waterway starts here in Trenton. In summer, visitors in all kinds of boats crowd to the marina to set off on an excursion on the waterways that crisscross the centre of the province all the way to Georgian Bay.

Brighton

Most people who pass through Brighton only spend a short time here, opting instead for the lovely beaches at Presqu'île Provincial Park. This peaceful hamlet, which has a rather charming, old-fashioned look about it, is nonetheless a pleasant place to stop.

The area around Brighton, as far as Cobourg, is strewn with apple orchards, which create a charming pastoral atmosphere, especially in the spring, when the blossoms are out.

Presqu'île Provincial Park ★

Presqu'île Provincial Park *(R.R. 4, Brighton, K0K 1H0, ☎475-2204)* was created in order to protect a thin strip of land that extends into Lake Ontario and is flanked by vast swamps, which attract a variety of bird species. There are wooden piers, from which ornithologists of all ages can view some of the local species at close range. Wooden benches and panels providing information on the wildlife make an outing here both pleasant and instructive. Visitors eager to enjoy the refreshing waters of Lake Ontario won't be disappointed either, since the park has long sandy beaches. Campsites are available for overnight stays.

Cobourg

Cobourg lies in the heart of the countryside on the shores of Lake Ontario. At first glance, it looks like a simple little town. On your way through, however, you will discover some impressive buildings, which bear witness to a prosperous past, when Cobourg's port was one of the busiest in the region, and flour mills, sawmills and car factories fuelled the local economy. One of the most noteworthy of these elegant

Cobourg Town Hall

edifices is the majestic, Palladian-style **town hall** ★ *(Victoria Hall, 55 King St. W.)*, designed by architect Kivas Tully in 1860. During these years, Ontario's towns underwent a period of growth, and needed larger municipal buildings. Huge sums of money were allocated for the construction of these new buildings. In fact, townspeople seem take as much civic pride in the amount spent on the projects as in the city halls themselves. With this background knowledge, it becomes easier to understand why a relatively small community would have such an imposing town hall! This large building houses the provincial courts, a concert hall and an art gallery whose exhibits include handicrafts and paintings by Canadian artists. A few steps away stands **St. Peter's Church**, a lovely example of Gothic Revival architecture, begun in 1851.

For a relaxing stroll or picnic next to the peaceful waters of Lake Ontario, head to the lovely sandy beach at **Victoria Park**. You can also enjoy a pleasant stroll on the pretty streets around the park, which are shaded by elms and willows.

Port Hope ★

It is easy to be enchanted by Port Hope's charming town centre, with its string of craft and antique shops. The village dates back to 1788, when Peter Smith settled here. A few years later, in 1793, he was followed by a group of Loyalists, who actually founded the town. A few beautiful old buildings bear witness to the past, including **St. Mark's Church**, erected in 1822, as well as some pretty houses built in the different architectural styles that were fashionable in Ontario in the 19th century. These treasures of brick and stone have been painstakingly restored in the last several decades, and the town now has some of the prettiest and best preserved buildings in the region.

Situated about 20 kilometres north of Port Hope, **Rice Lake** is a vast expanse of water known for its lovely beaches and fishing. The lake is one of the links in the Trent-Severn Seaway, and is a hub for numerous outdoor activities during the summer.

If you are going to Toronto, keep heading west. If not, you can go north and start Tour C, which covers the Kawartha Lakes.

Oshawa ★

Oshawa, the last town on this tour, lies about fifty kilometres from Toronto, whose presence is already tangible. This town has flourished as a result of its automobile industry, which was launched at the beginning of the century, when Robert McLaughlin began manufacturing cars here, and has since become the most highly developed in Ontario. When General Motors purchased his plant, he became director of the company's Canadian division. Since then, GM has been the town's largest employer.

Like many industrial towns in North America, Oshawa is a drab-looking place. It does, however, have a few interesting attractions, most related to McLaughlin and the automobile industry.

The **Robert McLaughlin Gallery** ★ *(free admission; Tue, Wed and Fri 10am to 5pm, Thu until 9pm, Sat and Sun noon to 4pm; Civic Centre, Centre St., ☎905-576-3000)* displays some lovely paintings by contemporary Canadian artists, including abstract pieces by members of the Painters Eleven, who made a name for themselves in the 1950s. These artists' technique was to paint quickly, drawing only on the inspiration of the moment, in order to infuse their work with a feeling of intensity.

You can step into the world of automobiles at the **Canadian Automotive Museum** ★ *($5; Mon to Fri 9am to 5pm, Sat and Sun 10am to 6pm; 99 Simcoe St. S., ☎905-576-1222)*, a totally nondescript building containing over sixty antique cars.

The **Oshawa Community Museum** *($2; Jul and Aug, noon to 5pm, Sun 1pm to 5pm, closed Sat all year; Sep to Jun, Mon to Fri noon to 4pm, Sun 1pm to 5pm; Simcoe St. S; in Lakeview Park, ☎905-436-7624)* is made up of three historic little houses once owned by the Robinson, Henry and Guy families respectively. It presents several small exhibits, including one on electricity.

If you only have time to see one attraction in Oshawa, head straight to **Parkwood Estate** ★★ *($6; Jun to Sep, Tue to Sun 10:30am to 4:30pm, Sep to May, Tue to Sun 1:30pm to 4pm; 270 Simcoe St. N., ☎905-579-1311)*, the sumptuous former residence of R.S. McLaughlin. The house stands in the midst of a magnificent garden featuring a harmonious combination of stately trees, hedges and verdant stretches of lawn, crowned by a lovely fountain. The outstanding garden is an indication of the opulence of the house itself, whose 55 beautifully decorated rooms make for a captivating visit.

Tour B: Quinte's Isle ★

Quinte's Isle abounds in lovely pastoral scenes, which you'll discover as you round a bend in the road or explore the shores of the island. With its peaceful hamlets, vast, fertile fields and long sandy beaches, Quinte's Isle is sure to appeal to city-dwellers in search of beautiful natural landscapes. Although many visitors come here to savour the bucolic atmosphere in summer, the island has not become touristy. It is crisscrossed by a few roads, which are perfect for bicycling.

Starting in Kingston, this tour follows the Loyalist Parkway (Route 33) through picturesque little towns and continues along the Adolphus Reach North Channel right up to the lake,

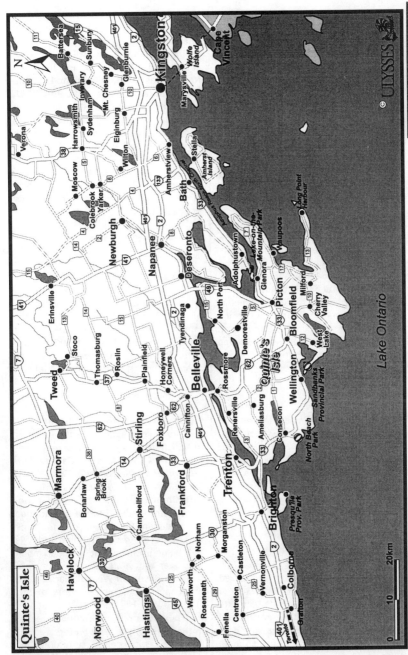

Quinte's Isle

© ULYSSES

where a ferry takes you across to Quinte's Isle.

If you arrive on the island via Route 49, you will pass through the Mohawk territory of **Tyendinaga**. On the way, you'll come across a surprising but very elegant Anglican church topped by a pretty Gothic tower.

Amherstview

Just outside Kingston, you will be surrounded by fields and apple orchards as far as the eye can see. Amherstview, the first town you will come to, has a long history that goes back to the time of Ontario's settlement. William Fairfield, a Loyalist fleeing from Vermont, established himself here in 1793, building beautiful **Fairfield House** *(west of Amherstview, ☎384-2813)*, which is one of the oldest in the region. Notice the roof and its long gallery that resembles those found on houses in Québec built during the same period.

Bath

The houses here line the channel, and each strives to be more charming than the last. Bath is really one of a kind. One of the first towns in the region, its pretty old houses date back to the 18th century. Upon entering Bath, there is a pleasant park with lovely green spaces and pretty views of the channel.

Adolphustown

The last town on Highway 33, named after the seventh son of King George III, Adolphus Frederick, by the Loyalists who settled here in 1784. At the end of the road, a **ferry** *(free; every day)* takes passengers and their cars to Quinte's Isle.

Glenora

The first community you'll encounter on this peaceful island will be the modest hamlet of Glenora. By following Route 7 east, you will come to **Lake-on-the-Mountain Park** *(☎393-3319)*, named after an unusual lake located at the top of a rocky escarpment, 61 m above the water level of the Bay of Quinte. The lake was probably created by a dissolution of limestone before the last glaciers receded. This park is only open during the day, but is a wonderful place for a picnic, with a splendid view of Lake Ontario.

Continue west to Picton.

Picton

Picton is more or less the nerve centre of the island, since all the major roads intersect here. It is also the largest town on the island, with 4,000 inhabitants. The place still has a rural look about it, though, and consists chiefly of a few handsome historic buildings and some shops and restaurants.

Picton still has some magnificent 19th-century buildings, some of the loveliest of which are located in **Macaulay Heritage Park ★** *(Tue to Sun 10am to 4pm in summer; at the corner of Church and Union, ☎476-3833)*. **St. Mary Magdalene Church** is built in the Gothic Revival style. Made of stone and topped by an elegant bell tower, it dates back to 1825. The tower standing today is not the original one, but has been modified over the years. It owes its existence to Reverend William Macaulay, a prominent figure in the history of this little town. His home, a splendid Regency-style red brick house erected in the 1830s, has been restored and is decorated with period furniture. The dining room, study and bedrooms are particularly interesting.

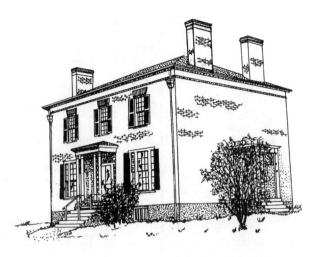

Macaulay Heritage House

Route 17 leads to the southern part of the island and Millford.

Around South Bay

From Picton, the road threads its way through vast fields giving way to stands of maple trees that turn a vivid red in autumn. The glittering waters of Prince Edward Bay suddenly lie before you as you go around a bend in the road. Peaceful towns have sprung up here and there, among them **Milford**, with its charming boutiques. From Milford, you can take Route 10, and then Route 13, which runs the length of **Long Point**, right to the end of this long strip of land jutting into Lake Ontario. Needless to say, beautiful views are to be had from here.

Retrace your steps to Milford.

Pushing further west into the back country, you will reach the other side of Quinte's Isle. Here, **Sandbanks Provincial Park ★** *(R.R. 1, ☎393-3319)* protects the fragile ecosystem of the

impressive sand dunes that rise as high as 25 metres (see p 143). The park is also known for its two magnificent sand beaches that are no doubt the most beautiful in Ontario. Camping is permitted here, but it's best to reserve in advance since the park is very popular.

Take Route 12 to Bloomfield.

Bloomfield ★

Although you'll pass through Bloomfield before you know it, you're sure to notice its string of lovely red brick houses dating from the 19th century, which give its main street an irresistible charm.

This village is ideal for shopping, since the main street is a jumble of little boutiques vying for your attention. Each shop has appealing window displays and contains many little treasures. The stately buildings are reminders of the town's prosperity in the 19th century, when no fewer than 12 mills operated here.

Wellington

Although it doesn't have as much character as Bloomfield, neighbouring **Wellington** is a bit bigger and therefore better equipped to meet visitors' needs. It is also located just a short distance from the lovely beaches of **Sandbanks Provincial Park** and **North Beach Park** (see p 143). Both have long sandy beaches perfect for taking a dip, sunbathing or having a picnic.

On Main Street, you'll find the **Wellington Museum** *($1; Jul and Aug, every day 10am to 4pm; rest of the year, Sat and Sun 10am to 4pm; Main St., ☎399-5015)*, which was once a Quaker church. The Quakers took refuge in this area around 1784, when their lands were being confiscated in the United States.

If you continue on Route 33, you'll reach Trenton.

Tour C: The Kawartha Lakes ★

This region has been geared towards tourism since 1876, when vacationers started coming here to enjoy the peaceful natural setting of Kawatha, whose Amerindian name means "Land of Shining Water." Kawatha has since become Kawartha, but has managed to retain its unique character, having successfully combined the beauty of a still unspoiled natural setting with the comfort of a few charming little villages where visitors can dine and sleep. Many pleasure-boaters pass through this region on the Trent-Severn Waterway, making for some fascinating activity around the locks.

Peterborough

In 1825, Governor Peter Robinson led 2,000 Irish immigrants to the site of present-day Peterborough, on the shores of Little Lake and the Otonabee River, and founded the town that still bears his first name. Peterborough itself is a rather gloomy-looking place, which serves as a stopping point for motorists travelling between Ottawa and Toronto. Visitors using the Trent-Severn Waterway, however, will see the town in a more attractive light, since it has three locks, including an amazing **hydraulic lift lock** ★ *(☎705-750-4950, ≈705-750-4958)*, an elevator dating from 1904, which still lifts boats some 20 m above water so that they can continue on to Georgian Bay. Peterborough is also the home of **Trent University**.

Renovations were carried out by architect Ron Thom during the 1960s. The sandstone buildings were constructed on a lovely site along the Otonabee River. Among the most attractive are the modern ensemble of buildings that make up Champlain College.

One of the city's charming little museums is the **Canadian Canoe Museum** ★ *(910 Monaghan Rd., ☎705-748-9153)*, which has a wonderful collection of kayaks and canoes. The canoe, so central to the life of Native Americans and the first colonists, is one of the hallmarks of Canadian history. The exhibits show the evolution of canoe-making, from traditional bark canoes to modern ones. Of course, the museum also inevitably touches on aspects of the fur trade, and of the history of the country in general.

Several kilometres east of Peterborough, **Lang Pioneer Village** *(May to Sep every day; from Hwy. 7 take County Rd. 34 south for 6 km; ☎705-295-6694)* is an interesting his

Peterborough

● ATTRACTIONS

1. Hydraulic Lift Lock
2. Trent University
3. Canadian Canoe Museum
4. Lang Pioneer Village
5. Peterborough Square Complex
6. Hutchison House
7. Centennial Museum

0   500   1000m

torical reconstruction. Guides in period costumes and machinery bring the 20 buildings to life and recreate a 19th-century atmosphere. A great place for a family excursion on a pleasant summer day.

In the centre of town, the modern shopping centre, **Peterborough Square Complex** ★ was built in 1973 and

integrated in to old Market Hall. This former market, dominated by its clock tower, was built in 1889 and designed by architect John Belcher.

If you have a little time to spare, you can visit **Hutchison House Museum** *(May to Dec, Tue to Sun 1pm to 5pm; Jan to Mar, Mon to Fri 1pm to 5pm; 270 Brock St., K9H 2P9,*

☎705-743-9710), the former home and office of Peterborough's first resident doctor. Now restored, it contains some mementos of the city's early days.

Centennial Museum ($2.50; Mon to Fri 9am to 5pm, Sat and Sun noon to 5pm; 300 Hunter St. E., west of the locks, PO Box 143, K9J 6Y5, ☎705-743-5180, ≈705-743-2614) traces the history of the city, from the beginning of colonization to the 20th century, with particular emphasis on the difficult life of the early immigrants.

Take Route 28 from Peterborough to Lakefield.

Lakefield

Lakefield lies at the point where the Otonabee River flows into Lake Katchenawooka, the first lake on the Trent-Severn Waterway. The river's tumultuous waterfalls are now controlled by a lock. Lakefield's only attraction is its charming town centre, made up of pretty little red brick houses.

To reach Petroglyphs Provincial Park, take the 28 to Burleigh Falls, then the 36 toward Woodview.

Petroglyphs Provincial Park ★

The Ojibwa who once lived in this region left behind scores of petroglyphs carved in white marble. They used these symbols to tell the young the story of life. **Petroglyphs Provincial Park** (Woodview, K0L 3E0, ☎705-877-2552) was founded in order to protect these testimonies to the Ojibwa past, which are five to ten centuries old. Visitors can admire a few of the 900 petroglyphs found in the park, which are now inside a large building.

Retrace your steps and continue on Route 36 to Bobcaygeon.

Youngs Point

You can make a short stop to enjoy the natural scenery at Youngs Point. Don't miss its pleasant park on the river, where you can stretch your legs and watch the pleasure boats going through the locks.

Curve Lake Indian Reserve

After Youngs Point, take Route 20 west to Route 507 north. Then take Route 22 along the shores of Buckhorn Lake. This long strip of land belongs to the Ojibwa and covers an area of some 400 hectares between Chemong Lake and Buckhorn Lake. The Whetung Reserve has a small art gallery and a museum where different aspects of Ojibwa culture are represented. There is also a gift shop that sells an array of Native American handicrafts.

Bobcaygeon ★

After passing through Peterborough, the road winds through a dense, seemingly uninhabited forest interspersed with peaceful hamlets. Bobcaygeon is one of these picturesque little villages, whose quaint downtown is sure to charm you. It also has the first lock to be built on the canal (1883), surrounded by a pleasant park shaded by large trees and benches from which you can watch the boats pass by.

Lindsay

Lindsay is the most populous town in the Kawartha Lakes region after Peterborough, but still retains its small town charms. Though the town is pretty, the main attraction here is definitely the promenade alongside the locks on the Scugog River.

Those wishing to go boating on the Trent-Severn Waterway can climb aboard the *Skylark VIII*. A variety of cruises are offered, including one to Fenelon Falls (see further below).

Fenelon Falls

The town of Fenelon Falls is not particularly interesting in its own right. Its impressive 7-m high namesake **waterfall ★**, is another story. The deafening roar of the rushing water is audible as soon as you enter the town. A pleasant park has been laid out by the falls.

 OUTDOOR ACTIVITIES

 Swimming

Tour B: Quinte's Isle

Sandbanks Provincial Park ★ *(R.R. 1, Picton, K0K 2T0, ☎393-3319)* is known mainly for its magnificent sandy beaches, which stretch along the shores of Lake Ontario and are literally overrun with sun-worshippers and water sports enthusiasts on hot summer days.

If the beaches at Sandbanks Park are too crowded for you, head to **North Beach Park** *(R.R. 3, Consecon, K0K 1T0, ☎393-3319)*, whose beach may not be as beautiful as the ones in Sandbanks Park, but is attractive nonetheless.

 Cruises

Tour C: The Kawartha Lakes

The **Trent-Severn Waterway** stretches 386 km, and offers a unique and enjoyable way of exploring the Ontario landscape (see p 134). For further information or to plan a trip, write to:

Trent-Severn Waterway
P.O. Box 567, Peterborough K9J 6Z6, ☎(705) 742-9267.

If you don't have a boat but would like to spend a few hours on the Waterway, you can take a cruise from Lindsay or Fenelon Falls.

Skylark VIII Boat Tours
Wellington St., Lindsay,
☎(705) 324-8335, $15.

Fenelon Falls Cruise
Tickets available on Oak Street, ☎(705) 887-9313, $14.

 Hiking

Tour A: Along the Shores of Lake Ontario

The **Ganaraska Trail** begins at Port Hope and winds some 450 kilometres through the interior before ending at Georgian Bay. Running along the Ganaraska River, it crosses the magnificent Ganaraska pine forest and the Kawartha Lakes region. You'll see lots of beautiful countryside, but some sections of the trail are classified as difficult.

Ganaraska Trail Association
12 King St., Orillia, L3V 1R1, ☎416-757-3814, www3.sympatico.ca/hikers.net.

Another very pretty hiking trail around Port Hope is the **Waterfront Trail**, which starts at Stoney Creek, at the outskirts of Toronto, and follows the shore of Lake Ontario to Trenton. This lengthy trail (325 km) offers some magnificent panoramas along the way, but requires planning and preparation. You can always settle for going just part of the way.

 Bird-watching

Tour A: Along the Shores of Lake Ontario

Presqu'île Provincial Park ★ covers a large stretch of swampland, which attracts all sorts of birds. Wooden footbridges have been built so that the animals can be observed in their natural habitat. Amateur ornithologists can thus enjoy a close look at a variety of species, including barnacle geese and about twenty species of ducks. To ensure that your visit is an enjoyable one, the park has been equipped with benches and information panels describing some of the species found here.

 Bicycling

Tour B: Quinte's Isle

Quinte's Isle is perfect for cycling, especially since it's so peaceful and traffic is never heavy. Cyclists are free to explore every corner of this large island, travelling across fields or along Lake Ontario. It is also very easy to plan a longer excursion of several days. In short, the island lends itself to cycling, no matter what your level.

If you hit a snag, you can have your bicycle repaired at **Bloomfield Bicycle Co.** *(Main St.)* in downtown Bloomfield.

 Fishing

Tour A: Along the Shores of Lake Ontario

In winter, when its frozen surface is covered with fishing shacks, the Bay of Quinte bustles with activity. **Belleville** and **Trenton** play host to the ice-fishing buffs who descend on the area. You can rent the necessary equipment near the marinas of these two towns, as well as in many of the villages located by the bay.

Turner's Tackle
R.R. 2 Carrying Place,
☎394-2705.

Foster's
R.R. 2, Picton, ☎476-7290.
Fishing equipment rentals in winter and summer.

Quinte Marina
1 Marina Rd., Deseronto,
☎396-3707
Rents out fishing shacks for ice fishing and all other necessary equipment.

Tour B: Quinte's Isle

Quinte's Isle is known for its lovely rural landscape, but is also popular with fishing buffs, who have discovered that there are some good catches to be made in the surrounding waters. From the shores of Hay Bay and near Wellington, you can land yourself a pike or even a salmon.

ACCOMMODATIONS

Tour A: Along the Shores of Lake Ontario

Belleville

Another place to keep in mind is the **Ramada Inn on the Bay** *($95; =, ≈, ℛ, △, ᕃ, ✕;11 Bay Bridge Rd., K8N 4Z1, ☎968-3411)*, pleasantly located on the banks of the Moira River and with comfortable rooms.

A big red-brick building set in the heart of Belleville, the **Clarion Inn** *($109; =, ℛ; 211 Pinnacle St., K8N 3A7, ☎962-4531 or 800-CLARION, ⇒966-5894)* is somewhat massive-looking. The inn mainly has suites. Each of the 50 suites is originally furnished according to a different theme (Ethos Suite, Northern Lights Suite, etc.).

Brighton

Presqu'île Provincial Park *($19.75; ☎474-4324, ⇒ 475-4324)* has some lovely campsites, which are well-shaded and only a short distance from the beach.

A few kilometres from the park, is a charming little B&B — the **Apple Manor B&B** *($60 bkfst incl.; 96 Main St., ☎475-0351)*, which boasts a beautiful garden.

Cobourg

At first sight, you might hesitate to stay at the **Woodlawn Inn** *($$$; 420 Division St., K9A 3R9, ☎905-372-2235, ⇒372-4673, www.woodlawninn.com)* because of the busy street on which it is lo-

cated. However, this red brick house is surrounded by a magnificent garden, which minimizes the noise. Built in 1835, the place has been carefully renovated. Its 16 rooms are tastefully decorated and impeccably kept. This classy establishment also has a restaurant (see p 148)

Port Hope

 "Magnificent" is the word that will spring to mind when you set eyes on the **Hillcrest** *($110 bkfst incl; =, ≈, △, ⊛; 175 Dorset St. W., L1A 1G4, ☎905-885-7367, ⇒885-8167)*, a gorgeous Art-Nouveau-style inn. Six majestic columns flank the entrance which leads into an exquisite foyer that gives you an inkling of the beauty and elegance to be found in rooms. Some rooms have fireplaces, while others have balconies or lovely high ceilings. All are furnished with antiques and have private bathrooms. There couldn't be a more comfortable place to stay. Guests have access to a large day room, a heated swimming pool, a sauna, and a magnificent garden right on the lake.

Oshawa

Being an industrial town, Oshawa is hardly a vacation spot. Visitors can nevertheless find comfortable accommodation at the **Travelodge** *($85; =, ≈, ⊛, ✕; 940 Champlain Ave., L17 7A6, ☎905-436-9500 or 800-578-7878, ⇒436-9544)*.

Tour B: Quinte's Isle

There are a number of charming places to stay on Quinte's Isle, including some lovely B&Bs set in the heart of the countryside and a few well-maintained campgrounds.

The campground at **Sandbanks Provincial Park** *($22.75; ☎393-3319)* has some truly beautiful sites right on Lake Ontario. As this place is not exactly a well-kept secret, reservations are strongly recommended.

Picton

🦞 The **Merrill Inn** *($95-$265 bkfst incl.; 343 Main St. E., K0K 2Y0, ☎476-7451 or 800-567-5969)* is inside one of Picton's lovely Victorian houses. This red-brick building was built in 1878 for Edwards Merrill and his family. The pretty rooms of this appealing little inn are all decorated with antiques.

If you would like to stay outside the village, in the heart of the countryside, head to the **Isaiah Tubbs Resort** *($825 per week, $179/room; West Lake Rd., K0K 2T0, ☎393-2090 or 800-267-0525, ≈ 393-1291)*. In addition to a few simple cottages, this waterside hotel complex has pleasant rooms and apartments, located inside handsome wooden buildings and equipped with all the modern comforts. The place has been designed to meet all guests' needs, with conference rooms and a host of athletic facilities, including tennis courts and swimming pools. The setting is as peaceful as can be, and in order to make the most of the location, the restaurant and several terraces look out onto the water.

🦞 Just outside of Picton, you will notice a lovely stone house surrounded by a large garden. **Waring House** *($105 bkfst incl.; R.R. 8, K0K 2T0, ☎476-7492, ≈476-6648)* is over 100 years old, but, of course, has undergone quite a few renovations

during this time. It is now a beautiful B&B with a delicious restaurant (see p 148). Inside, everything has been done to make this an elegant place to stay: some of the finest cuisine in the area, a courteous welcome, and tastefully decorated rooms, furnished with handsome antique furniture.

After leaving Picton, on the way to Bloomfield, you will come across **Groove Cottage** *($79 bkfst incl.; ≡; R.R. 1, K0K 2T0, ☎393-3974)*. Set back from the road at the top of a little hillock, the house has a tranquil natural setting, with only some large trees to share in the tranquillity. Built in 1860, this attractive wooden house has a large room where antiques are sold. The guestrooms are located upstairs, are attractively decorated with antique furniture, and are very comfortable.

Bloomfield

The lovely **Honey's Bed & Breakfast** *($55 bkfst incl.; ≡; 292 Main St., K0K 1G0, ☎393-2373)* is in a charming little house with four well-maintained rooms and a comfortable day room where you can unwind.

The **Bloomfield B&B** *($60 bkfst incl.; 341 Main St., K0K 1G0, ☎393-1392)* is a red-brick building with pretty blue shutters. Its white porch is the perfect place to relax and enjoy the day. The place is truly charming, but only rents out two rooms, both attractively furnished.

Tour C: The Kawartha Lakes

Peterborough

During summer vacation, visitors looking for inexpensive accommodation can stay in the residence halls at **Trent**

University *($; 310 London St., K9J 7B8, ☎705-748-1260).*

Peterborough's **Holiday Inn** *($$$-$$$$; ≡, ≈, ℛ, ⊛, △, &, ✕; 50 George St. N., K9J 3G5, ☎705-743-1144 or 800-465-4329, ≈705-740-6557 or 740-6559, www.holiday.inn.com)* is easy to find located right at the edge of town. This big hotel is fully equipped to accommodate families, and also has two swimming pools.

Lakefield

The slightly rustic **Beachwood Resort** *($190 ½b; ℛ; R.R. 1, K0L 2H0, ☎705-657-3481, www.beachwoodres ort.com)*, outside Lakefield, will appeal to visitors looking for a natural setting. Located alongside Deer Bay and surrounded by lovely conifers, it offers an escape from the urban hustle and bustle.

Bobcaygeon

The **Princess Motel** *($55; ≡, △; 96 Main St., K0M 1A0)* is easy to find; its the long blue building in the centre of Bobcaygeon. The rooms are decorated in a rather nondescript manner, but are well kept and are overall decent.

 The building now known as the **Bobcaygeon Inn** *($69.95; ≡, ℛ; 31 Main St., K0M 1A0, ☎705-738-5433)* has been accommodating visitors since the 1920s. Although it has been renovated, its rooms are decorated with antiques and still have an old-fashioned charm about them. The place also boasts an outstanding location, right at the edge of the water.

Fenelon Falls

If you're looking for total comfort and a first-class natural setting, **Eganridge Inn & Country Club** *($160 bkfst incl.; ℛ, ≡; R.R. 3, K0M 1N0, ☎/≈705-738-5111, www.eganridge.com)* is the place to go. Located in a magnificent, carefully renovated log manor (Dunsford House) built in 1937, its guestrooms have preserved their olden-days charm, but have all the modern comforts. The antique-looking furniture adds a classic touch. The place is absolutely idyllic, especially with its elegant garden and superb view of the sparkling waters of Sturgeon Lake. There is a golf course and a delicious Swiss restaurant. Guests can also stay in cabins which are very comfortable, have a rustic decor, and blend in well with their surroundings. Special golf packages are available.

Lindsay

Those who decide to stay in Lindsay will find comfortable lodgings at the **Days Inn** *($89.95; ≡, ≈, ℛ, &; R.R. 4, K9V 4R4, ☎705-324-3213 or 800-268-2278, ≈ 324-9121).*

✕ RESTAURANTS

Tour A: Along the Shores of Lake Ontario

Belleville

You will probably have noticed the lovely **Limestone Café** *($$; 184 Front St., ☎966-3406)* as you walk along the town's main street. Inside, stone walls give the dining room a nice touch. Here, you can enjoy a good meal in a pleasant environment. The menu features European dishes.

The **Angus Steak House** *($$$; 211 Pinnacle St., ☎962-4531)* has a very large dining room decorated in a style reminiscent of the turn of the century. It offers a wide selection of consistently good, all-you-can-eat dishes, such as roast beef.

Cobourg

Chipper's *($; 103 King St. W., ☎905-372-9784)* is certainly not the place to go for an unforgettable meal, but it will satisfy that craving for a burger. It has a solid reputation with the locals.

If you can't stand the thought of eating French fries again, go to **Casey's** *($$; 1 Strathy Rd., ☎905-372-9784)*, which is only slightly more elegant than Chipper's, but serves good grilled meats with vegetables on the side.

For an excellent meal that is not exorbitantly priced, head to the **Woodlawn Inn** *($$$; 420 Division St., ☎905-372-2235)*. The Victorian decor is a little excessive, but warm and welcoming nonetheless, and will no doubt win you over. The refined menu lists delicious dishes that will tingle your tastebuds.

Port Hope

🏛 Whether you're looking for a place to eat, or simply have an afternoon tea, **The Owl and the Pussycat** *($; 127 Walton St., ☎905-885-8702)* is a delightful choice. This small restaurant is also an antique store where you can have a bite and browse through the shop. There is also a small terrace.

Another place to have a simple but good meal in town is **Jim's Pizza and**

Pasta *($-$$; Walton St.)*, which has a pleasant dining room and a terrace.

Oshawa

For a good, healthy meal, head to **Cultures** *($; Simcoe St. corner of Athol St., ☎905-728-5356)*, which serves yummy sandwiches and salads.

For a good, nourishing meal, try **Fazio** *($$-$$$; 33 Simcoe Street, ☎905-571-3042)*, where you can savour simple Italian dishes in a large, but somewhat impersonal dining room.

Tour B: Quinte's Isle

Picton

🏛 The **Waring House** *($$$; R.R. 8, ☎476-7492)*, a superb 19th-century house, is both a pretty inn and a pleasant restaurant. The dining room has big picture windows looking out onto the neighbouring fields, providing a serene atmosphere in which to enjoy your meal. Most of the dishes are prepared with local ingredients, most notably fish from the surrounding area. Classics like beef Wellington are also available.

Bloomfield

The charming town of Bloomfield is a wonderful place to satisfy your hunger. **Mrs. Dickenson's** *($; Main St., ☎393-3356)*, a cafe open only during the day, has a simple menu featuring sandwiches and succulent desserts. This is a perfect place to relax.

Walking along the main street, you will notice the **Bloomfield Brasserie** *($; Main St.)*, which serves simple dishes like quiche, sandwiches and salads, as well as good desserts. The tables are set up in a dining room with large windows facing the street. You can also eat outside on a tiny terrace that only has one or two tables.

Year after year, **Angeline's** *($$$; 29 Stanley St. W., te. 393-3301)* manages to live up to its long-standing reputation as the best restaurant on the island. People come here to savour a handful of French specialties, such as lamb with garlic. The restaurant, furthermore, is a charming place to spend a delightful evening.

Tour C: The Kawartha Lakes

Peterborough

Not far from the Eaton Centre, which literally dominates downtown Peterborough, is **Häaselton** *(394 George St.)*, where you can relax for a bit while sipping a nice cappuccino. Also a perfect spot for lunch, the place serves simple and tasty food like soups and sandwiches, made with healthy ingredients.

The youthful, unpretentious atmosphere at **Hot Belly Mama's** *($; on Water St. at Simcoe)* lends itself well to enjoying a good meal at lunchtime. The menu features quiche and skewered shrimp.

Gazebo *($-$$; 150 George St. N., ☎705-743-1144)*, the restaurant in the Holiday Inn, has a very pleasant location right beside the pool and Little Lake. Grill dishes feature prominently on the menu, as well as simple meals that will appeal to the whole family.

Bobcaygeon

With a great view of the locks, **Big Tomato** *($-$$; Bobcaygeon Inn,*

31 Main St., ☎705-738-5433) is the place to go for pizza, pasta or a hamburger. The restaurant is not too elegant, but the simple decor (plastic tablecloths, a view of the water) gives it a seaside holiday ambiance.

Fenelon Falls

With its absolutely exquisite setting, the restaurant at **Eganridge** *($$$; R.R.3, ☎705-738-5111)* makes for a memorable dining experience. The delightful dining room has large bay windows with a view of the garden and Sturgeon Lake, while the menu, featuring French, Mediterranean and Californian cuisine, changes with the seasons to make sure that the ingredients are at their freshest. Don't miss out in this gourmet feast if you can afford it.

 ENTERTAINMENT

Tour A: Along the Shores of Lake Ontario

Cobourg

City Hall *(Victoria Hall, 55 King St. W.)* Has a concert hall where operettas and other musical performances are put on by different companies.

 SHOPPING

Tour A: Along the Shores of Lake Ontario

Port Hope

Port Hope's downtown streets are lined with inviting shop displays that will easily pull you in. No fewer than 40 antique shops have sprung up here, and you're certain to find a little something to take home if you rummage through their wares. Most of these shops are on Walton Street.

If your taste in home furnishings is more contemporary, head to **Country Accents** *(78 Walton St.)*.

Tour B: Quinte's Isle

Bloomfield

For quilts, embroidered tablecloths, candlesticks, dishes and all sorts of other great gift ideas, head to **Green Gables** *(286 Main St., ☎393-1494)*.

Across the street, **Christmas in the Village** *(287 Bloomfield Main, ☎393-2828)* sells all types of decorations.

Tour C: The Kawartha Lakes

Peterborough

If you need to buy any equipment for your trek into the forest, check out thequality merchandise at the **Wild Rock Outfitter** *(Charlotte St.)*.

Youngs Point

Another good place to find the latest in outdoor equipment is the **Lockport Trading Company** *(by the locks at Youngs Point, ☎652-3940)*.

Curve Lake Indian Reserve

The **Whetung** *(☎6577-3661)* Indian reserve is one of the best places for aboriginal crafts.

TORONTO

The honour of being the first European to discover Lake Ontario and to trample the ground that would become the largest city in Canada falls to Étienne Brûlé, a French explorer sent by Samuel de Champlain. Brûlé's expedition took place in 1615, at the beginning of the French colonization of North America. Like many of his predecessors, Brûlé was in search of navigable route across the continent to the riches of the Orient. At the time, a native village called *Teiaiagonon* was established on the site now known as Toronto. The natives who knew and had inhabited this region for more than 10,000 years were well aware of the advantages of this site that the Hurons called *Toronto* (meeting place): its excellent natural port and easy access to Lake Ontario and Lake Huron by foot or by canoe.

The French and later the British, also came to appreciate the site's advantages. As of 1720, the French set up a fur trading post. About 30 years later, the British, in an attempt to counter competition from their commercial rivals, constructed a fort. The French ultimately burned their Fort Rouillé in 1759 as they beat a hasty retreat from advancing British troops.

In order to realize the potential of this excellent site, the British purchased it from the Mississauga Indians in 1787 for 1,700 pounds sterling. John Graves Simcoe, the first governor of Upper Canada, needed a capital for the new province; the location had to be well-protected and far from the American border to avoid potential invasion. In 1793, he chose this site. A small fort called York was built, and the area's new status as capital attracted a few colonists. The 700 people that had settled here by 1812 succeeded in pushing back the Americans, who had declared war on Britain the year before, but not before the town had been occupied for a few days and destroyed.

In 1834, the city was incorporated and renamed Toronto. Its population was 9,000 at the time. During the 19th century, Toronto underwent a rapid expansion, particularly from 1850-1860 with the construction of the railway between Montreal and New York. The railway signalled the beginning of the industrialization of Toronto and its surroundings, which has continued in successive waves right up until the present. Simultaneously, the city continued to assert its commercial prowess and became the capital of the new province of Ontario with the Canadian Confederation in 1867.

At the beginning of the 20th century, Toronto gained a reputation that it just couldn't seem to shake. It became known as "Toronto the Good", rather fitting especially after the 1906 legislation on the "Day of Lord" which forbade the city's residents from any work or diversions on Sundays. Torontonians thus have a reputation for being reserved and hard-working. As home to several banks, investment companies, financial heavyweights and countless factories, the city attracted an increasing number of immigrants and by 1914 was the second largest city in Canada, after its big rival Montreal. Immigration to Toronto was on hold for nearly two decades following the years of growth that succeeded the First World War as first the Great Depression, and then the Second World War shook things up.

The urban face that characterizes Toronto today began to develop in the 1950s under the administration of Frederik Gardiner. Gardiner oversaw the laying out of parks, an expansion of the subway system and the construction of expressways for automobile traffic. In effect, he created a pleasant and livable city. Over the following decades, Toronto flourished, surpassing Montreal and becoming the largest city in Canada.

Toronto's growth over the last 20 years has literally redefined the city. It has blossomed into a city with a decidedly cosmopolitan air. Nowhere else in Canada are there as many different ethnic communities, a characteristic that distinguishes the city from the rest of Ontario and also with the Toronto of old. This cultural mosaic has created a dynamic microcosm, making Toronto the heart of culture in English-speaking Canada.

Six tours are have been outlined to facilitate your visit of Toronto: Tour A, "The Waterfront," Tour B, "The Theatre and Financial Districts," Tour C, "Front Street and St. Lawrence," Tour D, "Queen Street West and Chinatown," Tour E, "Around Queen's Park" and Tour F, "Bloor and Yorkville." You'll also find an introduction to Toronto's many vibrant neighbourhoods and a list of attractions located around the city.

FINDING YOUR WAY AROUND

Getting to Toronto

Lester B. Pearson International Airport

See p 37

Bus Station

610 Bay Street, ☎416-393-7911.

Train Station

65-75 Union Street West
between York St. and Bay St.
across from the Royal York Hotel
☎800-361-1235

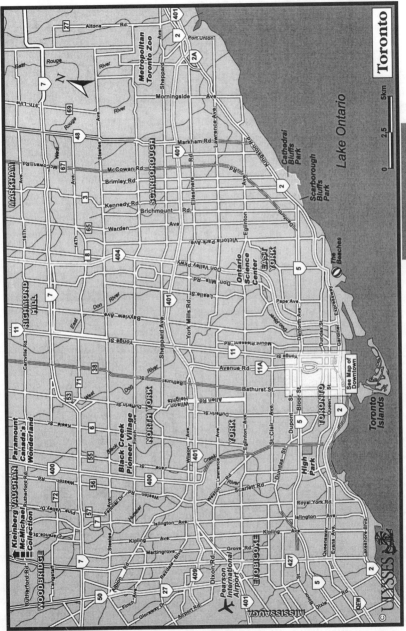

TORONTO

By Car

Most people arriving by car from east or west will enter the city on Highway 401, which crosses the northern part of the city. Coming from the west, take Hwy. 427 south to the Queen Elizabeth Way (QEW), continue east to the Gardiner Expressway, and exit at York, Bay or Yonge Streets for downtown. Coming from the east, the quickest way to reach downtown is on the Don Valley Parkway; continue to the Gardiner Expressway, then exit at York, Bay or Yonge Streets. Those coming from the United States will follow the shores of Lake Ontario on the QEW to the Gardiner Expressway. Rush-hour traffic can be very heavy on Toronto's highways, especially on the Don Valley Parkway.

Renting a Car

Avis
Hudson Bay Centre at Yonge and Bloor
☎416-964-2051

Budget
141 Bay St.
☎416-364-7104 or 363-1111

Hertz
128 Richmond St. E.
☎416-363-9022

Thrifty
134 Jarvis
☎416-868-0350

National
40 Dundas St. W.
☎416-591-8414

Getting Around Toronto

On Foot

Toronto's underground city, called the **PATH**, is the largest in the country. It weaves its way under the streets from Union Station on Front Street all the way to the Atrium on Bay at Dundas Street. The perfect escape for those cold winter days, it provides access to shops, restaurants (see map).

By Car

Toronto's grid-system of streets makes it easy to get around. Yonge (pronounced *young*) Street is the main north-south artery and it divides the city between east and west. Street addresses that have the suffix "East" or "E." lie east of Yonge and vice versa; 299 Queen St. W. is therefore a few block west of Yonge. Toronto's downtown is generally considered to be the area south of Bloor, between Spadina and Jarvis.

Public Transportation

Toronto's public transportation system is run by the **Toronto Transit Commission**, the **TTC**; it includes a subway, buses and streetcars. There are three subway lines: the yellow Yonge University line is U-shaped and runs north-south, with the bottom of the U at Union Station; the green Bloor Danforth line runs east-west along Bloor and Danforth from Kennedy Road to Kipling Road; the blue Scarborough RT line runs north and east up to Ellesmere Road. There is also the Harbourfront LRT, which runs from Union Station along Queen's Quay to Spadina. Finally, the GO commuter train links the suburbs of metropolitan Toronto with

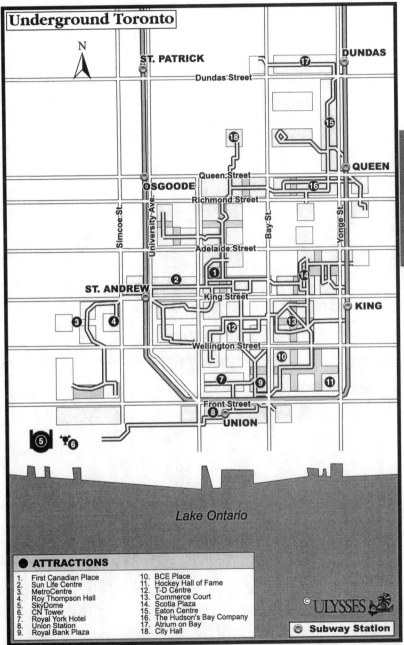

Underground Toronto

N

ST. PATRICK

DUNDAS

Dundas Street

QUEEN

OSGOODE

Queen Street

Richmond Street

Simcoe St.

University Ave.

Bay St.

Yonge St.

Adelaide Street

ST. ANDREW

King Street

KING

Wellington Street

Front Street

UNION

Lake Ontario

TORONTO

● **ATTRACTIONS**

1. First Canadian Place
2. Sun Life Centre
3. MetroCentre
4. Roy Thompson Hall
5. SkyDome
6. CN Tower
7. Royal York Hotel
8. Union Station
9. Royal Bank Plaza
10. BCE Place
11. Hockey Hall of Fame
12. T-D Centre
13. Commerce Court
14. Scotia Plaza
15. Eaton Centre
16. The Hudson's Bay Company
17. Atrium on Bay
18. City Hall

© ULYSSES

◎ **Subway Station**

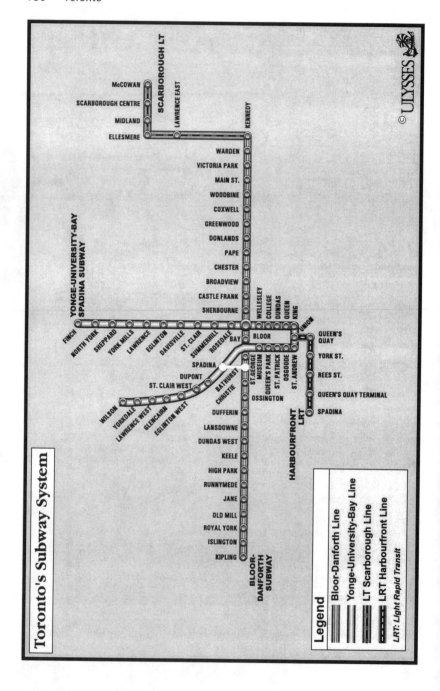

Toronto's Subway System

downtown. All of these trains and subways are safe and clean. Buses and streetcars run along the city's major arteries. You can transfer between buses, streetcars and subways without paying another fare, but you will need a transfer, so always take one, just in case. Pick up a copy of the *Ride Guide*, as well. It shows most of the major attractions and how to reach them by public transportation.

A single **fare** is $2 for adults, $1.35 for students (you must have a TTC student card) and seniors and 50¢ for children under 12. Five adult tickets or tokens cost $8, 10 student or senior tickets or tokens cost $10.70 and 10 child tickets or tokens cost $4. If you plan on taking several trips in one day, buy a Day Pass for $6.50, which entitles you to unlimited travel on that day. Sundays are really economical, since one Day Pass can be used by two adults, or by a family (two adults and four children, or one adult and five children). A monthly pass costs $83 for adults and $73 for students and seniors.

Bus and streetcar drivers do not give change; you can purchase tickets at subway booths and certain stores (Shopper's Drug Mart).

For route and schedule information call ☎393-4636; for fare and general information call ☎393-TONE(8663).

PRACTICAL INFORMATION

The **area code** for Toronto is **416** unless otherwise indicated.

Tourist Information

The main offices of **Tourism Toronto** are at Queen's Quay Terminal *(207 Queen's Quay, Suite 590,* *M5J 1A7,* ☎*203-2500 or 800-363-1990)* but this location is mostly that, offices, plus a few brochures. The staff are nevertheless very helpful and will gladly answer any questions you might have. A more complete tourist office, run by Ontario Travel, is located on the lower level of the Eaton Centre at Queen and Yonge Streets; the **Visitor Information Centre** *(☎800-668-2746)* is open year-round, Monday to Friday 10am to 9pm, Saturday 10am to 5pm and Sunday noon to 5pm.

The **Traveller's Aid Society** *(in Union Station, on the arrivals level, ☎366-7788; at Pearson International Airport, Terminal 1 ☎905-676-2868, Terminal 2 ☎905-676-2869, Terminal 3 ☎905-612-5890)* is a volunteer organization that can provide information about hotels, restaurants, sights and transportation.

 EXPLORING

Tour A: The Waterfront ★★★

Being near a major body of water often determines the location of a city, and Toronto is no exception. For many years, however, the city of Toronto neglected its waterfront. The Gardiner Expressway, the old railway lines and the numerous warehouses that disfigured the shore of Lake Ontario offered few attractions in the eyes of residents. Fortunately, large sums of money were spent to return this area to life, and it is now home to a luxury hotel, many shops, and numerous cafés bustling with constant activity.

Harbourfront Centre ★ *(free admission, 410 Queen's Quay W.; ☎973-4000 for information on special events)* is a good example of the changes on Toronto's waterfront. It is easily reached by the new Union Station trolly running west toward Spadina Avenue. Since the federal government purchased 40 hectares (100 acres) of land located along the shores of Lake Ontario, dilapidated old factories and warehouses have been renovated, turning this into one of Toronto's most fascinating areas. Apart from the pretty little cafés and the numerous shops, there are also a variety of shows and cultural events that are the pride of Torontonians.

A few steps away, at the foot of York Street, is **Queen's Quay Terminal ★★★** (207 Queen's Quay W.), where boats leave for trips around the bay and the Toronto Islands. Queen's Quay is a former warehouse that has been completely renovated and modified to house a theatre devoted exclusively to dance as well as about 100 restaurants and shops.

From Queen's Quay Terminal, head over toward the lake and the **Power Plant Contemporary Art Gallery ★** (235 Queen's Quay W.), with its collections of paintings, sculptures, photographs and modern videographic works. Next door is the red-brick **Du Maurier Theatre Centre** (231 Queen's Quay W.), behind which is the **Tent in**

the Park, where various concerts and plays are presented all summer long. A little further west is the **York Quay Centre ★** (☎973-3000), with restaurants and other establishments. Be sure not to miss the **Craft Studio** (York Quay Centre, free admission) where you can observe craftspeople at work and perhaps make some purchases. Right near Lake Ontario, sailboats and motorboats can be rented at the **Harbourside Boating Centre** ($50 or more for three hours; 283 Queen's Quay W., ☎203-3000), with prices varying according to the size and type of boat. Sailing lessons are also offered. In the winter, the bay is transformed into a gigantic skating rink. You can rest at one of the many bars and restaurants of **Bathurst Pier 4**, which has water sports as its theme, or else go on to explore some of the sailing clubs.

Inaugurated in 1998, the **Toronto Waterfront Museum** (245 Queen's Quay W., ☎392-6827) has replaced the former Marine Museum. Good use has been made of this lakefront location, using old warehouses dating from the 1920s, renewed to their original state. Visitors can discover exhibits on Lake Ontario wreckages, historical battles, and the changing face of Toronto's Harbourfront.

● ATTRACTIONS

1. Princess of Wales Theatre
2. The Royal Alexandra
3. Union Building
4. Roy Thompson Hall
5. Metro Hall
6. St. Andrew's Presbyterian Church
7. Sun Life Tower
8. First Canadian Place / Toronto Stock Exchange
9. Toronto-Dominion Centre
10. Old Toronto Stock Exchange
11. Bank of Nova Scotia
12. National Club Building
13. Canada Permanent Building
14. Northern Ontario Building
15. Canadian Imperial Bank of Commerce
16. Number 15
17. Royal Bank Plaza
18. Union Station
19. Royal York
20. Air Canada Centre
21. Hockey Hall of Fame-BCE Place-Bank of Montréal
22. Gooderham Building
23. St. Lawrence Market
24. Farmer's Market
25. St. Lawrence Hall
26. St. James Cathedral
27. King Edward Hotel
28. Market Square
29. Elgin and Wintergarden Theatres
30. Pantages Theatre
31. Massey Hall
32. St. Michael's Cathedral
33. Mackenzie House
34. Eaton Centre
35. Old City Hall
36. New City Hall
37. Nathan Phillips Square
38. Campbell House
39. CityTV and MuchMusic
40. Kensington Market
41. Art Gallery of Ontario
42. The Grange
43. Art Museum of Toronto
44. Ontario College of Art
45. Provincial Parliament
46. University of Toronto
47. University College
48. Knox College
49. Students' Administrative Council Building
50. Hart House
51. Philosopher's Walk
52. Flavelle House
53. Victoria College
54. St. Michael's College
55. Maple Leaf Gardens
56. York Club
57. Bata Shoe Museum
58. Royal Ontario Museum
59. George R. Gardiner Museum of Ceramic Art
60. Park Plaza Hotel
61. Church of the Redeemer
62. Metropolitan Toronto Library
63. Yorkville Public Library
64. Firehall No. 10
65. Village of Yorkville Park
66. Casa Loma
67. Spadina
68. Allan Gardens

◯ ACCOMMODATIONS

1. Bond Place Hotel
2. Crown Plaza Toronto Centre
3. Delta Chelsea
4. Four Seasons Hotel Toronto
5. Holiday Inn on King
6. Hotel Inter-Continental Toronto
7. King Edward Hotel
8. Marigold Hostel
9. Neil Wycik College Hotel
10. Novotel
11. Park Plaza Hotel
12. Radisson Plaza Hotel Admiral
13. Royal York
14. Sheraton Centre Toronto
15. Strathcona Hotel
16. Toronto Marriott Eaton Centre
17. Venture Inn
18. Victoria University
19. Westin Harbour Castle

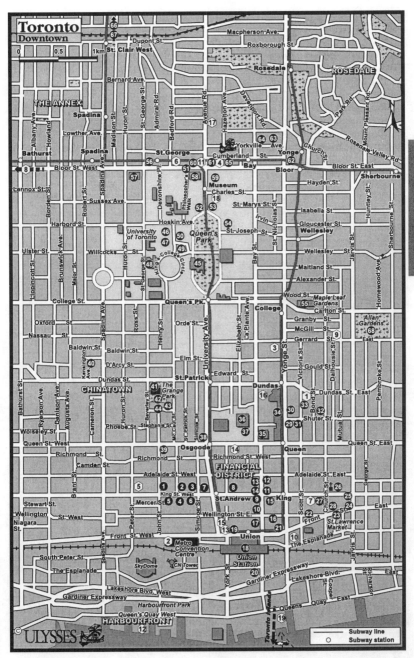

The very popular **Harbourfront Antique Market** ★★ is open to visitors every day except Monday *(May to Oct, Tue to Sat 11am to 6pm, Sun 8am to 6pm; Nov to Apr, Tue to Sat 11am to 5pm, Sun 8am to 6pm; 390 Queen's Quay W., ☎260-2626)*. This makes for a most interesting visit. You may spend hours perusing its countless antique shops with their many valuable items, perhaps discovering some minor marvel you simply cannot do without.

At the foot of Bay Street, just behind the Harbour Castle Westin Hotel, a ferry will take you to the **Toronto Islands Park** ★★★ *(open year-round; Metro Parks general information ☎392-8186; ferry return fares $4; schedule: May to Sep, first departure 8am then every 30 min or 15 min during peak hours, last ferry to the city from Hanlan's Point is at 9:30pm, from Centre Island 11:45pm, from Ward's Island 11:30pm; call for departure times for rest of the year ☎392-8193)* which lies on a group of 17 islands collectively known as the Toronto Islands, a short 8-minute ferry ride from Toronto Harbour. Three ferries, each departing from the Mainland Ferry Terminal at the foot of Bay Street, service the three biggest islands, Hanlan's Point, Centre Island and Ward's Island; bridges connect the other islands, which are occupied by private homes, yacht clubs and an airport. Bicycles are permitted on all of the ferries, except, on occasion, the Centre Island ferry, which gets very crowded on weekends. Bikes can be rented at Hanlan's Point and at the pier, while canoes, rowboats and pedal-boats can be rented on Long Pond east of Manitou Bridge.

A stone's throw from The Centre Island Ferry Dock is one of the islands' main attractions, the **Centreville Amusement Area** *(free admission to grounds, charge per ride, day pass available)*, an old-fashioned amusement park with a classic ferris wheel, bumper cars and pretty 1890s merry-go-round. Another child-pleaser is **Far Enough Farm** *(late Apr to mid-May, Sat and Sun; mid-May to Sep, every day; ☎363-1112)*, a petting zoo with barnyard animals just a short distance beyond the rides. The formal Avenue of the Islands extending from Manitou Bridge to the pier and the beach is lined with flower beds, reflecting pools, fountains and beautiful grassy expanses with signs inviting you to "please walk on the grass." Two licensed restaurants are located on the islands, The Island Paradise Restaurant (see p 193) and The Iroquois Restaurant (see p 193). Paved, scenic trails crisscross the island, to the delight of walkers, joggers, in-line skaters, cyclists, cross-country skiers and even snowshoers. To the west, they lead towards Hanlan's Point and beautiful sunsets year-round passing **Gibraltar Point Lighthouse**, Toronto's oldest remaining structure along the way. Ward's Island lies to the east and is accessible along a paved trail or a picturesque waterfront boardwalk. During the summer months, an amusing tram, one of the only motorized vehicles on the islands, offers historical guided tours from Centre Island to Hanlan's Point free of charge. Sandy **beaches** ring the lake side of the islands from Ward's Island to Hanlan's Point Beach; remember that swimming is prohibited in the channels and lagoons. The calmest and cleanest beach is on Ward's Island. Tennis, frisbee-golf, softball diamonds and wading pools round out the other outdoor possibilities. Finally, one of the highlights of this rural oasis is the spectacular view, day or night, of Toronto.

From Harbourfront Centre, it is just a few steps to reach the SkyDome and the CN Tower.

Adorable Boreal owls such as this one can be spotted
along Ontario's numerous hiking trails.
– *T. Beck*

A spectacular sunset over Lake Ontario, one of the five Great Lakes.
– J. Burke

Serenity reigns at this little hideaway nestled in Algonquin Park.
– P. Quittemelle.

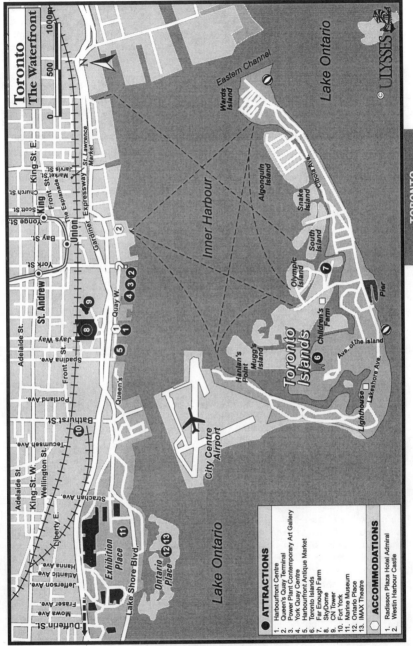

Toronto
The Waterfront

0   500   1000m

N

Lake Ontario

Eastern Channel

Wards Island

Inner Harbour

Algonquin Island

Snake Island

South Island

Olympic Island

Children's Farm

Toronto Islands

Hanlan's Point

Mugg's Island

7

6

Ave. of the Island

Lighthouse

Lakeshore Ave.

Pier

Cibola Ave.

City Centre Airport

Lake Ontario

Exhibition Place

Ontario Place

11

12 13

Dufferin St.

Mowa Ave.

Fraser Ave.

Jefferson Ave.

Atlantic Ave.

Hanna Ave.

Strachan Ave.

Liberty E.

Lake Shore Blvd.

Wellington St.

King St. W.

Adelaide St.

Tecumseh Ave.

Bathurst St.

Portland Ave.

Spadina Ave.

Front St.

Queen's Quay

Quay W.

5

8

9

1

4 3 2

2

Union

Front St.

The Esplanade

Gardiner Expressway

St. Lawrence Market

Market St.

Jarvis St.

King St. E.

Church St.

Scott St.

Yonge St.

Bay St.

York St.

St. Andrew

King

Jays Way

Adelaide St.

TORONTO

● ATTRACTIONS

1. Harbourfront Centre
2. Queen's Quay Terminal
3. Power Plant Contemporary Art Gallery
4. York Quay Centre
5. Harbourfront Antique Market
6. Toronto Islands
7. Far Enough Farm
8. SkyDome
9. CN Tower
10. Fort York
11. Marine Museum
12. Ontario Place
13. IMAX Theatre

◇ ACCOMMODATIONS

1. Radisson Plaza Hotel Admiral
2. Westin Harbour Castle

ULYSSES

The **SkyDome** ★★ *(guided tour: $9; every day 9am to 4pm; tour schedules may vary depending on events; 1 Blue Jay Way, ☎341-3663)*, the pride of Toronto, is the first sports stadium in the world with a fully retractable roof. In poor weather, four panels mounted on rails come together in 20 minutes despite their 11,000 tonnes, to form the SkyDome's roof. Since opening in 1989, this remarkable building has been home to the American League's Toronto Blue Jays baseball team and to the Canadian Football League's Toronto Argonauts. The Toronto Raptors, one of two Canadian-based teams in the National Basketball Association, also play here pending construction of a new indoor arena near the SkyDome.

Depending on the requirements of different sports, the SkyDome can be converted quickly to welcome 52,000 baseball fans or 53,000 football fans. For special events, it can fit up to 70,000 people. For concerts and other events not requiring as great a capacity, out comes the Skytent, a giant cloth that divides the stadium to improve the sound quality. Finally, no spectator, even those who get stuck in the poorer seats, need miss any of the action thanks to the Jumbotron, an enormous screen 10 metres high and 33 metres wide.

To learn more about the SkyDome's technical aspects, guided tours are offered every day *(☎341-2770)*, lasting about an hour-and-a-half. You will see a collection of objects excavated when the foundations for the new stadium were being dug in 1986 and a 20-minute documentary film on the SkyDome's construction titled *The Inside Story*, which relates, perhaps with a bit too much drama, how architect Roderick Robbie and engineer Michael Allen developed the concept of the retractable roof. The tour also includes a visit to the press box and a

peak into one of the corporate boxes, which the marketing people call SkyBoxes and rent for a mere $1 million for 10 years, not counting tickets, refreshments or food!

The **CN Tower** ★★★ *(observation deck $13; summer every day, 8am to midnight; autumn, 10am to 10pm; winter Sun to Thu 11am to 8pm, Fri to Sat 11am to 10pm; Front St. W., ☎360-8500)*. No doubt the most easily recognizable building in Toronto, the CN Tower dominates the city from a height of 553.33 metres (1,815 feet), making it the highest observation tower in the world. Built originally by Canadian National Railways to help transmit radio and TV signals past the numerous downtown buildings, it has become one of the city's main attractions. To avoid long lines, go early in the morning or late in the day, especially in the summer or on weekends. On an overcast day, it is best to postpone your visit.

CN Tower

The foot of the tower offers a panoply of activities, including **Q-Zar** *($8)*, a game in which you chase your adversaries and try to eliminate them with a laser gun, the **Simulator Theatre** *($8)* which projects you at high speed inside an enormous flipper, and **Virtual World** *($8, discounts available)*, a games arcade whose name says it all.

You can also climb to the observation deck in an elevator that lifts you off the ground floor at a speed of six metres per second, equivalent to the takeoff of a jet aircraft. Located 335.25 metres up and set on four levels, the observation deck is the nerve centre of the tower. The first floor houses telecommunications equipment, while the second floor has an outdoor observation deck and a glass floor for those who are not afraid of heights. The third floor has an indoor observation deck and elevators (for a $2.25 supplement) going to the **Space Deck**, floating 447 up and forming the world's highest public observation post. The view from the top is splendid, of course. On a clear day, you can see over a distance of 160 km and even make out Niagara Falls. Finally, the fourth floor has a bar and restaurant with seating for up to 400 people. Because of the great height, you may feel the tower sway in the wind. This is perfectly normal and enhances the resistance of the entire structure.

To continue your tour of the waterfront, head west toward Fort York. By car, you can reach Fort York along Lakeshore Boulevard, turning right on Strachan, right on Fleet Street and then left on Garrison Road. Streetcar number 511 along Bathurst Street also provides easy access.

It was on the shores of Lake Ontario, at **Fort York** ★ *($4.75; early Oct to mid-May, Tue to Fri 10am to 4pm, mid-May to late Sep, Tue to Sun 10am to 5pm; ☎366-6127)* that Toronto began. Built in 1783 by Governor John Graves

Simcoe in response to a looming American threat, Fort York was destroyed by American invaders in 1813 and rebuilt soon afterward. As relations with the United States improved rapidly, it gradually lost its purpose. In the 1930s, the city of Toronto renovated it extensively to turn it into a tourist attraction. Nowadays, Fort York is the site of the largest Canadian collection of buildings dating from the War of 1812. A visit includes a tour of the barracks which are furnished as they were when they housed officers and soldiers, as well as a small museum with a short informative video of the history of the fort. Guides in period dress re-enact military manoeuvres in the summer.

Several years ago, Fort York was at the centre of another battle, this one pitting the city of Toronto against real estate developers who wanted to move the site to make way for the Gardiner Expressway. The decision to preserve Fort York's authenticity was like a wake-up call for the city of Toronto, which began to see the importance of preserving the many pieces of history that dot its urban landscape, such as its splendid streetcar system. Though the expressway and warehouses that now surround Fort York are rather uninspiring and a far cry from the waterfront location it once enjoyed, it is interesting to see how Toronto has developed from this little fort into the sprawling metropolis it is today.

Head down to the lake. Continue west along Lakeshore Boulevard, beyond the grounds of the Canadian National Exhibition, to Ontario Place.

Ontario Place ★ *(free admission except during special events; day passes offer unlimited access to various attractions except for bungee-jumping and sailboarding; May to Sep, Mon to Sat 10:30am to midnight, Sun 10:30am to 11pm; 955 Lakeshore Blvd. W.,*

☎314-9900; from late May to early September, a bus service links Union Station with Ontario Place). Designed by Eberhard Zeidler, Ontario Place consists of three islands joined by bridges. Five structures are suspended several metres above the water and bustle with activities for the young and the not so young. An enormous white sphere stands out clearly from the other buildings; inside is the **Cinesphere**, an **IMAX cinema** *(☎965-7711)* with an impressive six-story-high movie screen. Ontario Place has a marina with a capacity for about 300 boats, centred around the *HMCS Haida*, a World War II destroyer.

If you have children, head to the **Children's Village**, with its playgrounds, pool, waterslides, waterguns, bumperboats, Nintendo centre, LEGO creative centre, cinema and other attractions. The not-so-young will appreciate the **Forum**, an outdoor amphitheatre with various musical shows each evening.

Tour B: The Theatre and Financial Districts ★★

Start at the corner of King and John, the stretch of King Street from here to Simcoe Street is also known as Mirvish Walkway, after the father and son duo of discount-store magnates who refurbished the area by saving the Royal Alex from the wrecking ball and by filling in the empty warehouses with restaurants for hungry theatre-goers.

Start out at the **Princess of Wales Theatre** *(300 King St. W, ☎872-1212).* This spanking new theatre was built in 1993 expressly for the musical *Miss Saigon* by none other than the Mirvishes (see box). Though no tours are offered, it is worth taking a peak inside at the minimalist decor of moon and stars in the lobby, which is well-suited to the famous musical that still plays here.

Continue next to **The Royal Alexandra** ★★ *(260 King St. W, ☎872-3333).* Plastered along the walls of Ed Mirvish's various food emporiums between these two theatres is a collection of newspaper articles attesting to the entrepreneur's various exploits (see box). The Royal Alexandra was named after the king's consort, and is now popularly known as the Royal Alex. This is one of the most important theatres in the city and has been a favourite haunt of Toronto's elite ever since it opened in 1907. Its rich Edwardian styling and beaux-arts decor of plush red velvet, gold brocade and green marble were restored in the 1960s by Toronto discount-sales magnate Ed Mirvish.

Just a few steps to the east and you'll find yourself in front of the offices of Swiss Re Holdings. This edifice is typical of the mini Classic Revival palaces that were all the rage around 1907 when this building was erected. Known as the **Union Building** *(212 King St. W.)*, it originally housed the Canadian General Electric Company.

Across the street rises **Roy Thompson Hall** ★★ *(45 min guided tours Mon to Sat 12:30pm; $3; 60 Simcoe St., ☎593-4822)*, one of the most distinctive buildings in Toronto's cityscape. The space-age 3,700-square-metre (40,000 square feet) mirrored-glass exterior was designed by Canada's Arthur Erickson and gets mixed reviews, having been compared to an upside-down mushroom and a ballerina tutu. The interior is, however, another story, boasting striking luminosity, a glamorous lobby and exceptional acoustics, which the resident Toronto Symphony orchestra and Mendelssohn Choir show off beautifully. Touted as the New Massey Hall while under con-

Ed Mirvish

Ed Mirvish is a man of initiative. Born in Virginia, his family moved Toronto when he was nine years old. At the age of 15, his father died and Ed took over the management of the family grocery store. Mirvish's personal retail ventures would prove to be on a much grander scale, however. Garish yet delightful in all its neon splendour, his flagship **Honest Ed's** discount store opened for business more than 40 years ago, and high volume and low markup have since been the foundations of his business. Shoppers profit from "daily door crashers" where 2-litre bottles of Coca-Cola might sell for 5¢. When zoning laws prevented Mirvish from razing the decaying mansions along Markham Street behind his store, he transformed them into **Mirvish (Markham) Village**. The buildings now house art galleries and bookstores. Mirvish is also known as a philanthropist of sorts. His growing interest in music, the ballet and the theatre prompted him to save the historic Royal Alexandra Theatre in 1963, and to purchase and refurbish the Old Vic in London, England. His son David now runs the Royal Alex, and the pair recently built a brand new theatre, The Princess of Wales Theatre especially for the musical *Miss Saigon*.

struction, the hall was ultimately named after newspaper magnate Lord Thompson of Fleet, whose family made the largest single donation.

A large courtyard stretches out to the west of Roy Thompson Hall, it is bordered to the west by **Metro Hall** (facing the Princess of Wales), and to the south by **Simcoe Place** (the large square building to the left) and the **CBC Broadcast Centre** (the tall building to the right).

Back on King Street, on the southwest corner of Simcoe Street rises **St. Andrew's Presbyterian Church**, built in 1876. The church used to share this intersection with Government House, Upper Canada College, and a rowdy watering hole, leading the corner to be known as "Legislation, Education, Damnation and Salvation." Today, its Scottish Romanesque Revival sandstone exterior contrasts sharply with the steel and mirrored glass that surround it as you make your way into Toronto's financial district. Ironically, the Sun Life Tower ensured the church's survival by

paying some $4 million to build above and below it.

The tour now continues into Toronto's heart, its **financial district** where money, the thing that makes many local residents run themselves ragged, is the leading preoccupation. The district extends between Adelaide Street to the north and Front Street to the south and between University Avenue to the west and Yonge Street to the east.

The intersection of King and Bay Streets is the symbolic and geographical centre of Toronto's financial district. The four corners of this intersection are occupied by four of Canada's five national banks: the Bank of Nova Scotia, on the northeast corner; the Canadian Imperial Bank of Commerce on the southeast; the Toronto-Dominion Bank on the southwest and the Bank of Montreal on the northwest.

Historically, high finance in Toronto has always been centred around this area. It all started at the intersection of Yonge and Wellington in the mid-

1800s, when the only form of advertisement available to financial organizations was architecture. Image was everything in those days, and a sense of solidity and permanence was achieved through majestic entrance halls, cornices, porticoes and the like. By the early 1900s the hub had shifted north to King and Yonge where the sleekness of Art Deco was in vogue. As the district expanded to the west, Bay Street's skyscrapers were built right up against the street, creating a northern version of the Wall Street canyon. In the last two decades, the steel and glass towers have become the centrepieces of vast windswept courtyards. In recent years, these concrete parks have been in direct competition with the ever-expanding underground walkway system known as the PATH, and the debate continues as to the merits of these impersonal tunnels, which shuttle office workers hither and thither.

The first tower of steel and mirror, the **Sun Life Tower** ★★ *(150-200 King St. W)*, stands opposite St. Andrew's Church at the corner of Simcoe and King Streets. The sculpture in front of it is the work of Sorel Etrog. Continue along King Street to York Street. On the northeast corner stands the tower of august marble known as **First Canadian Place** ★. Though its stark exterior and squat base are not very appealing, the interior commercial space is bright and airy. The **Toronto Stock Exchange** ★★ *(free admission; Mon to Fri 9:30am to 4pm, guided tours at 2pm; 130 King St., ☎947-4670)* the focal point of Canadian high finance, is located inside. The Visitors' Centre is located on the ground floor of the Exchange Tower, in the reception area. This is one of the more interesting stops in the district as visitors can watch the action on the trading floor from an observation gallery.

Halfway between York and Bay, the **Standard Life** and **Royal Trust** buildings rise up on the south side of King Street next to the impressive **Toronto-Dominion Centre** ★★ *(55 King St. W)*, on the southwest corner of King and Bay. The work of famous modernist Ludwig Mies van der Rohe, it was the first international skyscraper built in Toronto in the mid-1960s. These plain black towers may seem uninspiring, but the use of costly materials and the meticulous proportions have made T-D Centre one of the most renowned forms in Toronto's cityscape. The first phase of construction dates between 1963 and 1969, when two towers, 46 and 56 stories high, were erected. These modern towers gave rise to the construction of other buildings of this type in Toronto's city core, and elsewhere in Canada. In the 1970s and 1980s, three other towers (not designed by Mies van der Rohe) were built between King and Wellington Streets West.

Stroll along Bay Street to see the beautiful Art Deco façade of the **Old Toronto Stock Exchange** *(234 Bay St.)*, which has been cleverly preserved and blends well with the surrounding skyscrapers. Its mural on the theme of "work" is especially interesting.

Continue a little further north along Bay Street.

Occupying the northeast corner and extending along King is the **Bank of Nova Scotia** ★ *(44 King St. W)*, built in 1949-51 using Art Deco plans that had been shelved before the war. Heading north up Bay, the next building is the unassuming Neo-Georgian **National Club Building** *(303 Bay St.)*. The club was founded in 1874 to promote the Canada First movement, which challenged the notion of a union with the

United States. On the west side of Bay is the former Trust and Guarantee Co., now the **Bank of Montreal** *(302 Bay St.)*. A few steps farther north is the **Canada Permanent Building** ★★ *(320 Bay St.)*. The splendour of the vaulted entrance and coffered ceiling seem to flout the hard times that were being ushered in in 1929, when the building was going up. The lobby is a triumph of Art Deco styling; don't miss the bronze elevator doors portraying antiquity figures.

North of Adelaide, on the left is the **Northern Ontario Building** *(330 Bay St.)*, a classic 1920s skyscraper. The **Atlas Building** ★ *(350 Bay St.)* is next up the block. Its small lobby is decked out in lovely brass-work.

Retrace your steps and continue along King Street West.

Head east on Adelaide Street. Cross the back courtyard of the red-tinted trapezoid known as the **Scotia Plaza** ★ *(30 King St. W)* and walk through the lobby back to King Street. The eastern façade of the Bank of Nova Scotia is visible inside this more recent addition which fits into the surroundings quite harmoniously.

You will come to the **Canadian Imperial Bank of Commerce** ★★ *(25 King St. W.)*, built between 1929 and 1931. With its 34 stories, it was once the tallest building in the British Empire. Today, this handsome Romanesque-Revival-style tower meshes well with its modern backdrop, Commerce Court. Step into the main hall to admire its stunning coffered ceiling, gilded moulding and wrought-iron details.

Just a short distance away is the grand former head office of the **Royal Bank** *(2 King St. E)*, now a retail store. Designed by Montréal architects Ross and Macdonald, it features classic Greek styling. Across King Street stands the **Canadian Pacific Building** *(1 King St. E)*. Continuing down Yonge, you'll come to the **Trader's Bank** *(61-67 Yonge St.)*. With its 15 stories, it was Toronto's first real skyscraper when it was built in 1905. Ironically its design sought to reduce the appearance of height in the building. The **Bank of British North America** building *(49 Yonge St.)*, at the corner of Yonge and Wellington, is another notable edifice.

Cross Yonge and Wellington Streets and make your way west along the latter. On the south side, at number 15, you'll find the oldest building on this tour. Originally the Commercial Bank of Midland District, then the Merchant's Bank, it is now simply known as **Number 15** ★★, or depending who you talk to, Marché Mövenpick (see p 195). Greek Revival in style, it was designed in 1845 by the same architect as St. Lawrence Hall (see p 170).

At Bay Street, turn left and proceed to Front Street.

The designers of the **Royal Bank Plaza** ★★ *(200 Bay St.)* chose to have these two triangular towers beautify the Toronto skyline rather than rival each other in height. At 26 and 41 stories tall, respectively, these towers are covered in golden mirrored glass, in which laminated thin sheets of gold change the colour of the building according to the time of day. A huge public atrium links the two towers.

Make your way towards Front Street and Union Station to begin Tour C.

Tour C: Front Street and St. Lawrence ★

It was in the rectangular area formed by George, Berkley, Adelaide and Front streets that Commander John Graves

TORONTO

Simcoe of the British army founded the town of York in 1793. Today it is better known as Toronto. This part of the city, close to Lake Ontario, was for many years the business centre of the growing city. At the end of the 19th century, economic activity slowly moved toward what is today known as the financial district (see p 165), leaving behind a partially deserted area. Like Harbourfront (see p 157), the St. Lawrence neighbourhood has undergone major renovations over the last couple of decades, financed by the federal, provincial and municipal governments. Today, a cheerful mixture of 19th- and 20th-century architecture characterizes an area where the city's various socio-economic groups converge.

Union Station ★★ *(65-75 Front St. W.)* ranks first among Canadian railway stations for its size and magnificent appearance. It was built in the spirit of the great American railway terminals, with columns and coffered ceilings inspired by the basilicas of ancient Rome. Work on the station began in 1915 but was completed only in 1927. This was one of the masterpieces of Montréal architects Ross and Macdonald. Its façade on Front Street stretches more than 250 metres, hiding the port and Lake Ontario in the background.

Early in the century, Canadian Pacific began the construction of a chain of luxury hotels spanning the length of Canada's national railway. This is how Toronto's **Royal York Hotel ★** *(100 Front St.)* came to be in 1927, located directly in front of Union Station. Its Romanesque-Revival-inspired design, with a Chateau-style roof, is typical of the grand Canadian Pacific hotels. The lobby showcases the hotel's elaborate and rich decor. As with Union Station, this hotel is the work of architects Ross and MacDonald.

Heading south along York Street, you will reach the **Air Canada Centre** *(40 Bay St.)*. Officially opened in 1999, it now houses the city's hockey team, the Toronto Maple Leafs.

Retrace your steps.

At the corner of Front and Bay, rises the **Royal Bank Plaza** (see p 167). Continuing east on Front Street, the **Canada Trust Tower** is on the left and the **Canada Customs Building** on the right, at the southwest corner of Front and Bay streets.

Enter **BCE Place ★★** by the courtyard located east of the Canada Trust Tower. BCE Place stretches from Bay Street to Young Street and is made up of twin towers linked by a magnificent five-story glass atrium supported by an enormous structure of white metal ribs. This bright and airy space is a delightful place to rest for a few moments or grab a bite from the lower level fast-food counters. For something unique, head instead to the Marché Mövenpick (see p 195), a happy blend of restaurant and market where diners move from stall to stall and choose the dishes that seem most appealing. The Chamber of Commerce building, built in 1845, has been well preserved and blends harmoniously into its modern backdrop.

BCE Place also encloses the entrance to the famous **Hockey Hall of Fame ★** *($10; summer, Mon to Fri 10am to 5pm, Sun 10am to 6pm; rest of the year, Mon to Fri 10am to 5pm, Sat 9:30am to 6pm, Sun 10:30am to 5:30pm; 30 Yonge St., ☎360-7765)*, a veritable paradise for hockey fans. All sorts of items from the beginnings of this sport up to the present are on display. Do not miss the Bell Great Hall, at the centre of which is the original Stanley Cup, North America's oldest professional sports trophy, donated by Lord Stanley of Preston in 1893. More

Gooderham Building

than 300 plaques pay homage to the various players who have made their mark on professional ice hockey. Other highlights inside include a reconstitution of the Montréal Canadiens' dressing room as well as some of hockey's most exciting moments on video screens. There are also exhibits on the evolution of hockey equipment through the decades, with goaltender's masks, hockey sticks, skates and sweaters bequeathed by some of the greats.

At the corner of Yonge and Front Streets is the exterior of the old building of the **Bank of Montreal ★★**. The Hockey Hall of Fame is actually located in this building, though the only entrance is through BCE Place. Built in 1886 by architects Darling and Curry, the Bank of Montreal building is one of the oldest 19th-century structures still standing in Toronto. Designed during a prosperous and optimistic period, its architecture, which conveys a sense of power and invulnerability, was typical of the era, with imposing masonry, splendid porticos and gigantic windows. Until the construction of a new building in 1982, this was the Bank of Montreal's headquarters in Toronto.

At the southeast corner of Yonge and Front streets, is the **O'Keefe Centre**, soon to be renamed the Hummingbird Centre. With 3,200 seats, it is one of Toronto's most important theatre, ballet and opera centres. One block east, the **St. Lawrence Centre** also serves as a site for many concerts and plays each years. Despite its imposing façade, it offers a much more intimate interior.

A little further east along Front Street, beyond Berczy Park, is the amusing *trompe l'oeil* fresco painted at the back of the **Gooderham Building** ★ *(49 Wellington St.)*. This mural, created by Derek Besant in 1980, has become a well-known sight in Toronto. Contrary to popular belief, it does not portray the windows of the Gooderham Building but rather the façade of the Perkins Building, located across the street at 41-43 Front Street East. The Gooderham is often called the Flatiron Building because of its triangular structure, recalling the shape of its famous New York namesake, which it precedes by several years. The building's shape was dictated by the fact that it sits on a triangular lot at the corner of Wellington Street, which follows the grid pattern established by the British during the founding of York, and Front Street, which runs parallel to the north shore of Lake Ontario. Built for George Gooderham, a businessman who made his fortune in distilleries, this building stands out for its mural and for its castle-like architecture. It still houses many offices.

Look back now from where you came and contemplate the interesting vista of the Flatiron Building framed by the office towers of the financial district and the CN Tower.

Across Front Street, the gleaming façades that now harbour shops and cafes are merely those of simple warehouses. The **Beardmore Building** *(35-39 Front St. E.)* is one of the more noteworthy of a series of buildings that once formed the heart of the warehouse district in the middle of the 19th century.

At the corner of Jarvis Street, is the **St. Lawrence Market** ★★ *(91 Front St. E.)*. Built in 1844, it housed the city hall until 1904, the year Henry Bowyer Lane converted it to a public market.

Expanded in 1978, St. Lawrence Market is famed today for the freshness of its fruits and vegetables, fish, meats, sausages and cheeses. This giant red-brick building actually completely envelops the former city hall, which is still perceptible in the façade. The best time to go is on Saturday, when the fish is freshest and area farmers arrive at 5am to sell their products across the street at the **Farmer's Market**.

Walk up Jarvis Street, and turn right on King Street.

St. Lawrence Hall ★ *(151 King St. E.)* was Toronto's community centre in the latter half of the 19th century. This Victorian structure was built to present concerts and balls. Among the celebrities who performed here were Jenny Lind, Andelina Patti, Tom Thumb and P.T. Barnum. For several years, St. Lawrence Hall was also home to the National Ballet of Canada.

Lovely **St. James Park**, a 19th-century garden with a fountain and annual flower beds, lies a few steps to the west. While seated on one of its many benches, you can contemplate **St. James Cathedral** ★★ at the corner of Church and King streets, Toronto's first Anglican cathedral. Built in 1819 with help from a government loan and from the alms of the faithful, it was destroyed in the 1849 fire that levelled part of the city. The St. James Cathedral you see today was built on the ruins of its predecessor, based on a design by architect Frederich Cumberland, who wanted to invoke religious superiority. It has the highest steeple in all of Canada and the second highest in North America, after St. Patrick's Cathedral in New York. The yellow brick façade accentuates the Gothic shapes of the cathedral, giving it a rather sober character. The interior is far more elaborate. The marble choir stall, where

Bishop Strachan's is interred, is truly magnificent.

Continue west along King Street, turning right at Toronto Street.

Toronto Street was one of the city's most beautiful streets in the 19th century. Nowadays, some buildings still provide a glimpse of the charm and elegance this street once radiated. Note the building of the **Argus Corporation** *(10 Toronto Street)*, with its portico of four symmetrical Ionic columns and its neoclassic architecture resembling a Greek temple. This building served as a post office, a customs office and a branch of the Bank of Canada, before being transformed into offices.

Retrace your steps back to King Street.

The splendid **King Edward Hotel ★★** *(37 King St. E.)* (see p 189), between Church Street and Leader Lane, was designed in 1903 by E.J. Lennox, architect of the Old City Hall (see p 173), Massey Hall (see p 172) and Casa Loma (see p 184). With its Edwardian style, its wonderful mock marble columns on the ground floor and its magnificent dining rooms, the King Edward was one of Toronto's most luxurious hotels for nearly 60 years until with the decline of the surrounding area it fell into disrepair. It was the splendid Café Victoria (see p 195) which ultimately saved the hotel from the wrecker's ball. Today, with the revitalization of the area, the King Edward is once again drawing a fashionable clientele with its superb rooms and its two wonderful restaurants.

Return now toward St. James Cathedral, in front of which extends the **Toronto Sculpture Garden**. Walk through the garden and back to Front Street, admiring the various sculptures along the way. Once back on Front you'll find yourself at **Market Square ★**

(80 Front St. E.) right next to the city's first market. Of more recent construction, it blends in remarkably well with the historic surroundings. Market Square houses with numerous shops and luxury apartments.

Tour D: Queen Street West and Chinatown ★★★

This tour starts at the corner of Yonge and Queen Streets where Queen West begins. **The Bay** department store occupies the southwest corner and the whole south side of Queen all the way to Bay. The building originally housed the Simpson's department store, until hard economic times forced its closure and most Simpson's stores became Bays. This was the largest retail establishment in Canada in 1907, when the nine-story addition along Queen was added. The original six-story building (1895) at Yonge and Queen features some lovely terra cotta decorations. An Art Deco addition in 1928 lead to glamorous renovations throughout the store, of which the entrance at Richmond and Yonge is a fine example.

Head north on Yonge Street. On the left is the exterior of the six-story shopping mecca, the Eaton Centre; on the right you'll soon come upon two more of Toronto's majestic theatres, the Elgin and Wintergarden and the Pantages.

Before visiting the Elgin and Wintergarden, take a look at the **Bank of Montreal** *(173 Yonge St.)* on the corner. This stylish Edwardian building dates from 1909.

The **Elgin and Wintergarden Theatres ★★** *($4; one-hour tours; Tue 5pm, Sat 11am; 189 Yonge St., ☎363-5253 or 872-5555)* together form the last operating double-decker theatre complex in the world. Opened in 1914, they began as vaudeville theatres; the Elgin downstairs was opulence galore, while the Wintergarden upstairs was one of the first "atmospheric theatres," with trellised walls and columns disguised as tree trunks supporting a ceiling of real leaves. After a stint as a movie house, these treasures were restored by the Ontario Heritage Centre and now once again serve as live theatre houses.

Once the biggest vaudeville house in the British Empire, the **Pantages Theatre** *($4; one-hour tours Mon, Tue and Fri 11:30am, Sat 10:30am; 263 Yonge St., ☎362-3218)* had many reincarnations as a picture palace and then a six-theatre movie house. In 1988-89, it was restored to its original splendour. It is perhaps best-known, however, as the home of Andrew Lloyd Webber's *Phantom of the Opera*. This grandiose production is first-class, and the show and venue complement each other nicely.

Backtrack down Yonge Street, turn left at Shuter Street and walk two blocks to Massey Hall.

Massey Hall *(178 Victoria St., at Shuter St., ☎593-4828 or 872-4255)*, originally Massey Music Hall, is renowned for its exceptional acoustics. Though the Toronto Symphony Orchestra has moved out (see p 200), Massey Hall is still a venerable venue for musical acts.

Two of Toronto's great churches lie one block to east.

Though there were relatively few Catholics in Toronto in the 19th century, **St. Michael's Catholic Cathedral ★** *(57 Bond St.)* a building that lacks the presence of the Anglican cathedral or the nearby United church, was constructed between 1845 and 1867. The sometimes overbearing architecture of Victorian Catholic churches is evident

here in the multiple openings of the spire, the massive dormers and the polychrome interior. The painted starry vault was completed in 1870. To the south, facing Queen Street, the **Metropolitan United Church** (1870) is seen as a challenge to both the Anglican (see p 170) and Roman Catholic cathedrals and thus represents the commercial and social power of Toronto's Methodist community (the Methodists, along with the Congregationalists and two-thirds of the Presbyterians formed the United Church in 1925). It dominates the area, due to its grand proportions and location in the middle of a block-square park.

Continue up Bond St. towards Dundas, stopping in at Mackenzie House along the way.

By 1837, fruitless attempts to establish responsible government and growing impatience with England, had left the Canadian colony in crisis. The colonial emancipation movement was lead by Louis-Joseph Papineau in Lower-Canada (Québec) and by William Lyon Mackenzie in Upper Canada (Ontario). Mackenzie had arrived in Toronto from Scotland in 1820. Before becoming the city's first mayor, he ran a newspaper called *The Colonial Advocate* which so enraged the Family Compact that his print shop was ransacked and his type, dumped in Lake Ontario. After losing the mayorship in 1836, he lead an abortive rebellion against the oligarchy, then fled to the United States. **Mackenzie House ★** *($3.50; Tue to Sat 9:30am to 5pm, Sun and holidays noon to 5pm; 82 Bond St., Dundas subway, ☎392-6915)*, a modest Georgian-style residence built in 1857, was offered to him by a group of followers upon his return in 1859. The odd placement of the house is due to the fact that it was once part of a row of identical residences. The Toronto Historical Board has since restored the house and now maintains a museum here. Guides in period dress re-enact the daily life of a middle-class Toronto household in the 1860s. It is furnished with antique furniture and also features a reconstruction of Mackenzie's print shop, complete with the offending printing press. Mackenzie's grandson was William Lyon Mackenzie King, Canada's longest serving Prime Minister.

Walk along Dundas to Yonge Street and turn left.

Even if you have no desire to go shopping, at least poke your head into the **Eaton Centre ★★**, running along Yonge Street between Queen and Dundas. And if you do need something, by all means linger in this glass-roofed arcade which even a few sparrows have decided is more pleasant than outside. Here, so-called streets have been stacked five-stories high and lined with pristine benches and trees. Look up and you will see Michael Snow's exquisite flock of fibreglass Canada geese, called *Step Flight*, suspended over the Galleria. Framed by two 30-story skyscrapers and two subway stations (Dundas and Queen Stations) and occupying six million square feet, the Eaton Centre contains more than 320 stores and restaurants, 2 parking garages and a 17-theatre cinema complex.

Once you've had your fill of the shops, exit the Eaton Centre via Trinity Square, at the northwest corner of the mall.

This lovely space was almost never created. The **Church of the Holy Trinity ★★** (1847), the **Rectory** (1861) and the **Scadding House** (1857) are some of Toronto's oldest landmarks, and the original plans for the Eaton Centre called for their demolition. Fortunately, enough people objected and the huge mall was built around the grouping. Holy Trinity was a gift from an anonymous woman in England who stipulated that free seating be guaranteed in the church. Its excellent acoustics are renowned and helped create the beautiful music on the Cowboy Junkies album *The Trinity Sessions*. The rectory and the house of Rev. Henry Scadding, the first rector of Holy Trinity, complete the vista. The latter had to be moved to make way for the Eaton's department store.

Head down James Street towards the back of **Old City Hall ★★** *(60 Queen St. W.)* designed by A. J. Lennox in 1889. As you make your way around the building towards the front on Queen Street, look up at the eaves below which the architect carved the letters "E J LENNOX ARCHITECT" to ensure that his name would be remembered. Lennox won a contest to design the building but the city councillors denied his request to place his name on a cornerstone; to get back at them, he had disfigured versions of their faces carved above the front steps so that they would be confronted with their gargoyle-like selves every day! By the time all these personal touches were revealed, it was too late to do anything about them.

The vast sandstone edifice was built on a square plan around a central square and is probably the most exacting example of Richardsonian neoclassicism in Canada. The style was developed in the 1870s and 1880s in the United States by architect Henry Hobson Richardson and was based on French Romanesque. It defined itself by a use of mass and volume and surfaces that are generally not smooth. The numerous vaulted openings are framed by small engaged columns which lend a medieval and picturesque air to buildings of this style. Its elegant tower ornamented with a clock rises above the centre of Bay Street, the heart of high-finance in Toronto.

TORONTO

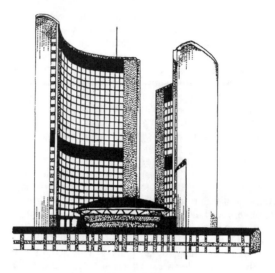

New City Hall

In 1965, the municipal administration of Toronto moved out of its Victorian city hall and into **New City Hall ★★** *(100 Queen St. W.)*. A modernist masterpiece that quickly gained a certain notoreity and became as symbolic of Toronto as the CN Tower. Once again, a contest was held to choose an architect and this time the winner was Finn Viljo Revell, a master of Scandinavian post-war rationalist thinking. Its two curved towers of unequal length are like two hands protecting the saucer-shaped structure which houses the Council Room.

Stretching out in front of New City Hall is **Nathan Phillips Square ★** a vast public space named after the mayor of Toronto who blessed Toronto with many new installations at the beginning of the 1960s. A large pool of water straddled by three arches is transformed into a skating rink in the winter. Nearby, stands "The Archer" by Henry Moore, and the Peace Garden designed in 1984 by the Urban Design Group. This small green space serves as a frame for the Eternal Peace Flame which flickers in a half-destroyed shack that is meant to remind us of the effects of war and symbolize the population's desire for peace.

Cast-iron gates enclose **Osgoode Hall ★★** *(116-138 Queen St. W.)* and its shaded garden, reminiscent of a royal palace of the British Empire, though it was originally built to house the Law Society of Upper Canada and the provincial law courts. Built in stages from 1829 to 1844 according to plans by different architects, its façade is nevertheless a lovely ensemble. Its layout is in the Palladian style though the decorative elements are those of an Italian Renaissance palace as was the style with London high-society at the time. The neoclassical vestibule can be visited as well as the magnificent law library by checking at the ticket office at the entrance.

Not far from Osgoode Hall, **Campbell House ★** *(160 Queen St. W.)* was the private club of a select group of Ontario lawyers, the Advocates Society. The house was built in 1822 for Judge William Campbell and is one of the oldest in Toronto. Its brick façade combines traditional Georgian elements with Adamesque fantasy, like the oval bull's-eye window of the pediment that lightens the structure. The inside, open to visitors, is decorated with lovely woodworking and mantlepieces with delicate trimming typical of the art of the Adam brothers, the pair of Scots who swept Great Britain with their antiquated refinement at the end of the 18th century.

Make your way along Queen Street West, lined with trendy shops, cafés and bars for most of its length, it is also the home of **CityTV** and **Muchmusic** *(299 Queen St. W.)*, "the nation's music station." The former Wesley Building was built for a publishing company in 1913-15, note the grotesque readers and scribes that adorn its façade. Renovated in 1986 to accommodate Muchmusic, a music-video television network, the building is now a hive of activity, with "v-jays" often animating their shows right on the sidewalk, and a televised fashion-show-cum-dance-party known as the "Electric Circus," every Friday night. Another intriguing feature is the Speakers' Corner video booth where you can applaud or criticize whatever cause you like, and maybe even end up on national television.

Take the time to stroll along **Queen West ★★** and admire the hip and avant-garde boutiques. There are even a few interesting architectural highlights, as most of these shops occupy late-19th-century buildings. Number 371-373, now Peter Pan Restaurant (see p 197) was built in 1890 and originally housed a grocery store. It boasts some lovely stained glass. Numbers 342 to 354 are collectively known as the Noble Block (1888), after Mrs.

Emma Noble, a widow who once owned the property.

At this point you can head north on Spadina. The five blocks between Queen and Dundas might not look like much, but they contain some of the best bargains in town, from designer clothes to designer food, from evening wear to kitchenware. At the intersection of Spadina and Dundas, you will find yourself in the heart of Toronto's **Chinatown ★★**. The community radiates from this point north to College Street, south to Queen and east to Bay, and is the largest Chinatown in North America. The neighbourhood actually began around Elizabeth Street where New City Hall now stands. It gradually moved west to Spadina, though signs of it remain all along Dundas. The best time to explore the fascinating tea shops, herbalists and Chinese grocers is on Sunday, when the sounds of Cantonese pop music, the mounds of fresh vegetables, the racks of roasted duck and the smell of ginseng tea transport you to another world. Sunday is also the day when most Chinese families head out for brunch, though they call it dim sum, and there are no scrambled eggs or baked beans to wade through!

Before straying too far along Dundas, however, check out **Kensington Market ★★**, located all along Kensington Street. This bazaar epitomizes Toronto's multi-ethnicity. It began as a primarily Eastern European market, but is now a wonderful mingling of Jewish, Portuguese, Asian and Caribbean. The lower half of Kensington is mostly vintage clothing shops, while the upper portion boasts international grocers peddling fresh and tasty morsels from all over the world. Perfect for picnic fixings!

Whether you decide on a picnic or dim sum, make sure to save time for an edifying afternoon at the Art Gallery of Ontario and The Grange.

The Art Museum of Toronto was founded in 1900, but was without a permanent home until 1913, when The Grange (see below) was bequeathed to the museum. A new building was added in 1918, and the first exhibition of Canada's renowned Group of Seven (see p 28) was held in 1920 at what was by then known as the Art Gallery of Toronto. A significant chapter in Canada's and Toronto's cultural histories was thus written. In 1966, the museum received provincial support and was officially rebaptized the **Art Gallery of Ontario ★★★** *($5; May to Oct, Tue and Thu to Sun 10am to 5:30pm, Wed 10am to 10pm, holiday Mon 10am to 5:30pm; Oct to May, Wed 10am to 10pm, Thu to Sun 10am to 5:30pm, holiday Mon 10am to 5:30pm; 317 Dundas St. W., ☎977-0414).* Successive renovations and additions over the years have each tried to reinvent the AGO, adding new elements and hiding old ones. The Gallery is now laid out in a collection of buildings, which were successfully united in 1989 by architects Barton Myers and Associates, and finally do justice to the splendid treasures they contain, collections donated by wealthy Ontarians over the years.

The 1989 renovations known as Stage III added close to 50% more exhibition space. The permanent collection is now installed so that visitors can tour the Gallery from the 15th century to the present day. It features contemporary art, Inuit sculptures and the beautiful Tanenbaum Sculpture Atrium, where a façade of The Grange is exposed. The Henry Moore Sculpture Centre is one of the museum's greatest treasures. Donated by the artist himself, it is the largest public collection of Moore's work in the world. The Canadian historical and contemporary collec-

tions contain major pieces by such notables as Cornelius Krieghoff, Michael Snow, Emily Carr, Jean-Paul Riopelle, Tom Thomson and the Group of Seven — Frederick Varley, Lawren Harris, Franklin Carmichael, A. Y. Jackson, Arthur Lismer, J. E. H. MacDonald and Frank H. Johnson. The museum also boasts masterpieces by Rembrandt, Van Dyk, Reynolds, Renoir, Picasso, Rodin, Degas and Matisse, to name a few.

Adjacent to the Art Gallery of Ontario stands its original home, **The Grange ★** *(admission with AGO; May to Oct, Tue and Thu to Sun noon to 4pm, Wed noon to 9pm; Oct to May, Wed noon to 9pm, Thu to Sat noon to 4pm; Grange Park, south of the AGO, ☎977-0414).* The Georgian-style residence was built in 1817-18 by D'Arcy Boulton Jr., a member of Toronto's ruling elite, the much-reviled Family Compact. The city of Toronto was barely thirty years old at the time, but by 1837, the year of Mackenzie's rebellion, The Grange had become the virtual seat of political power and thus symbolized the oppressive colonial regime in Upper Canada. In 1875, Goldwin Smith, an Oxford scholar, took up residence here. Seen as a liberal intellectual in his day, his suspicion of other religions and races have since revealed him to be a bigot. He nevertheless entertained some very eminent visitors at The Grange, including a young Winston Churchill, the Prince of Wales (later Edward VII) and Matthew Arnold. When Smith died in 1910, he willed the house to the Art Museum of Toronto which occupied it for the next 15 years. The gallery then used it for offices until 1973 when it was restored to its 1830s grandeur and the whole house was opened to the public. It rear façade was integrated into the AGO's sculpture gallery in 1989. This gentleman's house, with its grand circular staircase and fascinating servants quarters, was one of Toronto's first brickwork buildlings.

The **Ontario College of Art** *(100 McCaul St.)* once occupied the look-alike building to the east of The Grange. The college's more recent addition faces McCaul Street.

End your day with a hearty meal on Baldwin Street in Chinatown's residential area. The block to the east of McCaul harbours some fantastic little restaurants (see p 196).

Tour E: Around Queen's Park ★★

Each of the ten provinces has its own legislative assembly, Ontario's is located in the **Provincial Parliament ★★** *(1 Queen's Park)*, located at the centre of Queen's Park in the middle of University Avenue. The red sandstone building (1886-1892) was designed in the Richardsonian neo-Romanesque style (see Old City Hall, p 173) by architect Richard A. Waite of Buffalo who is also responsible for several Canadian buildings including the old headquarters of the Grand Trunk Railway on McGill Street in Montreal (the Gérald-Godin building). Notice the amusing crowning towers of the central part of the parliament which exhibit the inventiveness of 19th-century architects who were preoccupied with eclecticism and the picturesque. Take a walk around the building before entering to explore the typical 1890s public spaces with their highly sculpted dark wood exteriors.

From Queen's Park Crescent W. walk along Hart House Circle to Kings College Circle.

The some forty buildings of the **University of Toronto ★★** *(between Spadina Rd. to the west, Queen's Park Cresc. to the east, College St. to the south and Bloor to the north)* are spread about a vast and very green English-style campus. Awarded a charter in 1827, the institution didn't really get going until the construction of its first building in 1845 (no longer standing). However, religious rivalries slowed down the progress of the university as each denomination wanted its own institution for higher learning. In the following decade there were six universities, each one barely getting by. It wasn't until partial unification in the 1880s that the campus began to expand. Today, the University of Toronto is considered one of the most important in North America.

The oldest building on campus is **University College** *(15 Kings College Circle)* built in 1859 by architects Cumberland and Storm. The result was a picturesque neo-Romanesque ensemble with particularly noteworthy detailed stone carving. The beautiful Norman portal is also quite magnificent. Neo-Romanesque was something new in Canada at the time and thus was not associated with any specific religious or social movements; it therefore met the needs of the university leaders who wanted to create a secular environment, open to everyone.

Continue around King College Circle past **Knox College** *(59 George St.)* with is pretty leaded casement windows and rough sandstone exterior to Hart Tower Road.

The lovely Victorian **Students' Administrative Council Building** *(12 Hart House Circle)* was built in 1857. It originally housed the Toronto Magnetic and Meteoriligical Observatory and originally stood on the other side of the Front Lawn. It was moved and reconstructed in 1908.

Among the many university buildings, **Hart House** *(7 Hart House Circle)* is particularly noteworthy. Donated by the Massey Foundation, it was an undergraduate men's activity centre until 1972, when women were finally allowed to become members. It was designed by architects Sproatt & Rolph in the Gothic style; the Soldiers' Memorial Tower, by the same architects, was added in 1924. Completing the vista of English Gothic buildings is **Trinity College** *(6 Hoskin Ave.)*, by architects Darling and Pearson (1925), with its chapel by Sir Giles Gilbert Scott, well known for his cathedral in Liverpool. These last four buildings, with their many stone ribs, lead windows and peaceful courtyards were inspired by the pavilions of Oxford and Cambridge. A few other buildings of various styles also merit a look. **Massey College** *(4 Devonshire Place)*, built in 1963, successfully maries a medieval atmsophere with modern architecture. Walk up Devonshire Place to Bloor to see the highly Victorian exterior of the **Royal Conservatory of Music** *(273 Bloor St. W.)* with its dormers, chimneys and corbels.

Beyond Varsity Stadium and through the Alexandra Gates, which originally stood at Bloor and Queen's Park, lies a winding road called **Philosopher's Walk ★**. The Taddle Creek once flowed where the philosopher now walks. Step through the gates and the clamour of Bloor Street quickly fades away and is replaced by the wafting sounds of music students practising their scales at the Conservatory. A contemplative stroll next to the newly planted oak trees brings you back to Hoskin Avenue. Turn left on Hoskin, then left again on Queen's Park Crescent W.

Flavelle House *(78 Queen's Park)* was built in 1901 for Joseph Flavelle, and was for many years the grandest of Toronto's mansions. It is now used by the university's faculty of law.

Continue along Queen's Park Crescent to Victoria College and St. Michael's College.

The rich, finely crafted Romanesque **Victoria College** *(73 Queen's Park)* is very inviting for a scholarly building; it is just one of the buildings of Victoria University. This grouping, which includes Burwash Hall rimming the site to the east and north, Annesley Hall on Queen's Park and Emmanuel College to the west, is considered one of the most successful on the campus.

The collection of buildings that make up the University of St. Michael's College occupy a lovely site at the corner of Queen's Park and St. Joseph Street. This Catholic school was founded by the Basilian Fathers from France; **St. Michael's College** *(50 St. Joseph St.)* and **St. Basil's Church** *(50 St. Joseph St.)*, both built in 1856, were its earliest buildings. The college was the first to affiliate itself with the University of Toronto in 1881, and thus claims the oldest buildings on campus.

Continue your stroll eastbound along Carlton Street.

This will bring you to **Maple Leaf Gardens** *(60 Carlton Street)*, home to the local hockey team, the Maple Leafs, from 1931 to February 13, 1999. The team now plays in the larger sports complex, the Air Canada Centre (see p 168).

Continue along Jarvis Street, an area that is home to various restaurants and Bed and Breakfasts.

Tour F: Bloor and Yorkville ★★★

This tour covers the areas around Bloor and Yorkville, one of Toronto's prettiest and most swank neighbourhoods. In addition to its posh residences and chic boutiques, Yorkville is also home to some of Toronto's best museums.

The area north and west of Bloor and Bedford was once the Village of Yorkville, incorporated in 1853 and existing as a separate town until 1883, when it was annexed to the city of Toronto. It was a stylish bedroom community that lay within a short distance of the growing metropolis to the south. However, the encroachment of that metropolis eventually saw the transformation of many of Yorkville and Bloor Streets' loveliest homes into office space and a relocation of the city's elite to more exclusive areas farther north. For the first half of this century this area was a middle-class suburb. The first signs of the area's trend-setting status began to appear in the postwar era, as the 19th-century residences were transformed into coffeehouses and shops, and Yorkville became the focus of Canada's folk music scene. During the 1970s and 1980s, Yorkville became on of the city's most upscale neighbourhoods. Visit it for the great window-shopping in its many stylish boutiques, or relax in one of its pretty sidewalk cafés.

Start at the corner of St. George and Bloor Streets, just a few steps from the St. George subway station. This corner lies at the southwestern extremity of The Annex (see p 184), an area containing many wonderfully preserved 19th-century homes. The impressive red brick and stone building on the northeast corner is now home to the **York Club ★**, but was once a private home. It is the most distinguished Richardsonian Romanesque house in Toronto and was built in 1889 for the wealthiest man in the province at the time, George Gooderham. The architect, David Roberts also designed the distinctive Godderham Building (see p 170), also known as the Flatiron

building, on Front Street. The York Club moved into the house in 1909, making it the first secular institution tolerated in the area.

Kitty-corner to the York Club is the new home of the **Bata Shoe Museum ★★★** *($6; Tue to Sat 10am to 5pm, Thu until 8pm, Sun noon to 5pm; 327 Bloor St. W., ☎979-7799)*. This is a whimsical start to a serious museum touring excursion and a great place to get a few ideas before you hit the major shopping! The first museum of its kind in North America, it holds 10,000 shoes and provides an extraordinary perspective on the world's cultures. The new building was designed by architect Raymond Moriyama to look like a shoe box, and the oxidized copper along the edge of the roof is meant to suggest a lid resting on top. There are four permanent exhibits: "All About Shoes," is touted as a sumptuous feast of footwear with shoe trivia, shoe history and shoes of the rich and famous; "Inuit Boots: A Woman's Art," takes a look at "Kamiks" and the importance of footwear in the Arctic; "The Gentle Step: 19th Century Women's Shoes" examines the evolution of women's footwear at the dawn of the modern age; "One, Two, Buckle My Shoe" exhibits illustrations of shoes from children's books. Some of the more memorable pieces of footwear on display include space boots of Apollo astronauts, geisha platform sandals and a pair of patent leather beauties that once belonged to Elvis Presley.

Walk along Bloor Street to the Royal Ontario Museum, past Varsity Stadium and the campus of the University of Toronto, on the right.

The **Royal Ontario Museum ★★★** *($10, families $22, free admission Tue 4:30pm to 8pm; Mon to Sat 10am to 6pm, Tue 10am to 8pm, Sun 11am to 6pm; 100 Queen's Park, ☎586-5549 or*

TORONTO

586-5551; Museum Subway; parking is expensive) is Canada's largest public museum, as well as a research facility. The ROM, as it is often called, preserves some six million treasures of art, archaeology and natural science. After extensive renovation, restoration and the opening of new galleries, the ROM is now able to display these treasures in a manner befitting their inestimable worth. Upon entering the impressive free-Romanesque-style building, visitors' eyes are drawn up to the Venetian glass ceiling that depicts a mosaic of cultures. The ceiling is the only part of the museum that was not built using materials from Ontario. Continuing into the museum, the eyes are drawn up once again by the towering totem poles flanking the lobby, one of which is 80 feet tall, and whose top reaches just six inches below the ceiling! With exhibits on everything from bats to dinosaurs and Romans to Nubians, your first stop should be the Mankind Discovering Gallery, where the layout and workings of the ROM are explained. Visitors have a somewhat mind-boggling range of choices which include: the Dinosaur Gallery, a favourite with amateur paleontologists of all ages; the Maiasaurus exhibit, an ongoing project where onlookers can observe palaeontologists reconstructing a real dinosaur skeleton; the Evolution Gallery; the Roman Gallery, displaying the largest collection of its kind in Canada; the Textile Collection, one of the best in the world; the East Asian galleries, where you'll find one of the museum's most precious gems, the Chinese Art and Antiquities Collection, containing a Ming Tomb and the Bishop White Gallery, whose walls are covered with Buddhist and Daoist paintings; the Discovery Gallery, a treat for children, with hands-on displays featuring authentic artifacts; the Ancient Egypt Gallery and Nubia Gallery, which boast the consummate and ever-intriguing mummies and ancient relics; the

Sigmund Samuel Canadiana Collection of decorative arts, recently relocated to the ROM from its location on the campus of the University of Toronto; and the last big crowd-pleaser is the Bat Cave, a walk through an all too realistic replica of the St. Clair limestone cave in Jamaica, complete with all too realistic replicas of swooping bats. The possibilities of discovery and exploration at the ROM are endless!

Head back up Queen's Park to the next attraction.

On the east side of Queen's Park Avenue, the **George R. Gardiner Museum of Ceramic Art ★★** *($5; year-round Tue to Sat 10am to 5pm, Sun 11am to 5pm; in summer Tue until 7:30pm; 111 Queen's Park, ☎593-9300)* boasts a striking collection of porcelain and pottery. The ground floor showcases some very interesting South American ceramic pieces from the pre-Columbian era, as well as French, Italian, English, and German earthenware, porcelain, and pottery from the 16th, 17th, and 18th centuries. Especially interesting is the magnificent collection of characters from the *Commedia dell'Arte* as well as Swan Service, a dining set of no less than 2,200 pieces.

The luxurious **Park Plaza Hotel** *(4 Avenue Rd.)* (see p 192), built in 1926, stands at the northwest corner of Avenue and Bloor. The rough stone walls, sweeping slate roof and belfry of the **Church of the Redeemer** *(162 Bloor St. W)* occupy the northeast corner of Bloor and Avenue. Rising behind it is the **Renaissance Centre**, which, though it dominates the church, also gives it a commanding presence over this busy corner. The **Colonnade**, to the east, was the first building on Bloor to combine commercial, residential and office space.

The stretch of Bloor Street from Queen's Park/Avenue to Yonge is a collection of modern office buildings, shopping malls and ultra-chic boutiques and galleries including such notables as Holt Renfrew, Chanel, Hermès, Tiffany's and Hugo Boss. According to some, Bloor Street is Toronto's Fifth Avenue, so make your way along it as quickly or as leisurely as you wish (see p 203). Most of Bloor Street's façades are clearly more recent additions, though some have been preserved and jazzed up in keeping with the chic boutiques that have moved in. Two interesting building façades, however, await rehabilitation. The former curved façade of the **University Theatre**'s *(100 Bloor St. W.)* and the modest red-brick Neo-Georgian façade of the **Pearcy House**'s *(96 Bloor St. W.)* modest red-brick Neo-Georgian façade now apparently house a parking lot. At one time the plan was to transform the two into the venue for Toronto's annual film festival, but for now, parking is paying the bills.

At Yonge Street, turn left and head towards the trendy Yorkville area.

Before hitting the shops, you'll come upon the **Metropolitan Toronto Library** *(789 Yonge St.)* on the corner of Yonge and Asquith, a large building of brick and glass that is very popular with Torontonians and visitors alike since it is open to the public. It does not look like much from the street, though inside a profusion of plants and bright spaces, make it feel just like home. The building was designed by architect Raymond Moriyama in 1973.

Heading west along Yorkville now, you'll come to the grand **Yorkville Public Library** *(22 Yorkville Ave.)* built in 1907 and remodelled in 1978. The bold porticoed entrance still dominates the façade just as it did when this library served the village of Yorkville.

Right next door is the old **Firehall No. 10** ★ *(34 Yorkville Ave.)*, built in 1876 and then reconstructed (except for the tower, used to dry fire hoses) in 1889-90. This red and yellow brick hose house once served the village of Yorkville and is still in use. The coat of arms on the tower was salvaged from the town hall; the symbols on it represent the vocations of the town's first councillors: a beer barrel for the brewer, a plane for the carpenter, a brick mould for the builder, an anvil for the blacksmith and a bull's head for the butcher.

As you browse through the shops, take a look at the Georgian-style houses at **numbers 61-63** and **77**, the Queen Anne porch of **number 84**, the Victorian house that once served as the Mount Sinai Hospital at **number 100** (and is now awaiting the renovating hands of a good-willed developer) and the jazzed-up row of Victorian houses at **number 116-134**.

An exceptional collection galleries, shops and cafés line Yorkville, Hazelton and Cumberland. Intrepid explorers may want to stop in for a bit of armchair travelling at Ulysses Travel Bookshop at 101 Yorkville. More architectural gems, too numerous to list, remain on Hazelton Avenue. These have all been faithfully restored, some so much so that they look like new buildings; nevertheless, the results are aesthetically pleasing and worth a look. Of particular note are **Hazelton House** *(33 Hazelton Ave.)*, which originally housed the Olivet Congregational Church at the end of the 19th century, and now contains shops, galleries and offices, and the Carpenter Gothic-style **Heliconian Club**, a women's arts and letters club founded in 1909.

After exploring Hazelton Avenue, continue along Yorkville to Avenue Road.

Turn left on Avenue and then left again on Cumberland Avenue.

The **Village of Yorkville Park** *(Cumberland St. between Avenue Rd. and Bellair St.)*, a new addition to Toronto's cityscape, it is a fascinating example of urban ecology. Divided into 13 sectors, it represents local history and regional identity. A walk through the park from west to east begins in the Amelanchier Grove and leads through the Heritage Walk (Old York Lane), the Herbaceous Border Garden, the Canadian Shield Clearing & Fountain, the Alder Grove, the Ontario Marsh, the Festival Walk, the Cumberland Court Cross Walk, The Crabapple Orchard, The Fragrant Herb Rock Garden, The Birch Grove and the Prairie Wildflower Gardens before ending up in the Pine Grove. The highlight of the walk is certainly the village rock in the Canadian Shield sector. The rock is approximately one billion years old and weighs 650 tonnes. It comes from northeast of Gravenhurst, in the Muskoka Lakes region (see p 211).

Looking south, as you traverse the park, you can peer across the parking lot and through the façades of the University Theatre and Pearcy House (see p 181), two more pieces of Toronto's architectural heritage that are awaiting redevelopment.

Toronto: City of Neighbourhoods

Many people view Toronto as a bastion of Anglo-Saxon culture, as Canada's financial hub or as the home to the Blue Jays and the CN Tower, but few realize that it is also a city of neighbourhoods. From Rosedale to Cabbagetown, from the Beaches to Little Italy, not to mention the city's many Chinatowns, Toronto's neighbourhoods have become its newest attraction. While some areas are defined by their architectural ex-travagance or lack thereof, a perhaps more interesting handful are defined by the people that live there. Toronto's ethnicity is a marvel; with some 70 nationalities and more than a hundred languages, the city is emblematic of the Canadian mosaic, and restaurant-goers are the happier for it!

Toronto's best-known ethnic neighbourhood is **Chinatown** (see p 175). There are actually six Chinatowns in greater Toronto, but the most exciting and vibrant is probably the one bound by University, Spadina, Queen and College. During the day, fresh vegetables line the sidewalks around the intersection of Spadina and Dundas, the area's core, while at night, the bright yellow and red lights are reminiscent of Hong Kong. Picturesque, adjacent **Kensington Market** is often associated with Chinatown. The vintage clothing stores and specialty food shops from Europe, the Caribbean, the Middle East and Asia are veritable must-sees.

Italians make up the city's largest ethnic group, and their spiritual home is **Little Italy**, located on College Street near Bathurst, where trattorias and boutiques add a bit of the Mediterranean to this Canadian metropolis. The neighbourhood extends to **Corso Italia**, on St. Clair Avenue, west of Bathurst. This vibrant mix of traditional shops and designer Italian boutiques is a marvellous spot for a real cappuccino or Italian *gelato*.

Greektown is also known as *The Danforth*, after the road that runs through it. Greektown is perhaps a misnomer anyway since the community is now home to Italians, Greeks, East Indians, Latin Americans and Chinese. The Greeks still dominate, however, when it comes to restaurants, and Greektown, with its late night fruit markets, specialty food shops, taverns and summer cafés, is a real culinary experience.

Between the Lakeshore and Dundas Street West, Roncesvalles Avenue is known as **Little Poland**, a pleasant area of grand trees and stately Victorians. This is where you can catch an Eastern European film or savour traditional home-made cabbage rolls and pirogies at one of the many cafés.

The traditional *azulejos* (ceramic tiles) and a glass of port will make you think you are in Portugal when you visit the area around Dundas Street West, Ossington Avenue, Augusta Avenue and College Street, an area known as **Portugal Village**. The bakeries here sell some of the best bread in town, while cheese stores, fish markets and lace and crochet shops occupy every other corner.

Little India is a collection of spice shops, clothing stores, restaurants and movie houses along Gerrard Street, east of Greenwood Avenue. These establishments are frequented by Toronto's East Indian community, which is now spread throughout the city.

The area around Bathurst Street north of Bloor Street is the commercial district known as the **Caribbean Community**. Great food shops sell delicious treats, including the savoury patty (pastry turnover with a spicy meat filling) and *roti* (flat bread with meat, fish or vegetable filling) of the islands.

Toronto has the largest population of gays and lesbians in Canada, and is a surprisingly welcoming place considering the city's occasionally stodgy reputation. The **Gay Village** is centred around the corner of Church and Wellesley Streets. Another popular hangout is Hanlan's Point on the Toronto Islands.

Both of Toronto's most distinguished and affluent neighbourhoods lies just north of the downtown area. **Rosedale** is bound by Yonge Street to the west, the Don Valley Parkway to the east, Bloor Street to the south and St. Clair Avenue to the north. North of St. Clair Avenue, the posh area known as **Forest Hill** begins, extending north to Eglinton, east to Avenue Road and west to Bathurst Street.

Rosedale began as the estate of Sheriff William Jarvis, and was so named by his wife Mary after the wild roses that once abounded here. The wild roses and the original house overlooking the ravine are now gone, replaced by a collection of curved streets lined with exquisite residences representing quite a variety of architectural styles. Rosedale was once considered too far from town, but today its natural ravine setting is one of its major assets. Some of the prettiest residences lie on South Drive, Meredith Crescent, Crescent Road, Chestnut Park Road, Elm Avenue and Maple Avenue.

The former village of Forest Hill was incorporated into the city of Toronto in 1968. Perhaps in keeping with its name, one of the village's first bylaws back in the twenties was that a tree be planted on every lot. This haven of greenery is home to some of the city's finest dwellings; many of the loveliest grace Old Forest Hill Road. The community is also home to one of the country's most prestigious private schools, Upper Canada College, which has produced such luminaries as authors Stephen Leacock and Robertson Davies.

Cabbagetown was once described as the "biggest Anglo-Saxon Slum" and was for many years an area to be avoided. The area has been transformed in recent years, however and is now the epitome of gentrification in

Toronto. Its name originated with Irish immigrants who arrived here in the mid-19th century and grew cabbages right on their front lawns. Cabbagetown's residential area lies around Parliament Street (its commercial artery), and extends east to the Don Valley, and north and south between Gerrard and Bloor Streets. It contains grand trees and quaint small-scale Victorian homes, many of which have historic markers. Winchester, Carlton, Spruce and Metcalfe Streets are all lined with true gems. **Allan Gardens**, with its Victorian botanical garden, **Riverdale Farm** *(free admission)*, an old-fashioned zoo, and two cemeteries, **St. James Cemetery**, and the **Necropolis**, or "city of the dead," are also part of the community.

Extending north and west of the intersection of Bloor Street and Avenue Road to Dupont and Bathurst Streets is an area that was annexed by the city of Toronto in 1887, and is now appropriately called **The Annex**. As this was a planned suburb a certain architectural homogeneity prevails; even the unique gables, turrets and cornices are all lined up an equal distance from the street. Take a stroll along Huron Street, Lowther Avenue and Madison Avenue to get a true feel for the Annex's architectural character, which residents have long fought to preserve. Save a few ugly apartment high-rises along St. George Street, their efforts have been quite successful. A few addresses stand out among the hundreds of attractive homes in the Annex, including the York Club (see p 179) and of course Casa Loma and Spadina.

Canadians are known for their reserve, modesty and discretion. Of course there are exceptions to every rule and one of these is certainly **Casa Loma** ★★ *($9; every day 9:30am to 4pm; 1 Austin Terrace, ☎923-1171)* an immense Scottish castle with 98 rooms built in 1914 for the eccentric colonel

Sir Henry Mill Pellatt (1859-1939) who made his fortune by investing in electricity and transportation companies. Pellatt owned among others the tramways of São Paolo, Brazil! His palatial residence, designed by the architect of Toronto's Old City Hall, E.J. Lennox, includes a vast ball room for 500 guests with a pipe organ, a library with 100,000 volumes and an underground cellar. The self-guided tour leads through various secret passages and lost rooms. Great views of downtown Toronto can be had from the towers.

To the east of Casa Loma, atop the Davenport Hill and accessible by the Baldwin Steps is **Spadina House** ★ *($5; Jun to Dec, Mon to Fri 9:30am to 5pm, Sat and Sun noon to 5pm; Jan to May, Tue to Fri 9:30am to 4pm, Sat and Sun noon to 5pm; 285 Spadina Rd., ☎392-6910)* another house-turned museum of Toronto's high society. This one is smaller, but just as splendid for those who want to get a taste of the Belle Époque in Canada. Built in 1866 for James Austin, the first president of the Toronto Dominion Bank, the grounds include a solarium overflowing with luxuriant greenery and a charming Victorian garden, in bloom from May to September. The residence has been renovated several times and features several glassed-in overhangs which offered its owners panoramic views of the surroundings which the natives called *Espanidong*, and the English *Spadina* (pronunced *Spadeena*). Toronto Historical Board guides have lead visitors on tours of the estate since 1982 when the last member of the Austin family left the house.

Last but not least, there are **The Beaches** (Toronto really does have everything!). This is perhaps Toronto's most charming neighbourhood, for obvious reasons — sun, sand, a beach-side boardwalk, classic clapboard and

Casa Loma

shingle cottages and the open water all lie just a streetcar ride away from the hectic pace of downtown. Bound by Kingston Road, the Greenwood Raceway, Victoria Park Avenue and Lake Ontario, The Beaches are more than just a neighbourhood, they are a way of life. Weary travellers will revel in the chance to sunbathe on the hot sand, take a quick dip in the refreshing water and as the sun sets, do some window-shopping and lounge about on a pretty patio.

Other Sights

High Park *(for information ☎392-1111)*, located in the western part of the city and bound by Bloor Street to the north, The Queensway to the south, Parkside Drive to the east and Ellis Avenue to the west, is Toronto's Central Park. It is accessible by both subway (Keele or High Park stations) and streetcar (College or Queen). Toronto's largest park, High Park features tennis courts, playgrounds, bike paths and nature trails;

skating and fishing on Grenadier Pond; rare flora; wildlife indigenous to the area plus animal paddocks where buffaloes, llamas and sheep are kept; a beach on Lake Ontario; a swimming pool and finally historic Colborne Lodge and the Howard Tomb and Monument (see below). "Shakespeare Under the Stars" is one of the park's most popular summer attractions *(for park information ☎392-1111)*.

Colborne Lodge ★ *($3.50; May to Sep, Tue to Sun noon to 5pm; Sep to Apr, Sat and Sun noon to 5pm; year-round for booked groups; these hours change often so call ahead; High Park, ☎392-6916)*. Completed in 1837, this Regency-style residence was built and lived in by architect John Howard. Its lovely three-sided veranda offered clear views of Lake Ontario and the Humber River. Howard ceeded 67 hectares to the City of Toronto in 1873. The other 94 hectares that now make up High Park were acquired separately. The house is now open to the public and run by guides in period dress. The **Howard Tomb and Monument**, close by, is surrounded by an iron fence designed by Christopher Wren that once surrounded St. Paul's Cathedral in London, England.

Montgomery's Inn ★ *($3; year-round Tue to Fri 9:30am to 4:30pm, Sat and Sun 1pm to 5pm; 4709 Dundas St. W., ☎394-8113, Islington subway)* began receiving guests in 1832. Built by an Irish military captain, it is one of Toronto's best examples of Loyalist architecture. Afternoon tea is served *($3; 2pm to 4:15pm)* with all the trimmings by costumed staff who also bake bread, hook rugs and stitch quilts.

Ontario Science Centre ★★★ *($8; every day 10am to 6pm, 770 Don Mills Rd., ☎429-4100, www.osc.on.ca)*. Since its opening, September 27, 1969, the Science Centre has welcomed over 30 million visitors, young and old. Designed by architect Raymond Moriyama, it houses 650 different expositions. The best part about the centre is its many hands-on exhibits and experiments. These interactive exhibits are spread throughout 11 categories: The Living Earth, Space, Sport, Communication, Food, The Information Highway, Technology/Transportation, The Human Body, Science Arcade, Matter/EnergyChange, and Earth. One of the biggest crowd-pleasers is the electricity ball that stands your hair on end. Scientists at heart will also discover the chemistry of cryogenics while the Starlab planetarium transports them to the four corners of the galaxy. They'll learn to make their own paper as well as about the evolution and the impact on humanity of the printing press. The steps involved in making metal objects are described at the foundry on site, and finally the numerous applications of lasers in the modern world are explored. The OSC has an OMNIMAX theater with an enormous 24-m wide dome with a powerful hi-fidelity sound system.

For an enjoyable change of scenery, within 30 minutes from the heart of downtown Toronto head to the **Toronto Metropolitan Zoo** ★★ *($12; follow Hwy. 401 to Exit 389, then take Meadowvale Dr., ☎392-5900)* where you can see some 4,000 animals from the four corners of the globe and take advantage of this lovely 300-hectare park. The African pavillion is particularly interesting, since it is located in a large greenhouse where the climate and vegetation have been recreated. Canadian wildlife is also well represented, and several species that are adapted to the local climate roam free in large enclosures.

Black Creek Pioneer Village ★ *($8; May to Aug, every day 10am to 5pm; Sep to Nov, Mar and Apr, Wed to Sun 10am to 5pm; Dec every day 10am to 4:30pm; 1000 Murray Ross Pkwy., at Jane St. and Steeles Ave. W., ☎905-736-1733, from Finch subway station take bus 60 to Jane St.)* is about 30 minutes from downtown. Period buildings include an authentic mill from the 1840s with a 4-tonne waterwheel that grinds up to one hundred barrels of flour a day, a general store, a town hall, a print shop and a blacksmith; all of these are manned by friendly animators going about their business dipping candles, shearing sheep and baking goodies that you can sample. In the summer, enjoy a horse-drawn carriage ride, and in the winter bundle up for skating, tobogganing and sleigh rides.

The first one of its kind in the country, **Paramount Canada's Wonderland** ★★ *(Pay One Price Passport: guests aged 7-59 $37.95; grounds admissions ticket $19.95; May, Sep and Oct, Sat and Sun 10am to 8pm; Jun to Labour Day, every day 10am to 10pm; 9580 Jane St., Vaughan, ☎905-832-7000, 30 min from downtown, Rutherford exit from Hwy. 400* and follow the signs, or Yorkdale or York Mills subway then take special GO express bus) is the answer if you have a day to kill and children to please. Gut-wrenching rides include the Vortex, the only suspended roller coaster in Canada and the renowned Days of Thunder which puts you behind the driver's seat for a simulated stock car race. The park also features a waterpark called Splash Works with 16 rides and slides, and live shows at the new Kingswood Theatre (☎905-832-8131). Recently purchased by Paramount, Star Trek characters now wander through the park along with more Canadian idols like Scooby Doo and Fred Flintstone. The restaurant facilities may not be to everyone's liking so pack a lunch.

The **McMichael Collection** ★★★ *($7; mid-Oct to May, Tue to Sun 10am to 4pm; May to mid-Oct, every day 10am to 5pm; take Hwy. 400, then Major Mackenzie Dr. to Islington Ave., ☎893-1121)* houses one of the most magnificent collections of Canadian and native art in Canada and draws many visitors to the peaceful hamlet of Kleinberg on the outskirts of Greater Toronto. A magnificent stone and log house built in the 1950s for the McMichaels is home to the collection. Art-lovers from the start, their initial collection of paintings by the grand Canadian masters are at the heart of the museum's present collection. The large and bright galleries present an impressive retrospective of the works of Tom Thomson as well as the Group of Seven. A visit here allows you to admire and contemplate some of the best works of these artists who strove to reproduce and interpret in their own way Ontario's wilderness. Inuit and native art is also well represented, notably the work of Ojibwa painter Norval Morrisseau, who created his own "pictographic" style.

The Don River Valley wends its way through Toronto to Lake Ontario and conceals a network of beautiful parks linked by bridges and trails. **Edwards Gardens** *(parking at Leslie St. and Lawrence Ave. E.; information ☎397-1340)* is one of Toronto's first garden parks and features rock gardens, perennials, rose gardens, small waterfalls and dense forest. The river flows south past **Wilket Creek Park** and **Ernest Thompson Seton Park**. The Ontario Science Centre overlooks the latter. Near Don Mills Road, **Taylor Creek Park** extends to the east all the way to Warden Woods. All of these parks are wonderful places for walking, bicycling, jogging, cross-country skiing and even bird-watching.

Scarborough Heights Park and **Cathedral Bluffs Park** command breathtaking views of Lake Ontario from atop the scenic bluffs, while **Bluffer's Park** offers scenic and spacious beaches and picnic areas.

 OUTDOOR ACTIVITIES

 Bicycling

The **Martin Goodman Trail**, a 22-kilometre jogging and cycling path, follows the shore of Lake Ontario from the mouth of the Humber River west of the city centre, past Ontario Place and Queen's Quay to the Balmy Beach Club in The Beaches. Call ☎367-2000 for a map of the trail.

Bicycle and jogging paths also weave their way through Metropolitan Toronto's parks. For maps and information on the trails call ☎392-8186.

Toronto Island Bicycle Rental
Centre Island ☎203-0009
$5 an hour

In-line Skating

Toronto's streets may be a bit hazardous for this sport, but the scenic paths on the Toronto Islands and near the water in The Beaches and in The Bluffs are ideal.

Rent 'n' Roll
Queen's Quay Terminal
☎203-8438

This shop rents the skates and all the necessary equipment (pads) for $10/hour. You will need at least 3 hours to tour the islands. They also offer lessons.

 Skating

There are several enchanting places to go ice-skating in the city. These include the rink in front of New City Hall, Grenadier Pond in High Park and York Quay at Harbourfront. For information on city rinks call ☎392-1111.

 Golf

There are five municipal golf courses (two executive and three regulation), which operate on a first-come first-served basis. One of these is the **Don Valley Golf Course** (☎392-2465), a challenging regulation course with several water and bunker hazards. For general information on public courses call ☎367-8186.

For something more challenging, take a little jaunt out to Oakville, to the **Glen Abbey Golf Club** (green fees and cart $145, discount rates in off-season and on weekends after 2pm $85; 1333 Dorval Dr., ☎905-844-1800). This spectacular course was the first to be designed by Jack Nicklaus. The rates are high, but it's a real thrill to play where the pros play. This is the home of the Canadian Open Championship.

  Hiking and Cross-Country Skiing

Toronto's many ravines are wonderful spots to explore by foot or on skis. A lovely trail begins in Edwards Gardens and meanders along the Don River to Taylor Creek. Pedestrians can gain access to the Don River Valley from Leslie Street between Lawrence and Eglinton, from Gateway Boulevard behind the Ontario Science Centre, from Moore Avenue near Mount Pleasant Cemetery and from the Gerrard Street overpass.

Much more pristine than the Don River Valley, **Highland Creek** to the east of Scarborough is also lined with scenic walking trails. This area is known for its spectacular fall colours. The woodsy trails of **Morningside Park** are perfect for cross-country skiing.

 ACCOMMODATIONS

Tour A: The Waterfront

SkyDome Hotel (*$169; ≡, ℛ, ≈, ⊘, ⌂; 1 Blue Jay Way, M5V 1J4, ☎341-7100 or 800-441-1161, ⇴341-5090*) has 346 rooms with panoramic views, 70 of which face the inside of the stadium. The latter cost more, but what a view! The hotel also has a choice of restaurants and a bar with a view of the playing field. The rooms, decorated in modern style, are very comfortable. Valet and room service are available day and night.

Old salts will feel at home at the **Radisson Plaza Hotel Admiral** (*$175; ≡,

®, ≈; *249 Queen's Quay W., M5J 2N5,* ☎*203-3333 or 800-333-3333,* ≈*203-3301).* The decor of this charming hotel displays a seafaring motif, with the rooms giving guests the impression they are aboard a cruise ship. The view of the bay from the fifth-floor pool is quite magnificent. Regular shuttle service is offered between the hotel and the downtown area.

The **Westin Harbour Castle** *($189; ≡, ≈, ℜ, ⊘, △, tv; 1 Harbour Sq., M5J 1A6,* ☎*869-1600 or 800-228-3000,* ≈*869-1420)* used to be part of the Hilton hotel chain. In 1987, Westin and Hilton decided to swap their respective Toronto hotels. Located on the shore of Lake Ontario, in a calm and peaceful spot, the Westin Harbour Castle is just a few steps from the Harbourfront Centre and the ferry to the Toronto Islands. To help guests reach the downtown area, the hotel offers a free shuttle service; it also lies next to a streetcar line.

Tour B: The Theatre and Financial Districts

The location of the **Hotel Victoria** *($75-95; ℜ, ℛ, tv; 56 Yonge St., M5E 1G5,* ☎*363-1666,* ≈*363-7327)* is particularly appealing, midway between the financial district and Union Station. The hotel offers simple rooms at very affordable prices. Though the hotel does not have its own parking area, there are public parking lots nearby.

The **Holiday Inn on King** *($120; 370 King St. W., M5V 1J9,* ☎*599-8889)* has typical rooms with pleasant, modern decor though they lack charm. Some have balconies.

The **Toronto Hilton International** *($130; ≡, ®, ≈, ℜ, ⊘, △, tv; 145 Richmond St. W., M5H 3M6,* ☎*869-3456 or 800-445-8667,* ≈*869-0291)* resembles many other Hilton hotels, with its pastel decor. It offers comfortable, clean, well-equipped rooms. The Hilton is also the place where many visiting sports teams stay, among them the Montréal Canadiens, the Los Angeles Kings and the Oakland A's.

Tour C: Front Street and St. Lawrence

The **Essex Park Hotel** *($89; ≡, ≈, ℜ, ⊘, △; 300 Jarvis St., M5B 2C5,* ☎*977-4823 or 800-567-2233,* ≈*977-4830)* squeezes about 100 rooms into a rather small space, but it manages to retain a special old-world charm. Rooms are small but very comfortable, and service is excellent.

For a pleasant hotel located in the heart of downtown, just a few steps from the Royal York Hotel and a few minutes' walk from the waterfront, head to the **Strathcona Hotel** *($99; ≡; 60 York St., M5J 1S8,* ☎*363-3321,* ≈*363-4679).*

French hotel chain **Novotel** *($115; ≡, ®, ℜ, ⊘, △, tv; 45 The Esplanade, M5E 1W2,* ☎*367-8900 or 800-668-6835,* ≈*360-8285)* enjoys an ideal Toronto location, just minutes from Harbourfront, the St. Lawrence and O'Keefe (Hummingbird) Centres, and Union Station. Comfort is assured at this hotel, except perhaps on the Esplanade side where noise from the restaurants and terraces has a tendency to filter into the rooms.

Built in 1903, making it the oldest hotel in the city, the **King Edward Hotel** *($125; ≡, ℜ, ⊘, tv; 37 King St. E., M5C 1E9,* ☎*863-9700 or 800-534-4300,* ≈*367-5515)* is still among Toronto's most attractive. Various different rooms are available from sumptuous suites, each with their own unique decor, to typical no-frills hotel rooms; unfortunately, neither offer much in terms of views. The magnificent lobby, two ballrooms and restaurants make up for this, however. Airport buses stop here regularly.

The **Cambridge Suites Hotel** *($150 bkfst incl.; ≡, ≈, ⊛, K, ℝ, ⊘, △, tv; 15 Richmond St. E., M5C 1N2, ☎368-1990, ⊶601-3751)* offers sumptuous 51 m² (nearly 550 square feet) suites in area, all equipped with microwave ovens, refrigerator and complete sets of dishes. Deluxe suites offer whirlpool baths.

With its renovated guest rooms, its 34 banquet rooms (each decorated differently), and its 10 restaurants, it is easy to understand why the **Royal York Hotel** *($169; ≡, ≈, ⊘, △, tv; 100 Front St. W., M5J 1E3, ☎368-2511, 800-828-7447 or 800-441-1414)* is one of Toronto's most popular hotels. The sumptuously decorated lobby is a good indication of the opulence you'll find in the guest-rooms.

Tour D: Queen Street West and Chinatown

If you are visiting Toronto during the summer months and you want a clean, economic place to sleep, you can take advantage of the 425 rooms at **Victoria University** *($60 bkfst incl.; ⊘, tv; 140 Charles St. W., M5S 1K9, ☎585-4524, ⊶585-4530)*. Guests also have a laundromat, cafeteria and sports facilities at their disposal.

The **Beaconsfield** *($69 sb, $99 pb bkfst incl.; 38 Beaconsfield Ave., M6J 3H9, ☎535-3338)*, set in a superb Victorian house dating from 1882 in a quiet little neighbourhood near Queen Street, is a good place to turn if you are looking for something different from the big hotels, including a delightful breakfast accom-

panied by music. Rooms are charming and imaginatively decorated.

The **Bond Place Hotel** *($89; ≡, ℝ, tv; 65 Dundas St. E., M5B 2G8, ☎362-6061, ⊶360-6406)* is doubtless the most ideally located hotel for enjoying the rhythm of the city and mixing with the busy throng at the corner of Dundas and Yonge streets.

The **Delta Chelsea** *($129; ≡, ⊛, ≈, ℝ, ⊘, tv; 33 Gerrard St. W., M5G 1Z4, ☎595-1975 or 800-268-9070, ⊶585-4366)* is very popular with visitors and justly so, for it offers comfortable rooms at reasonable prices, and guests under 18 can share their parents' room free of charge. The new tower draws business travellers thanks to its business centre with ergonomically designed chairs, fax machines and telephones.

Tour E: Around Queen's Park

From May to August, at the **St. George Campus** of the **University of Toronto** *($60; K, ℝ, ℝ, ⊘; 214 College St., M5T 2Z9, ☎978-8045)*, you will find an excellent, low-cost alternative to expensive hotels. The university has lodgings that can accommodate four to six persons, each with a fully equipped kitchenette. They are located near a cafeteria, a pub and a physical fitness centre.

Toronto has many reasonably priced Bed and Breakfasts. **Homewood Inn** *($60 bkfst; 65 Homewood St., M4Y 2K1, ☎920-7944, ⊶920-4091)* is one of these – a quaint home located in a peaceful residential neighbourhood. Well kept. Somewhat busy interior decor. Breakfast is served in a large, well-lit dining room. Guestrooms are satisfactory.

A few steps away from busy Jarvis Street, is **Mulberry Tree** *($60 bkfst; ○; 122 Isabella St., M4Y 1P1, ☎960-5249, ⇒960-3853)*, tucked away in a quiet area. You will first be struck by the pretty red brick exterior, and once inside, you will enjoy tasteful decor, clean rooms, and a good breakfast.

Victoria's Mansion *($95; tv; ℝ; 68 Gloucester St., M4Y 1L5, ☎921-4625, ⇒925-0300)* is a beautiful turn-of-the-century home located on a quiet street close to lively neighbourhoods. Its elaborate exterior gives a somewhat inaccurate idea of its modestly decorated interior and plainly furnished suites. Vicotria's is particularly well suited for long-term stays, since each room is equipped with a kitchenette and desk, offering a comfort similar to that of a small apartment.

The Days Inn Carlton *($99-$135; ≈, ℛ, ○; 30 Carlton St., M5B 2E9, ☎977-6655, ⇒977-0502)* is a few steps away from a former city institution, Maple Leaf Gardens, once jam-packed with hockey fans. While the decor is nothing special, the rooms are clean and comfortable.

A few blocks away is the **Primerose Best Western** *($179; tv; ≈, ○, ℛ, bar; 111 Carlton St., M5R 2G3, ☎977-8000, ⇒977-6323)*. With its modern, but somewhat austere decor, the lobby gives a preview of the 300 rooms, which, although well furnished, are adequately comfortable.

An enormous complex including 40 shops, restaurants and bars as well as two cinemas houses the **Sheraton Centre Toronto** *($239; ≈, ≈, ℛ, ⊘, ○, tv; 123 Queen St. W., M5H 2M9, ☎361-1000 or 800-565-0089, ⇒947-4874)*. This very comfortable hotel has many rooms, the most attractive of which are in the two towers, served by private elevators. The lobby is perhaps most surprising, with its magnificent two-acre indoor garden. You will also have access to the network of indoor passageways linking many downtown points.

If you prefer to have everything under the same roof, the brand new **Toronto Marriott Eaton Centre** *($209; ≈, ≈, ℛ, ⊛, ○, ⊘, tv; 525 Bay St., M5G 2L2, ☎597-9200, ⇒598-9211)* will fit the bill. Linked to the famous Eaton Centre, a shoppers' mecca and one of the city's major attractions (see p 173), the Marriott Hotel offers very big, well equipped rooms (they even have irons and ironing boards). If you wish to relax, there are two ground-floor lounges, one with pool tables and televisions.

Tour F: Bloor and Yorkville

For an alternative to the big, expensive hotels, try the **Marigold Hostel** *($22.25/person in dormitory bkfst incl.; sb; 2011 Dundas St. W., M6R 1W7, ☎536-8824 after 7pm)*. This charming little hotel is often filled with young travellers and students who prefer to save a bit of cash and can forego a private bathroom.

The **YWCA** *($47 bkfst incl.; 80 Woodlawn Ave. E., M4T 1C1, ☎923-8454)* is open only to women, who can choose between dormitories, semi-private or private rooms.

Hostelling International *($24; K, tv, ℛ; 76 Church St., M5B 1Y7, ☎971-4440 or 800-668-4487, ⇒971-4088)* is open day and night, with a total of 175 affordable beds in dormitories and semi-private rooms. There are a television lounge, laundry facilities, a kitchen and a restaurant with a pool table and darts, as well as a small terrace.

From mid-May to mid-August, the **Neil Wycik College Hotel** *($49; ℜ, △; 96 Gerrard St. E., M5B 1G7, ☎977-2320 or 800-268-4358, ⌐977-2809)* opens its student residences to travellers. Rooms are simple and offer only the basics, but guests have room-cleaning service, a television lounge and a laundromat at their disposal.

🦡 The **Amblecote** Bed and Breakfast *($79 bkfst incl.; 109 Walmer Rd., M5R 2X8, ☎927-1713)* is a little jewel hidden in the trendy Annex district west of Yorkville, on a quiet street lined with stately homes. Dating from the early 20th century, this superb house has been fully renovated after a period of neglect. The new owners, Paul and Mark, worked hard to restore it to its former glory. There are beautiful antiques throughout, including the guest rooms. Those at either end are especially splendid, bright and spacious.

Near the stylish boutiques and swank restaurants of Yorkville is the **Venture Inn** *($99 bkfst; 89 Avenue Rd., M5R 2G3, ☎964-1220, ⌐964-8692)*. While it is perhaps lacking some of the charm of other neighbourhood institutions, its rooms are comfortable and reasonably priced. As if to compensate for its lacklustre exterior, its interior is warmly and tastefully decorated. Its furniture is mostly pine, creating a more rustic ambiance, thus distinguishing it from other establishments in this category.

The **Quality Hotel by Journey's End** *($129; ≡, tv; 111 Lombard St., M5C 2T9, ☎367-5555, ⌐367-3470)* caters to people on a budget who want simple but comfortable rooms at a reasonable price.

The rooms at the **Park Plaza Hotel** *($185; ≡, ℜ, ⊘, tv; 4 Avenue Rd., M5R 2E8, ☎924-5471 or 800-268-4927, ⌐924-4933)* have been tastefully renovated, and the bathrooms, decked out in marble. The hotel is pleasantly and conveniently located in the heart of Yorkville, just a few minutes' walk from the Royal Ontario Museum (see p 179).

Just a few steps from the Royal Ontario Museum (see p 179) and from Yorkville Street, you will be seduced by the **Inter-Continental Toronto** *($189; ≡, ≈, ℜ, ⊘, △, tv; 220 Bloor St. W., M5S 1T8, ☎960-5200, ⌐920-8269)*, with its vast, tastefully decorated rooms and its exemplary service.

The brand new **Metropolitan Hotel** *($225; ≡, ⊛, ≈, ⊘, △, tv; 108 Chestnut St., M5G 1R3, ☎977-5000 or 800-668-6600, ⌐977-9513; www.metropolitan.com)* is one of the most interesting additions to the Toronto hotel scene. Entering the lobby, you will discover an inviting atrium, giving you an idea of what to expect in the thoroughly pleasant rooms.

If you are looking for a top-of-the-line luxury hotel, the **Four Seasons Hotel Toronto** *($280; ≡, ⊛, ≈, ℜ, ⊘, tv; 21 Avenue Rd., M5R 2G1, ☎964-0411 or 800-268-6282, ⌐964-2301)* is one of the most highly rated hotels in North America. This spot is faithful to its reputation, with impeccable service and beautifully decorated rooms. It also has a sumptuous ballroom with Persian carpets and crystal chandeliers. The hotel restaurant, **Truffle** (see p 199), with Uffizi sculptures at the entrance portraying two wild boars, will satisfy your desires with some of the best food in Toronto.

Near the Airport

Morning Glory Bed and Breakfast *($65 bkfst incl.; 1545 Jane St., ☎533-6120)* occupies a charming Edwardian house with pretty stained glass windows and big, comfortable rooms. Weather permitting, you can have your breakfast on the outdoor terrace. Outdoor parking is available.

A lovely Georgian house with two elegant white columns accommodates the **Palmerston Inn** *($85 bkfst incl.; 322 Palmerston Blvd., M6G 2N6, ☎920-7842, ⇒960-9529)*. Located on one of the city's few quiet streets, this Bed and Breakfast offers eight rooms for non-smokers only, five of them air conditioned and all are decorated with period furniture.

The **Sheraton Gateway Hotel at Terminal Three** *($99-155; ≡, ⊛, ℛ, ⊘, tv; Toronto AMF, PO Box 3000, Mississauga, L5P 1C4, ☎905-672-7000 or 800-565-0010, ⇒905-672-7100)*, linked directly to Terminal 3 at Toronto's Pearson International Airport, is the best located hotel for in-transit passengers. It has 474 attractively decorated rooms and is fully soundproofed, with panoramic views of the airport or the city of Mississauga.

For middle-budget travellers, **Quality Suites** *($150; bkfst incl.; ≡, ℛ. tv; 262 Carlingview Dr., Etobicoke M9W 5G1, ☎674-8442 or 800-668-4200, ⇒674-3088)* offers pleasant, unpretentious rooms at a reasonable price. Although a little far from the airport, it offers one of the best quality-to-price ratios in the area. Travellers without cars need not worry, for a bus links the hotel and the airport every half-hour.

The **Best Western Carlton Place Hotel** *($160; ≡, ⊛, ≈, ℛ, ⊘, tv; 33 Carlson Court, Etobicoke M9W 6H5, ☎675-1234 or 800-528-1234, ⇒675-3436)* offers decent, comfortable rooms at reasonable prices within close proximity of the airport.

 RESTAURANTS

Tour A: The Waterfront

A few steps from the Centreville amusement park the **Iroquois** restaurant *($; Toronto Islands, ☎203-8795)* is often invaded by crowds of happy children who come for a pizza or a hamburger.

Not to be missed is the Toronto franchise of **Planet Hollywood** *($-$$; 277 Front St. W., ☎596-7827)*, located at the foot of the CN Tower. This chain of restaurants, co-owned by many Hollywood celebrities, serves hamburgers, pizzas, salads, and similar fare. At Planet Hollywood, the decor seems to be just as important, if not more so, as the food. Walls are adorned with American pop culture memorabilia, and the famous restaurant owners are featured in movie clips projected on giant screens.

The **Island Paradise Restaurant** *($$$; next to the Centre Island ferry, ☎203-0245)* is popular for its outdoor terrace and spectacular views of Lake Ontario and of Toronto, which can be enjoyed while delighting in a choice of chicken dishes or a steak. Open until the departure of the last ferry.

Imagine having a meal with Toronto at your feet. This is what awaits you atop the CN Tower, at the **360** *($$$$; CN Tower, 301 Front St. W., ☎362-5411)* revolving restaurant, which offers good food as well as one of the finest views of the city. The menu features both continental cuisine and seafood.

Tour B: The Theatre and Financial Districts

Plantation *($; 121 King St. W., ☎861-0808)* is an ideal place to stop to savour a coffee or a dish made from fresh, quality ingredients. High ceilings, large windows, and fresco replicas all make this a fine place to eat.

🦞 The owner of the **Bibiche Bistro** *($$; 1352 Danforth St., ☎463-9494)* is so friendly that will you soon forget the very ordinary decor. Such things are inconsequential anyway, especially with such fabulous entrees and desserts.

Café Brussel *($$; 786 Broadview Ave., ☎465-7363)* is a little café where you can sit and sip a good Belgian beer to the sounds of jazz. From soup to dessert, everything is prepared on the premises. The mussels are especially good.

Fenice *($$; 319 King St. W., ☎585-2377)* invites you to enjoy delicious Italian dishes, prepared with fresh ingredients, and to delight in a warm atmosphere, to the strains of classical music.

The famous Honest Ed Mirvish will take you on a trip back in time to the grand old days of the Victorian era at **Ed's Warehouse** *($$-$$$; 270 King St. W., ☎937-3939)*, decorated with antiques. Remember, everything at Honest Ed's is for sale; do not hesitate to ask the price if something catches your eye. Besides the decor, this restaurant, spread over five floors in two buildings, will satisfy every taste: it includes Ed's Chinese, Ed's Seafood, Old Ed's, Ed's Italian and Ed's Folly.

The Keg *($$-$$$; 515 Jarvis St., ☎964-6609)* is located in a superb former residence on Jarvis Street. Traditional cuisine with specialties including steak and roast beef is served in this charming atmosphere.

Soul Machossa *($$-$$$; 499 Church St., ☎922-3859)* is anything but your typical fast-food-type pizzeria. The atmosphere is definitely more suited to a romantic evening for two. The menu offers a deliciously different choice of toppings.

🦞 A few steps from St. Lawrence Hall, you'll savour Italian food worthy of the finest palates at **Biaggio** *($$$; 155 King St. E., ☎366-4040)*. This elegant restaurant serves some of the best fresh pasta in town. After grappling with the tempting array of dishes on the menu, it's on to the excellent wine list, a no more easier task. Fortunately, the waiter will be more than happy to make a few suggestions.

The **Senator** *($$$$; closed Mon; 249 Victoria, ☎364-7517)* has survived the recent explosion of the Toronto restaurant scene and still serves one of the best steaks. Classy, refined setting.

Tour C: Front Street and St. Lawrence

In response to Toronto's growing infatuation with good coffee, **Starbucks** *($; 81 Front St. E., ☎955-9956)*, the famous Seattle-based chain, has recently opened several branches in Toronto. With its excellent coffee, it has become so popular among Torontonians that it is sometimes hard to find a seat on one of the cosy couches that furnish the place.

Some places are truly timeless. This is the case of **Shopsy's** *($-$$; 33 Yonge St., ☎365-3333)*, a delicatessen that opened in 1921 and has captured the hearts and stomachs of Torontonians with its traditional breakfasts and its hot dogs. It is located a few steps from the Hockey Hall of Fame, at the corner of Yonge and Front streets.

At the **Mövenpick Market** *($$-$$$; inside BCE Place, ☎366-8986)*, you can choose from a tasty array of dishes each more tempting than the last, and prepared right before your eyes. After finally deciding on your meal, you may face the problem of finding a table, for this spot is very popular

Le Papillon *($$-$$$; 16 Church St., ☎363-0838)* is a true delight, with its tempting menu combining the delicacies of French and Québec cuisines. The *crêpes* are especially good.

A water theme prevails at **Acqua** *($$$; BCE Place, 10 Front St. W., ☎368-7171)*. The attractive and rather unusual decor of this fashionable restaurant, certainly adds to the enjoyment of the tasty dishes drawn from the culinary traditions of the Mediterranean and California.

The historic and classic decor of the **Café Victoria** *($$$-$$$$; King Edward Hotel, 37 King St. E., ☎863-9700)* is enchanting. A certain level of intimacy is achieved at the carefully set tables, despite the loftiness of the room. The meal, a veritable feast ending with a delicious dessert, is sure to be memorable.

Tour D: Queen Street West and Chinatown

The relaxed setting at **Kalendar's Koffee House** *($; 546 College St., ☎923-4138)* is ideal for an intimate tête-à-tête over coffee and cake, or a light lunch. The menu lists an array of interesting sandwiches and simple dishes.

On Sunday morning, the **Chinatown International** *($-$$; 421 Dundas St. W., ☎593-0291)* bustles with activity as Chinese families come for the traditional *dim sum*. This is a special occasion to enjoy a unique and succulent experience.

The funky retro decor of **La Hacienda** *($-$$; 640 Queen St. W., ☎703-3377)* recalls the best of the fiftites and sixties and is really quite charming. The solid, though simple menu consists mostly of Mexican dishes, including a few vegetarian varieties.

Squirly *($$; 807 Queen St. W., ☎594-0574)* is a charming restaurant where you can go for a good meal in a relaxed, unpretentious atmosphere without emptying your pockets. The dining room boasts a fun kitschy decor, while on fine summer days you may prefer the pretty outdoor terrace in back.

Queen Street West is one of Toronto's liveliest streets after dark, and the **Bamboo** *($$; 312 Queen St. W., ☎593-5771)* is one of the most colourful restaurants around. To reach the dining rooms, you have to squeeze through a narrow passageway linking the "temple" to the street. You can then choose between a two-level outdoor terrace or one of two indoor dining rooms. This one-of-a-kind restaurant, with food spanning Caribbean, Malay, Thai and Indonesian flavours, also offers shows. Thus you can enjoy specialties such as *satay* (chicken brochettes with spicy peanut sauce) before heading out onto the dance floor and swaying to the captivating rhythms of reggae or salsa.

TORONTO

Bertucci's *($$; 630 College St., ☎537-0911)* is a friendly little Italian restaurant with very simple decor. People come not for the decor, however, but to eat delicious pasta dishes while enjoying a level of service worthy of the finest hotels.

The friendly **College Street Bar** *($$; 574 College St., ☎533-2417)* boasts a tasty Mediterranean menu and lively atmosphere. This hot spot is frequented by a young crowd, and many folks just stop in for drinks and atmosphere.

On certain days, the little **Lee Garden** *($$; 358 Spadina Ave., ☎593-9524)* is so crowded you'd think all of China has squeezed in here. People come for the delectable Chinese cuisine, especially the seafood and duck dishes.

Cavernous and austere decor, exquisite presentation, attitude, mood lighting and an interesting interpretation of southwestern cuisine, all pretty much sum up the dining experience at **Left Bank** *($$; 567 Queen St. W., ☎504-1626)*.

🦪 **Margaritas** *($$; 14 Baldwin St, ☎977-5525)* provides quite an escape with its infectious Latin music and its tasty dishes including Toronto's best *nachos* and delicious *guacamole*; it's like a piece of Mexico in the heart of Toronto. The lively atmosphere makes the dull urban grey of the city seem far away.

Soft lighting, white tiles, fresh-cut flowers and simple chairs with gold-stencilled crisp white slipcovers come together to create a romantic ambience in which to enjoy the Italian specialties at **Pony** *($$; 488 College St., ☎923-7665)*. The veal and calamari are particularly noteworthy.

Taro Grill *($$; 492 Queen St. W., ☎504-1320)* is one of those places where you go not only to eat but also to be seen. This is one of the trendier spots in town. The show is continuous, with the chef visible in the open kitchen.

On Queen Street, **Tiger Lily's** *($$; 257 Queen St. W., ☎977-5499)* has an established clientele fond of their good, inexpensive dishes. This Noodle House, as part of its name suggests, prepares Asian pasta dishes of all kinds and for all tastes.

Only about 30 people can squeeze into the fun surroundings of the tiny dining in **The Tempest** *($$-$$$; 468 College St. W., ☎944-2440)* at one time. You can expect to have a good time despite the sometimes slow service. Fortunately, the desserts, especially the cheesecake, will reward your patience amply.

🦪 The smooth jazz sounds of the **Bistro Select** *($$$; 328 Queen St. W., ☎596-6405)* will tempt you to stay for hours. But this Parisian-style bistro offers more than a warm, relaxing atmosphere. A clientele of connoisseurs is also drawn to its impressive menu. There is something to please you at all times of year, especially in the summer when you can enjoy the pleasant outdoor terrace.

The **Bodega** *($$$; 30 Baldwin St., ☎977-1287)* serves resolutely gastronomic French dishes made with the freshest of ingredients. The wall coverings, the lace and the music that wafts across the dining room contribute to a genuinely French atmosphere.

Mediterranean dishes and a comfortable and pretty New Age dining room await at the **Kensington Kitchen** *($$$; 124 Harbord St., ☎961-3404)*. This is a good spot to remember for fine summer days, when you can enjoy the same specialties on the rooftop terrace.

Toronto is home to many excellent Chinese restaurants, but few can compare to **Lai Wah Heen** *($$$; 108 Chestnut St., Metropolitan Hotel, ☎977-9899)*. Its menu features mostly Cantonese *haute cuisine*. Remarkable attention to detail is shown in both preparation and presentation. A place of great refinement for its food, decor, and service. Dim Sum is also served in the mornings.

Peter Pan *($$$; 373 Queen St. W., ☎593-0917)* offers an authentic 1930s decor as well as delicious and imaginative dishes, where pasta, pizza and fish are reinvented. Service is courteous.

There is nothing quite like a good *sushi* or *sashimi*, like the kind prepared at the **Sushi Bistro** *($$$; 204 Queen St. W., ☎971-5315)*. Sitting at the sushi bar, the chef prepares these delicious mouthfuls of raw fish with a stunning degree of skill right before your eyes. A festive atmosphere takes over as the evening wears on and patrons take the stage at the *karaoke* bar.

Tour E: Queen Street West and Chinatown

There is nothing quite like a tender grilled sirloin steak from **Barberian's** *($$$$; 7 Elm St., ☎597-0225)*. Steak dominates the menu here, which may seem a little bare to anyone hoping for other choices. Reservations recommended.

Tour F: Bloor and Yorkville

You may be surprised to discover a traditional diner in the Yorkville area, facing the chic Harry Rosen clothing store. **Flo's Diner** *($; 10 Bellair St., ☎961-4333)*, like most establishments of this type, is a good spot for hamburgers. In the summer, you can sit on the rooftop terrace.

You will think you have been invited into the living room of a stylish house for a delectable dessert at the **Pyramid Cakery** *($; 2519 Yonge St., ☎489-2246)*. Let your sweet tooth guide you, and treat yourself not only to a divine piece of cake, but also to a cup of the establishment's famous hot chocolate.

Yorkville is certainly one of Toronto's best neighbourhoods to stroll about. Beautiful homes and stylish boutiques line its streets, along with charming restaurants such as **Café Nervosa** *($$; Yorkville St. at Belair St.)*. Its menu features mostly pizza and panini, making this ideal for a lunchtime visit.

For hamburgers, pasta, or even just a drink, **J.J. Muggs** *($$; 500 Bloor St. W., ☎531-8888)* is *the* place on busy Bloor Street — if there is something going on you'll find out about it here.

Queen's Pasta Café *($$; 2263 Bloor St. W., ☎766-0993)* is a friendly little restaurant with a young, relaxed clientele. Pasta holds the place of honour here.

As expected, oysters are front and centre at the **Crown Oyster Café** *($$-$$$; 2253 Bloor St. W., ☎760-0816)*. Even if you are not a lover of this mollusk, rest assured that the menu offers delicious alternatives such as filet of sole. Service is impeccable.

Jacques L'Omelette, also called **Jacques Bistro du Parc** *($$-$$$; 126-A Cumberland Ave., ☎961-1893)*, is a charming little spot located upstairs

TORONTO

in a fine Yorkville house. The very friendly French owner offers simple but high-quality food. The fresh Atlantic salmon and the spinach salad are among the more pleasant surprises on the menu. It may be a bit difficult to locate this spot, but well worth the effort.

Remy's *($$-$$$; 115 Yorkville Ave., ☎968-9429)* is busy year-round. You can eat at the bar, a streetside table, or in the large dining room at the back of the restaurant. The menu is varied, running the gamut of peanut chicken to hamburgers and sandwiches.

The **Bellair Café** *($$$; 100 Cumberland Ave., ☎964-2222)* is a big bar and bistro with bay windows looking out onto the street perfect for people-watching. The decor is in shades of pink with wooden floors and furniture. Towards the back, on the left, a pleasant dining room with modern furnishings and lighting greet guests who prefer a quieter atmosphere. The menu offers some interesting surprises such as mushroom *risotto* with duck.

Mövenpick *($$$; 133 Yorkville Ave., ☎926-9545)* is a big, tastefully decorated Swiss restaurant with innovative dishes and reasonable prices, considering the quality. You can feast on the same specialties as at the Marché (see p 195) but minus the hectic cafeteria layout. Sunday brunch here is a must, but there can be a long wait.

In a funky 1960s decor, **Opus** *($$$; 37 Prince Arthur, ☎921-3105)* serves refined and modern cuisine described as "contemporary Canadian," mixing traditional recipes with other culinary traditions. Exceptional wine list.

🦞 **Sassafraz** *($$$; 100 Cumberland, 924-2222)*, a restaurant with a hip design, is now one of the most fashion-able places in Yorkville. While the decor and ambiance will certainly add to your dining experience, it is first and foremost the food, a delightful blend of Californian and French cuisines, that gave Sassafraz its reputation.

Yamato *($$$; 18 Belair St., ☎927-0077)* features Japanese cuisine with a twist – the chef prepares your meal right before your eyes! The menu includes classics, such as teriyaki steak and vegetable tempura, always fresh and tasty.

Boba *($$$-$$$$; 90 Avenue Rd., ☎961-2622)* is an inviting and charming little restaurant which has acquired a solid reputation thanks to its fine cuisine and courteous service. In-house specialties include beef, duck, and lamb, and its desserts are particularly delicious.

North 44 *($$$-$$$$; 2537 Yonge St., ☎487-4897)* is one of the *in* restaurants with the hip Toronto crowd. This is not just a place to see and be seen, however, since its food is also exquisite. The chef culls from several culinary traditions to create a decidedly innovative menu.

🦞 For a memorable evening, the **Auberge du Pommier** *($$$$; 4150 Yonge St., ☎222-2220)* offers a quiet, elegant atmosphere and refined French cuisine, including specialties such as caviar and *foie gras*. Meals here can be accompanied by one of the fine wines from the excellent list.

🦞 **Bistro 990** *($$$$; 990 Bay St., ☎921-9990)* is a meeting place for *nouvelle cuisine* lovers, and is among the best restaurants in the city. Its pleasant decor is Mediterranean style, and its menu features one delectable dish after another. The duck and lamb, as well as the desserts, are all worthwhile.

Truffle *($$$$; Four Seasons Hotel, 21 Avenue Rd., ☎964-0411)* is perhaps not within everyone's budget, but if you can swing it, the food is well worth it. The restaurant's reputation for being among the best eating spots in town is well-deserved.

Rosedale

Toronto and Montreal: these long-time rivals have one good thing in common – **Moishes** *($$$; 77 Adelaide St. W., ☎363-3509)*. The specialty of the house, a tender, succulent steak, will delight any gourmet. A quiet ambiance and impeccable service add to your dining experience.

  ENTERTAINMENT

Bars and Nightclubs

The **Loose Moose** *(220 Adelaide St. W., ☎971-5252)* serves typical pub-grub, burgers and wings, but is more recommended as a popular pick-up joint! A small dance floor and the latest top-40 hits set the pace.

The Big Bop *(651 Queen St. W., ☎504-6699)* is packed every week-end night with a young crowd (the capacity is 800 people!), who let loose to oldies on the first floor and rock 'n' roll, dance and house upstairs. The decor is eclectic to say the least. This is a major meat market for the 19-25-year-old set!

Just the name might be enough to keep some people away from the **Bovine Sex Club** *(542 Queen St. W., ☎504-4239)* and enough to attract some others. An alternative crowd hangs out here.

A rich and lavish decor sets the tone at **Bemelman's** *(83 Bloor St. W., ☎960-0306)*. A trendy crowd of young professionals appreciates the extensive list of martinis (shaken or stirred) and the outdoor terrace, for hot summer nights.

Whiskey Saigon *(250 Richmond St. W., ☎593-4646)* is one of Toronto's consummate dance halls. Retro, rap, reggae and rock all have their place here.

Toronto's most popular student hangout is the **Brunswick House** *(481 Bloor St. W., ☎964-2242)*. Large-screen televisions, shuffleboard, billiard tables, lots of beer and a character named Rockin' Irene are the mainstays here. Jazz and blues create a more mellow atmosphere at **Albert's Hall** upstairs. **Rotterdam** *(600 King St. W., ☎868-6882)* is a beer-lover's dream-come-true, with over 40 brews on tap, and many more in bottles. Young and old fill up the outdoor patio on summer nights.

Toronto's highest piano lounge, **The Acquarius Lounge** *(55 Bloor St. W., 51st floor, ☎967-5225)* sits atop the ManuLife Centre. The drinks and cocktails are pricey, but then again the view is spectacular. Proper dress required.

The **Hard Rock Café** *(1 Blue Jays Way, ☎341-2388)* is all about the great days and famous names of rock 'n' roll. Its decor is eclectic and includes objects and instruments which, apparently, once belonged to Paul McCartney, Janis Joplin, and other such legends. This bar, also a restaurant, has a splendid view of the Sky Dome.

Peel Pub *(276 King St. W., ☎977-0003)* is like one big student party! Its cheap beer will quench the most extreme thirst. Food is served until late at night.

Horizons Barn, located at the top of the **CN Tower**, offers a breathtaking view of Toronto's skyline, which, at night, is a riot of light. A must-see spectacle.

If you have not had the chance to stay at the **Royal York**, but want to admire its timeless elegance, you can enjoy a drink in one of its bars. Both the Lobby Bar and the Library Bar give a taste of the classic charm of this turn-of-the-century hotel. An excellent place to sit and relax before catching a train at Union Station located directly in front of the hotel.

In front of Roy Thompson Hall, **Elephant & Castle Pub** *(212 King St. W., ☎598-4455)* offers all the warm charm typical of an authentic English pub.
If you are looking for something more than just a bar, **Yuk Yuk's Comedy Cabaret** *(2335 Yonge St., ☎967-6425)* has live comedy performances sure to tickle the funny bone.

Local and international celebreties give shows at the **Montreal Bistro-Jazz Club** *(65 Sherbourne St., ☎363-0179)*, considered one of the city's finest jazz clubs.

Top O' the Senator *(253 Victoria St., ☎364-7517)*, a jazz bar which first opened its doors in the 1920s, is a real Toronto institution. International jazz stars perform regularly here. Inside the same building is the Victory Lounge, a cigar lounge with a quieter ambiance.

The Bamboo *(312 Queen St. W., ☎593-5771)* is the choice venue for Caribbean music, especially reggae, salsa, and calypso. At 10pm, this pretty restaurant is transformed into a bar, attracting a varied clientele. Although the dance floor is somewhat small, this is made up for by the always-exhilarating music.

While **Sassafraz** *(100 Cumberland St., ☎964-2222)* is best known as a stylish restaurant, it is also popular with a young, hip, urban crowd for its great ambiance and exceptional view of Yorkville.

C'est what? *(67 Front St. E., ☎867-9499)*, located in the basement of an older building, is a charming pub with regular live blues, jazz, funk and rock performances. Great selection of beer and scotch.

Gay Bars

Woody's *(467 Church St., ☎972-0887)* is a popular meeting place for gay men. Set in the heart of the gay village, the atmosphere is casual and friendly.

Boots/Kurbash *(592 Sherbourne, ☎921-0665)* is a popular and intense dance bar frequented by a gay and straight clientele. Theme nights include fetish nights and other intriguing possibilities.

Cultural Activities, Sport and Festivals

Concert Halls and Theatres

Roy Thompson Hall
60 Simcoe St., ☎593-4828.
The Toronto Symphony Orchestra and Toronto Mendelssohn Choir both perform in the exceptional acoustic of this hall.

When the big names in theatre come to Toronto they come to the following three theatres:

Royal Alexandra
360 King St. W., ☎872-3333.

Princess of Wales Theatre
300 King St. W., ☎872-1212.

Pantages Theatre
263 Yonge St., ☎872-3333.
Home of the lavish production of *The Phantom of the Opera*

Young People's Theatre
165 Front St. E., ☎864-9732.
This is the only theatre in Canada devoted solely to children.

Massey Hall
178 Victoria St., ☎593-4828.

O'Keefe Centre
1 Front St. E., ☎872-2262.
For presentations by the Canadian Opera Company and the National Ballet of Canada.

Canadian Opera Company
239 Front St., ☎363-8231 or 393-7469

For popular music concerts:

SkyDome
1 Blue Jay Way, ☎963-3513.

Maple Leaf Gardens
60 Carlton St., ☎977-1641.

Exhibition Stadium
☎393-6000.

Tickets for these and other shows are available through:

Ticketmaster
☎870-8000.

T.O. Tix
at the corner of Yonge and Dundas streets, ☎596-8211.
Reduced-price tickets for same-day musical and theatrical events.

Sporting Events

The **Blue Jays,** the only Canadian team to have carved out a place of honour in major league baseball, are part of the American league and play at the Skydome (see p 162). A young team with a lot of talent, including Carlos Delgado.

The **Maple Leafs** are one of the six original teams in the National Hockey League (NHL), and have been playing at their new home in the Air Canada Centre since February 1999. After ranking near the bottom of the league for the past several seasons, the team now has a very respectable lineup thanks to players like Mats Sundin and goalie Curtis Joseph.

The **Argonauts** belong to the Canadian Football League and fight it out at the Skydome, where the Blue Jays also play. This major player in Canadian football lost their star quarterback Doug Flutie to the National Football League (American Football) in 1998, when he joined the Buffallo Bills.

The **Raptors**, meanwhile, take on the best teams in the National Basketball League at the Air Canada Centre. Apart from the Vancouver Grizzlies, they are the only Canadian teams in this American league.

Early June is the time for the **Toronto International Dragon Boat Race Festival**, when Lake Ontario hosts these historic races, ☎364-0046.

The Molson Indy
Mid-July, ☎260-9800.

Canadian International Marathon
End of October, ☎972-1062.

TORONTO

Festivals

Canadian Springtime Craft Show & Sale
End of March, ☎960-3680.

North by Northeast
Mid-June, ☎469-0986.
More than 300 folk, rock, blues and funk groups gather in the bars and venues of Toronto for this music festival.

Benson & Hedges International Fireworks Festival
Mid-June through July, ☎442-3667.

Du Maurier Downtown Jazz
End of June, ☎363-8717 or 363-5200.

Caribana (Caribbean festival)
End of July and beginning of August, ☎925-5435.

Canadian National Exhibition
End of August/beginning of September, ☎393-6000.

International Film Festival
beginning of September, ☎967-7371. For tickets: Film Festival Box Office, ☎968-FILM.

 SHOPPING

Toronto is the perfect place for window-shopping along busy streets lined with elegant boutiques and little shops that sell interesting merchandise. You can find just about anything in the city's myriad stores and shopping centres. However, to find exactly what you're looking for, you have to know where to go. This section provides you with brief descriptions of some of the stores found in the various neighbourhoods. While the list is, of course, far from complete, it will point you in the right direction where you will find that perfect buy.

Tour A: The Waterfront

Your first stop should be the **Queen's Way Shops** (207 Queen's Way) on Queen's Way. This shopping centre is set up in the old warehouse district and contains numerous boutiques.

Antiques

If you have the time and enjoy rummaging through old-fashioned items, antiques and other treasures from another era, head to the **Harbourfront Antique Market** (390 Queen Quay W., ☎260-2626) which has some hundred antique sellers, some with very handsome wares.

Crafts

For aboriginal handicrafts, try **Arctic Canada** (207 Queen Quay W., ☎260-7889), a shop that sells attractive pieces, especially prints and sculptures, as well as leather and fur apparel.

Beer, Wine and Liquor

Two useful addresses to remember: **Beer Store** (350 Queen Quay W.) For beer, and the **Liquor Control Board of Ontario** (2 Cooper St., corner of Yonge St. and Queens Quay) for wine and liqueurs.

Clothing

Travellers have been coming to **Tilley Endurables** (Queen`s Quay Shop, ☎203-0463) for a long time. The line has a reputation for designing clothes that are perfectly suited to travellers' needs, made with waterproof material that don't wrinkle. Tilley's heavy-duty hats are perhaps the most popular.

Tour B: The Theatre and Financial Districts

Outdoors

Mountain Equipment Co-op *(400 King St. W.,* ☎*340-2667)* frequented by outdoor buffs who know where to find quality merchandise (backpacks, clothing, sports equipment) at good prices.

Tour C: Queen West and St. Lawrence

Eaton Centre *(220 Yonge St.)* is so well-known in Toronto that it has almost become an attraction in itself. With some 320 stores, it is a must for shopping of any kind. Among the more interesting boutiques are Harry Rosen, Mexx, Banana Republic and Gap for clothes, Bowrings for home furnishings, Disney Store for children and the Liquor Control Board of Ontario for wine and liqueurs.

Near the Eaton Centre is another Toronto institution, **The Bay** *(176 Yonge St.)* department store, with nine storeys bursting with all kinds of items.

Gifts

Selling books, decorative items and jewellery, the gift shop of the **Art Gallery of Ontario** *(317 Dundas St. W.,* ☎*979-6648)* is worth checking out. High quality items can be found in the several rooms, including unique gift ideas for adults and children of all ages.

Music

Sam the Record Man *(347 Yonge St.)* is a good place for rock, pop, rap – and pretty much any other musical style.

Clothing

Boutiques catering to a young and well-off clientele can be found along Queen Street. Among them, La Cache is especially well-known for their hats and scarves and cotton and linen clothing for women, while Gap clothes and Roots leather jackets and wool sweaters are also popular.

Tour F: Bloor and Yorkville

Bloor Street

Holt Renfrew has one of the best selections of men's, women's and children's fashions by famous Canadian, American and European designers, as well as beauty products and quality accessories.

Clothing

Bloor Street is a succession of clothing stores, including some of the world's biggest names in fashion. Your eye will inevitably be attracted by the alluring window displays. Among the most prestigious shops are **Chanel Boutique** *(131 Bloor St. W.,* ☎*925-2577)*, **Max Mara** *(131 Bloor St. W.,* ☎*928-1884)*, **Emporio Armani** *(50 Bloor St. W.,* ☎*960-2978)* and **Hermès** *(131 Bloor St. W.,* ☎*968-8626)*.

Other stores also have stylish collections, many with a more relaxed look. Among them, **Banana Republic** *(80 Bloor St. W.,* ☎*515-0018)*, **Club Monaco** *(157 Bloor St. W.,* ☎*591-8837)*, **Gap** *(Bloor St. W.)* and

Roots *(95A Bloor St. W., ☎323-3289)* are sure to have something that appeals to you, and shopping here won't break the bank.

Books

Toronto has its share of mega-bookstores where you can spend hours browsing and still not have had enough time to check out everything. Two such establishments are located in this area: **Chapter's** *(110 Bloor St. W., ☎920-9299)* and **Indigo Books, Music and Café** *(55 Bloor St. W., ☎925-3536)* whose superb design is bound to dazzle you.

Beer, Wine and Liquor

To stock up on beer, wine and liqueurs, go to the **Liquor Control Board of Ontario** *(55 Bloor St. W., Manulife Centre)*.

Jewellery

Bloor Street has three elegant jewellers: **Birks** *(55 Bloor St. W., ☎922-2266)*, **Cartier Boutique** *(101 Bloor St. W., ☎967-1785)* and **Tiffany & Co.** *(85 Bloor St. W., ☎921-3900)*. You can't go wrong no matter which one you visit, since all of them offer a beautiful selection of jewellery, including watches, bracelets and glittering gems.

Gifts

You can realize your zaniest dreams at **The ROM Shops** *(100 Queen's Park Cresc., ☎586-5551)* which sells some of the museum's collection. Of course, the items for sale are reproductions of the "real thing," but they are painstakingly crafted and make fabulous gifts. Books, jewellery and decorative objects are also for sale.

The Gardiner Museum *(111 Queen's Park Cresc.)* is known for its magnificent collection of porcelain and pottery, and draws collectors and afficionados. The gift shop caters to this clientele with a lovely selection of porcelain and ceramic pieces by contemporary artists.

Home Decorations

Lalique is a French jeweller and designer who became known at the turn of the century for his moulded glass objects. His name lives on through his collection of glass works (vases, lamps, table settings) that will accentuate the decor of the most elegant home. In Toronto, you can find some of these masterpieces at **Lalique Boutique** *(131 Bloor St. W., ☎515-9191)*.

Discount Stores

Known for half a century for the place to find bargain deals on merchandise of all sorts, **Honest Ed's** *(581 Bloor St. W., ☎537-1574)* is an absolute must for anyone looking to save. Here you'll find a huge inventory of a wide assortment of items, including everything from food to clothing.

Leather Goods

Over the years, the name **Louis Vuitton** *(100 Bloor St. W., ☎968-3993)* has become synonymous with quality luggage and leather goods. It goes without saying that the prices are upscale.

Music

Looking for a new CD? You are almost guaranteed to find it at **HMV** *(50 Bloor St. W., ☎324-9979)* which has a boggling selection of albums representing just about every musical genre.

Yorkville Avenue

Yorkville is the best area in Toronto for walking around and stopping in at charming boutiques. On colder days, you can opt instead for the **Hazelton Lanes** *(55 Avenue Rd.)* shopping centre which has shops like Mondi, Polo, Ralph Lauren and Versace.

Antiques

Hazelton Lanes is one of Toronto's prettiest streets, largely because of the charming boutiques that are found here. Among them there are several antique dealers whose wares are worth browsing through if you are interested in period furniture.

Crafts

Whether you are looking for mocassins, leather or fur apparel, prints or sculptures by aboriginal artists, you are sure to find it at **The Arctic Bear** *(125 Yorkville)*.

Yorkville has several shops worth checking out if you like native art: **The Guild Shop** *(118 Cumberland St., ☎921-1721)* and **Feheley Fine Arts** *(14 Hazelton Lanes, ☎323-1373)*.

Antique Prints

There is nothing ordinary about **Antique Prints** *(Hazelton Lanes)* which has a collection of vintage prints, some of which are over 100 years old. You are sure to find something you like among the beautiful pieces that add a wonderful classic touch to any home.

Toys

The Toy Shop is crammed with educational toys, dolls, teddy bears and doll houses with miniature furniture – in short, with everything to delight the little ones.

Clothing

Successful Montréal women's clothing designer **Marie Saint-Pierre** *(161 Cumberland St., ☎513-0067)* has opened a little shop in the Queen City some of her most stylish designs are sold.

Children's Clothing

You can find some designers who cater specifically to children – and their parents, who are sure to swoon over their creations. **Caramel Camels** *(Hazelton Lanes)* has a good selection of apparel for the little princes and princesses. Careful, though: the prices are sky-high.

TORONTO

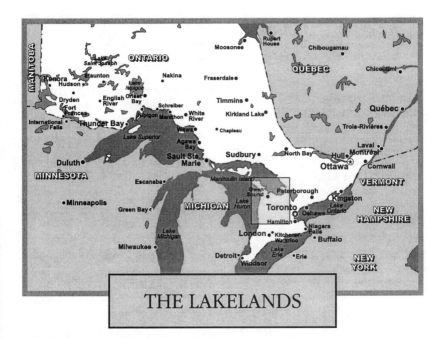

THE LAKELANDS

For many years, the area north of Toronto, called the "Lakelands," has been popular with visitors seeking a respite from the fast pace of city life in beautiful natural surroundings. There are three distinct regions in this territory, each with its own extraordinary scenery. The first region, the Muskoka Lakes, is closest to Toronto and offers high quality tourist facilities that blend into the landscape. Luxurious residences, harbours for pleasure boats and charming villages are the main attractions in this area where rich Torontonians have their cottages. The region further north borders on magnificent Georgian Bay. This area attracts visitors all year long because, in addition to its lovely beaches, it has the only downhill ski centre for many kilometres. It is also well known as the heart of the territory that was once occupied by the Huron Nation. Historical restorations help explain what this aboriginal people's social structure, customs and traditions were like before

it was destroyed after the arrival of the first Europeans. The third region, the eastern shore of Lake Huron, has some pleasant little towns. However, its main attractions are the magnificent beaches at the edge of the enormous lake that stretches as far as the eye can see.

There are three suggested tours for this region: Tour A: "Barrie and the Muskoka Lakes," Tour B: "Around Georgian Bay," and Tour C: "Along the Shores of Lake Huron". All three offer lots of lovely countryside.

 FINDING YOUR WAY AROUND

Tour A: Barrie and the Muskoka Lakes

The tour starts at Barrie, about a hundred kilometres north of Toronto, then continues north, through the towns of

Orillia, Gravenhurst, Bracebridge and
Huntsville.

By Car

Take the 400 from Toronto to Barrie,
then pick up the 11.

Bus and Train Stations

The train to North Bay runs through this
region, via Barrie and Orillia. Once
again, buses are a very efficient and
inexpensive means of travelling short
distances, since they stop in many
towns.

Orillia: 150 Front St.,
☎(705) 326-4101.

Gravenhurst: 150 Second Street,
☎(705) 687-2301.

Huntsville: At the corner of Main and
Centre.

Tour B: Around Georgian Bay

Bus Stations

Owen Sound: 1020 3rd Ave. E.,
☎(519) 376-5375.

Collingwood: 70 Hurontario,
☎(705) 445-4231.

Tour C: Along the Shores of Lake Huron

By Car

This tour follows the shores of Lake
Huron from Grand Bend to
Southampton on Hwy 21.

PRACTICAL INFORMATION

Tour A: Barrie and the Muskoka Lakes

Area Code: 705.

Tourist Information

Simcoe County Building
Midhurst, ON, L0L 1X0, ☎726-8502,
≠726-3991.

Tour B: Around Georgian Bay

Area code: 519 or **705.** The former is
indicated in this chapter. If no area
code is indicated, it is 705.

Tourist Information

HTA - Simcoe County Building
1110 Highway 26, Midhurst, ON,
L0L 1X0, ☎726-8502 or
☎(800) 487-6642, ≠726-3991.

Tour C: Along the Shores of Lake Huron

Area Code: 519

Tourist Information

**Southwestern Ontario Travel
Association**
4023 Meadowbrook Dr., Suite 112,
London, ON, N6L 1E7,
☎(519) 652-1391 or ☎(800) 661-6804,
≠(519) 652-0533.

HTA - Simcoe County Building
1110 Highway 26, Midhurst, ON,
L0L 1X0, ☎726-8502 or
☎(800) 487-6642, ≠726-3991.

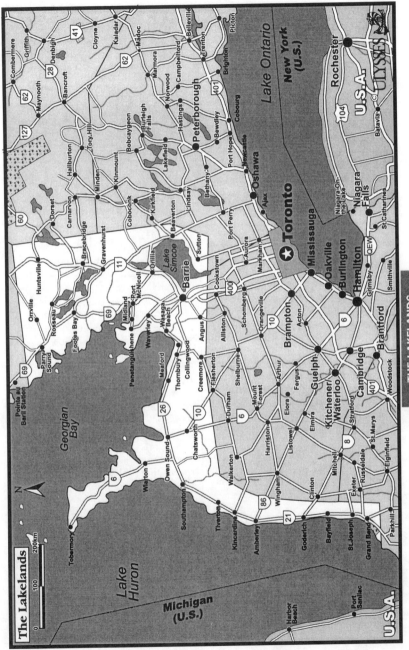

EXPLORING

Tour A: Barrie and the Muskoka Lakes ★★

For nearly a century now, the lovely Muskoka Lakes region has been attracting vacationers, who come here for the charming villages and unobtrusive but well-developed tourist infrastructure. This tour will take you from Toronto to Barrie and Orillia, and then farther north, into the Muskoka Lakes region, from Gravenhurst to Huntsville.

Take the 400 from Toronto to Barrie.

Barrie

Outside the greater Toronto area, the highway continues north along Lake Simcoe. It skirts round Kempenfelt Bay, which stretches westward like a long arm of the sea, at the end of which lies Barrie, the most populous town in the region. Although the outskirts of Barrie can seem somewhat stark at first sight, you will be pleasantly surprised by the downtown area, which is attractively located alongside the bay.

Those fond of water sports can head to **Centennial Park**, whose lovely sandy beach is often packed on hot summer days.

The **Simcoe County Museum** *($4; Mon to Sat 9am to 4:30pm, Sun 1pm to 4:30pm; Route 26, Midhurst, ☎728-3721)*, located some 8 km north of town, offers a survey of local history, starting with the region's first inhabitants and continuing up to the 20th century. The reconstruction of an 1840's commercial street is by far the most interesting of the major displays.

Orillia ★

The site of present-day Orillia, located at the meeting point of Lakes Simcoe and Couchiching, was inhabited by Ojibwa Indians for many years. Around 1838, the natives were driven out of the region by European colonists, at which point an urban area began to develop. Surrounded by woods and water, it was naturally geared toward the forest industry and agriculture. Then, toward the end of the 19th century, another lucrative industry began to flourish here: tourism. Ever since, visitors have been flocking to Orillia, lured by its attractive location on the shores of Lake Couchiching. The town also became known through the writings of Stephen Leacock (1869-1944), who lived here.

In 1908, Stephen Leacock purchased a plot of land on Lake Couchiching and had a magnificent house built. At the **Stephen Leacock Museum ★** *($7; Jun to Sep, every day 10am to 7pm; Sep to Jun, Mon to Fri 10am to 5pm; turn off Hwy. 12B at Forest Ave., follow this road to Museum Dr., 50 Museum Dr., ☎329-1908, ≈326-5578, www.trans data.ca/~leacock)*, now open to the public, visitors can see where the author wrote some of his works, and even examine a few of the actual manuscripts. The rooms are decorated with period furniture.

Leacock taught history and economics at McGill University (Montreal), but is known primarily for his literary output, characterized by wit and irony. *Sunshine Sketches of a Little Town* will be of particular interest to visitors, since the stories take place in a fictional town called Mariposa which was later revealed to be the town of Orillia.

Near the marina, stretched along Lake Couchiching, is a beautiful **park ★** with a promenade, a few benches and a small beach. The *Island Princess*, which docks at the marina, takes visitors on cruises on the lake.

The **Orillia Opera House** *(at the corner of West and Mississaga, ☎326-8011)*, a red, turreted building built in the late 19th century, towers over Mississaga Street in downtown Orillia. Don't be fooled by its name, though; only plays are presented here.

Gravenhurst ★

Gravenhurst was once a modest lumberjack village. Like the neighbouring towns, however, it has been reaping the benefits of the public's infatuation with this region since the late 19th century. Visitors began coming here for the lovely natural setting and built the beautiful Victorian homes that still grace the streets. As the gateway to the Muskoka Lakes region, Gravenhurst welcomes throngs of summer visitors attracted by its peaceful atmosphere and air of days gone by. Gravenhurst lies on the shores of Lake Muskoka, short cruises of the lake aboard the *R.M.S. Segwun* are offered (see p 223).

A variety of activities can be enjoyed at **Gull Lake** (see p 232).

Gravenhurst was the birthplace of the eminent Canadian doctor Norman Bethune. To learn more about his accomplishments, stop by **Bethune Memorial House** *($2.25; mid-May to Oct, every day 10am to 5pm; Nov to Apr, Mon to Fri 10am to 5pm; 235 John St. N., ☎687-4261)*, where he grew up. Here, you'll find articles relating to different aspects of his life, as well as some of the technical innovations for which he was responsible, including the mobile blood transfusion unit.

Norman Bethune

Norman Bethune (1890-1939) was not your usual doctor, and his social ideals drove him to work abroad, alongside the Spanish army. There, he made a name for himself by inventing mobile blood transfusion units, which were extremely useful during the war, since they made it possible to care for the wounded in the field. In 1938, he joined the Chinese revolutionary army and was placed in charge of the medical unit. This phase of his life was destined to be a short one, however, for he died the following year, at the age of 49, of blood poisoning.

Bracebridge

Located on the banks of the Muskoka River, Bracebridge is a very pretty town graced with elegant houses and attractive shops and centred around a magnificent park shaded by stately trees. At the edge of town, the Muskoka River empties into Lake Muskoka. Visitors are well served here, as the charming streets are lined with comfortable hotels and B&Bs.

Huntsville ★

Huntsville is a picturesque town located at the meeting point of Vernon and Fairy Lakes. In order to make the most of the setting, the downtown area has been laid out on the shores of both lakes, which are linked by a small bridge. On one side, you can browse through charming shops, while on the other, you can enjoy lunch on one of several attractive waterfront terraces. The town has a few decent places to stay, but most visitors opt for the su-

THE LAKELANDS

perb hotel complexes in the surrounding countryside.

The **Muskoka Pioneer Village** *($7; 10am to 4pm mid-May to Jun and Sep, Sat and Sun, Jul and Aug, every day; Brunel Rd., ☎789-7576)* is a reconstruction of an early 19th-century village. It is made up of 18 little buildings, including a smithy, an inn and a general store, where the local settlers' daily life is re-enacted. Although it is less impressive, the museum is open year-round *(free admission)*.

Tour B: Around Georgian Bay ★★

Separated from Lake Huron by the Bruce Peninsula, Georgian Bay is a vast expanse of fresh water. This part of the lake is teeming with fish, and the forested shores are home to a variety of animals. It was naturally an attractive area for the Huron, who established their villages along these shores. Conditions were perfect for their life style of hunting, fishing, agriculture and trade. However, the area was coveted by other aboriginal nations, which led to many territorial disputes. With the arrival of the Europeans in the 17th century, these quarrels turned into full-blown battles that resulted in the annihilation of the Huron Nation. The last Hurons were forced out of the territory. Today, the restored villages teach visitors about the history, customs and traditions of this aboriginal people. In addition to historical attractions, the Georgian Bay area has many delightful vacation towns and beautiful outdoor areas. One such area, the Blue Mountains, has been a favourite with downhill skiers for many years. Georgian Bay is no less popular in the summer, when people head to the water to enjoy outdoor pastimes.

Owen Sound

This little town, formerly known as Sydenham, was renamed after Admiral Owen, who made the first hydrographic studies of Georgian Bay, thus making it safer for boats to sail on the Great Lakes. Although Owen Sound has the advantage of being located alongside this magnificent body of water, with its lovely scenery, a number of factories have been built along part of the shoreline here, giving some sections of town a gloomy look. The more attractive downtown area has rows of red-brick buildings and businesses.

For a stroll through a pleasant stretch of greenery, go to **Harrisson Park ★**, which has picnic tables, a restaurant and a number of ponds with ducks and wild geese paddling about in them.

Owen Sound is also known as the birthplace and childhood home of the great Canadian landscape painter Tom Thomson (1877-1917). The **Tom Thomson Art Gallery ★** *(donations welcome; Mon to Sat 10am to 5pm, Sun noon to 5pm; 840 1st Ave. W., ☎519-376-1932)* is devoted to this artist, whose magnificent paintings reveal a highly personal interpretation of the Canadian wilderness, particularly the Canadian Shield. The museum displays a fine collection of his paintings, as well as a number of works by other Canadian painters, including members of the Group of Seven.

At the **County of Grey-Owen Sound Museum** *($4; Jul and Aug, Mon to Sat 9am to 5pm, Sun 1pm to 5pm; Sep to Jun, Tue to Fri 9am to 5pm, Sat and Sun 1pm to 5pm; 975 6th St. E., ☎519-376-3690)*, visitors can learn about the early settlement of Owen Sound and its surrounding area, from 1815 to 1920.

Head east on Hwy 26.

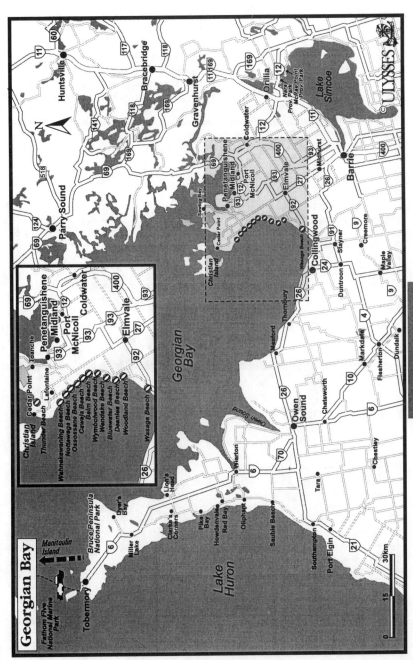

The Niagara Escarpment

The Niagara Escarpement is actually a huge geological basin created about 400 million years ago, when shallow seas covered this area. Over the years, the sea bed became carpeted with coral and bone fragments, which formed a solid layer of dolomite, a calcareous mineral. When the water receded, the dolomite did not erode as rapidly as the rocks below it. Eventually there was nothing left to support it and it collapsed, forming a vast bowl, whose rim runs from New York State all the way to Georgian Bay.

Meaford

The town of Meaford grew up on the shores of Georgian Bay and makes the most of this superb location with its lovely marina that is perfect for strolling and watching the waves. The town also has some attractive houses from the last century that have survived all this time with their charm intact. However it is the annual Georgian Theatre Festival that attracts talented players – and appreciative audiences – to Meaford every summer. In the downtown area, the imposing red-brick **Meaford Opera House** is a must.

Collingwood ★

Collingwood, also located on the shores of Georgian Bay, was an important shipbuilding centre at the beginning of this century. When that industry started to decline, the town managed to capitalize on its location near the Blue Mountains and the lovely beaches on the bay, and develop a prosperous tourist industry. This little town now has everything a vacationer could ask for — pretty shops, a comfortable inn and delicious restaurants. The city has preserved several handsome buildings from the end of the 19th and early 20th centuries. You can admire these stone Victorian houses by taking leisurely strolls through the shady streets. With its attractive beach with a playground for children, **Sunset Park** is a

pleasant spot for spending hot summer days

Collingwood's popularity stems from its proximity to the **Blue Mountain ★★** resort, with its family-oriented downhill ski centre and summertime mountain biking trails, golf course and water slides. There is something for the whole family to enjoy all year round.

The **Collingwood Museum** *(free admission; 9am to 6pm every day, corner of St. Paul St. and Hwy. 26, ☎445-4811, ≈445-9004)* offers a brief overview of the region's development, with particular attention to the shipbuilding industry.

Among the possible outdoor excursions is a visit to the **Scenic Caves** *($7.50; May 1 to Oct 10, at 5pm; from Collingwood, take Blue Mountain Rd. to Scenic Caves Rd. and turn left, ☎446-0256)*. Here, you will get an idea of the geological formations in the region. Descending into limestone caves that were formed by glaciers over millions of years, you will be able to have a close look at specific rock formations. Above ground, the site has been landscaped and offers some magnificent scenic views of Georgian Bay and Collingwood.

From Collingwood, you may continue east toward Midland by taking Route 92 east. You can also head south to

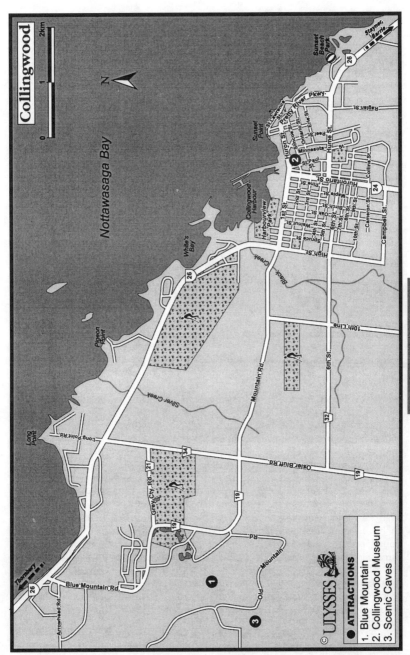

Collingwood

Nottawasaga Bay

N

0 1 2km

© ULYSSES

ATTRACTIONS

1. Blue Mountain
2. Collingwood Museum
3. Scenic Caves

THE LAKELANDS

larger cities such as Kitchener-Waterloo (see p 237). On the way, you will come across charming hamlets like Creemore. Take Route 24 south to Maple Valley, then follow Route 9 east.

Creemore ★

If there is one single most charming village in this corner of Ontario, it has to be Creemore. With its tree-lined streets and majestic 18th-century Victorian houses, the town's charm is simply irresistible. The downtown area is just as seductive: interesting shops and attractive restaurants entice customers with inviting window displays. This peaceful village invites you to steal a few hours to enjoy the atmosphere of a bygone era and have a pleasant lunch.

Wasaga Beach ★★

Magnificent Wasaga Beach, a strip of sand stretching about 14 km along Georgian Bay, which has been protected by the creation of a provincial park, is a virtual paradise for vacationers who enjoy water sports. Although there are some lovely summer homes along the beach, part of it has unfortunately been overdeveloped, so a jumble of cheap-looking souvenir shops and unattractive motels detracts somewhat from the beauty of the landscape. This area is nonetheless a good place to have fun, and is popular with the younger crowd who enjoy its lively atmosphere.

The **Nancy Island Historic Site** *(mid-Jun to early Sep, every day 10am to 6pm; Moseley St., for info call Wasaga Beach Provincial Park ☎429-2516 or 429-2728)* tells the story of the *HMS Nancy*, a sailing ship that went down in the bay in 1814 during the War of

1812. In addition to seeing the wreckage of the ship, visitors will learn about 19th-century fur-traders and their way of life.

Wasaga Beach Provincial Park *(P.O. Box 183, L0L 2P0, ☎429-2516)* protects a long, magnificent strip of golden sand along Georgian Bay, where you can lounge about or go swimming in the rather chilly water. Although the beach itself is extremely pleasant, the surrounding area has unfortunately been developed in a rather haphazard manner.

Take the 92, then turn left onto the 93.

Midland ★★

Now a peaceful little town, Midland once lay at the heart of Huronia, just a few kilometres from the site where the fearsome Iroquois martyrized and killed a large number of Hurons, as well as the Jesuit priests who had come here to convert them to Christianity. Thanks to several historical reconstructions, one of which is particularly fascinating, visitors can relive the colony's early days. The town itself is very pretty, with several hotels, and is a good place to stay in the Georgian Bay area.

Although it is not as big as Sainte-Marie Among the Hurons, the **Huronia Museum and Huron Indian Village** *($6.42; King St. S., Little Lake Park, P.O. Box 638, L4R 4P4, ☎526-2844, ☎527-6622)* nevertheless offers an introduction to Huron society, complete with a reconstructed Amerindian village.

You can board the ***Miss Midland*** *(adult $14, 2.5 hours; town dock, ☎526-0161)* for a cruise in the bay, during which you can take in the magnificent sight of the 30,000 Islands.

The other local attractions lie 5 km east of town. Unfortunately, no public transportation is available, so visitors who don't have a car will have to take a taxi.

Standing by the side of the highway is the **Martyr's Shrine** *(Hwy. 12, near Sainte-Marie)*, a Catholic sanctuary dedicated to the first Canadian martyrs, including Jean de Brébeuf, Gabriel Lalemant and Antoine Daniel. The fascinating historic site of Sainte-Marie Among the Hurons lies on the opposite side of the road.

Sainte-Marie Among the Hurons ★★ *($9.75; May to Oct every day 10am to 5pm; Hwy. 12, 5 km east of Midland, ☎526-7838)*. When colonists first arrived here, the Georgian Bay region was inhabited by Hurons, who were among the first native nations in Ontario to come into contact with Europeans (French explorer Étienne Brûlé came here around 1610). The natives and the French were on such good terms with each other that Jesuit missionaries came to the region in 1620 to try to convert the Hurons to Christianity, and founded a mission here in 1639. Their efforts had profound repercussions on Huron society, which split into two groups — those who had been converted and those who hadn't. The resulting disputes upset the social structure. In addition, many natives fell victim to illnesses brought over by the Europeans (influenza, smallpox, etc.), further destabilizing the society.

The Hurons were thus in a weakened state when it came time to fight the ferocious Iroquois, who were determined to take control of the fur trade. In 1648, the Iroquois attacked the mission, captured, tortured and killed Jesuit missionaries Jean de Brébeuf, Antoine Daniel and Gabriel Lalemant, and massacred the Hurons. In 1649,

the last Hurons and Jesuits abandoned the mission and fled to Quebec City.

Sainte-Marie Among the Hurons is an excellent reconstruction of the mission as it appeared in the 1630s. The site includes the village, its longhouses and the various tools used by the Hurons. Guides in period dress (Jesuit priests, colonists, natives) offer an idea of what daily life was like here. After touring the mission, you can further increase your knowledge of Huron society by visiting the museum located on the premises.

Wye Marsh Wildlife Centre (see p 223).

Continue heading north on the 93.

Penetanguishene

Penetanguishene, a charming little hamlet on the shores of the bay, was originally a trading post. Later, during the War of 1812, British soldiers took refuge here after fleeing the forts that had been seized by the Americans. The village also attracted a certain number of French-speakers, who still make up a small part of the local population.

Discovery Harbour ★ *($5.50; May to Sep, every day 10am to 5pm; 93 Jury Dr., ☎549-8064)* illustrates the naval and military history of this city. The site consists of a rebuilt British naval outpost that stood here between 1817 and 1856. Guides in period costumes will take you through the officers' quarters as they were in 1845, and explain life at the post during that time. Finally, you can take a cruise on the *HMS Tecumseh* or the *HMS Bee*, replicas of ships of the period.

Double back and take a left on the 12, then another left on the 69, which leads to Parry Sound.

Beaver

Parry Sound ★

The coastline of Georgian Bay becomes more and more jagged the farther north you go, its shores notched by the mouths of various rivers. The scenery changes as well, with fertile farmland giving way to the bare rocks and twisted pines that characterize the Canadian Shield. This untamed wilderness has something harsh yet poetic about it, which is sure to linger in your memory. In the 1850s, people began settling here in order to capitalize on the region's vast woodlands, and a small village named Parry Sound developed. The forest industry fuelled the local economy, and the area prospered. Parry Sound is now a perfectly charming vacation spot, as well as the point of departure for cruises around the 30,000 Islands. With its delightful inns and numerous other amenities, this little village the perfect place to relax in complete comfort while enjoying the magnificent scenery of this part of Ontario.

The scenery of the 30,000 islands that dot Georgian Bay is typical of the Canadian Shield, featuring twisted pines and bare rocks of the same type that inspired Tom Thomson and the Group of Seven. In fact, many people have been enchanted by the landscapes here,

including wealthy vacationers, who began purchasing the islands one by one until 1929, when the **Georgian Bay Islands National Park** ★ *(P.O. Box 28, Honey Harbour, POE 1E0, ☎756-2415)* was created in order to keep 59 of them in the public domain. These unspoiled areas are only accessible by boat; if you don't have one, you can take a water taxi from Honey Harbour or one of the private boats that set out from the marinas of coastal towns like Penetanguishene and Midland. The only campsites and hiking trails you'll find are on Beausoleil Island. No matter where you go, however, always make sure to bring along sufficient food and water.

Tour C: Along the Shores of Lake Huron ★

The second-largest body of fresh water in Canada, exceeded in size only by Lake Superior, the 59,800 square kilometres of Lake Huron majestically dominates the landscape on this tour. Pretty little towns that come alive in the summer punctuate this stretch of shoreline. But what visitors really come for are the magnificent long beaches that form an unbroken chain of wide white-sand beaches that are perfect for sunbathing. From Tobermory to Grand Bend,

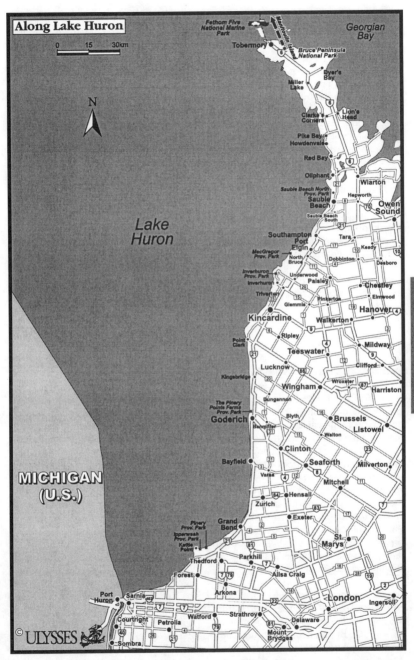

Along Lake Huron

0   15   30km

N

Lake Huron

MICHIGAN (U.S.)

© ULYSSES

Fathom Five National Marine Park

Tobermory

Georgian Bay

Bruce Peninsula National Park

Dyer's Bay

Miller Lake

Lion's Head

Clarke's Corners

Pike Bay
Howdenvale

Red Bay

Oliphant

Wiarton

Sauble Beach North Prov. Park

Hepworth

Sauble Beach

Owen Sound

Sauble Beach South

Southampton
Port Elgin

Tara

Keady

Desboro

MacGregor Prov. Park

North Bruce

Dobbinton

Inverhuron Prov. Park

Underwood

Paisley

Chesley

Inverhuron

Triverton

Glemmis

Pinkerton

Elmwood

Hanover

Kincardine

Walkerton

Ripley

Mildway

Point Clark

Teeswater

Lucknow

Clifford

THE LAKELANDS

Kingsbridge

Wingham

Wroxeter

Harriston

Dungannon

The Pinery Points Farms Prov. Park

Goderich

Blyth

Brussels

Listowel

Benmiller

Walton

Clinton

Bayfield

Seaforth

Milverton

Varna

Mitchell

Zurich

Hensall

Grand Bend

Exeter

St. Marys

Pinery Prov. Park

Ipperwash Prov. Park

Kettle Point

Parkhill

Thedford

Forest

Ailsa Craig

London

Ingersoll

Arkona

Port Huron

Sarnia

Watford

Strathroy

Delaware

Courtright

Petrolia

Mount Brydges

Sombra

this vast territory has everything fans of water sports and huge natural parks could desire.

The first part of this tour winds through the Bruce Peninsula, a long piece of land that is actually a continuation of the Niagara escarpment extending into Lake Huron. At times, this escarpment reaches heights of 100 metres, creating splendid vantage points for admiring the scenery along the winding roads of the peninsula. The peninsula is also rimmed with beaches, to the great delight of those who like swimming and water sports. Next, the route follows the shoreline, where the scenery is equally magnificent, and the beaches are, as always, fantastic.

Only one road crosses the Bruce Peninsula; Route 6 runs from Tobermory to Wiarton.

Tobermory

With fewer than 1000 residents, the little village of Todermory stands at the far end of the Bruce Peninsula. Nevertheless, it becomes a hub of frenetic activity in summertime, with vacationers thronging to its port to take advantage of the facilities and, above all, to enjoy the inviting waters of Lake Huron. The town also gets lively when the ferry to Manitoulin Island arrives and leaves. Many visitors stop here on the way to the superb Fathom Five National Park that includes the renowned Flowerpot Island. Others wind up here after a long and fascinating hike, since this is the end of the Bruce Trail.

Bruce Peninsula National Park ★★
(P.O. Box 189, Tobermory, N0H 2R0, ☎519-596-2233) covers a large portion of the 80-km peninsula that stretches into Lake Huron, forming part of the shoreline of Georgian Bay. Within this vast park, there are tracts of private

property as well as stretches of untouched wilderness where you can find a mixed forest and unusual flowers, including about forty different kinds of orchids. The animal life is no less fascinating; the park is home to deer, beavers, the dangerous massasauga (a venomous snake), and as many as 170 species of birds. You can venture into the heart of the park on one of a number of hiking trails, including the Bruce Trail (see p 223) and the Cyprus Lake trails. Visitors also have access to beaches (on Cyprus Lake and Dorcas Bay) and campsites.

A series of islands, 19 in all, trail off the tip of the Bruce Peninsula; these are actually the last peaks of the Niagara Escarpment. These limestone masses have eroded over the years, and now form odd-looking rocky pillars, the best known and most strangely shaped of all being Flowerpot Island. **Fathom Five National Marine Park ★★** *(P.O. Box 189, Tobermory, N0H 2R0, ☎519-596-2233)* encompasses this entire area.

All these rocky islets are completely wild, except for Flowerpot Island, where campsites and paths have been cleared. Hidden around them lie the wrecks of a number of ships that went down in the sometimes treacherous waters of Lake Huron in the late 19th and early 20th centuries. You can take part in a scuba diving excursion or go for a ride on a glass-bottomed boat to view these sunken ships.

Wiarton

The first good-sized village you will come to on your tour of the Bruce Peninsula, Wiarton has some attractive little red-brick houses and can be considered a pleasant first stop on your visit to the region. There is also a port

Flowerpot Island

THE LAKELANDS

nearby, as well as a long, lovely sandy beach.

From Wiarton, take Route 13 to Sauble Beach.

Sauble Beach

A resort village has developed haphazardly along this magnificent sandy beach ★, which stretches 11 km. Unfortunately, the sad-looking little houses do not exactly enhance the natural beauty of the place. In any case, all activity here is centred around the beach, which is sure to appeal to visitors looking for a lively atmosphere.

Southampton

The first small town along Lake Huron, Southampton gives you a good indication of the scenery in store for you on the second part of the tour: a little cluster of houses and businesses in cozy proximity to a wonderful promenade set up along the lake. You will want to spend hours here watching the passing boats, or the sun as it goes down in myriad shades of orange. The entire town seems to be oriented towards the sparkling waves. The town also boasts of a long beach rimmed with dunes that shelter a rich ecosystem. But its reputation rests on its lighthouses, in particular the popular **Chantry Island Lighthouse**, which has watched the traffic on the lake for ages. This lighthouse was renovated in 1998 in order to create the Lighthouse Keeper's Home Museum.

Port Elgin

Port Elgin is another typical little resort town, with nothing particularly charming about it, aside from its lovely, long sandy beach, which is packed on hot summer days. Its beach is all the more popular because the water is calm; perfect for family outings.

Kincardine

Kincardine is also attractively located alongside a superb sandy beach washed by relatively warm waters that are perfect for swimming. The town itself is a typical pretty little waterside resort with an attractive marina that is a pleasant place to go for a stroll and watch the boats off in the distance.

Goderich ★

Between 1820 and 1830, the British government, concerned about poverty on the British Isles and the large number of immigrants to the region from the United States, attempted to increase colonization of Upper-Canada. It set up a grant system to encourage emigration to its possessions in North America. These subsidies resulted in the creation of enterprises like The Canada Company, which bought up several hundred thousand hectares of land, including some 400,000 hectares along Lake Huron, and used every means possible to convince colonists to settle in the area. This is how the city of Goderich came into being in 1827. The city still has several elegant residences that date from the 19th century, especially in the area close to the lake. There are also museums, including the **Huron County Museum** *($4; Mon to Fri, 10am to 4:30 pm; 110 North St., ☎519-524-2686)*, that tell the stories of the early colonists. While this part of the city has great appeal for tourists, the outskirts of town give an entirely different impression. The main highways leading into town are bordered with fast food restaurants and large uninteresting stores.

Bayfield ★

Tall trees, pretty houses, some of them over 100 years old, a delightful inn and a few antique shops... That about sums up this charming little hamlet, which is sure to appeal to romantic souls in search of villages with a 19th-century look about them. In addition to streets that seem to have been untouched for decades, Bayfield has a busy port where you can relax and observe boats of all sizes.

Grand Bend

This little village of fewer than 800 inhabitants undergoes a transformation come summertime, when its magnificent beach attracts scores of water sports enthusiasts, and hungry vacationers flock to the fast-food restaurants lining its main street. The town is essentially limited to these two areas, and would surely go unnoticed if it weren't for its superb stretch of golden sand. Its surrounding area is of greater interest, however. Here, you'll find a magnificent pine forest, part of which is protected by the superb Pinery Provincial Park.

The **Pinery Provincial Park ★** *(R.R. 2, NOM 1T0, ☎519-243-3099)* was created in order to protect a magnificent forest of stately conifers on the shores of Lake Huron, south of Grand Bend. You can explore this forest by foot or on skis, since trails are maintained here year-round. Water sports enthusiasts will enjoy the lovely sandy beaches. Camping.

You can stay on Route 21 until the intersection with Route 7, which goes to Sarnia (see p 290).

 # OUTDOOR ACTIVITIES

 ## Hiking

Tour B: Around Georgian Bay

One hiking trail follows the railroad from Collingwood to Meaford-Heberg; in the winter, it becomes a cross-country ski trail. The 32-km **Georgian Trail** runs along the Niagara Escarpment.

Tour C: Along the Shores of Lake Huron

Part of the Bruce Trail runs through Bruce Peninsula National Park, alongside the cliffs overlooking Georgian Bay. There are a number of other trails in the park as well, including four in the Cyprus Lake area. The 7-km Cyprus Lake Trail loops around the lake, while the other three lead to the shores of the peninsula, where you can take in a magnificent panoramic view of the cliffs and Georgian Bay (all three intersect with the Bruce Trail).

 Bicycling

Tour C: Along the Shores of Lake Huron

A brochure entitled *Cycling Lake Huron Shoreline*, published in collaboration with the Lake Huron Shoreline Tourist Committee, suggests several possible itineraries in the Port Elgin and Kincardine areas. These tours are a good way to take in the area's beautiful scenery. Some are 8 km-long and suitable for all levels of cyclists, while others cover nearly 80 km and require greater preparation.

To obtain a copy of the brochure, call:

Kincardine Tourism Information
☎(519) 396-2731

Port Elgin Tourist Information
☎(519) 832-2332

 Bird-watching

Tour B: Around Georgian Bay

Despite their lowly reputation, swamps play a vital role in the survival of an entire ecosystem. The dual purpose of the **Wye Marsh Wildlife Center ★** *($5; late May to Sep, every day 10am to 6pm, until 4pm during the rest of the year; Hwy. 12, near Sainte-Marie Among the Hurons, ☎526-7809)* is to protect the marshes in this area and increase public awareness of the importance and fragility of this fascinating world. There are trails through the woods and the swamps so that visitors can observe all sorts of birds like chickadees some of which get along particularly well with human beings, and will not hesitate to eat seeds out of your hand.

 Scuba Diving

Tour C: Along the Shores of Lake Huron

Fathom Five National Marine Park, located at the tip of Bruce Peninsula, has everything scuba divers could ask for: clear waters, islands, caves (some underwater) and ship wrecks. Excursions start at the Tobermory dock.

 Cruises

Tour A: Barrie and the Muskoka Lakes

The *Island Princess* offers cruises on **Lake Couchiching** out of **Orillia**:

Orillia Boat Cruise
At the foot of Mississaga St., ☎325-2628, winter ☎538-0910; $13.50, www.obcruise.com

In **Gravenhurst**, you can set out to discover some of the beautiful scenery of the **Muskoka Lakes** on a real 19th century steamboat (reservations recommended).

R.M.S Segwun
Town pier, ☎687-6667; about $20

Tour B: Around Georgian Bay

A cruise around the Georgian Bay Islands (from Midland, Penetanguishene or Parry Sound) is a wonderful opportunity to get a taste of magnificent scenery.

PMCL Cruises
30,000 Island Boat Cruise
Municipal Dock, Midland, ☎526-0161, www.pmcl.on.ca/

Georgian Queen cruises
town dock, Penetanguishene, ☎549-7795; $14.

Island Queen
Municipal Dock, Parry Sound, ☎746-2311 or (800) 506-2628; $17.

From Penetanguishene, you can take to the waves on splendid sailboats, or ride the *HMS Tecumseh* and the *HMS Bee*, replicas of period ships. Make reservations in advance: the boats are not always in port *(93 Jury Dr., ☎549-8064)*.

Tour C: Along the Shores of Lake Huron

Less daring types and those who don't have a scuba diving certificate can still explore the depths of Lake Huron from aboard the **Great Blue Heron** *(departures 11am and 2:30pm; Tobermory, Little Tub Harbour, ☎519-596-2999)*, a glass-bottomed boat.

 ## Horseback Riding

Tour A: Barrie and the Muskoka Lakes

The stables at the Deerhurst Resort offer trail rides through the lovely forest around the **Muskoka Lakes**.

Deerhurst Riding Stable
R.R. 4, Huntsville, ☎789-6411, ext. 4335; one hour, adults $35.

 # Cross-country Skiing

Tour C: Along the Shores of Lake Huron

The Bruce Trail is maintained during winter, so that skiers can make the long journey all the way across southwest Ontario.

There are also trails in certain parks, like the **Pinery Provincial Park** *(Grand Bend, ☎519-243-2220)*. These are shorter than the Bruce Trail, of course, but nonetheless pleasant for an outing in the woods on a fine winter day.

 # Downhill Skiing

Tour B: Around Georgian Bay

For downhill skiing, the place to go is the **Blue Mountain Resort** *(R.R. 3, Collingwood, L9Y 3Z2, ☎445-0231, ≈444-1751, www.bluemountain.ca)*, which has the highest vertical drop in the region (219 m). Some of the trails are open for night skiing as well.

A number of shops in the area sell, rent and repair equipment, so you'll have no trouble finding everything you need.

 # ACCOMMODATIONS

Tour A: Barrie and the Muskoka Lakes

This region has been welcoming visitors for many years, and thus has all sorts of charming inns and luxurious hotel complexes. It is nonetheless possible to

Toronto's old city hall, which dates from 1889, is shadowed
by a mirrored skyscraper towering over it.
– *M. Grahame*

One of the prett
houses in
Niagara-on-
the-Lake.
– *Emma*

In St. Jacobs,
near Kitchener-
Waterloo, it is
common to
see traditional
Mennonites,
such as this
elderly couple,
riding horse-
drawn
carriages
alongside
more modern
vehicles.
– *P. Quittermelle*

find inexpensive accommodation here, although the choice is somewhat limited.

Orillia

Mara *($; PO Box 2178, L3V 6S1, ☎326-4451)* and **McRae Point** *($; PO Box 2178, L3V 6S1, ☎325-7290)* Provincial Parks both have attractive natural campsites.

The **Lakeside Inn** *($75; 86 Creighton St., L3V 1B2, ☎325-2514)* is more like a motel than a charming inn, but its location on the banks of Lake Couchiching makes it a pleasant place to stay.

Although its roadside location is not very appealing, the **Highwayman Inn** *($95; 201 Woodside Dr., L3V 6T4, ☎326-7343)* is easy to reach and meets modern standards of comfort.

Gravenhurst

Slightly removed from the centre of town, the **Pinedale Inn** *($78; ≈, ≈; 200 Pinedale Lane, P1P 1B4, ☎687-2822)* has long buildings with simply decorated but pleasant rooms. The main attraction here is the location, on the shores of Gull Lake.

The **Muskoka Sands Inn** *($189; ≈, ≈, ℜ, ◉, ○, ७; Muskoka Beach Rd., ☎687-2233 or 800-461-0236, ⇔687-7474)* lies in a very peaceful setting outside of Gravenhurst, on the shores of Lake Muskoka. The cabins and buildings containing the rooms are scattered across its extensive grounds. Guests will also find lots to do here, since the complex has a beach, swimming pools and tennis courts.

Bracebridge

On your way into town, you'll pass the **Muskoka Riverside Inn** *($119; ≈, ℜ, ○, ७; 300 Ecclestone Dr., ☎645-8775 or 800-461-4474, ⇔645-8455)*, a large, uninspiring place that nonetheless meets modern standards of comfort and even has a few bowling lanes.

🦞 The more elegant **Inn at the Falls** *($130; ≈, ℜ; 1 Dominion St., P1L 1R6, ☎645-2245, ⇔645-5093)* offers rooms furnished with antiques. It is made up of several old houses, each more charming than the last, and all facing onto a quiet little street that leads to the Muskoka River, near the falls.

Huntsville

Arrowhead Park *($20.75; Route 11, ☎789-5105)*, located a little father north, has 388 campsites.

The **Sunset Motel** *($70; ≈, ◉; 69 Main St., P0A 1K0, ☎789-4414)*, at the edge of town, is a typical motel with modern rooms that are comfortable and reasonably priced, albeit lacking in charm.

On King William Street, you will find a series of motels. Among these, the spruce-looking **Huntsville Motor Home** *($72; 19 King William St., ☎789-4431)* is definitely your best bet.

The most attractive places to stay, however, are located in a small valley a few kilometres outside of town. Take Route 60 to the 3, which will take you to a vast stretch of greenery punctuated by large hotel complexes.

🦞 The elegant **Grandview** *($154; ≈, ≈, ℜ, ○, ◉; R.R. 4, P0A 1K0, ☎789-4417 or 800-461-4454, ⇔789-6882)* was once a private residence. It has since been converted into a magnificent hotel complex where everything has been designed to ensure guests' satisfaction. The charmingly decorated rooms and varied choice of activities, ranging from golf to walks in the woods, make a stay here both fun and relaxing.

The **Deerhurst** *($199;* ≡*,* ≈*,* ℛ*,* △*,* ⊛*; 1235 Deerhurst Dr., P0A 1K0, ☎789-6411 or 800-461-4393, ⌐789-2431)* hotel complex lies on the shores of Peninsula Lake, in an outstanding natural setting where you can savour clean air and a tranquil atmosphere. The complex is made up of three-story buildings with extremely comfortable rooms, some of which are equipped with a kitchenette and a fireplace. To ensure that guests are entertained as well as comfortably lodged, all sorts of activities are planned.

Route 60 continues deeper into the forest, and on to the **Cedar Grove** *($105/person fb; ℛ, ⊛, ✕; PO Box 5104, P1H 2K5, ☎789-4036 or 800-461-4269, ⌐789-6860)*, a series of charming, rustic little cabins set on the shores of Peninsula Lake.

Tour B: Around Georgian Bay

Owen Sound

The **Inn on the Bay** *($100; ℛ, &; 1800 2nd Ave. E., N4K 5R1, ☎519-371-9200)* stands at the far end of a dreary-looking industrial area, overlooking the waters of Owen Sound. The building has been cleverly designed so that every room has a lovely view of the bay. This place boasts the most attractive setting in town, and is therefore often full on weekends.

If you don't mind missing out on the view, you can find slightly less expensive accommodation at one of the hotels on the edge of town. The **Comfort Inn** *($93; &, ✕; 955 9th Ave. E., N4K 6N4, ☎519-371-5500, ⌐371-6483)* and the **Travelodge** *($80; ℛ, &, ✕; 880 10th St. E., N4K 1T4, ☎519-371-9297, ⌐376-1567)* are among the most pleasant of these, with fairly comfortable rooms.

Thornbury

The **Carriages Riverside Inn** *($95 bkfst incl.; 27 Bridge St., N0H 2P0, ☎/⌐519-599-3135)*, on the banks of the Beaver River, is a lovely red brick house built in 1865 by a merchant named Thomas Andrews. Visitors can enjoy a relaxing stay in a charming little room, soaking up the peaceful atmosphere of the village.

Collingwood

There are several places to stay at the foot of the Blue Mountains, the least expensive being the **Blue Mountain Auberge** *($20-$119 in high season; R.R. 3, L9Y 3Z2, ☎445-1497, ⌐444-1497)*, whose no-frills dormitories are decent for the price. The reception is sometimes less than friendly and the lobby disorderly, but at these prices we won't quibble at details. If you are willing to pay more, the Auberge also has rooms *($79.95)* that are somewhat expensive for the comfort they offer.

If staying in charming surroundings is more important to you than being close to outdoor activities, you will leave **Beild House Inn** *($99 bkfst incl.; 64 Third St., L9Y 1K5, ☎444-1522, ⌐444-2394)*. The house, which dates back to the beginning of the century, has been artfully renovated so that every room provides the utmost in comfort. From the large sitting room with its fireplace to the wall-papered guestrooms that are furnished with antiques and have eiderdown comforters on the beds, this inn sees to every detail of your well-being. The lovely interior decoration is not its only attraction: the home-cooked breakfast served here is absolutely delicious, and there is a spa in the basement.

There are several hotels in the village of Collingwood as well. The **Best Western** *($99.95; ≈, △; 1 Balsam St., L9Y 3J4, ☎444-2144, ⇰444-7772)* has relatively attractive and comfortable rooms with modern furnishings.

At the edge of town, on the way to Blue Mountain, there is a large group of fairly new buildings that includes a hotel, the **Cranberry Inn** *($109; 19 Keith Ave., L9Y 4T9, ☎/⇰445-6600 or ☎800-465-9077)*. Well away from the commotion of the city, this place provides peace and quiet. The modern rooms are comfortable and clean. There are condos for longer stays, and a special rate that includes golf is also available.

The **Mountain Spring Lodge** *($109; ≈, ≡, K; R.R. 3, L9Y 3Z2, ☎444-7776 or 800-444-8633, ⇰444-6533)* is another good choice if you're looking for a small apartment for a day or more. Although not as well located as the Blue Mountain Inn, it is still near the slopes. The buildings, furthermore, are charming and include a fireplace, as well as comfortable modern furniture.

The **Blue Mountain Inn** *($139; ≈, ℜ, _⊛, K, △, ♡; R.R.3, L9Y 3Z2, ☎445-0231, ⇰444-1751, www.bluemountain.ca)* hotel complex is undoubtedly the best-known establishment in the region. Its location at the foot of the ski slopes is certainly ideal. The comfortable and conveniently arranged rooms are in a long modern building. Apartments with kitchenettes are also available. This place is popular year-round. Apart from skiing in winter, there are water slides, a nearby golf course and mountain biking in summer.

Wasaga Beach

All sorts of nondescript, charmless motels lie close to the beach. For more peace and quiet, we recommend staying in one of the neighbouring towns instead.

On Mosley Street, the **Lakeview Motel** *($65; 44 Mosley St., L0L 2P0, ☎429-5155)* is one possibility, but don't expect a very warm welcome from the owner. The place does have the advantage of being located near the beach, however.

Just a touch more chic, the **Luau Motel** *($109; ≈; Mosley St., L0L 2P0, ☎429-2252, ⇰429-6141)* provides standard motel-style accommodations in a one-storey building with separate entrances from the parking lot. Numerous flower boxes have been added in an effort to beautify the decor. The rooms are very clean.

Midland

There are a few modern hotels in town, most of which are located along the road leading to Sainte-Marie Among the Hurons. None of these places is particularly charming, but the **Best Western Highland Inn** *($109; 924 King St., L4R 4L3, ☎526-9307, ⇰526-0099)* has decent rooms.

Parry Sound

The **Jantje Manor** *($60; 43 Church St., P2A 1Y6, ☎746-5399)* is one of those places whose cozy atmosphere makes

THE LAKELANDS

for a memorable stay. The courteous service and period decor are two more reasons why this is one of the best places in town.

🦐 Heading east on Route 124, you'll pass right by Manitouwabing Lake, where the superb **Inn at Manitou** *($226 fb; ≈, ℜ, △, ◉, ◑; McKellar, POG 1CO, ☎389-2171, ⇒389-3818)* hotel complex lies hidden away in the wilderness. With its thirteen tennis courts, gym and elegant rooms, this is the perfect place to spend the vacation of your dreams.

Tour C: Along the Shores of Lake Huron

Tobermory

Many tourists just make a brief stop here, since the town has no special attractions. As a result, there are very few comfortable places to stay. Most are motels, many of them near the dock of the *Chi-Cheemaun* ferry, that are fine for a one-night stay before continuing your trip.

Port Elgin

If the idea of staying in a charming 19th-century house appeals to you, try the **Winnspire Inn** *($$$; 276 Mill St., NOH 2CO, ☎519-389-3898)*, which has a pretty antique decor.

Goderich

Campers can pitch their tents at **Point Farms Provincial Park** *(R.R. 3, N7A 3X9, ☎519-524-7124)*.

Benmiller

🦐 Route 31, a small road just a few kilometres from Goderich, leads to Benmiller, a little town founded in 1840, which would probably be deserted if it weren't for the outstanding **Benmiller Inn** *($179 bkfst incl.; ≈, ℜ, △, ◉, ◑; R.R. 4, N7A 3Y1, ☎519-524-2191 or 800-265-1711, ⇒519-524-5150)*. Guests stay in the impeccably renovated houses of the area's first colonists. A truly unique experience.

Bayfield

The **Albion Hotel** *($125; Main St., NOM 1GO, ☎519-565-2641)* in Bayfield is set in a charming house built at the beginning of the century. The place underwent major renovations in 1998 to give its rooms added comfort and sparkle.

🦐 A beautifully renovated old 19th-century house, the **Little Inn of Bayfield** *($125; Main St., P.O. Box 100, NOM 1GO, ☎519-565-2611 or 800-565-1832, ⇒519-562-5474)* is quite simply delightful. There are 30 rooms, all equally charming. Some of the rooms have little extras, such as a whirlpool or a fireplace. This place really has what it takes to please guests, especially since it is located on a lovely quiet avenue and has a superb restaurant (see p 232).

Grand Bend

If you have a tent, you can camp out in magnificent **Pinery Provincial Park** (see p 222).

If you continue past Grand Bend on the 21, you'll come to a golf course and a small hill, at the top of which lies the lovely **Oakwood Inn** *($89-$139; ≈, ℜ, △, ◉, ◑, ◑; Hwy. 21, Box 400, NOM 1TO, ☎519-238-2324 or 800-387-2324, ⇒519-238-2377)*. With its long wooden buildings and its garden shaded by majestic trees, this place has a rustic charm perfectly suited to the region. The interior, furthermore, has been decorated to create an inviting atmosphere.

The **Bonnie Doone Manor-on-the-Beach** *($89-$160;* ✖; *16 Government Rd., P.O. Box 550, NOM 1T0,* ☎*519-238-2236,* ➴*519-238-5252)* boasts an outstanding location alongside Grand Bend's magnificent beach, looking out onto Lake Huron, which stretches as far as the eye can see. This charming little inn only has about a dozen rooms and is sure to please visitors longing for a natural setting and some peace and quiet.

✖ RESTAURANTS

Tour A: Barrie and the Muskoka Lakes

Barrie

Weber's *($; 11 Victoria Street,* ☎*734-9800)* is a veritable burger institution in town that is sure to satisfy ravenous and not so ravenous hunger attacks.

Tara *($$; 128 Dunlop Street East,* ☎*737-1821),* located downtown, serves up delicious Indian food. All the effort is concentrated on the excellent cuisine, such that the uninspired decor is soon forgotten.

Orillia

Weber's *($; Highway 11, RR 3,* ☎*325-3969)* is a local road-side institution at the edge of town, where you can enjoy a good charbroiled burger.

If you're more in the mood for a healthy meal, head downtown to the aptly named **Evergreen** *($; Mississaga St.),* which serves delicious, nutritious sandwiches, salads and the like.

For breakfast or a quick snack, try **Café au Lait** *($; Mississaga St.),* which serves tasty baked goods and cappuccinos.

 Frankie's *($$; 83 Mississaga St. W.,* ☎*327-5404),* a lovely restaurant with a relaxed atmosphere serves delicious, innovative Italian cuisine with fresh ingredients.

The chef at **Carmine's** *($$$; 64 Mississaga St. W.,* ☎*326-0464)* also prepares Italian dishes — veritable feasts, which guests savour in an elegant, tastefully decorated dining room. According to some, this is the best restaurant in town.

Bracebridge

In fine weather, the terrace at the **Muskokan** *($; at the corner of Kimberley and Manitoba)* is definitely one of the most pleasant places in the area for lunch. Seated in the delightful shade offered by stately trees and parasols, you can start off your day with a good, simple meal.

The well-located restaurant of the **Inn at the Falls** *($$$$; 1 Dominion St.,* ☎*645-2245)* boasts a beautiful view of the Muskoka River. Comfortably seated in the elegant dining room, you can enjoy this magnificent setting while savouring such irresistible dishes as beef tournedos in a chanterelle sauce and grilled swordfish. Although each dish is more delicious than the last, try to save some room for dessert — you'll be glad you did.

Huntsville

The banks of the Muskoka River, with its wooden terrace and string of restaurants, whose main attraction is their idyllic location, is the perfect spot for a noontime meal. **Blackburn's Landing** *($)* serves simple fare like hamburgers, pasta and salads, as does the **Pasta & Grill** *($)*, next door.

Tall Trees *($$; 87 Main St., ☎789-9769)*, located in the centre of town, does not boast as beautiful a setting, but is a pleasant place to go for supper. There is something for everyone on the menu, including prime rib, fish and grilled chicken and shrimp.

Tour B: Around Georgian Bay

Owen Sound

In the heart of Harrisson Park, you'll find a big house containing a **restaurant** *($)* with an extremely affordable menu.

The **Inn on the Bay** *($-$$; 1800 2nd Ave. E., ☎519-371-9200)* is perfect for breakfast and a glorious sunrise over the water..

Norma Jean *($-$$; 243 8th St. E., ☎519-376-2232)* is a pleasant little restaurant whose walls are adorned with posters and statuettes of Marilyn Monroe. The perfect place to go for a bite with friends, it has quite a strong following, no doubt drawn by the tasty burgers, salads and beef dishes.

More elegant and also more expensive, the **Louis Steak House** *($$$; 1610 16th St. E., ☎519-376-4430)*, in its superb Victorian surroundings, is unquestionably the best restaurant in town. While savouring one of the house specialties, beef Wellington or pepper steak, you'll enjoy a muted atmosphere

and courteous, albeit slightly chilly, service.

Collingwood

To get the most out of a beautiful sunny day, have a meal at the **Admiral's Post** *($-$$; 2 School Lane)* where the shady terrace is set up well away from the street. On rainy days, there is the welcoming atmosphere of the dining room, decorated in the style of an English pub. There is nothing extravagant on the menu which features items like fish and chips, sandwiches and steak. This is also a good spot to have a beer at the end of the day.

Another attractive restaurant with an enticing terrace, **Terracotta** *($-$$; corner of Pine and Second Streets)* has a steady flow of customers in search of a good meal at prices that are not outrageous. There is a selection of good, simple dishes like sandwiches and salads, but there are also more ample suggestions such as chicken cacciatore and steak Madagascar. The decor is very pleasant, with original paintings and plants, and the atmosphere is warm and welcoming.

Christopher's *($$-$$$; 167 Pine, ☎445-7117)* is sure to catch your eye, as it occupies a magnificent house built in 1902 as a wedding present. It has lost none of its character over the years, and is perfectly suited to an intimate meal at lunchtime *($-$$)*, when quiche and pasta dishes are served, or in the evening, when the menu is more elaborate.

Another wonderful place is the **Spike and Spoon** *($$$; 637 Hurontario, L9Y 2N6, ☎446-1629)*, which is also set up inside a lovely Victorian house and serves specialties worthy of the most discriminating palate.

Another deluxe establishment in a magnificent former residence, **Georgian Renaissance** *($$$-$$$$; 188 First St., ☎446-3337)* puts you in the lap of luxury. First, the dining room is tastefully decorated. Next, the menu offers such tempting dishes that you will develop an appetite just from reading it! There is a fantastic selection of exquisite dishes such as snails, salmon poached in white wine and *canard moscovite* (duck Moscow-style).

Around Collingwood

Collingwood has an incredible number of fine restaurants, but if you are among those who swear by French cuisine, and by French cuisine only, **Chez Michel** *($$-$$$$; take Hwy. 26 for approx. 10 min., ☎443-9441)*, just outside town, is a must. Here, it is not the building that attracts your attention, although it is tastefully decorated, but rather the menu. You can start your gastronomic adventure with snails *bourguignonne* (with butter and garlic), followed by a main course like rack of lamb with herbs, salmon with leeks and saffron, or sweetbreads with Madeira sauce. All these savoury dishes will delight even the finest palate. Be careful to save some room for desserts – they are heavenly! There is lemon mousse with berry coulis for those who really could not eat another bite, while for heartier appetites there are crêpes filled with *crème pâtissière et framboise* (confectioner's custard and raspberries), served with coulis. Delicious!

Creemore

As you head into town, you will surely be tempted to stop and relax for a bit on the lovely terrace of the **Mad River Tea House** *($; ☎466-3526)*. The menu includes sandwiches, a large selection of teas, and the choice of several cakes, so you can stop here at any time of the day. Inside, there are a few tables and a small store.

Midland

Midland Fish & Chips *($; 311 King St., ☎526-9992)* might not serve gourmet cuisine, but some people claim that the breaded fish is the best in the region.

Parry Sound

A whole series of good restaurants can be found alongside the marina, where you can set out for a cruise on the bay. These have the added advantage of offering a magnificent view of the water, which stretches as far as the eye can see. **Just like Mama's** *($; 10 Bay St., ☎746-6525)*, a little bistro that serves Italian specialties, is perfect for lunch.

If being near the water has put you in the mood for some delicious fresh fish, opt for the **Bay Street Cafe** *($$; 22 Bay St., ☎746-2882)*.

Tour C: Along the Shores of Lake Huron

Wiarton

Adorable little shops and restaurants are clustered together on the main street. For an enjoyable meal, stop in at the **Three Friends Café** *($-$$)* where the menu includes simple dishes like sandwiches and pastas. The old-fashioned furniture helps to create a warm atmosphere.

THE LAKELANDS

Goderich

Downtown Goderich, bordered by a circular street, has a unique charm about it. It is home to several restaurants, including **Van Dely's** *($)*, which serves tasty, nutritious dishes at lunchtime.

Benmiller

If you're passing through Benmiller and money is no object, stop for a meal at the **Benmiller Inn** *($$$-$$$$; R.R. 4, ☎519-524-2191)*, where each dish is more delicious than the last. Both the menu and the wine list are sure to pique your appetite.

Bayfield

The restaurant at the delightful **Little Inn of Bayfield** *($$$; Main St., ☎519-565-2611)* is sure to win you over with its old-fashioned look and mouth-watering menu, you'll wish you could order one of everything on the menu! Whether you settle on rabbit braised with Merlot, Bordeaux-style lamb or one of the other consistently delicious dishes, you are guaranteed a satisfying meal.

Grand Bend

The dining room at **Sanders on the Beach** *($$; near the beach)* has big picture windows, enabling guests to enjoy a splendid view of the lake. If it's a find summer day, however, you might prefer to sit outside on the terrace, which also offers a magnificent view.

ENTERTAINMENT

Tour A: Barrie and the Muskoka Lakes

Barrie

At the **Kempenfest Festival** *(early August; ☎739-9444)*, over 200 exhibitors display crafts, antiques and objets d'art.

Orillia

The **Orillia Opera House** *(at the corner of West and Mississaga, ☎326-8011)* presents good theatrical productions all summer long.

The **Leacock Heritage Festival** *(☎325-3261)*, held in late July and early August, offers an opportunity to enjoy a few evenings of comedy, theatre and music.

Bar

Lipsmackers, with its lovely waterfront terrace, attracts a young clientele, who come here to have a drink and enjoy the setting.

Gravenhurst

Gull Lake is the scene of a variety of events, including outdoor concerts, on Sundays in July and August, performed on a floating stage.

Tour B: Around Georgian Bay

Meaford

The Georgian Theatre Festival *(☎519-538-3569)* is a good opportunity to see several excellent productions, from the end of June to the beginning of August, at the Meaford Opera House *(12 Nelson St. E.)*.

Collingwood

Winter or summer, the **Admiral's Post** *(2 School Lane)* is a great place to stop in at nightfall for a beer with friends in a relaxed atmosphere.

If you prefer to end the day with a pleasant evening at the theatre, find out what is playing at the **Collingwood Theatre** *(☎444-6376)*, where plays are performed all summer long.

 ## SHOPPING

Tour A: Barrie and the Muskoka Lakes

Orillia

On your way through the Rama reserve, you'll pass by the **Rama Moccasin & Craft Shop** *(R.R. 6, ☎325-5041)*, which is typical of the stores found on native reserves. Don't be put off by the building's wacky appearance (the parking lot is adorned with wooden bears and tepees); the place sells lovely native crafts, including Ojibwa moccasins, *mukluks*, Inuit and Iroquois sculptures, prints and all.

Tour B: Around Georgian Bay

Collingwood

At **Clerkson's** *(94 Pine St., ☎445-7814 or 445-2212)*, set up inside a big, beautiful house, you can treat yourself to some handicrafts, decorative objects or perhaps even a piece of antique-style furniture.

Midland

The **Wye Marsh Wildlife Centre** has a bookstore with a wide selection of books on birds and nature in general. sorts of jewellery.

Tour C: Along the Shores of Lake Huron

Goderich

The centre of town is full of charming shops, and you're sure to find a little something at **Cooker's Mercantile** *(48 West St.)*, which sells kitchen products. For clothes and toys, try **Something Irresistible** *(168 Courth House Sq., ☎524-5972)*.

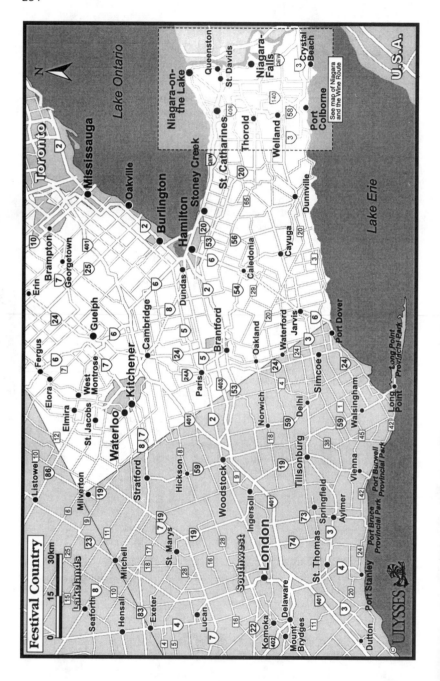

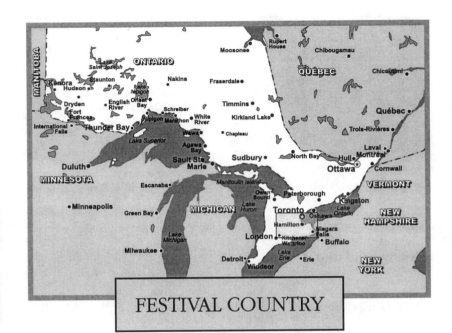

FESTIVAL COUNTRY

One urban area leads into the next at the eastern end of Lake Ontario. The city of Toronto dominates the landscape for many kilometres in all directions. And, just as you think you have finally left Toronto city traffic behind, you enter one of the larged towns that surround the metropolis. Among these are the very pleasant towns of Oakville, Burlington, and above all, Hamilton, which is tucked away at the end of the lake. There are some interesting places to visit along this route, but the real treasures in this part of Ontario are found on the southern shore of the lake. Little by little, urban areas give way to vast, furrowed fields and vineyards that grow some very good wine. Finally, you reach the area's most splendid natural attraction, Niagara

Falls, which has impressed visitors from all over the world for more than a hundred years. Finally, this chapter takes you to the Kitchener-Waterloo region and its surrounding areas with their magnificent rural landscape of fertile farmland.

Three different tours are described here. The first, "Kitchener-Waterloo and surroundings," takes you through this city and the charming hamlets around it. The second, "Hamilton and surroundings," tries to show you the best of this industrial region, and includes Oakville, a pretty vacation town. Finally, the third, "Niagara and the Wine Route" is unquestionably the most popular tour in the province, winding through a superb region of vineyards and stopping at Niagara Falls.

FINDING YOUR WAY AROUND

Tour A: Kitchener-Waterloo and Surroundings

By Car

From Toronto: Take Highway 401 to Kitchener-Waterloo.

Bus Stations

Kitchener-Waterloo: 15 Charles St., ☎(519) 741-2600.

Brantford: 64 Darling St., ☎(519) 756-5011.

Train Stations

Kitchener-Waterloo: 126 Weber St. (corner of Victoria and Weber), ☎(800) 361-1235.

Brantford: 5 Wadworth St.

Tour B: Hamilton and Surroundings

By Car

From Toronto: Take the Queen Elizabeth Way (QEW).

Bus Station

Hamilton: 36 Hunter St.

Train Station

Burlington: 1199 Waterdown Rd. (corner of Hwy. 403 and Waterdown Rd.), ☎(800) 361-1235.

Tour C: Niagara and the Wine Route

By Car

From Toronto: Take the Queen Elizabeth Way (QEW), which leads to Hamilton and St. Catharines.

Bus Stations

St. Catharines: 7 Carlisle St.

In summer, there is daily bus service between Niagara-on-the-Lake and both St. Catharines and Niagara Falls. If you don't have a car, the only way to get to Niagara-on-the-Lake during the rest of the year is by taxi.

Niagara Falls: 4555 Erie Ave., ☎(905) 357-2133.

PRACTICAL INFORMATION

Tour A: Kitchener-Waterloo and Surroundings

Area code : 519

Niagara and Mid-Western Travel Association
180 Greenwich Street, Brantford, ON, N3S 2X6, ☎756-3230 or ☎(800) 267-3399 (within Canada and the United States), ≈756-3231.

Southwestern Ontario Travel Association
4023 Meadowbrook Dr., Suite 112, London, ON, N6L 1E7, ☎652-1391 or ☎(800) 661-6804, ≈652-0533.

Tour B: Hamilton and Surroundings

Area code : 905

Niagara and Mid-Western Travel Association
180 Greenwich Street, Brantford, ON, N3S 2X6, ☎(519) 756-3230 or ☎(800) 267-3399 (within Canada and the United States), ⇆(519) 756-3231

Tour C: Niagara and the Wine Route

Area code : 905

Niagara and Mid-Western Travel Association
180 Greenwich Street, Brantford, ON N3S 2X6, ☎(519) 756-3230 or ☎(800) 267-3399 (within Canada and the United States), ⇆(519) 756-3231.

 EXPLORING

Tour A: Kitchener-Waterloo and Surroundings

Intensive colonization of the territory west of Toronto did not get underway until the 19th century. However, members of the Mennonite religious community, the first immigrants to settle here, began arriving at the end of the 18th century. They came from the United States where they were subject to reprisals by government authorities for having refused to take up arms during the War of Independence. These newcomers settled on fertile agricultural land in the heart of southwestern Ontario. English, Scottish and German settlers arrived in the following years and founded villages and cities, one by one. Today, Kitchener-Waterloo is the largest of these. This region of extensive farmlands that stretch as far as the eye can see has been dubbed the "greenhouse of Ontario". The Mennonite population has, for the most part, been able to preserve its traditional way of life. This gives the area a distinctive character that makes travelling here a pure delight.

Kitchener-Waterloo ★★

In the wake of the American Revolution, those individuals who had declined to fight alongside the American troops were persecuted. The Mennonites, who had refused to take up arms for religious reasons, thus decided to emigrate to Ontario, where they could purchase fertile land at low prices. This first wave of immigrants arrived at the very end of the 18th century. Other colonists, mainly of German origin, also settled in the region, founding towns like Kitchener. Even today, a good part of the population of Kitchener-Waterloo is of German descent. In fact, every year the city hosts the largest *Oktoberfest* outside Germany.

Originally, Kitchener and Waterloo were simply neighbouring towns, but as they both grew, they merged into one large urban area, so authorities decided to join them officially. Kitchener-Waterloo thus has two downtown areas, one on King Street near Erb Street East (Waterloo) and the other along King Street West around Queen Street (Kitchener); although there are places where the two towns still seem like separate entities rather than a united whole. Kitchener-Waterloo is a pleasant city with several noteworthy tourist attractions.

Turn onto Erb Street West from King Street (Waterloo).

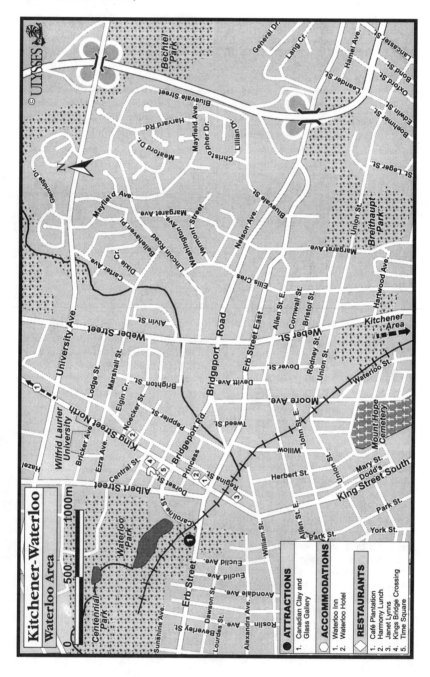

Kitchener-Waterloo
Waterloo Area

0   500   1000m

ATTRACTIONS
1. Canadian Clay and
   Glass Gallery

ACCOMMODATIONS
1. Waterloo Inn
2. Waterloo Hotel

RESTAURANTS
1. Café Plantation
2. Harmony Lunch
3. Janet Lynns
4. Kings Bridge Crossing
5. Time Square

© ULYSSES

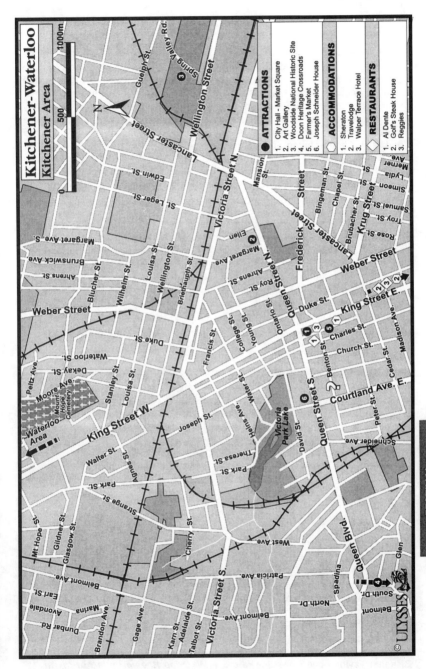

Kitchener-Waterloo

Kitchener Area

N

0   500   1000m

ATTRACTIONS

1. City Hall - Market Square
2. Art Gallery
3. Woodside National Historic Site
4. Doon Heritage Crossroads
5. Farmer's Market
6. Joseph Schneider House

ACCOMMODATIONS

1. Sheraton
2. Travelodge
3. Walper Terrace Hotel

RESTAURANTS

1. Al Dente
2. Golf's Steak House
3. Reggies

FESTIVAL COUNTRY

© ULYSSES

The Mennonites

In 1536, in the Netherlands, a parish priest by the name of Menno Simons broke with the Catholic church and founded an Anabaptist sect, whose adherents came to be known as Mennonites. Because they were pacifists who refused to be baptized, Mennonites were persecuted for their religious beliefs, which seemed revolutionary in those intolerant times. As a result, they emigrated in the hopes of finding a more hospitable country. Hoping to find a more accepting environment, they followed the example of William Penn, who had settled in the United States. They prospered in this new territory, until they were again persecuted in the aftermath of the War of Independence because they had refused to take up arms. At the end of the 18th century, many of them left the United States for Ontario, where they established little communities and farmed extensively.

Today, the Mennonites have strong roots in the Kitchener-Waterloo region. It is easy to recognize the more conservative branch of the doctrine: the men are bearded and wear wide-brimmed hats, and women always wear dresses and bonnets. Many shun mechanized transportation, and can been seen driving one- or two-horse buggies. They are often seen on the country roads around St. Jacobs and Elmira. Although it is this segment of the group that attracts the most attention, many Mennonites are completely integrated into modern society and are not visibly identifiable.

The **Canadian Clay and Glass Gallery** ★ houses several collections of ceramic and glass objects, including one donated by the Indusmin silica company. Also on display are a number of works by Canadian artists like Denise Bélanger-Taylor, Irene Frolic, Joe Fafard and Sadashi Inuzuka. The museum has occupied the present building, designed by Vancouver architects John and Patricia Patkau, since 1993.

Continue along King Street, which becomes King Street West outside of Waterloo (the north part of town).

City Hall stands at the corner of King and Queen, along with a shopping arcade known as Market Square, where the local **Farmer's Market** *(☎741-2287)* is held every Saturday morning (see p 272).

Head south on Queen Street.

A visit to the **Joseph Schneider Haus** *($1.75; Wed to Sat 10am to 5pm, Sun 1pm to 5pm, open every day in Jul and Aug; 466 Queen St. S., ☎742-7752, www.region.waterloo.on.ca.jsh)*, the former home of a German Mennonite, will give you an idea how simply 19th-century Mennonites lived. There are guides on the premises to explain the rustic, austere lifestyle of members of this community.

Retrace your steps and continue along Queen Street North.

Next, you will come to the **Kitchener-Waterloo Art Gallery** *(donations welcome; Tue, Wed, Fri and Sat 10am to 5pm, Thu 10am to 9pm, Sun 1pm to 5pm; 101 Queen St. N., Kitchener ☎579-5860)*, whose collection, spread over seven rooms, is quite modest on the whole. Most of the works exhibited are paintings by contemporary artists. The gallery regularly hosts temporary exhibitions as well.

The **Woodside National Historic Site ★** *($2.50; May to Dec, every day 10am to 5pm; 528 Wellington St. N., ☎571-5684)*. William Lyon Mackenzie King, Prime Minister of Canada from 1921 to 1930 and from 1935 to 1948, spent part of his childhood here, between the ages of five and eleven. After touring the house, which has been restored and refurnished to look just as it did when Mackenzie lived here, you can take a stroll around the magnificent wooded grounds.

Head south (towards the 401) on Homer Watson Road from Queen's Boulevard.

The **Doon Heritage Crossroads** *($5.50; early May to early Sep, every day 10am to 4:30pm, weekends only until late Dec; Homer Watson Rd., ☎748-1914, www.region.waterloo.on.ca/doon)* is a reconstruction of a typical 19th-century village, as found in this part of Ontario. It consists of several buildings, including a general store, a train station and a farm complete with animals.

Head north on Hwy. 8.

St. Jacobs ★

The charm of St. Jacobs, or Jacobstettel, as it used to be called, is in its main street, which is lined with crafts shops whose windows alone are fascinating enough to grasp your attention for hours. This Mennonite village, which has managed to preserve its old-time appearance, is overrun year-round by visitors lured here by the pretty shops and the peaceful atmosphere pervading the streets.

To learn more about the Mennonites can go to the **Visitor's Centre** *($3; May to Oct, Mon to Fri 11am to 5pm, Sat 10am to 5pm, Sun 1:30pm to 5pm; Nov to Apr, Sat 11am to 4:30pm, Sun 2pm to 4:30pm; with reservation; 33 King St., ☎664-3518)*, which presents a half-hour film on the subject.

Twice a week, the local farmers gather at the **St. Jacobs Farmers' Market and Flea Market** *(year-round Thu and Sat 7am to 3:30pm, Jun to Aug also on Wed 8am to 3pm, ☎265-3353)* to sell farm produce and handicrafts. Not only is this a picturesque scene, but it's also the perfect opportunity to purchase some delicious local foodstuffs.

FESTIVAL COUNTRY

Head north on the 8, which becomes Hwy. 86 for part of the way.

Elmira

Although less charming than its two neighbours, Elora and St. Jacobs, Elmira is nonetheless a pretty town, which was founded in the previous century by the first Mennonites to settle in Ontario. The Mennonite presence is still evident here, especially in the lovely farms and churches on the outskirts of town.

Head east on Route 86, not to be confused with Hwy. 86.

West Montrose

The modest little hamlet of West Montrose is best known as the home of Ontario's last **covered bridge ★**, known in this region as the "kissing bridge." Designed by John Bear in 1880, this bridge is 60 m long and is still open to local traffic.

Take Hwy 21. to Elora.

Elora ★

Elora was founded in 1832 on the banks of the Grand River, on a site suitable for a mill. This magnificent stone structure has since been converted into a charming inn, which serves as a focal point for the local tourist industry. It is surrounded by shops in little stone houses, where you can purchase all sorts of knick-knacks.

The steep limestone walls of the **Elora Gorges ★** *($3.25; Elora Rd., NOB 1S0, ☎846-9742)* are a beautiful sight, which you can take in from the area hiking trails in the summer or the cross-country trails in the winter. Camping.

Continue along Hwy. 21.

Fergus

Fergus was founded on the banks of the Grand River by Adam Fergusson in 1830. Fergusson built a mill here, which brought the area a certain amount of prosperity. This little village, which shows a strong Scottish influence, still has many lovely limestone buildings dating from the previous century. Among these, don't miss the beautiful **St. Andrews Presbyterian Church**. Built of stone from the surrounding area in 1862, it has thick walls and an elegant spire that rises above the downtown area. It is usually a quiet place, but gets quite lively during the **Highland Games**, which are held in August.

Hwy. 6 leads south to Guelph.

Guelph ★

Scottish novelist John Galt, known for his works on Lord Byron, made several trips to Upper Canada for the Canada Company. He even lived here from 1826 to 1829, at which time he founded the town of Guelph (1827) on the shores of the Speed River. To create a pleasant environment, he incorporated large parks and wide arteries into the town's design, something highly unusual in those days. Today, this dynamic city is known for its university, the **University of Guelph**, whose magnificent buildings are located south of the Speed River.

The **MacDonald Stewart Arts Centre ★** *(358 Gordon St., ☎837-0010)*, located on the university campus, has a lovely collection of Canadian and Inuit art, which is displayed in spacious, well laid-out rooms and complemented by clear written commentaries.

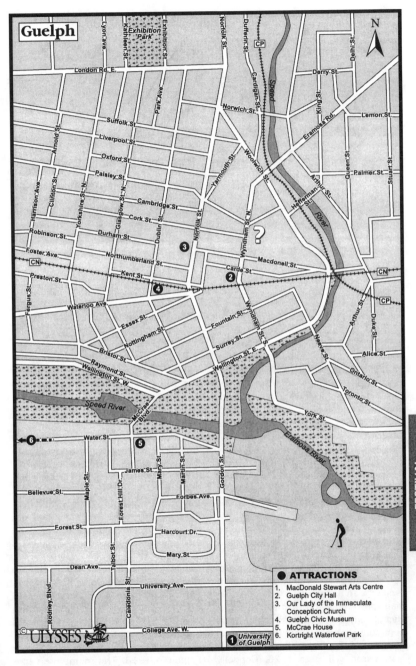

Guelph

● **ATTRACTIONS**
1. MacDonald Stewart Arts Centre
2. Guelph City Hall
3. Our Lady of the Immaculate
    Conception Church
4. Guelph Civic Museum
5. McCrae House
6. Kortright Waterfowl Park

Our Lady of the Immaculate Conception

On the winding streets of downtown Guelph, you'll find several interesting commercial and public edifices, including **Guelph City Hall ★** *(59 Carden St.)*, which looks out onto a small public square. This elegant neo-Renaissance style building, designed by architect William Thomas, was erected in 1857.

An imposing church, **Our Lady of the Immaculate Conception ★★**, towers over City Hall. In the 19th century, most parishioners of Ontario's Catholic churches were Irish who had fled the potato famine, and French Canadians who had come here from Québec in search of a brighter future. This church is the masterpiece of Irish architect Joseph Connolly, and owes its existence to an enterprising French-Canadian priest by the name of Father Hamel. Since the families of the local communities were larger than average, the place had to be big. Its construction lasted from 1876 to 1926. Connolly opted for the Neo-Gothic style of the

cathedral of Cologne in Germany. The only part of the church that truly reflects a Germanic influence, however, is the upper apse at the back of the building, which is surrounded by numerous apsidioles.

The **Guelph Civic Museum** *($3; Jun to Aug, every day 1pm to 5pm; Sep to May closed Sat; 6 Dublin St. S., ☎836-1221)* is in a superb stone building that dates from 1847. It recounts the history of the town since its founding by John Galt in 1827. Various objects, photographs, toys and clothing are on display.

The **McCrae House** *($3; Mon to Fri 1pm to 5pm; 108 Water St., ☎836-1482)* is the former residence of John McCrae, a doctor who fought in World War I and wrote the famous poem "In Flanders Fields" as a result of that experience. He was born in this house, but died in France in 1918. The rooms are decorated as they were at the end of the 19th century.

The **Kortright Waterfowl Park** (see p 259).

From Guelph, you can make a side trip to Acton. Take Route 7 east.

Acton

The little town of Acton has a charming central area dominated by a red-brick church with a white bell tower that dates back to 1894. However, shopping is really the main attraction here. Acton is famous for its clothing and other leather goods. Many beautiful articles can be bought here at reasonably low prices.

Backtrack as far as Guelph, then take Route 24 towards Cambridge.

Cambridge

Cambridge was founded in 1973, when three little towns (Galt, Hespeler and Preston) on the banks of the Grand and Mill Rivers were merged into one. The rivers are Cambridge's pride and joy, for they are lined with lovely parks. If you walk along the Grand River, you will also find three of the town's most beautiful churches, **Central Presbyterian Church** ★, erected by the riverside in 1880; **Trinity Anglican Church**, which was built by James Fraser in 1844 and still has its original nave, and **Knox Presbyterian Church**, built in 1869. All three are located around **Park Hill**, which also boasts some magnificent houses, making it one of the most pleasant areas in town. Nearby lies downtown Cambridge, which has some pretty buildings, but is flanked by big, ugly factories.

N.B.: when we speak of downtown Cambridge, we refer to Main, Water and Ainslie Streets, not far from the river. Because the cities are very close together, it is possible to mistake it for downtown Hespeler, in the Queen Street area, or downtown Preston, which is on and around King Street.

To get to Stratford, take the 8, which leads first through Kitchener.

Brantford

This rather gloomy-looking town was named after Joseph Brant, whose native name was Thayendanegea. Its downtown area appears to have been abandoned by the local shopkeepers. Anyway, people come here to learn more about Iroquois culture, not for the buildings.

In the 17th century, the Iroquois confederation known as the Five Nations managed to wipe out the native tribes living in southwestern Ontario and take over their land. In the late 1800s, however, the Mississaugas drove the Iroquois back to their original territory south of the Great Lakes.

During the American Revolution, the Six Nations (the Tuscaroras had since joined the other five), based in the northeastern United States, declared themselves neutral, with the exception of a few warriors, like Joseph Brant, who fought alongside the British. Nevertheless, in the wake of the English defeat, all of the Iroquois had to leave the United States. As a gesture of thanks for the Iroquois' assistance during the war, Great Britain granted them 202,350 ha of land along the Grand River. Two thousand natives thus returned to the region, and 450 of them settled on the site now occupied by Brantford. In 1841, British colonists

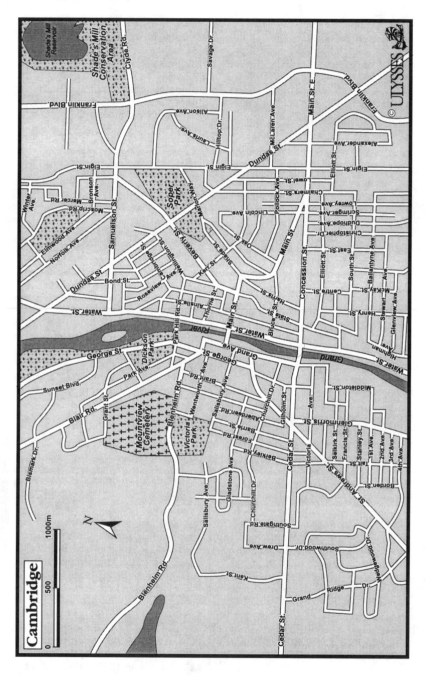

purchased back part of the land and took up residence here.

From Hwy. 2, which runs through the centre of town, head south on Market Street, then make an immediate right onto Mohawk Street.

At the edge of town, you will see a small white church known as the **Royal Chapel of the Mohawks ★**, which is the oldest Protestant church in Ontario. It was erected by King George III to thank the Iroquois for their assistance during the American Revolution.

Continue along Mohawk Street to the Woodland Cultural Centre.

The **Woodland Cultural Centre ★** *($4; Mon to Fri 8:30am to 4pm, Sat and Sun 10am to 5pm; 184 Mohawk St., ☎759-2650, ext. 241)* traces the history of the Six Nations. Articles on display include tools, clothing, *wampum* (traditional belts) and handicrafts. A short visit here is a pleasant way to learn about Iroquois customs and traditions.

The Invention of the Telephone

The brilliant inventor took an interest in teaching a language to deaf-mutes, since his wife Mabel suffered from that handicap. In 1874, while creating an artificial ear that could record sounds, he developed the invention that would make him famous. The first telephone call was made in 1876.

Alexander Graham Bell was born in Edinburgh, Scotland in 1847 and moved to Brantford with his parents in 1870. The **Bell Homestead** *($2.75; Tue to Sat 9:30am to 4:30pm; 94 Tutela Heights, ☎756-6220)*, where he lived from 1870 to 1881, is open to the public. It is decorated the same way it was in those years, and houses a number of Bell's inventions.

To learn more about the colonization of this region, head to the **Brant County Museum and Archives** *(Wed to Fri 9am to 4pm, Sat 1pm to 4pm, May to Aug also open Sun 1pm to 4pm; 57 Charlotte St., ☎752-2483 or 752-8578)*, which displays various tools and other articles that belonged to the early settlers. The museum is particularly informative in regards to Iroquois captain Joseph Brant (1742-1807). Temporary exhibits are also presented.

Built in 1837, **Myrtleville** *($2.25; ☎752-3216)* is one of the impressive homes in Brantford that is open to the public. It lets you see all the period furnishings in the dining room, parlour, children's and parents' bedrooms, and get an idea of what daily life was like in those times. Costumed guides are on hand. The grounds are also open to the public, and you can take a stroll through the lovely garden.

From Brantford, head west on the 53, then take the 401 to London or to Mississauga in the other direction. The 403, just north of Brantford, also intersects with the 401.

Tour B: Hamilton and Surroundings

There are two large cities to the west of Lake Ontario, Toronto and Hamilton. The stretch of road leading through Toronto's suburbs and Hamilton's industrial outskirts is not very appealing, but you can't avoid it if you want to go to Niagara Falls. There are, however, a few noteworthy attractions along the way, including the Royal Botanical Gardens in Hamilton.

FESTIVAL COUNTRY

Mississauga

Fans of contemporary architecture, should make a detour to Mississauga on their way to Hamilton. The **Mississauga City Hall** ★★ *(1 City Centre Dr.)*, which doubles as a community and cultural centre, is the most daring post-modernist structure in the country. Built by architects Jones and Kirkland between 1982 and 1987, it is dominated by a 20-story clock tower. Make sure to go inside to see the Great Hall, all in black marble. The Mississauga City Hall symbolizes the aspirations of this suburban town, which, as a result of continuous urban expansion, is on its way to becoming more populous and more affluent than the Queen City, Toronto.

Between these two industrial areas is a surprising little treasure: Oakville. It is a lovely vacation town that is sure to please.

Oakville ★

Auspiciously situated on the shores of Lake Ontario, Oakville will enchant visitors longing for a weekend in the open air. After having passed through the industrial zones of Toronto or Hamilton, it is a pleasant surprise to come upon such a lovely city. The city's attractions become more apparent the closer you get to downtown and the **marina** where a large number of sailboats and superb yachts are moored. Park at the corner of Water and Robinson Streets and go for a quiet walk beside the sparkling waters. The downtown area, which boasts a succession of interesting shops and restaurants, can easily be explored on foot. Without a doubt, Oakville is the star attraction in this corner of Ontario.

Burlington

The westernmost shore of Lake Ontario is occupied by Burlington to the north, and Hamilton to the south. Set side by side, and linked by Beach Boulevard, these two cities could almost be considered a single urban area. Burlington, the less populous of the two, is a peaceful residential town with little to offer in terms of tourist attractions, except perhaps for the little **Joseph Brant Museum** *($2.75; Tue to Sat 10am to 4pm, Sun 1pm to 4pm; 1240 North Shore E. Blvd., ☎634-3556)*, the last home of the Mohawk captain for which it is named.

Hamilton ★

Up until the arrival of the first colonists, who did not begin settling this area until the end of the 18th century, the site now occupied by Hamilton was the focal point of an Amerindian conflict. The Iroquois had virtually wiped out the Neutrals who had first inhabited the area. In turn, however, the Iroquois were driven out by white colonists. In 1815, George Hamilton drew up the plans for the city. Hamilton flourished in the 20th century, thanks to the steel, automobile and home appliance industries, among others. These industries left their mark on the city, whose surrounding landscape is vast, stark and dreary.

Hamilton is nonetheless pleasantly located on Lake Ontario, whose shores are lined with lovely parks, including **Bayfront Park** and **Dundurn Park** where you can enjoy a stroll or a bike ride, relax on a bench or at a picnic table, and watch the lively activity at the marina. Along with the residential neighbourhood on the hillside, with its superb Victorian homes, this is definitely the prettiest part of town. Downtown Hamilton and its surroundings,

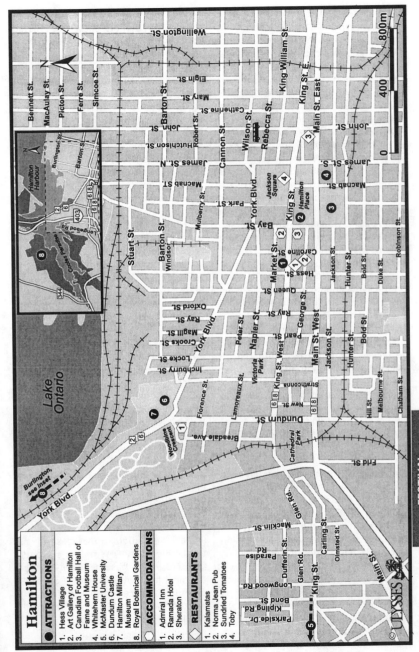

Hamilton

ATTRACTIONS
1. Hess Village
2. Art Gallery of Hamilton
3. Canadian Football Hall of Fame and Museum
4. Whitehern House
5. McMaster University
6. Dundurn Castle
7. Hamilton Military Museum
8. Royal Botanical Gardens

ACCOMMODATIONS
1. Admiral Inn
2. Ramada Hotel
3. Sheraton

RESTAURANTS
1. Kalamatas
2. Norma Jean Pub
3. Sundried Tomatoes
4. Toby

Lake Ontario

Hamilton Harbour

FESTIVAL COUNTRY

© ULYSSES

along King Street, are not particularly attractive places to explore on foot, except for **Hess Village ★**, a cluster of elegant houses, shops and restaurants.

There are, however, a few interesting places to visit in the centre of town, including the **Art Gallery of Hamilton ★** *($4, free on Thu 5pm to 9pm; Thur 10am to 9pm, Wed, Fri and Sat 10am to 5pm, Sun 1pm to 5pm; 123 King St. W., ☎527-6610, www.culturenet. ca/agh)*. Open since 1914, it houses paintings, prints and other works of art. Its collection of contemporary art is particularly rich, and makes for some fascinating viewing. Unfortunately, however, the written commentary accompanying the pieces can be a bit vague.

On the same square as the Art Gallery, you'll find the **Canadian Football Hall of Fame and Museum** *($3; Mon to Sat 9:30am to 4:30pm, from May to Sep open Sunday as well noon to 4:30pm; 58 Jackson St. W., ☎528-7566)*, which uses equipment, photographs and various mementos to trace the history of Canadian football and its evolution over the years.

Take St. James Street to Jackson Street West.

The classically inspired, Georgian-style **Whitehern** *($3.50; 41 Jackson St. E., ☎546-2018)* was erected in the late 1840s. In 1852, one Dr. McQueston purchased it, and the splendid house remained in his family's possession until 1968. Now open to the public, it has been restored to its original state, complete with period furnishings, and thus reflects the tastes of a prosperous 19th-century family.

St. Paul's Presbyterian Church ★ *(56 James St. N.)*, designed by the gifted architect William Thomas, is by far the most typically British of Ontario's 19th-century churches. Erected in 1854, it has an elegant sandstone steeple topped by a stone spire.

Founded in Toronto in the mid-19th century, **McMaster University** moved to Hamilton in 1928. The following year, construction was begun on **University Hall ★**, a lovely building similar to those found on the campuses of Oxford and Cambridge in England. Its façade is adorned with numerous gargoyles and masks symbolizing the various disciplines taught at the university.

Hamilton's most interesting attractions are hidden away outside the downtown area.

Head toward Burlington on York Boulevard.

Dundurn Castle ★★ *($6, entrance fee included in admission to military museum; one-hour guided tours; Mon to Fri 9am to 4pm; 610 York Blvd., Dundurn Park, L8R 3H1, ☎546-2872)*, generally viewed as the jewel of Hamilton, truly deserves to be called a castle, with its impressive dimensions and its architecture, a skilful blend of English Palladianism and the Italian Renaissance style characteristic of Tuscan villas. It was built in 1835 for Sir Allan MacNab, Prime Minister of the United Provinces of Canada from 1854 to 1856. Restored, furnished and decorated as it was back in 1855, this castle, with its 35 opulent rooms, reveals a great deal about upper-class life in the 19th century. The former servants' quarters in the basement are perhaps the most fascinating rooms of all, since they offer an idea of how difficult life was for those without which the castle wouldn't have functioned.

Keep heading toward Burlington on York Boulevard.

Another, smaller building on the castle grounds houses the **Hamilton Military Museum** *($2; Jun to Sep every day 11am to 5pm; Sep to May closed Mon, Sun noon to 5pm, Tue and Sat 11am to 5pm; ☎546-4974)*. Here, you will find a collection of the various uniforms worn by Canadian soldiers over the years.

You can enjoy a unique outing just a step away from downtown Hamilton, at the **Royal Botanical Gardens** ★★ *($7; outdoors every day 9:30am to 5pm, greenhouses every day 9am to 5pm; Plains Rd., at the intersection of Hwy. 6 and Hwy. 403; ☎527-1158, www.rbg.ca)*, where you can stroll about amidst luxuriant flowers and explore wonderfully preserved natural habitats. A large section of the park, which covers some 1,000 ha in all, is known as "Cootes Paradise," a stretch of marshes and wooded ravines crisscrossed by footpaths. In addition to this untouched area, you will find a variety of gardens, including a rose garden, the largest lilac garden in the world and a rock garden, where thousands of flowers bloom in the spring. The Royal Botanical Gardens are enchanting year round; in the winter, when the outdoor gardens are bare, you can visit the greenhouses, where various flower shows are presented.

Tour C: Niagara and the Wine Route

This tour covers the region to the west of the Niagara River, along the U.S. border. Control over this area was once crucial as far as shipping on Lakes Ontario and Superior was concerned, and the two forts that were built to protect it, Fort George and Fort Erie, still stand on either side of the river. Nowadays, however, the region is best known for its wineries and orchards, and for being home to the extraordinary Niagara Falls, which have continued to amaze people of all ages and inspire lovers and daredevils for decades.

St. Catharines

St. Catharines flourished with the construction of the Welland Canal in the 1820s. Situated at the mouth of the Niagara River, on the shores of Lake Ontario, this fair-sized town played an important role in Great Lakes navigation.

As in the case of the Rideau Canal in the Ottawa region (see p 65), the construction of the canal was deemed necessary after the War of 1812, in order to make Upper Canada more accessible. Strategic considerations aside, the canal was to provide an economic advantage as well. It would allow ships to pass from Lake Ontario to Lake Erie, which had been impossible until then, because the 99.5-metre-high Niagara escarpment stood in the way. The canal was begun in 1824 and became navigable in 1829. In later years it became apparent that this first canal was insufficient for lake traffic, and four new canals were dredged over the years, including the present one, which dates from 1932.

Forty-two kilometres long and equipped with eight locks, the canal enables ships from Lake Ontario and Lake Erie to travel from St. Catharines to Port Colborne. There are viewing areas all along it, the most interesting being the **Lock 3 Viewing Complex** ★ *(free admission; the canal is closed to ships from Dec to Mar; take the Glendale Avenue exit from the QEW and follow the signs)* in St. Catharines, where visitors can watch ships going through the lock from a large observation deck. At the neighbouring **St. Catharines Museum** *($3; summer, every day 9am to 9pm; rest of the year, Mon to Fri*

FESTIVAL COUNTRY

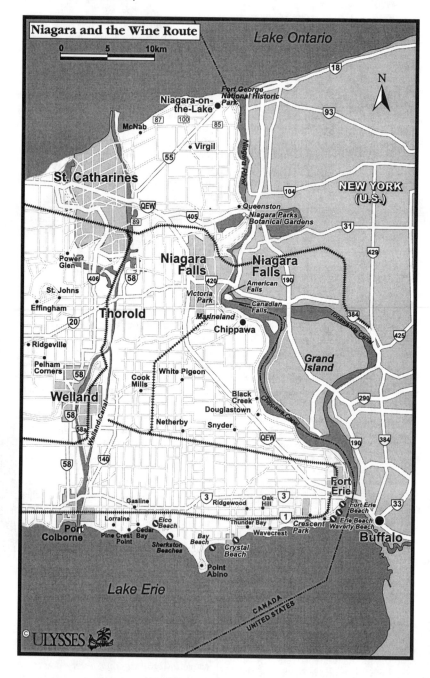

Niagara and the Wine Route

9am to 5pm; ☎984-8880), you can learn about the history of the canal and see a short documentary that explains how the lock works.

Take the 87 from St. Catharines to Niagara-on-the-Lake.

Niagara-on-the-Lake ★★

The history of Niagara-on-the-Lake dates back to the late 18th century, when the town, then known as Newark, was the capital of Upper Canada from 1791 to 1796. Nothing remains of that time, however, for the town was burned during the War of 1812, which pitted the British colonies against the United States. After the American invasion, the town was rebuilt and graced with elegant English-style homes, which have been beautifully preserved and still give this community at the mouth of the Niagara River a great deal of charm. Some of these houses have been converted into elegant inns, which welcome visitors attending the celebrated Shaw Festival (see p 271), or simply lured here by the town's English atmosphere.

After the American Revolution, the British abandoned Fort Niagara, which stands on the east side of the Niagara River. To protect their remaining colonies, however, they decided to build another fort. Between 1797 and 1799, Fort George was erected on the west side of the river. Within a few years, the two countries were fighting again. In 1812, war broke out, and the Niagara-on-the-Lake region, which shared a border with the United States, was in the eye of the storm. Fort George was captured, then destroyed in 1813, only to be reconstructed in 1815.

At the **Fort George National Historic Site ★** *($6; early Apr to late Oct, every* day; Nov to Mar, Mon to Fri, 9am to 4pm; Niagara Pkwy. S., ☎468-4257),* you can tour the officer's quarters, the guard rooms, the barracks and other parts of the restored fort.

The **Niagara Historical Society Museum** *($3; May to Sep, every day 9am to 5pm; winter, every day noon to 5pm; 43 Castlereagh, ☎468-3912)* displays a collection of tools and other everyday articles from the 19th century, as well as military weapons and uniforms.

You can also visit the lovely, Georgian-style **McFarland House** *($5; May to Sep, every day 10am to 6pm; Niagara Pkwy. S., 2 km south of town, ☎871-0540)*, built in 1800 for James McFarland and still decorated with furnishings dating from 1800 to 1840.

The special microclimate of the Niagara Peninsula allows plants that do not grow elsewhere in Canada to be cultivated – most notably the grapevine. Eighty percent of Canadian wines are produced here, some of which have won prestigious international awards. There are no less than ten vineyards in Niagara-on-the-Lake, and this region with its furrowed fields is perfect for walking, cycling or driving – not to mention discovering and enjoying some Ontario vintages.

Hillebrand Estates Winery
Highway 55, Niagara-on-the-Lake, ☎468-7123.

Konzelmann
1096 Lakeshore Dr., Niagara-on-the-Lake, ☎935-2866.

Stonechurch Vineyards
R.R. 5, Niagara-on-the-Lake, ☎935-3535.

Château des Charmes
1025 York Rd., St. David (near Queenston), ☎262-5202.

FESTIVAL COUNTRY

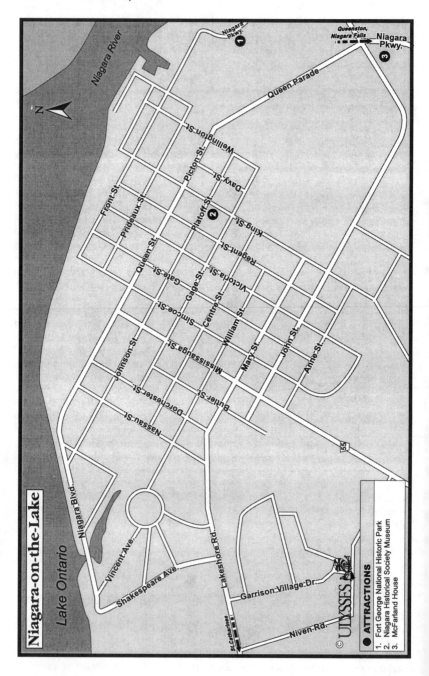

Niagara-on-the-Lake

Lake Ontario

Niagara River

N

Niagara Pkwy.

Queenston, Niagara Falls
Niagara Pkwy.

Queen Parade

Wellington St.

Picton St.

Davy St.

Front St.

Prideaux St.

Platoff St.

King St.

Queen St.

Regent St.

Gate St.

Victoria St.

Gage St.

Centre St.

Simcoe St.

William St.

Johnson St.

Mississauga St.

Mary St.

John St.

Anne St.

Dorchester St.

Butler St.

Nassau St.

55

Niagara Blvd.

Vincent Ave.

Shakespeare Ave.

Lakeshore Rd.

Garrison Village Dr.

St. Catharines

Niven Rd.

© ULYSSES

● **ATTRACTIONS**

1. Fort George National Historic Park
2. Niagara Historical Society Museum
3. McFarland House

Inniskillin Wines
R.R.1, Niagara-on-the-Lake,
☎468-3554.

Continue heading south on the Niagara Parkway, which runs alongside the Niagara River to Queenston.

Queenston

A pretty hamlet on the banks of the Niagara River, Queenston consists of a few little houses and verdant gardens. It is best known as the former home of Laura Secord who became famous during the War of 1812, when, upon learning that the Americans were about to attack, she ran 25 km to warn the British army, which was thus able to drive back the enemy troops. Today, her name is associated first and foremost with a brand of chocolate.

Farther south, you'll reach the foot of Queenston Height. If you're feeling energetic, you can climb the steps to the statue of sir Isaac Brock, a British general who died in this area during the War of 1812, while leading his men to victory. You will also enjoy a splendid view ★ of the region.

A few kilometres before Niagara Falls, lie the **Niagara Parks Botanical Gardens** *(Niagara Pkwy, Box 150 Niagara Falls, L2E 6G2, ☎356-8554)*, a horticulture school whose beautifully kept gardens are open to the public.

Keep heading south to Niagara Falls.

Niagara Falls

The striking spectacle of the Niagara Falls has been attracting crowds of visitors for many years, a trend supposedly started when Napoleon's brother came here with his young wife. Right beside the falls, the town of the same name is entirely devoted to tourism, and its downtown area is a series of nondescript motels, uninteresting museums and fast-food restaurants, accented by scores of colourful signs. These places have sprung up in a chaotic manner, and no one seems to have given a second thought to aesthetics. There's no denying that the Niagara Falls are a natural treasure, but the town is best avoided.

The **Niagara Falls ★★★** were created some 10,000 years ago, when the glaciers receded, clearing the Niagara Escarpment and diverting the waters of Lake Erie into Lake Ontario. This natural formation is remarkably beautiful, with two falls, one on either side of the border. The American Falls are 64 m high and 305 m wide, with a flow of 14 million litres per minute, while Canada's Horseshoe Falls, named for their shape, are 54 m high and 675 m wide, with a flow of 155 million litres of water per minute. The rocky shelf of the falls is made of soft stone, and it was being worn away by at a rate of 1 m per year until some of the water was diverted to the nearby hydro-electric power stations. The rate of erosion is now about .3 m per year.

It would be hard not to be impressed by the sight of all that raging water plunging into the gulf at your feet with a thundering roar. This seemingly untameable natural force has been a source of inspiration to many a visitor. In the early 20th century, a few daring souls tried to demonstrate their bravery by going over the falls in a barrel or walking over them on a tightrope, resulting in several deaths. In 1912, these types of stunts were outlawed.

During the summer, a huge number of visitors arrive every day to see the falls. Many come by car, so there tend to be traffic jams while everyone searches for a place to park. There is a huge parking

FESTIVAL COUNTRY

lot at the entrance to the park – for a fee, of course *($9)*. To save a few dollars, you can brave the traffic downtown, where parking lots are cheaper.

In 1885, **Victoria Park** ★ was created in order to protect the natural setting around the falls from unbridled commercial development. This beautiful green space alongside the river is scored with hiking and cross-country ski trails.

There are **observation decks** ★★★ in front of the falls. The best one is located right across from the Niagara Parks Commission offices and the tourist information centre. The falls can also be viewed from countless other angles: read on...

The *Maid of the Mist* **Steamboat Company** ★ *($10.10; May to Oct, departures every 30 min; 5920 River Rd., PO Box 808, L2E 6V6, ☎358-5781)* takes passengers to the foot of the falls, which make the boat seem very small indeed. Protected by a raincoat, which will prevent you from getting drenched during the outing, you can view the American side of the falls and then the Canadian side, right in the middle of the horseshoe.

If you climb to the top of the **Skylon Tower** *($6.95; year-round, every day 8am to 1am; 5200 Robinson St., L2G 2A3, ☎356-2651, reservations ☎888-275-9714, www.skylon.com)*, you can view the falls ★★ at your feet, a truly unique and memorable sight. You can enjoy a similar view from the **Minolta Tower** *($6.95; every day from 8:30am on; 6732 Oakes Prom., ☎356-1501)*.

The **Spanish Aero Car** *($5; Mar to Sep 9am to 9pm, Oct and Nov 9am to 5pm; Niagara Pkwy; Niagara Parks Commission ☎356-2241)* offers a bird's-eye

view of the falls from a height of 76.2 metres.

For a closer look at the falls, head to the **Table Rock Panoramic Tunnels** ★ *($6; every day from 9am on; Victoria Park, ☎358-3268)*, which run behind the Canadian side.

How about soaring through the air over the falls? You can do just that, thanks to **Niagara Helicopters** *($75; 9am to 5pm, Nov to Mar 10am to 4pm, weather permitting; 3731 Victoria Ave., PO Box 636, L2E 6V5, ☎374-1221)*.

An **elevator** transports visitors all the way down to the rapids *(Great Gorge Adventure $5; May to Oct from 9am on; 4330 River Rd., ☎356-1221)*.

Niagara has countless museums, some of little interest. A number of them are located in the downtown area known as Clifton Hill.

If you have a little time to spare, visit the **Niagara Falls Museum** *($6.75; May to Sep, every day 9am to 10pm; Oct to Apr 10am to 5pm; 5651 River Rd., ☎356-2151)*, whose collection ranges from Egyptian mummies to souvenirs of daredevils who have tried to conquer the falls.

The **Imax Theatre** *($7.50; May to Oct, every day; 6170 Buchanan Ave., Niagara Falls Imax Theatre and Daredevil Adventure ☎358-3611, www.tourism niagara.com/imax)* shows a giant-screen film on the falls that feels like you're actually in them.

The second most popular attraction in town, next to the falls, of course, is the **Casino Niagara** *(5705 Falls Ave.)*. The exterior is far from sensational; in fact, the most remarkable thing about it is the parking lot. Inside, however, the succession of lively and noisy gaming

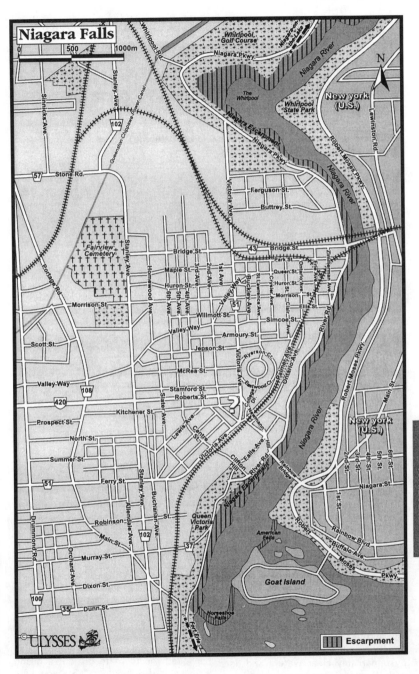

Niagara Falls

0 500 1000m

Whirlpool Golf Course

Niagara Pkwy.

The Whirlpool

Whirlpool State Park

New york (U.S.)

Niagara River

Niagara Escarpment

Niagara Pkwy.

Lewinston Rd.

Robert Moses Pkwy.

Niagara River

Slinicks Ave.

Stanley Ave.

102

Queenston Chippawa Power Canal

Whirlpool Rd.

57

Stone Rd.

Portage Rd.

Fairview Cemetery

Morrison St.

Scott St.

Valley Way

108

420

Prospect St.

North St.

Summer St.

51

Drummond Rd.

Orchard Ave.

100

35

Stanley Ave.

Homewood Ave.

Bridge St.

Maple St.

Huron St.

3rd Ave.

2nd Ave.

4th Ave.

5th Ave.

6th Ave.

Willmott St.

Valley Way

Buckley Ave.

Victoria Ave.

1st Ave.

Valley Way

Armoury St.

Jepson St.

McRea St.

Stamford St.

Roberts St.

Kitchener St.

Lewis Ave.

Crysler Ave.

Ferry St.

Robinson St.

Main St.

Murray St.

Dixon St.

Dunn St.

Buchanan Ave.

Allendale Ave.

Slater Ave.

102

37

Ferguson St.

Buttrey St.

Victoria Ave.

43

Bridge St.

Park St.

Queen St.

Huron St.

Morrison St.

Ellis St.

St. Lawrence Ave.

St. Clair Ave.

Simcoe St.

Ryerson Cr.

Eastwood Ct.

Palmer Ave.

Ontario Ave.

Erie Ave.

Ontario Ave.

Zimmerman Ave.

River Rd.

Niagara Escarpment

Clifton Hill

Falls Ave.

River Rd.

Oakes Dr.

Rainbow Bridge

Queen Victoria Park

American Falls

Goat Island

Horseshoe Falls

Fort Erie

Niagara River

New york (U.S.)

Main St.

1st St.

2nd St.

3rd St.

4th St.

5th St.

6th St.

Niagara St.

Rainbow Blvd

Buffalo Ave.

Robert Moses Pkwy.

N

© ULYSSES

Escarpment

rooms have a congenial decor. Open 24 hours a day (every day).

If you'd like to forget about the falls for a little while and watch some performing sea-lions, dolphins and whales instead, head to **Marineland** *($25.95; Apr to Oct 10am to 5pm; Jul and Aug 9am to 6pm; 7657 Portage Rd., ☎356-9565)*. The little zoo and carousels are sure to be a hit with the kids.

The road continues southward along the river to Fort Erie. It is flanked by a pleasant park, as well as a number of opulent houses, some of which are rather ostentatious.

Fort Erie

Fort Erie, a rather uninspiring little town, is located at the point where the Niagara River empties into Lake Erie. The Peace Bridge links it to Buffalo, in the United States, making it one of the major border stations in this region. Farther south, at the very end of the river, stands **Fort Erie** *($5; mid-May through Sep, every day 10am to 6pm; ☎871-0540)*, a stone structure that has been standing guard over the region since 1764. Partially destroyed over the years, it has been restored and now houses military equipment that belonged to English and American troops. In addition, a lovely park has been laid out around it.

Take the 1 from Fort Erie to Crystal Beach.

Crystal Beach

A popular summer resort for the well-heeled, this village boasts one of the loveliest beaches on Lake Erie, **Crystal Beach ★**, a long strip of sand washed by remarkably clear waters and lined with houses. The most beautiful of these are located near Point Abino, which stretches out into the blue waters of the lake and is studded with a few opulent vacation homes and a small lighthouse.

Follow the highway to Port Colborne.

Port Colborne

Port Colborne, located on the shores of Lake Erie, is home to the eighth and final lock on the Welland Canal. For a closer view of Lock 8, go to **Fountain View Park**. Aside from the lock, which is one of the largest simple locks in the world, the town has no real attractions to speak of.

At this point, you can head north on the 406, which will take you back to St. Catharines by way of Welland, or west toward London and Windsor on the 3.

 OUTDOOR ACTIVITIES

 Hiking

Tour A: Kitchener-Waterloo and Surroundings

Nearly 100 km long, the **Avon Trail** runs through a beautiful rural area. It leads from the Avon River into the heart of Mennonite country, passing through the lovely town of Stratford along the way. For further information, contact:

Avon Trail
P.O. Box 20018, Stratford, ON, N5A 7V3.

Its proximity to the Grand River has inspired the town to lay out a hiking trail along its banks. The **Cambridge**

Heritage River Trail is an easy two-hour excursion that allows you to get some fresh air and admire the peaceful riverside. It crosses the city from Waterworks Park to the Speed River. For a map of the trail call ☎740-4681, ext. 4229.

 Bicycling

The quiet, charming country roads of Festival Country are perfect for cycling. You can enjoy a ride through the fields in the St. Jacobs area, or tour the local vineyards. In most towns, you'll have no trouble finding a bike shop for any necessary repairs.

Tour C: Niagara and the Wine Route

Niagara Bicycle Touring *(tours start at the Pillar & Post Hotel ☎468-1300)* arranges three-hour bike trips through the Niagara-on-the-Lake region.

A road reserved for cyclists and pedestrians runs along the Niagara River (and the Niagara Parkway) from Niagara-on-the-Lake to Fort Erie, a distance of about 40 kilometres. Cyclists of all levels can enjoy this pleasant, peaceful ride.

 Birdwatching

Tour A: Kitchener-Waterloo and Surroundings

The **Kortright Waterfowl Park** *($2; Mar to Oct, Sat and Sun 9am to 5pm; 8 km north of Hwy 401; take Exit 195 and follow the signs, ☎824-6729)* is both a wilderness reserve and a research centre. This lovely, well laid-out area is a birder's paradise, with nearly one hundred species to spot.

 ACCOMMODATIONS

Tour A: Kitchener-Waterloo
and Surroundigns

Kitchener-Waterloo

There are several full-comfort hotels in town, but if you're looking for a charming inn, the neighbouring villages have more to offer.

The **Travelodge** *($92; ≈, ℜ, ⊛, ໖; 2969 King St. E., N2A 1A9, ☎894-5900 or 800-578-7878, ↝894-9144)* is located at the east edge of town. It is easy to spot, with its tall, red and white brick tower, which is very modern but has little character. The rooms are nevertheless quite pleasant.

The nearby **Walper Terrace Hotel** *($99; ℜ, ໖; 1 King St. W., N2G 1A1, ☎745-4321)*, by contrast, is a handsome building dating from 1893, whose charms are perhaps a bit outdated. Although not as luxurious as the more modern hotels, it is nevertheless comfortable.

Don't confuse the Waterloo Hotel with the **Waterloo Inn** *($100; ≈, ⃝, ℜ; 475 King St. N., N2J 2Z5, ☎884-0220, ↝884-0321)*. Built at the entrance to the town, its modern design has no particular allure, but it provides all the expected comforts.

The **Sheraton** *($129; ≈, ⊛, ⃝, ໖; 105 King St. E., N2G 3W9, ☎744-4141, ↝578-6889)*, located alongside Market Square, is unquestionably one of the most elegant places to stay in town. A modern hotel complex, it has spacious rooms and all the amenities. Large picture windows in the lobby look out onto a magnificent indoor swimming pool.

🦐 Although the aging facade of the **Waterloo Hotel** *($130; 2 King St. N., N2J 2W7, ☎885-2626, ⬧885-774)* is not terribly inviting, you will have a completely different impression once past the front doors. The lobby is furnished with beautiful antiques and has a majestic intricately carved hardwood staircase. Upstairs, each bedroom is different from the others, with beautiful furniture, high-backed armchairs and comfortable beds. The private bathrooms are modern and impeccably clean. This is by far the most charming place to stay in the city.

St. Jacobs

🦐 The **Countryside Manor** *($65 bkfst incl.; 39 Henri St., NOB 2NO, ☎664-2622 or 800-476-8942)* is one of those places you'll want to come back to. The owners are friendly, and you'll feel right at home in the pleasant rooms of their charming little house. The breakfasts, both copious and delicious, are equally memorable.

Right next to the Farmer's Market, this new hotel in the Best Western chain was built in 1998. The builders tried for a rustic effect by giving the **St. Jacob's Country Inn** *($99; ℜ, ℝ, ☉; 50 Benjamin Rd. E., ☎884-9295, ⬧884-2532)* a cedar-shingle roof. It does add a certain charm. Brand new, it is sure to please people who prefer the most up-to-date facilities.

Benjamin's Inn *($105; ℜ; 17 King St., St. Jacobs, NOB 2NO, ☎664-3731)* is a pretty building that has stood in the centre of town for over a century; it has been renovated in order to accommodate visitors. The rooms are furnished with antiques, and have a cozy charm that adds to the pleasure of being on vacation.

🦐 Stately trees adorn the garden of the **Jacobstettel Guest House** *($140 bkfst incl.; ℜ; 16 Isabella, NOB 2NO, ☎664-2208)*, a splendid Victorian house with about a dozen charming rooms, all decorated with antiques.

Elmira

The **Bristows Inn** *($89 bkfst incl.; 80 Arthur St. S., N3B 2N4, ☎669-1604)* has a particularly pleasant location on a peaceful residential street. A white and green house dating from the 19th century, it is as charming as can be. With only seven rooms, there is a decidedly family atmosphere for homesick types.

Elora

🦐 The stone mill by the falls around which the town of Elora grew is now the splendid **Elora Mill Country Inn** *($150 bkfst incl.; 77 Mill St. W., PO Box 218, NOB 1SO, ☎846-5356, ⬧846-9180)*. The place still plays a central role in the community, for its excellent reputation has long been attracting visitors, who come here for the tastefully decorated rooms and succulent cuisine.

Fergus

The distinguished **Breadalbane Inn** *($69-$175; ℜ; 487 St. Andrew St. W., ☎843-4770)* really stands out. The building was constructed in the 19th century for the family of George Douglas Fergusson. It has been converted into an inn, but all of the charm of yesteryear has been kept intact. There are eight pleasant rooms, each decorated in a unique and elegant way. The more expensive ones have added touches like canopy beds, fireplaces or whirlpools. There is also an excellent restaurant on the premises (see p 267).

Guelph

It may seem impossible to find a charming place to stay in Guelph. However, they do exist, and **Willow Manor** *($85 bkfst incl.; ≈; 408 Willow Rd., ☎763-3574)* is living proof. Set up in a tastefully renovated and decorated 19th-century stone residence, it has only five bedrooms. Each is ravishing, with a fireplace and comfortable bed. The special touches found in the bedrooms are complemented by a delicious breakfast served in the dining room or, even better on sunny mornings, beside the pool.

Although somewhat drab-looking, the **Best Western Emerald Inn** *($86; 106 Carden St., N1H 3A3, ☎836-1331 or 800-528-1234, ≈836-9627)*, has comfortable rooms and is well-located in the heart of downtown Guelph.

Cambridge

Located on a quiet residential street away from all the downtown activity, **Kress Hill House** *($80 bkfst incl. sb, $110 bkfst incl. pb; 127 Jacob St., ☎653-8728)* is a magnificent stone building with three well-maintained guestrooms. The warm welcome, good breakfast and charmingly furnished rooms are bound to win you over, and the house has a lovely garden shaded by mature trees.

Langdon Hall *($289; R.R. 33, N3H 4R8, ☎740-2100 or 800-268-898, ≈740-8161)*, in the countryside near Cambridge, is without question one of the most sumptuous inns in the region. Upon arriving, you will be greeted by a magnificent garden adorned with stately trees and thousands of flowers.

Then you'll see Langdon Hall itself, a large brick building containing 38 rooms, each exquisitely decorated in its own unique style.

Tour B: Hamilton and Surroundings

Burlington

Plains Road is not exactly enchanting, and is definitely not the kind of place where you would spend your dream vacation. The motels here are nonetheless inexpensive and have clean, albeit basic rooms. One option is the **City View Motel** *($65; 1400 Plains Rd., Burlington, L7T 1H6, ☎522-2483)*, whose decor is drab, to say the least.

If you're just passing through and want to avoid going into Burlington, you can stay in one of several hotels along the QEW, on the outskirts of town. The **Holiday Inn** *($140; pb, ≈, ℜ, △, ⊛, ✗; 3063 South Service Rd., L7N 3E9, ☎639-4443 or 800-HOLIDAY, ≈333-4033)* has rooms with functional furnishings and a private bath.

Hamilton

Hamilton has surprisingly few hotels and motels for a city of its size. The options are essentially limited to big chain hotels, which lack character, but are nonetheless quite comfortable. If you're on a tight budget and don't mind staying in a generic motel, you might be better off in Burlington.

Given the dearth of inexpensive accommodations in Hamilton, the rooms in the student residences at **McMaster University** *($35; 1280 Main St. W., L8S 4K1, ☎525-9140 ext. 24223)*, which can only be rented during summer, are perhaps one of the only low-budget options.

The **Admiral Inn** *($90; ℛ; 149 Dundurn St. N., L8R 3E7, ☎529-2311, ⇴529-9100)* has comfortable, modern rooms that are fairly typical of this kind of hotel, located on the way into a city. Its façade, on the other hand, is more unusual, with lots of picture windows, and as a result the lobby and restaurant are wonderfully bright and sunny.

Those who would rather stay downtown can choose from one of three Hamilton mainstays. The old **Howard Johnson Plaza Hotel** *($99; ≈, ℛ, ◐, ⊛, ♿, ✖; 112 King St. E., L8N 1A8, ☎546-8111 or 800-63-58, ⇴546-8144)* looks as if it has seen better days, but the rooms are nonetheless pleasant. If its old-fashioned look puts you off, head to the nearby **Ramada Hotel** *($110; ≈, ◐, ⊛, ♿, ✖; 150 King st. E., L8N 1B2, ☎528-3451, 800-603-0502 or 800-272-6232, ⇴522-2281)*, whose more modern-looking architecture and lobby might be more your style. In terms of comfort, the rooms are on a par with those at the Howard Johnson.

The **Sheraton** *($140; ≈, ℛ, ◐, ⊛, ✖; 116 King St. W., L8P 4V3, ☎529-5515 or 800-514-7101, ⇴529-8266)* is located near the Art Gallery of Hamilton. This lovely, modern, glass building, which literally dazzles in the sun, contains luxurious rooms.

Tour C: Niagara and the Wine Route

St. Catharines

There aren't many charming inns in town, so if that's what you're looking for, you're better off staying in Niagara-on-the-Lake. St. Catharines does, however, have a few modern hotels, like the **Highwayman Inn** *($99; ≈, ✖; 420 Ontario St., L2R 5M1, ☎688-1646)*, located alongside the highway.

Just outside of town, in a commercial district not far from Brock University, are the newly constructed buildings of the **Embassy Inn** *($109 bkfst incl.; ℛ, ≈, ◐; 3530 Schmon Pkwy, L2V 4Y6, ☎984-8484, ⇴984-6691)*. The large hotel, surrounded by a huge parking area, may lack the charm of rustic inns, but it perfectly meets the needs of business people. The suites are functional if slightly impersonal, and have a large living room, kitchen-dinette and bedroom. They also have all the conveniences of home, including irons and ironing boards, microwave ovens, televisions and hairdryers.

Niagara-on-the-Lake

If you have money to spare, you can really spoil yourself in Niagara-on-the-Lake, which has scores of quality inns. Visitors on a tight budget will have a harder time finding a place to stay, however.

Guest homes can be pleasant places to stay, both in town and in the surrounding areas. A hundred or more private homes offer this type of lodging. Some have only a room or two, while others offer luxurious quarters – there is something to suit every taste and budget. The **Niagara-on-the-Lake Chamber of Commerce & Visitor & Convention Bureau** *(153 King St. PO Box 1043, L0S 1J0, ☎468-4263, ⇴468-4930, www.niagara-on-the-lake.com)* will provide you with a list of these establishments and also offers a reservation service.

Here are just a few suggestions:

🏅 The **Ashgrove B&B** *($80 bkfst incl.; 487 Mississagua St., L0S 1J0, ☎468-1361)* is charmingly located at the edge of town where the countryside begins. Thus it provides a quiet atmosphere, but is still close to downtown. The rooms are tastefully decorated and there is a beautiful garden.

There is a lovely, white-stucco home with black shutters on Queen Street, just far enough away from the bustle of the city. This is the **Roger-Harrison House** *($110 bkfst incl.; 157 Queen St., LOS 1J0, ☎468-1615)*, whose guestrooms and common areas have an antique charm. Guests can use the living room and the library.

The majestic white-brick **Somerset B & B** *($190 bkfst incl.; 111 Front St., LOS 1J0)* faces Lake Ontario. A vast garden surrounding the property affords a superb view of the lake. The exceptional site is certainly an attraction, but it is not the only one. The rooms are elegantly decorated, well maintained and have balconies as well as private bathrooms.

The **Moffat Inn** *($79; ℜ; 60 Picton St., LOS 1J0, ☎468-4116)*, located near the centre of town, is a charming little white building adorned with green shutters. It has about twenty well-kept rooms, some with an attractive fireplace.

The **Olde Angel Inn** *($109; 224 Regent St., LOS 1J0, ☎468-3411)* occupies a building that dates back to the town's early days (1825). It stands on the site of another building erected a few years earlier, which was burned down during the War of 1812. This lovely place, adorned with green shutters and beautiful flowers, is now a comfortable inn, whose decor is not nearly as luxurious as that of some hotels in town, but has an appealing old-fashioned charm.

Although the modern decor of the lobby and the rooms may seem a bit cold, the **Colonel Butler Inn** *($110; 278 Mary St., LOS 1J0, ☎468-3251)* boasts all new furnishings and is extremely comfortable.

The inviting, and very elegant dining room of the Ristorante Giardino (see p 270), graced with superb picture windows, is easy to spot in the centre of town. The second floor is occupied by the **Gate House Hotel** *($160; ℜ; 142 Queen St., LOS 1J0, ☎468-3263, ⊷468-7400)*, which has about a dozen beautifully kept rooms. The style of rooms here differs from the usual old-fashioned look that seems to be popular in this town. The owners have opted for a designer decor that makes for a refreshing change.

A real local institution, the **Prince of Wales** *($175; ≈, ℜ, ◇, ◉, ⎣; 6 Picton St., LOS 1J0, ☎468-3246 or 800-263-2452, ⊷468-5521, www.prin ceofwhaleshotel.on.ca)* stands at the end of Queen Street, a commercial artery. This superb building, erected in 1864, has managed to retain its charm. In spite of its age, it is extremely elegant, from its richly decorated sitting and dining rooms to its pretty guest rooms. Renovations are planned for 1999 to give this place a facelift.

🦌 The vast, enchanting lobby of the **Pillar and Post Inn** *($190; ≈, ◷, ℜ, ◉, ◇, ⎣; corner of King and John St., 48 John St., PO Box 1011, LOS 1J0, ☎468-2123 or 800-361-6788, ⊷468-3551)* boasts plants, antiques and big skylights. The hushed atmosphere will make you feel like staying here for hours. This is just a foretaste of what you'll find in the rooms: beautiful wooden furniture, armchairs with floral patterns and even, in some cases, a fireplace. The owners have spared no effort in seeing to the comfort of their guests. A pool and an exercise room are at your disposal.

FESTIVAL COUNTRY

With its wide façade adorned with four white columns, the **Queens Landing Inn** *($195; ≈, ℛ, ⊛, ◌, ৬; 155 Byron St., PO Box 1180, corner of Byron and Melville St., L0S 1J0, ☎468-2195 or 800-361-6645, ⇁468-2227, www. vintageinns.com)* is somewhat ostentatious, but nonetheless elegant, standing there proudly alongside the Niagara River. It has 137 large, tastefully decorated rooms, each with a whirlpool bath and a fireplace. A first-class hotel by any standards.

Around Niagara-on-the Lake

With its orchards and vineyards stretching into the distance, the area between Niagara Falls and Niagara-on-the-Lake offers a peaceful contrast to the urban bustle of the two cities. At the heart of this pastoral haven, the **Grand Victorian B & B** *($189; ≈, ℛ; 4946 Clifton Hill, L2E 6S8, ☎358-3601)* promises a restful respite. The vast gardens are impressive, and the house is tastefully decorated, with large antique-filled rooms.

Niagara Falls

Niagara Falls, southwestern Ontario's tourist mecca, has at least a hundred hotels, most members of big North American chains, as well as a host of B&Bs. The local hotels are packed over summer vacation but empty during the low season, which is therefore a good time for bargain rates.

The most inexpensive place in town is without question the **Youth Hostel** *($21; 4945 Zimmerman Ave., L2E 3M2, ☎357-0770)*, an excellent option for visitors who are watching their pennies.

If you drive along the river before coming into town, you will pass a series of hotels offering modern standards of comfort and a lovely view of the rapids. The **Comfort Inn** *($179; ≈, ℛ, ✖; 4009 River Rd. L2E 3E5, ☎356-0131 or 800-565-0035)*, the **Days Inn** *($226; ≈, ℛ, ⊛, ◌; 4029 River Rd., L2E 3E5, ☎356-6666 or 800-263-2543, ⇁356-1800)* and the **Best Western Fireside** *($250; ≈, ℛ, ◌; 4067 River Rd., L2E 3E4, ☎374-2027, ⇁774-7746)*, all in a row, have similar rooms, although those in the Fireside are more charming, and each guestroom has a gas-burning fireplace.

There are a number of decent hotels in the centre of town, around Clifton Hill, but the location is not exactly peaceful. One worth trying is the **Venture Inn** *($189; ≈, ℛ, ⊛, ◌; 4960 Clifton Hill, PO Box 60, L2E 6S8, ☎358-3293 or 800-263-2557, ⇁358-3818, www. fallsresort.com)*, which offers adequate rooms in the heart of the action.

The nearby **FallsWay Quality Inn** *($189; ≈, ℛ; 4946 Clifton Hill, L2E 6S8, ☎358-3601)* has rooms of similar comfort. It goes without saying that establishments on this street are for guests seeking a lively atmosphere, morning, noon and night.

Other hotels are near all the action without being right in the middle of it, thus offering the advantage of being located on a somewhat quieter street than Clifton Hill. The **Travelodge Bonaventure** *($229; ≈, ℛ, ◌; 7737 Lundy's Lane, L2H 1H3, ☎374-7171 or 800-578-7878)* and the **Quality Hotel** *($249; ≈, ℛ, ◌; 5257 Ferry St., L2G 1R6, ☎356-2842)*, have clean, even pleasant rooms.

For a personal touch, Niagara Falls also has quite a few B&Bs, which are often much more charming than impersonal hotels. Located in a residential area facing the river, **Chandelier Inn** is another possibility. This lovely red-brick house with a gabled roof and finely wrought balconies also has a motel-style annex with extra rooms. You can also stay at the magnificent **Eastwood** *($$$$; River Rd., ☎354-8686, www.eastwood.com)*.

The **Old Stone Inn** *($189; ≈, ℛ, ⊛; 5425 Robinson St., L2G 7L6, ☎357-1234, ⇔357-9299)* is one of the few hotels in Niagara Falls with a little character. The lobby and the restaurant are located inside an old mill dating from 1904; the rooms, quite comfortable, in a more recent annex.

Outside Niagara Falls, there is a series of modern hotels along the river. One of these, the **Skyline Brock** *($175; ℛ; 5685 Falls Ave., L2E 6W7, ☎374-4444 or 800-263-7135)* is outstanding. Built in the twenties, it has a unique charm. A crystal chandelier and a majestic staircase grace the lobby. The rooms are quite comfortable, with modern conveniences.

Belonging to the same hotel chain, **Skyline Village Inn** *($125; ℛ, ≈; 4800 Bender Ave., L2G 3K1, ☎263-7135, ⇔357-4804)* is a concrete motel-style building that lacks the charm of the Skyline Brock. However, its rooms offer all the modern comforts and it is two steps away from the Casino.

The finest hotels stand at the top of the hill overlooking the falls, enabling guests to enjoy a beautiful view. They also offer the added advantage of a peaceful location, set away from the downtown area. The **Days Inn Overlooking The Falls** *($179-$249; 6361 Buchanan Ave., L2G 3V9, ☎357-7377)* has 239 comfortable rooms, the more expensive of which have a view of the falls (supplement of $30 to $60 is added to the price).

You can also opt for the elegantly decorated rooms of the **Renaissance** *($180; ≈, ℛ, △, ⊛; 6455 Buchanan Ave., L2G 3V9, ☎905-357-5200 or 800-228-9898, ⇔357-3422)*, a number of which, like those of the neighbouring hotels, offer a magnificent view of the falls.

🛏 At the very end of Oakes Street stands the beautiful **Sheraton Fallsview Hotel** *($195-$295; 6755 Oakes St., L2G 3W7, ☎905-374-1077 or 800-267-8439, ⇔374-6224, www.fallsview.com)*, which definitely has the best location of all. Each of the very comfortable rooms offers unimpeded views of the falls.

The newly constructed **Marriott** *($2200$250; ≈, ℛ, ⊛; 6740 Oakes Dr., L2G 3W6, ☎357-7300 or 888-501-8916, ⇔357-0490)* offers all the comforts, not to mention a view of the falls, or more precisely, a spectacular vista of the river stretching into the distance and torrents of water plunging down the precipice.

 RESTAURANTS

Tour A: Kitchener-Waterloo and Surroundings

Kitchener-Waterloo

To make it easier for you to locate the following restaurants, we have specified whether each one is located in Kitchener or Waterloo.

The façade of the **Harmony Lunch** *($; 90 King N., Waterloo, ☎886-4721)* looks as if it hasn't been touched since the place opened almost 50 years ago. Although this little restaurant looks rather uninviting at first, its "ham"burgers (literally made of ham) have won it a loyal clientele.

You will be amazed by the decor at the **Plantation** *($; 2 King St. N., Waterloo)* café. The vast dining room has imitation marble on the walls, punctuated by large, framed paintings with romantic themes. The furniture has been selected with comfort in mind, high-backed armchairs and cushioned benches are drawn up to wrought-iron tables. The place looks so inviting that you will want to settle in for a long, leisurely meal. The food is health-conscious and good. The menu offers fresh fruit salad, pasta with home-made sauces, and all sorts of cakes and teas. Perfect for breakfast or lunch!

For a quick bite to eat, try **Reggies** *($; 1 King St. W., Kitchener)*, where you can get a sandwich made to order. Wide choice of toppings.

The dining room of the **King Bridge Crossing** *($$; 77 King St. N., Waterloo, ☎886-1130)* is extremely cozy, with its comfortable armchairs, wallpaper and woodwork — just the kind of atmosphere that complements a good meal. The menu lists simple dishes like pasta, roast beef and hamburgers.

If you like innovative surroundings, you will enjoy **Times Square** *($$; 35 King St. N., ☎888-999)*, which is set up in a loft. The pipes on the ceiling have been painted and incorporated into the decoration scheme, while modern art is displayed on the brightly painted walls. Wooden tables add a softening touch and have colourful place settings. The overall effect is quite pleasing. However, decoration is not the only attraction here: the menu consists of well-prepared pasta dishes like *fettuccine prima vera* and spinach lasagna. There is a friendly bar on the second floor (see p 271).

On your way out of Kitchener, you'll see three restaurants side by side, in the building adjoining the Travelodge. All serve good, simple food; your only problem will be deciding among the Italian dishes at **Del Dente** *($$; 2980 King St. E., Kitchener, ☎893-6570)*, the grill at **Charcoal** *($$-$$$)* and the pasta bar at **Martini's** *($$)*.

🍴 If you're in the mood for the kind of tender, juicy steak that is a hallmark of American cuisine, head to **Golf's Steak House** *($$-$$$; open Mon to Sat 4pm to 11pm, Sun and holidays 4pm to 9pm, Sun brunch 11am to 2:20pm; 598 Lancaster W., Kitchener, ☎579-4050 or 579-4051)*. The dining rooms are attractively decorated, and a meal includes a steak (try the New York Sirloin), unlimited salad from the salad bar and the soup of the day.

The chef at **Janet Lynns** *($$$-$$$$; 92 King St. S., Waterloo, ☎725-3440)* definitely prepares some of the most sophisticated cuisine in town. The daily menu features mouth-watering specialties like grilled lamb and filet of pork with Beaujolais. To make a meal here that much more memorable, guests are seated in an elegant dining room, whose walls are adorned with colourful paintings.

St. Jacobs

🍴 The **Stone Crock** *($$; Mon to Sat 7am to 10:30pm, Sun 11am to 10:30pm; 41 King St., ☎664-2286)*, a Mennonite restaurant, has a modest dining room and a pleasant family atmosphere. The setup is simple: an all-you-can-eat, full-course meal including soup, salad bar, a choice of three main dishes (roast turkey, fried chicken or spareribs) and dessert for $13.95 per person.

🦞 There's something captivating about the atmosphere at **Benjamin's Inn** *($$-$$$; every day 11:30am to 9pm, closed Dec 25 and 26 and Jan 1; 17 King, ☎664-3731)*, and once you've taken a seat in the dining room, you'll feel like staying there for hours. Perhaps it's the rustic charm of the place, or the lovely fireplace. Or maybe it's the meal itself, made up of a succession of delicious dishes. Whatever the reason, you're sure to have a wonderful time here.

Elmira

Elmira has a **Stone Crock** *($$; Mon to Fri 7am to 8:30pm, Sun 11am to 8:30pm; 59 Church St., ☎669-1521 or 800-363-1881)* restaurant with the same setup as the one in St. Jacobs (see above).

Elora

🦞 The unpretentious **Desert Rose Café** *($; Metcalfe St.)* is the perfect place for a lunchtime snack, like a piece of quiche or a salad, or simply to treat yourself to a delicious dessert in the afternoon. The carrot cake and the butter tarts are especially worthy.

Not far from the stone mill is the perfectly charming **Lyander Tea House** *($)*. With pretty photographs on the walls and charming wooden tables, this is the perfect place to escape from the busy streets for a quiet bite to eat (cakes, salads, sandwiches and a selection of teas).

🦞 Alongside the river, is a real little gem called **La Cachette** *($$$; 13 Mill St., ☎846-8346)*, a French restaurant in a pretty house with two charming little dining rooms — one on the main floor, and the other on the second floor. The menu is even more appealing than the decor, listing succulent dishes like duck cutlet with apples and calvados and grilled lamb with *herbes de Provence*. During summer, you can enjoy your meal outside, by the side of the river, comfortably seated on the terrace.

Residents of Elora are truly spoiled when it comes to good restaurants. In addition to La Cachette, there's the **River Mill Inn** *($$$-$$$$; 77 Mill St. W., ☎846-5356)*, where you can enjoy a delicious meal in a dining room with a lovely view on the falls. The mouth-watering menu lists a variety of dishes, such as chateaubriand and lamb with a cheese filling.

Fergus

A familiar sight in the downtown area, **Jilly's Cafe** *($-$$; 216 St. Andrews St.)* would be much more appealing if the furniture were less like that found in old taverns, and more appropriate to a charming little restaurant. That said, the food is perfectly fine. Meat dishes, sandwiches and salads are on the menu.

🦞 Set up in a magnificent, renovated former residence, the restaurant at **Breadalbane Inn** *($$$-$$$$; 487 St. Andrew St. W., ☎843-4770)* is pleasing in every respect. The large dining room is furnished with antiques, and the long wooden tables and high-backed chairs make you feel comfortable right from the start. Then there is the wonderful menu, promising all sorts of delights. Finally, the food – dishes include rack of lamb and salmon with herbs – confirms it. This is an all-round wonderful restaurant!

FESTIVAL COUNTRY

Guelph

There are all sorts of charming places to enjoy a delicious meal in Guelph, which prides itself on having over a hundred restaurants. The following are a few of the finest and most pleasant ones on town.

The aptly named **Bookshelf Café** *($; 41 Quebec St.,* ☎*821-3333)*, located at the back of a bookstore, is a cosy little spot with big picture windows, a relaxed, youthful atmosphere and an appetizing menu.

Wimpy's *($; Wyndham St.)* is hardly elegant, but serves good burgers and has comfortable red vinyl bench seats.

The **Woolwich Arms Pub** *($-$$; 176 Woolwich St.,* ☎*836-2875)* is known for its delicious "specialty burgers" and attractive terrace, which is a pleasant place to eat on a fine summer day.

The **Georgian Creed's** *($$-$$$; 16 Douglas St.,* ☎*837-2692)*, hidden away on a quiet street a few steps from downtown Guelph, has a beautiful decor and serves delicious dishes that are sure to satisfy your palate.

Acton

The **Red Dog Cafe** *($; Mill St.)* is the perfect spot to have a sandwich or pasta, with its terrace that lets you see everything that's going on downtown. If it is raining, simply choose a table inside.

Cambridge

Cafe 13 *($-$$; 13 Main St.,* ☎*621-1313)*, located downtown in an old stone building, has a fairly typical pub-style menu featuring burgers and fries. It is an appealing place, however, and has a good selection of draft beer and scotch.

The **Riverbank Steakhouse** *($$$; 4 Parkhill Rd. W.,* ☎*740-2900)* is inside an old mill that has been completely renovated and boasts an enchanting location overlooking the Grand River. In order to make the most of the setting, the dining room has been laid out so that it opens onto the river, enabling guests to enjoy a magnificent view while savouring the restaurant's excellent cuisine. The meal promises to be equally delicious, with tender steak cooked to perfection. At lunch, a simpler menu with items like sandwiches and pasta is offered. On some nights, special "murder mystery" dinners are organized.

Brantford

The **Trattoria al Forno** *($-$$; 46 Dalhousie St.,* ☎*752-0555)* is a good place if you like Italian food. Specialties are pasta (lasagna, spaghetti bolognese or Alfredo), *pannini* and pizza cooked in a wood-burning oven. Don't be taken aback by the 1970s Italian-style decor (imitation marble, a fresco of Italy on the wall, aluminum chairs, red-and-white tablecloths, etc.). It is not so bad – provided you get a kick out of kitsch!

Tour B: Hamilton and Surroundings

Oakville

You know what kind of food to expect at **Omelette** *($; Lakeshore St.)* from its name. Large bay windows, a slate-tiled floor, brightly coloured walls and a few tables make up the basic decor of this charming little café.

🚲 **Nonna's** *($-$$; corner of Lakeshore St. and Navy St.)* has a wide selection of Italian specialties: *bruschetta,* assorted pastas and sauces, *panini* and more. There is no table service, so remember to order at the counter before getting too comfortably seated. But this lends a pleasant touch of informality to the restaurant.

Right next door, **Paradiso** *($$)* is a little trendier and more expensive. Its Italian food is perhaps a tad more refined, and always good.

Hamilton

You'll have no trouble finding a place to eat downtown on King Street, which is lined with fast-food restaurants. One option is **Toby** *($; King St., on Jackson Sq.)*, known for its big, tasty burgers.

Hess Village is the perfect neighbourhood for walking around and stopping for a meal in a pleasant restaurant. Some serve simple fare: **Norma Jean's Pub** *($-$$; George St.)* has an ordinary menu of hamburgers. Decorated with posters of Marilyn Monroe, this pleasant restaurant has a terrace facing the street.

The slightly more upscale **Kalamatas** *($-$$; Hess St.)* offers Mediterranean cuisine such as pasta in a cream sauce with sun-dried tomatoes and vegetables. Meals are served in a beautiful dining room or, weather permitting, on the terrace.

🚲 For something a little more sophisticated, you can try the classier **Sundried Tomatoes** *($$; at the corner of St. John and Main St. E.)*. The dining room, spacious enough so that guests have plenty of elbow room, is extremely pleasant. This place will appeal particularly to those with a penchant

for oysters, which have top billing on the menu.

If a good, tender steak is more up your alley, the **Shakespeare Steak House** *($$$; 181 Main St. E.,* ☎528-0689*)* supposedly serves the best in town.

Tour C: Niagara and the Wine Route

St. Catharines

Beantrees *($; 204 St. Paul St.,* ☎682-3357*)* must have the most eclectic clientele in St. Catharines. This little bistro, which is a perfect place for lunch, manages to attract students looking for a place to chat and while away the time; businesspeople, who stop in for a quick bite and shoppers lured inside by the impressive selection of tea.

Niagara-on-the-Lake

You can also stop by for a sandwich or a salad at **The Epicurean** *($; Queen St.)*, a simply decorated place with flowered tablecloths.

For just a coffee and a sandwich, the **Victoria** *($; Queen St.)* has a pleasant atmosphere.

🚲 On beautiful summer days, Queen Street is a magnet for window shoppers who may interrupt their leisurely strolls with a stop at one of the street's inviting terraces. It is sometimes hard to find a seat at the popular **Shaw Wine Bar and Cafe** *($-$$; Queen St.)*. However, you can always settle for the beautiful dining room with its large bay windows.

The elegant **Prince of Wales** *(6 Picton St.,* ☎468-3245*)* has two dining rooms. The first *($$$$)*, and more ritzy of the two, has a refined menu and is harmoniously decorated with antiques. The second *($$)* has a more relaxed atmosphere, a pub-style decor and a simple menu that's perfect for lunch, with selections like chicken fingers and salads. This is the perfect place for *Afternoon Tea ($9.95)*. Scones with cream, cucumber sandwiches, and of course, tea, are on the menu.

The dining rooms of **The Oban** *(160 Front St., ☎468-2165)* occupy most of the ground floor of a magnificent house. Some of the tables are set on a long veranda with big picture windows, and it is in this section of the restaurant *($$$-$$$$)* that you can sample some of the succulent dishes that have conquered both the hearts and the palates of so many people. Another room inside *($$)*, is more of a pub, with pictures covering the walls, antique furniture, all sorts of knick-knacks, a piano and a fireplace. Seated in a captain's chair or on a love seat, your plate on your knees or on a coffee table, you'll feel a bit like you're in your own living room. The menu lists simple dishes, such as chicken cacciatore and fried shrimp.

At the **Ristorante Giardino** *($$$$; 142 Queen St., ☎468-3236)*, you can enjoy a delicious Italian meal while comfortably seated in a magnificent room with big picture windows looking out onto the street.

Niagara Falls

Clifton Hill is lined with fast-food restaurants, which are devoid of charm, but will suit your needs if you're simply looking for a quick bite.

For ribs or roast chicken, visit **Tony's Place** *($; 5467 Victoria Ave.)*.

Victoria Park Restaurant *($-$$)* is pleasantly situated in the park beside the falls and faces the American side. Most people come for its location, but the food is also good, if simple (sandwiches).

In the same part of town, two other establishments offer respectable cuisine. **Parmigiana** *($$; Victoria Lane)*, stylishly installed in a little red-brick house, serves Italian food.

For a somewhat more refined meal, try the restaurant at the **Old Stone Inn** *($$-$$$; 5425 Robinson St., ☎357-1234)*, where you'll find a lovely dining room in a building dating back to the turn of the century. The menu lists an excellent selection of specialties from a number of different countries.

For beef (prime ribs), the second restaurant, **Montana** *($$-$$$; Victoria Lane)*, is less charming, but has good food.

The nearby **Casa D'Oro Dining Lounge** *($$$; 5875 Victoria Ave., ☎356-5646)* serves a decent selection of Italian specialties.

Finally, if your top priority is a view of the falls, your best bet is the restaurant in the **Skylon Tower** *($$$$; 5200 Robinson St., L2G 2A3, 356-2651, www.skylon.com)*. The menu features fish and meat dishes. Of course, you pay for the view, but what a view it is!

ENTERTAINMENT

Tour A: Kitchener-Waterloo and Surroundings

Kitchener-Waterloo

Bars and Nightclubs

At the end of the day, people flock to the **Kings Bridge Crossing** *(77 King N., Waterloo, ☎886-1130)* for a good meal, then top off the evening with a drink. If you don't want to eat here, you can take a seat in the bar section. The place features live music on certain nights.

Time Square *(35 King St. N.)* has a pleasant bar upstairs. You can settle in the rattan armchairs for a cozy chat or, if you prefer, join the action around the pool table.

Festivals

The **Oktoberfest**, the largest festival of its kind outside of Germany, serves as a reminder that a good part of the local population is of German descent. It is a major event in this region, during which all sorts of activities are organized, stalls selling sausages, sauerkraut and beer are set up and a festive atmosphere prevails.

Fergus

Festivals

The **Fergus Highland Games and Scottish Festival**, which celebrate the Scottish heritage of many local families, are held on the second weekend of August. The festivities include marching bands, concerts and a variety of tournaments.

Bars and Nightclubs

The **Breadalbane Inn** *(487 St. Andrew St. W.)* has one of the most charming little pubs imaginable. The perfect place to stop in for a beer.

Hamilton

Bars and Nightclubs

The **Gown and Gavel** *(Hess St.)*, which occupies one of the lovely Victorian houses in Hess Village, is something of a local institution and has a steady clientele of students.

A number of bars host live bands; you can find out who's playing where in the weekly paper *View*.

Niagara-on-the-Lake

Bars and Nightclubs

The **Oban** *(160 Front St., ☎468-2165)* is *the* place in town for a drink with friends, or even alone, ensconced in a comfortable armchair by the fireplace.

Festivals

The internationally renowned **Shaw Festival** *($21 to $60, reservations ☎468-2171 or 800-511-7429, ≈468-3804, www.shawfest.sympatico.ca)* has been held every year since 1962. From April to October inclusively, visitors can take in various plays by George Bernard Shaw at one of the three theatres in town, the **Festival Theatre**, the **Court House Theatre** and the **Royal George Theatre**.

Niagara Falls

Open 24 hours a day, only one establishment attracts so many late-night

FESTIVAL COUNTRY

customers: **Casino Niagara** *(5705 Falls Ave., www.casinoniagara.com)*. No less than 2,700 slot machines and 144 gaming tables cater to the gambling set.

Niagara Falls has its own **Hard Rock Cafe** *(beside the Casino)*. Faithful to the style of the well-known chain, this establishment is decorated with posters of rock stars and has vinyl booths.

 SHOPPING

Tour A: Kitchener-Waterloo and Surroundings

Kitchener-Waterloo

Market Square, located at the corner of King and Queen Streets, looks like your average shopping mall, but the place really comes alive every Saturday morning when the local **Farmer's Market** is held here. On the ground floor, you'll find all sorts of handicrafts, quilts, knitted goods and clothing; in the basement, a variety of foodstuffs, including honey, preserves, sausages, bread, cheese, etc.

St. Jacobs

St. Jacobs is full of **craft shops**, each one more enticing than the last. Rather than tell you where to go, we'll leave you the pleasure of poking around this maze of little stores on your own.

The local **Farmer's Market** *(Hwy. 17, at the west end of town)*, where handicrafts, foodstuffs and livestock are sold, is a show like no other.

Elora

Near the mill, you'll find shops selling clothing (**Magic Mountain Trading Co.**) and toys (**Bear Cupboard**; ☎846-9711). If you're not satisfied with the selection of teddy bears and dolls at the Bear Cupboard, try the **Doll House** *(81 Metcalfe, ☎846-9977)*, which has some beautiful items.

Guelph

There are some charming little shops on Quebec Street, including the **Bookshelf Café**, a restaurant and bookstore, and the **Maison de Madeleine**, where you can purchase unique and pretty decorative items for your home.

Ki Design *(40 Quebec St.)* is full of little treasures from the Orient, with *bonsaï* trees, kimonos and Japanese dishes and teapots.

Downtown has stores of all kinds, including an **Eaton's Centre** and other boutiques on Wyndham Street.

Acton

No visit to Acton would be complete without a stop at **Olde Hide House** *(49 Eastern Ave., ☎853-1031)*, a huge warehouse full of coats, clothing, handbags, briefcases and leather wallets. There is something to suit everyone: all prices and all styles. While, once, these items were manufactured here, they now are furnished by other enterprises.

Cambridge

The red-brick **Farmer's Market** is on the corner of Dickson and Ainslie, in downtown Cambridge. Local farmers come here to sell some of their produce.

Brantford

The little shop in the **Woodland Cultural Centre** *(184 Mohawk St., ☎759-2650)* has a good selection of native crafts, books and posters.

Tour B: Hamilton and Surroundings

Oakville

Lakeshore Street has a succession of enchanting shops with tempting window displays to lure you inside. Among the most interesting are **Harrisons of Oakville**, with stylish clothing for babies and children, the **Native Art Gallery**, with its fine collection of sculptures, engravings and masks and, finally, **Never Grow Up**, with its selection of teddy bears and dolls.

If you have a sudden craving for Belgian chocolates, stock up at **Bernard Callebaut**, where the confections are always delicious.

Hamilton

You can find just about everything is at the **Jackson Square** *(King St.)* shopping centre, which has an Eaton's and an HMV.

Tour C: Niagara and the Wine Route

St. Catharines

Elliot & Company is a charming little shop with a wide variety of pretty things (candles, vases, utensils, tablecloths, statuettes, frames, etc.). Some of the articles might not be all that useful, but they certainly are pretty.

Niagara-on-the-Lake

Downtown Niagara-on-the-Lake is home to all sorts of shops, each more enticing than the last, and a visit here wouldn't be complete without a little browsing.

J.W. Outfitters *(Queen St.)* looks like a simple souvenir shop, but inside you'll find terrific T-shirts and lovely posters of native art.

Greaves *(55 Queen St., ☎468-7831 or 468-3608)* specializes in jellies, jams and marmalades, all delicious. Right next door is pretty **Crabtree & Evelyn**, which sells bath and beauty products.

Something of an anomaly in a town like Niagara-on-the-Lake, **From Japan** *(187 Victoria St., ☎468-3151)* has a magnificent assortment of Japanese crafts.

The irresistible teddy bears, dolls and other toys at **The Owl & the Pussycat** *(Queen St.)* are a sure a hit with the kids.

For an unforgettable tasty treat, stop by **Maple Leaf Fudge** *(114 Queen St., ☎468-2211)*.

Niagara Falls

There aren't any charming little shops or attractive store windows here in the land of factory outlets, where you can find surplus inventory at bargain prices.

At the **Niagara Factory Outlets** *(1900 Military Rd.)*, you can find Mondi, Benetton, Levi's and Nautica merchandise, but be prepared to search through the racks, since not all of the stock is that interesting.

FESTIVAL COUNTRY

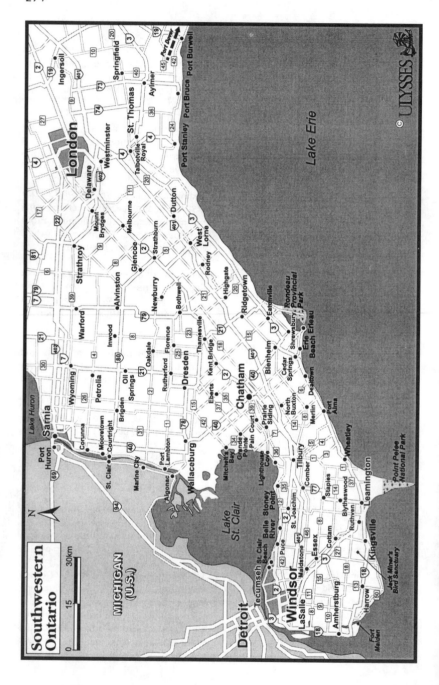

Southwestern Ontario

MICHIGAN (U.S.)

Lake Huron

Lake St. Clair

Lake Erie

Detroit

Windsor

London

Sarnia

St. Thomas

Chatham

Leamington

Point Pelee National Park

Rondeau Provincial Park

Jack Miner's Bird Sanctuary

© ULYSSES

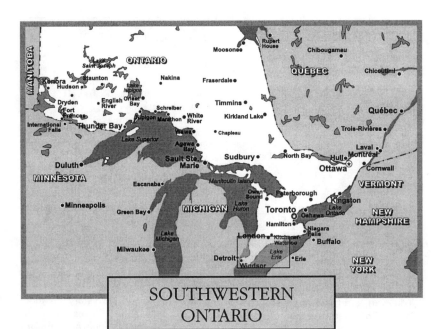

SOUTHWESTERN ONTARIO

Situated between Lake Erie and Lake Huron, southwestern Ontario is a wonderful place to enjoy the scenery of vast expanses of fresh water. The sparkling blue waves that delight beach-loving vacationers today were equally attractive to aboriginal tribes in former times who settled and prospered in this area. Fascinating tourist attractions, most notably around London, trace the history of these first nations. However, this fertile region is also near the navigation routes that were vital to the early colonists and they, too, wanted to settle here. The colonists founded little villages that eventually became lovely cities, such as London and St. Marys. Some of these towns are outstanding for the exceptional cultural initiatives they have undertaken. Stratford is one of these, with its famous Shakespeare festival that attracts huge crowds every summer.

Three tours are suggested for the southernmost part of the province.

Tour A: "London and Surroundings," presents this lovely city with its English charm, as well as the attractive little villages around it. Tour B: "Along the Shores of Lake Erie," will lead you on the discovery of beach resorts that have sprung up near beautiful stretches of sand and water. Lastly, Tour C: "The Far Southwest," explores this pretty region that was once the scene of conflict between England and the United States.

FINDING YOUR WAY AROUND

Tour A: London and Surroundings

By Car

From Toronto: Head west on Highway 2, which leads to London via Brantford.

Bus Stations

London: 101 York, ☎(519) 434-3245.

Stratford: 101 Shakespeare St.,
☎(519) 271-7870.

Train Stations

London: 197 York, at the corner of the
street.

Stratford: 101 Shakespeare St.

Tour B: Along the Shores of Lake Erie

By Car

The tour follows the shore of Lake Erie.
You can start from Crystal Beach
(see p 258) and take Route 3 to Port
Dover, or set out from London by taking the road to Port Stanley.

Tour C: The Far Southwest

By Car

From Toronto: Take the 401 West
towards Chatham, then pick up the 40,
which leads to the 3, the starting point
of the tour.

Bus Station

Windsor: 44 University St. E.,
☎254-7575.

Train Stations

Windsor: 298 Walker Rd., corner of
Riverside Dr., ☎(519) 256-5511.

Sarnia: 125 Green St.

PRACTICAL INFORMATION

Area Code: 519.

**Southwestern Ontario Travel
Association**
4023 Meadowbrook Dr., Suite 112,
London, ON, N6L 1E7, ☎652-1391 or
800-661-6804, ≈652-0533.

EXPLORING

Tour A: London and Surroundings ★★

A major centre of Iroquois culture in
Ontario, the London area boasts fascinating tourist attractions where visitors
can learn about Native history, customs
and traditions. Over 150 years ago, the
Iroquois began sharing this territory
with English colonists, who were lured
here by the fertile land. Once a modest
hamlet, London now has a rich architectural heritage that makes it one of
the loveliest towns in the region.

London ★★★

The industrious Colonel John Graves
Simcoe, the first Lieutenant-Governor
of Upper Canada, played an important
role in the development of the young
British colony. It was he who decided
to divide the present-day London region
into townships. His plan also included
the founding of London itself (1793),
which was supposed to become the
capital of Upper Canada, but never did.
He also lured farmers here from the
United States by selling them fertile
land at low prices. These so-called
"eleventh hour Loyalists," who arrived
after 1791, included a number of
Quakers and Mennonites (especially in
the Kitchener-Waterloo area).

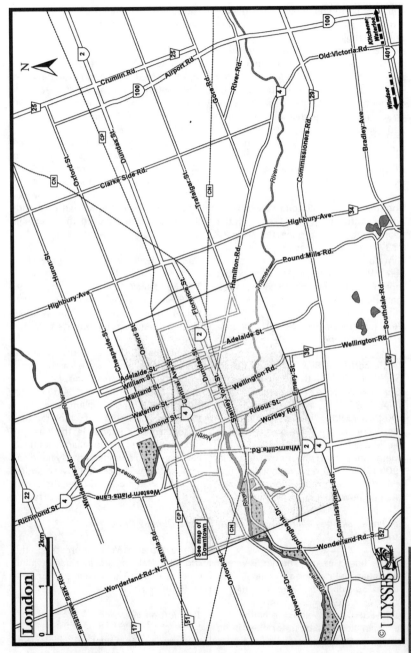

London

SOUTHWESTERN
ONTARIO

© ULYSSES

Unlike most towns, which go through a period of slow, steady growth before any prestigious public buildings are erected, London sprang immediately to life with the construction of an impressive government edifice known as the Middlesex County Courthouse (see further below) on a previously undeveloped piece of land that had been scouted out in the late 18th century as a potential site for a large town. This picturesque building was begun in 1828, and the town grew up around it over the following years.

The tour starts at **Victoria Park**, a large and beautiful stretch of greenery in the heart of town. After the Rebellion of 1837, the British troops who had been sent to London set up their quarters here. When they left in 1868, the town took over the land and turned it into a magnificent park.

Head west on Dufferin Street, then turn left on Richmond.

At the corner of Richmond and Fullarton, you will see the **Grand Theatre** *(Oct to Apr; 471 Richmond St., N6A 3E4, ☎672-8800 or 800-265-1593, www.grandtheatre. com)*, erected in 1901 on the site of the Masonic Temple and the Grand Opera House, which burned down in 1900. Since 1982, the building has undergone major renovations, and visitors can now take in a play here.

Continue along Fullarton to Ridout Street.

On the banks of the Thames River, is the elegant white **Eldon House** ★ *($5; Tue to Sun noon to 5pm; 481 Ridout St. N., N6A 2P8, ☎672-4580, ⌐660-8397)*, the oldest private residence in London, built for the Harris family in 1834. Now open to the public, it is still decorated with 19th-century furnishings. On Ridout Street,

there are a number of other lovely homes dating back to the town's first few years.

If you keep heading south on Ridout, you'll come to the **London Regional Art and Historical Museums** *(free admission; Tue to Sun noon to 5pm; 421 Ridout St. N., N6K 1S1, ☎672-4580, ⌐660-8397)*, a large, rather unusual-looking building designed by the architect Moriyama. It is shaped like a cross, with big picture windows that let in a lot of natural light. The art collection consists primarily of works by Canadian painters, while the second-floor rooms are devoted to an exhibit on the history of London.

Continue walking along Ridout North.

The **Middlesex County Courthouse** ★ *(399 Ridout St. N.)* is a former courthouse whose Neo-Gothic prison looks like a medieval castle with its towers.

The Middlesex County Courthouse is a solid brick building covered with stucco made to look like freestone. Like Montreal's Notre-Dame, built around the same time, it is an excellent example of the first attempts at architectural historicism in Canada. In the case of the courthouse, medieval accents have been added to a fundamentally neoclassical building. The central tower, added in 1878, was modelled after the tower of the Canadian Parliament in Ottawa.

Take Dundas Street.

At the corner of Wellington stands the **Old City Hall**, a neoclassical building erected in 1918 and enlarged by T.C. McBride in 1927.

Turn left on Waterloo.

Located in the midst of a pleasant stretch of greenery, the **First St. Andrew's United Church** ★ *(350 Queens*

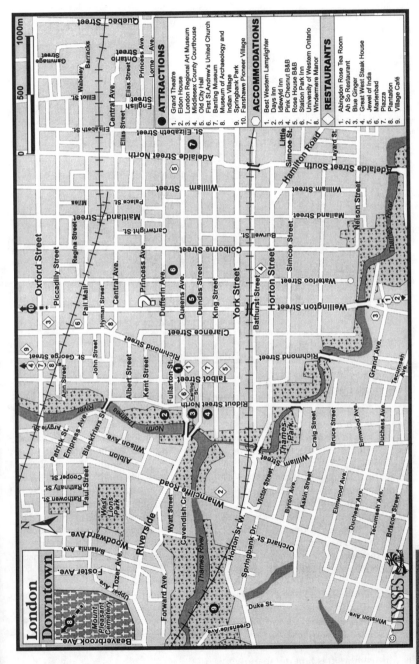

First St. Andrew's United Church

Ave.) was originally built for one of London's many Presbyterian communities. A brick building erected between 1868 and 1871, it has all the traditional neo-Gothic elements typical of Protestant churches, including ogival openings and a steeple topped by a spire. Inside, the nave has an austere, exposed wooden skeleton. Nearby, you'll find the neo-Renaissance manse, the former residence of the minister, or Reverend Doctor.

As you continue along Waterloo Street, take the time to admire the magnificent Victorian homes dating from the 19th and early 20th centuries.

If you have a little time to spare, you can take Dundas all the way to Adelaide Street instead of turning onto Waterloo. This will give you a chance to see the little **Banting Museum** *($3; Tue to Sat noon to 4:30pm; 442 Adelaide N., N6B 3H8, ☎673-1752, ⊷660-8992)*, devoted to the life and achievements of celebrated doctor Frederick Grant Banting (1891-1941), who, along with Scottish doctor John Macleod, won the Nobel Prize in medicine in 1923 for discovering insulin.

After passing through a peaceful residential neighbourhood, you'll reach the **Museum of Indian Archaeology ★** *($3.50; museum: summer, Mon-Sat*

Stratford

10am to 5pm; fall, Wed-Sun 10am to 4:30pm; winter, Sat and Sun 10am to 4:30pm, village: May to Aug, 10am to 5pm; 1600 Attawandaron Rd., N6G 3M6, ☎473-1360), which focuses on the archaeological excavations that revealed traces of native tribes dating back over 10,000 years. By presenting a survey of this research, the museum is able to teach visitors about the history, way of life and traditions of the First Nations. Outside, you'll find a reconstructed Iroquois village, complete with a longhouse.

Springbank Park *($4.75; May to Sep, every day 10am to 8pm; Springbank Dr. W.)* lies on the banks of the Thames. From here, you can set out on a river cruise aboard the *London Princess ($6.95 and up, ☎473-0363)*. The park is also home to the **Storybook Gardens** *($5.25 ☎661-5770)*, where you'll find a playground and a small zoo for children.

A visit to **Fanshawe Pioneer Village** *($5; May to Oct, every day 10am to 4pm; 2609 Fanshawe Park Rd. E., N5X 4A1,* ☎457-1296, ≈457-3364) is truly like taking a trip back in time. You'll find yourself in a small, 19th-century village amongst guides in period dress, who will take you on a tour of the 22 buildings, which include a blacksmith's shop and a general store.

To get to the village of Ska-Nah-Doht, take the 2 out of London to Delaware.

Delaware

Delaware is a modest hamlet with only a few little houses. The **Longwoods Road Conservation Area**, located 6 km to the south, is of greater interest. This large, wooded park not only has campsites, but is also home to the **Ska-Nah-Doht Village ★** *(Hwy. 2, ☎264-2420, ≈264-1562)*, an accurate reproduction of the kind of Iroquois village found here 1,000 years ago. Although this area was never actually inhabited by the Iroquois, the village will take you on an fascinating trip back in time.

Stratford ★★

A man named Tom Patterson, a shop-keeper with a passion for Shakespeare, is the one who came up with the idea of starting a Shakespeare festival (see p 298) here in 1951. Then a modest hamlet, Stratford has since become an enchanting little town, where crowds of visitors flock each year to see the plays and enjoy the charming setting. Its downtown area is very attractive, and splendid **Queen's Park ★★** lies stretched along the banks of the Avon, where ducks, swans and barnacle geese paddle about. The park is also home to the **Festival Theatre** *(May to Nov, ☎271-4040 or 800-567-1600, www.stratford_festival.on.ca)*, where some of the plays are presented.

Head south on Hwy. 7.

St. Marys ★

St. Marys has preserved so many of its 19th-century stone buildings that it is nicknamed "Stonetown." Built of locally quarried rock, these edifices are the pride of the city. One of the most re-markable is the Town Hall, dating from 1890, a time when the size of the municipal building was used to measure the importance of a town. Today it seems disproportionately large for a city with only 3,500 residents.

The Opera House, built in 1879, is just as imposing. It was originally intended to house shops on the main floor with a theatre on the second floor. How-ever, during the 20th century, it oper-ated as a mill. It has been renovated and now houses shops and private apartments. Take time to stroll along the streets of St. Marys, especially Church Street in the little downtown area. It has a charm all its own.

St. Thomas

A peaceful town of little interest to tourists, St. Thomas flourished in the late 19th century, with the construc-tion of the railway. A few Victorian buildings bear witness to that prosper-ous era. You can also take a stroll in **Pinafore Park** *($1.50; late May to early Sep; ☎775-2292)*, which has a zoo and some lovely gardens.

Tour B: Along the Shores of Lake Erie ★

Lake Erie is the southernmost border of Ontario, and is , incidentally, the most southerly area in Canada. A stopping point for migratory birds, this shore is lined with parks established to protect the varied and abundant wildlife and to showcase some of the area's scenic beauty. Birds are not the only beneficia-ries of this gorgeous shoreline dotted with golden sand beaches. In summer, vacationers flock here, too. Only some of Lake Erie's Ontario shoreline is cov-ered by this tour, which runs from Port Dover to Kingsville.

Port Dover ★

With its quaint cottages, downtown Port Dover seems a bit weathered, though charming. Bit by bit, the houses give way to the vacationers' favourite spot: the beach, which is always very lively. People come here to swim, browse in the downtown shops that sell mostly beach gear (T-shirts, hats, swimsuits, etc.) or just to watch the boat traffic in the marina.

From Port Dover, take Route 24 to Route 59, and turn left. This takes you to Long Point.

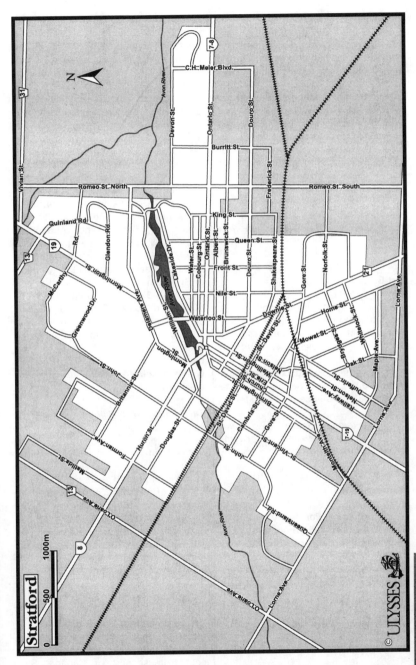

Stratford

© ULYSSES

Long Point ★

As it name suggests, Long Point is a long spit of land that extends into the lake. On both sides there are marshes with cattails and other plants, ideal for migrating birds. The marshes lead onto beautiful, long sandy **beaches ★** dotted with the occasional vacation home along the crescent-shaped shoreline. There are hardly any towns here; nature dominates in the scenery. Long Point Provincial Park lets you enjoy the natural beauty of this area.

Backtrack to the intersection of Route 42, which goes through Port Burwell.

Port Burwell

The little village of Port Burwell, on the shore of Lake Erie, would be passed over by most visitors were it not for the Port Burwell Provincial Park and its two beautiful sandy beaches. The town itself has little to offer besides a few attractive roads and the red-and-white lighthouse at the edge of the water.

Continue along Route 42. Take Route 19 (left) for a kilometre or two, to get to Port Bruce.

Port Bruce

Like Port Burwell, Port Bruce's claim to fame is its park, Port Bruce Provincial Park, which protects the long beaches that are so loved by swimmers and sunbathers. The town comes alive with the good weather and settles down again in the fall.

Take Route 24 west.

Port Stanley ★

South of London, you'll come to the charming village of Port Stanley, which is attractively located on the shores of Lake Erie. The village enjoyed a prosperous period during the first half of the 20th century, when vacationers would come here by train from London to enjoy the idyllic setting and attend the festivities held in the LP&S pavilion, where such celebrated musicians as Louis Armstrong and Duke Ellington performed. All that remains of that time are the lovely buildings downtown; there has been no train service between Port Stanley and London for years now, and the pavilion burned down in 1979. You can nonetheless relive the past by taking a trip to Union or St. Thomas on a little *train (\$9; Bride St., ☎782-3730)*. The town is not without charm, however. It has a magnificent long sandy beach with sand as soft as it is pale. Visitors flock here in summer to swim and lounge on the beach. Downtown is equally attractive, with handsome homes, restaurants and smart shops.

Take Route 20 to Highway 3 west.

Leamington

Leamington, which bears the unromantic title of National Tomato Capital, is best known as the gateway to wonderful Point Pelee National Park (see below), and has no tourist attractions as such. It is also a departure area for excursions to Pelee Island.

Point Pelee National Park ★★

At the southwestern tip of Ontario, a finger of land known as Point Pelee stretches into Lake Erie; this is the southernmost part of Canada. Surrounded by marshes, this point is home to a variety of wildlife, including all sorts of birds, especially in the spring and the fall, when a number of migratory species stop here. The area has been set aside as **Point Pelee National Park** *(from Leamington, take Hwy. 33; 1118 Point Pelee Dr., R.R. 1, Leamington, N8H 3V4, ☎322-2365, ≈322-1277)*, which has some pleasant hiking trails. As an added attraction, there are long wooden docks that lead deep into the marshes, making it possible to observe some of the nearly 350 species of birds found here in their natural environment. In September, monarch season, the park is filled with these orange and black butterflies. There are several beaches on Point Pelee as well.

Barnacle goose

Pelee Island

From Leamington, you can take the ferry heading for Pelee Island, which juts out of the sea and is the southernmost point in Canada. A few roads traverse this island whose climate favours grapevine cultivation. Here, you can visit the facilities of the **Pelee Island Winery's Wine Pavillion** *(20 East West Rd., ☎724-2469)*.

Kingsville

Each year, Kingsville is visited by crowds of barnacle geese, who stop here during their migratory flight. This phenomenon can be traced back to one Jack Miner, who began trying to attract these graceful winged creatures to his property in 1904. His efforts were successful, and this area, one of the first in Canada to be set aside for birds, was designated a national bird sanctuary in 1917. Today, **Jack Miner's Bird Sanctuary** ★ *(free admission; Mon-Fri 9am to 5pm year-round; north of Kingsville, west of Division Rd., ☎733-4034)* is still open to the public, and you can go there to observe the wild geese. Open year-round, it attracts large numbers of birds, especially in late March and from the end of October through November.

Tour C: The Far Southwest

This tour covers the strip of land flanked by Lakes Erie and St. Clair, alongside the United States, whose proximity has had a profound influence on the history of the region. Not only has the area often been the theatre of British-American conflicts, but it was also through here that many black slaves fled to Canada. The American influence is still very evident in this region, and some towns, like Windsor, live very much in the shadow of their imposing neighbour.

Amherstburg ★

The little town of Amherstburg, located at the mouth of the Detroit River, played an important role in local history when British troops were posted here at **Fort Malden** ★ *($2.50; every day 10am to 5pm; 100 Laird Ave., Box 38, N9V 2Z2, ☎736-5416, ≈736-6603)*, during the War of 1812, with orders to protect the English colonies in this area. Unfortunately, they were no match for the enemy forces, which succeeded in capturing the fort and destroying part of it. After being returned to Canada in 1815, it was reconstructed, and still stands guard over the river —symbolically, at least.

The **North American Black Historical Museum** *($4.50; mid-Apr to late Oct, Wed to Fri 10am to 5pm, Sat and Sun 1pm to 5pm; 277 King St., ☎736-5434)* was built in memory of the black slaves who fled to Canada from the United States. It tells the sad epic of the men and women who were taken by force from Africa and brought to America to work on plantations. Visitors will also learn about the underground railway taken by slaves to reach Canada.

Continue on the 18 to Windsor.

Windsor ★

Some people say that Windsor's greatest attraction is the Detroit skyline on the horizon. This is not simply a snide remark; Detroit, which stands on the opposite shore of the river of the same name, really does have something magical about it when viewed from here.

At the end of the 17th century, the French decided to set up a small trading post on the banks of the Detroit River. Due to their friendly relations with the local natives, the fort prospered. When France lost its American colonies to the British in 1763, however, the settlement was abandoned. Later, in 1834, the English began settling the east bank of the river, and native people began to realize that British expansion was indeed a reality. They founded a village named Sandwich, which later became Windsor. The town enjoyed its first period of prosperity with the construction of the Welland Canal, which enabled boats to sail into Lake Erie, and then with the arrival of the railway. It wasn't until the beginning of the 20th century, however, that the town really flourished, its population growing from 21,000 inhabitants in 1908 to 105,000 in 1928. This boom was largely due to the local automobile industry. Today, this industrial city has a rather depressing downtown area. There are a few pleasant spots, however, especially along the river, where a number of parks have been laid out. These include the magnificent **Coventry Gardens ★** *(Riverside Dr., at the corner of Pillette Rd.)*, adorned with beautiful flowers and the **Fountain of Peace**. Windsor also three **casinos** (see p 298).

If you are only staying in Windsor for a little while and can only visit one attraction, make it the **Art Gallery of Windsor ★★** *(free admission; Tue to Sat 10am to 5pm, Sun noon to 5pm; 3100 Howard Ave., N8X 3Y8, ☎969-4494, ⊷969-3632)*, which has an amazingly rich collection of true masterpieces by great Canadian artists. These magnificent paintings and sculptures are complemented by clear, detailed written commentary on various facets of Canadian art. The museum also boasts a superb collection of native art.

The former home of an influential man who played an important role in local politics in the late 19th century, the **François Baby House** *(free admission; May to Sep, Tue to Sat 10am to 5pm, Sun 2pm to 5pm; 254 Pitt St. W., N9A 5L5, ☎253-1812, ⊷253-0919)* presents a small exhibition on a few of the major events in Windsor's history.

Willistead Manor *($3.75; 1899 Niagara St., ☎253-2365)*, a splendid Tudor-style house built for Edward Walker,

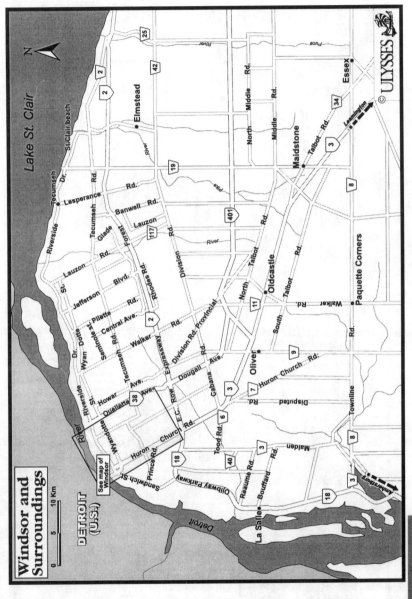

Windsor and Surroundings

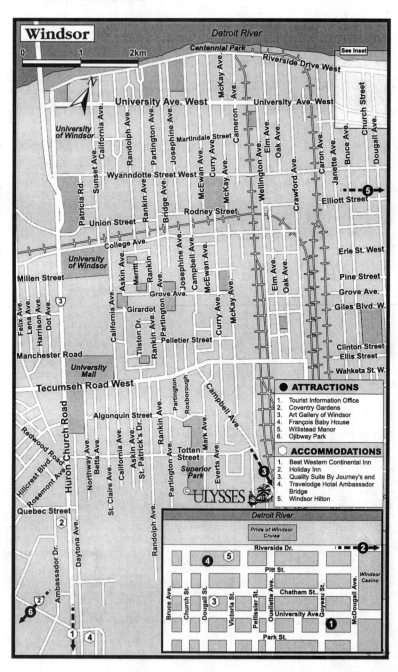

Windsor

0   1   2km

Detroit River

Centennial Park

Riverside Drive West

See Inset

University Ave. West

University of Windsor

University Ave. West

Church Street

Dougall Ave.

McKay Ave.

Cameron Ave.

Elm Ave.

Oak Ave.

Caron Ave.

Bruce Ave.

California Ave.

Randolph Ave.

Partington Ave.

Josephine Ave.

Martindale Street

Curry Ave.

McEwan Ave.

Wellington Ave.

Crawford Ave.

Janette Ave.

Sunset Ave.

Wyanndotte Street West

Rankin Ave.

Bridge Ave.

McEwan Ave.

McKay Ave.

Elliott Street

5

Patricia Rd.

Union Street

Rodney Street

College Ave.

Erie St. West

University of Windsor

Millen Street

Askin Ave.

Merritt

Rankin

Josephine Ave.

Campbell Ave.

McEwan Ave.

Elm Ave.

Oak Ave.

Pine Street

Grove Ave.

Giles Blvd. W.

Girardot

Grove Ave.

California Ave.

Tilston Dr.

Rankin Ave.

Partington

Pelletier Street

Curry Ave.

McKay Ave.

Clinton Street

Ellis Street

Felix Ave.

Lena Ave.

Harrison Ave.

Dot Ave.

3

Manchester Road

Wahketa St. W.

University Mall

Tecumseh Road West

Partington

Roxborough

Campbell Ave.

Redwood Road

Hillcrest Blvd.

Rosemont Ave.

Huron Church Road

Algonquin Street

Rankin Ave.

Mark Ave.

● ATTRACTIONS

1. Tourist Information Office
2. Coventry Gardens
3. Art Gallery of Windsor
4. François Baby House
5. Willistead Manor
6. Ojibway Park

Northway Ave.

Betts Ave.

St. Claire Ave.

California Ave.

Askin Ave.

St. Patrick's Dr.

Partington Ave.

Totten Street

Events Ave.

Superior Park

3

◻ ACCOMMODATIONS

1. Best Western Continental Inn
2. Holiday Inn
3. Quality Suite By Journey's end
4. Travelodge Hotel Ambassador Bridge
5. Windsor Hilton

©ULYSSES

Quebec Street

2

Ambassador Dr.

Daytona Ave.

Randolph Ave.

2

6

1

4

Detroit River

Pride of Windsor Cruise

Riverside Dr.

2

Pitt St.

4   5

Windsor Casino

Bruce Ave.

Church St.

Dougall St.

Victoria St.

Pellissier St.

Ouellette Ave.

Goyeau St.

McDougall Ave.

Chatham St.

3

University Ave.

1

Park St.

One of the natural wonders of the world,
the famous Niagara Falls.
– *T. Bognar*

Ontario is known for its many beautiful houses, such as this stone one, which belonged to Charles Ermatinger of Sault Ste. Marie.
– *Oriane Lemaire.*

Canada's four seasons are an attraction in themselves. Here, winter never seems to end on this snow-capped farm.
– *T. Beck*

son of distiller Hiram Walker, is one of the city's loveliest examples of early 20th-century architecture. Its opulent rooms are elegantly decorated with furnishings from the 1900s.

From downtown Windsor, take Riverside Drive to Broadway Street and turn left, then take a right on Matchette Road.

If you'd like to spend a day outdoors without leaving Windsor, go to the **Ojibwe Park and Nature Centre** *(free admission; ☎966-5852)*, where you'll find nature trails crisscrossing the forest and the prairie, with its vast fields of tall grass.

Take the 401 to the 21 and head west to Dresden.

Dresden

In the early 19th century, nearly 30,000 black slaves fled the United States and took refuge in Canada. Among them was Reverend Josiah Henson, who purchased a plot of land in this area and founded a shelter for fugitive slaves. His story inspired Harriet Beecher Stowe to write her celebrated novel *Uncle Tom's Cabin*. At the **Uncle Tom's Cabin** Historic Site ★ *($5; May to Oct, Mon to Sat 10am to 4pm, Sun noon to 4pm; 29251 Uncle Tom's Rd. R.R. 5, NOP 1M0, take Hwy. 21 West, 20 min. off Hwy. 401, exit 101, ☎683-2978, ⊷683-1256)*, you will find a number of buildings, including a church, the Reverend's house and a small museum.

Take Highway 21.

Oil Springs

Oil Springs is part of a region that once played an important role in the Cana-

dian petroleum industry. It was in this area, on the banks of Black Creek, that the country's first oil deposits were discovered (accidentally) in the 1850s. The land was then sold to James Miller Williams, who actually drilled a well. News of the discovery soon spread, and people started flooding into the area, hoping to strike it rich. Oil Springs was founded during this period. Within only two decades, however, the wells had already dried up, and the fledgling industry disappeared. To learn more about the Canadian oil industry, visit the **Oil Museum of Canada** *($3.75; May to Oct, every day 10am to 5pm; Nov to Apr, Mon to Fri 9am to 5pm; head east on Hwy. 21, 2423 Kelly Rd., NON 1P0, ☎834-2840)*.

Continue along Highway 21.

Petrolia

At the same time the oil industry was on the decline in Oil Springs, rich oil deposits were discovered in Petrolia, which in turn enjoyed a period of prosperity. Companies started drilling here in the 1860s, and the oil industry enabled the town to thrive up until the 1950s, at which point deposits discovered in Alberta made local production seem negligible. A number of superb buildings bear witness to Petrolia's golden years, including the **town hall** and **St. Philip's Catholic Church**, erected in 1887.

You can relive this bygone era by visiting the **Petrolia Discovery** *($3.75; May to Sep, every day 10am to 6pm, Sep and Oct 10am to 4pm; Petrolia St., west of Hwy. 21, P.O. Box 1480, NON 1R0, ☎882-0897, ⊷882-4209)*, on the site where the oil deposits to which the town owes its existence were discovered. To highlight this important period in the region's history, a 19th-century oilfield has been reconstructed.

In addition to seeing a well being pumped, you can learn about the history of petroleum in this part of Canada.

From Petrolia, take the 21 to the 402, which leads to Sarnia.

Sarnia

Sarnia is a rather dreary town, whose outskirts have a futuristic look, due to the area's thriving petrochemical industry. Fortunately, the beautiful parks along Lake Huron and the St. Clair River make it easy to forget about the factories, which are no doubt useful but disfigure the landscape.

 OUTDOOR ACTIVITIES

 Hiking

Tour A: London and Surroundings

You can discover the charms of the London region on the **Thames Valley Trail**, which stretches 60 km. For more information, contact:

Thames Valley Trail Association
P.O. Box 821, Terminal B, London, ON N6A 4Z2.

 Bicycling

Tour C: The Far Southwest

Point Pelee National Park is crisscrossed by cycling paths. Bicycles are available for rent here during summer.

 Bird-watching

Tour C: The Far Southwest

Large numbers of migratory birds stop alongside Lake Erie to gather their strength before setting out across this huge body of water, and as a result, outstanding bird-watching areas dot the shoreline.

Jack Miner's Bird Sanctuary *(north of Kingsville, west of Division Rd., ☎733-4034)* was created in 1904 in order to protect certain species of birds, particularly ducks and barnacle geese, which come here in large numbers.

Point Pelee National Park is another outstanding place to observe all sorts of birds – as many as 350 different species during the migrating seasons. It is laid out so that visitors can see as many birds as possible, with trails leading into the forest and wooden docks crisscrossing the marshes.

Rondeau Provincial Park *(R.R. 1, Morpeth, N0P 1X0, ☎674-1750)*, also located on the shores of Lake Erie, is another prime location for birding.

 Swimming

Tour B: Along the Shores of Lake Erie

All along the Lake Erie shore are nothing but a succession of long golden crescents of sand, perfect for basking in the sun or swimming. Vacation villages, where a pleasant holiday ambiance prevails throughout the summer, have opened up near several of these beautiful beaches.

Long Point

Very pleasant, this long promontory that juts out into the waters of Lake Erie is in fact made up of a series of long stretches of golden sand beaches. The town also boasts the **Long Point Provincial Park**, which not only lies near a lovely beach, but harbours a very pleasant campsite.

Port Burwell

The small town of Port Burwell boasts two beaches, a little one near the town centre as well as a second larger and more pleasant one in **Port Burwell Provincial Park**. You can spend the day here, but it costs $7.50. Visitors can use the changing cabins here.

Port Stanley

With its long crescent of soft sand lined with lavish homes, the superb Port Stanley beach has everything with which to delight holiday-makers. Its crystal-clear but cold waters make swimming a tempting prospect. Those who wish to spend a few hours here but have come unequipped can rent chairs *($5)*. Lifeguarded beach.

 ACCOMMODATIONS

Tour A: London and Surroundings

London

The **University of Western Ontario** *($35/day bkfst incl., $211/week bkfst and tax incl.; N6A 3K7, ☎661-3545)* is an economical solution during summer.

For lodgings right near downtown London, yet with the peace and quiet of a residential neighbourhood, head to the **Rose House B&B** *($45 sb, $65pb; 526 Dufferin, N6B 2A2, ☎433-9978)*, which has pretty, well-kept rooms.

In another, equally peaceful, part of town, **Pink Chestnut B&B** *($65 bkfst incl.; 1035 Richmond St., N6A 3J6, ☎673-3963)* is a handsome red brick home that has been transformed to accommodate tourists. Really charming and furnished with antiques, the Pink Chestnut has a relaxed and welcoming atmosphere.

If the place is full, you can try B&Bs one of the other twenty or so in town. A complete listing is available at the tourist office *(300 Dufferin Ave., ☎661-5000)*.

If you prefer a hotel but don't want to spend a fortune, try Wellington Street, outside the downtown area, which is lined with modern hotels with somewhat impersonal but nonetheless decent rooms. These include a **Days Inn** *($75; ≈; 1100 Wellington Rd., N6E 1M2, ☎681-1240 or 800-DAYS-INN, ≈681-0830)* and the **Best Western Lamplighter** *($80; 591 Wellington Rd. S., N6C 4R3, ☎681-7151, ≈681-3271)*.

🐌 Hidden away in the University of Western Ontario Research Park is a very pretty manor, built in 1925, that has been converted into an inn. **Windermere Manor** *($96 bkfst incl; 200 Collip Circle, N6G 4X8, ☎858-1391 or 800-997-4477)* often houses researchers and guests of the university. However, the magnificent park and the peacefulness of the surroundings (only 10 min. from town by car) can be enjoyed by other guests, as well. The rooms are surprisingly modern and quite comfortable. Suites with kitchenettes (with microwave ovens) are also available.

The **Idlewyld Inn** *($110; 36 Grand Ave., N6C 1K8, ☎433-2891)*, a splendid 19th-century house, has nothing in common with modern hotels. It has been renovated over the years, but has managed to retain its old-time charm. There are 27 rooms, each with its own unique decor.

The 22-storey tower of the **Westin** *(115; ℜ, ≈, ◯, ◔; 300 King St., ☎430-1661)* stands at the edge of the downtown area. It provides exceptionally large, comfortable rooms, decorated in the style found in many large North American hotel chains. The hotel has the added attractions of a pool and an exercise room.

The **Station Park Inn** *($125; K; 242 Pall Mall, corner of Richmond, N6A 5P6, ☎642-4444 or 800-561-4574, ≈642-2551)* lies near lovely Victoria Park, on Richmond, a pleasant commercial street. The pretty rooms inside this glass and brick building are equipped with kitchenettes. This place is perfect for visitors looking for a well-appointed room in one of the nicest areas in town.

There is one other top-notch hotel in town, the **Delta London Armouries** *($129; ≈, ℜ, ◉, ◯, ✗; 325 Dundas, N6B 1T9, ☎679-6111 or 800-668-9999, ≈679-6397)*, a converted armoury topped by a tall glass tower. Although somewhat surprising at first sight, the combination is nonetheless harmonious. The rooms, furthermore, are impeccable.

Stratford

During the finest months of the year, when the Shakespeare festival is in full swing, the local hotels are often full. Fortunately, there are plenty of B&Bs in town, each more attractive than the last. You can reserve a room in many of these places through the Stratford Festival Accommodation Bureau: P.O. Box 520, Stratford, N5A 6V2, ☎273-1600 or 800-567-1260, ≈273-6173.

You can stay in comfortable rooms in people's homes on peaceful Church Street. Here are some addresses in ascending order:

Angel's Inn *($75 bkfst incl; 208 Church St., N5A 2R6, ☎271-9651)*, gives you the chance to stay in a superb, Queen Anne red brick residence that dates back to 1889. There are three tastefully decorated and very quiet guestrooms. Guests can relax in front of the fireplace or on the terrace.

Inside one of the street's most attractive buildings, the impeccable **Stone Maiden Inn** *($180; 123 Church St., N5A 2R3, ☎273-7129)* will please the most exacting travellers. The yellow brick building itself is ravishing, and all its rooms are tastefully decorated. There is a splendid dining room, and the guestrooms all have charmingly decorated private bathrooms. Some rooms even have fireplaces. The establishment is very clean and the reception is extremely courteous.

Nearby, another pretty little house, **Attard's Heritage House** *($80 sb, $100 pb; 135 Church St., N5A 2R4, ☎273-5197, ≈273-2067)* dates from 1873. The rooms are charming and the atmosphere is peaceful.

A couple of doors down, **Maple of Stratford** *($75 bkfst incl.; 220 Church St., N5A 2R6, ☎273-9651)* stands out because of its delightful flower garden. The rooms are comfortable.

Stratford also has a few hotels:

On Front Street, a lovely, tree-lined residential area, **Carol's Place** *($75 bkfst incl.; sb; 105 Front St., ☎271-9724)* is a charming vine-covered cottage with a pleasant backyard.

Deacan House *($95 bkfst incl.; 101 Brunswick St., N5A 3L9, ☎273-2052)* promises an enjoyable stay. There is a large, charming living room with old-fashioned furniture to relax in, and the rooms are attractive and comfortable. With its terrace and mature trees, the garden is equally inviting.

Despite its name, there's nothing very Victorian about the **Victorian Inn** *($125; ≈, ℜ, ⊘, ﴾; 10 Romeo St. N., N5A 5M7, ☎271-2030 or 800-741-2135, www.victorian-inn.on.ca)*, a big, nondescript building made of white brick. It does, however, boast a superb view of the Avon River, as well as luxurious rooms and sports facilities.

On your way into town, you'll pass the **Festival Inn** *($105; ≈, ℜ, ﴾; 1144 Ontario St., Box 811, N5A 6W1, ☎273-1150 or 800-463-3581, ≈273-2111)*, a motel-style establishment, which is nonetheless quite pretty. Although its location is hardly charming, this place has comfortable, modern rooms.

Bentley's Inn *($140, $80 low season; ℜ; 99 Ontario St., N5A 3H1, ☎271-1121, ≈272-1853)*, located in the heart of downtown Stratford, is a lovely brick building dating from the beginning of the century. The rooms are well-kept and have an old-fashioned charm about them. This may not be the height of luxury, but it's still quite pleasant.

Also set in an older building, but with a somewhat outmoded decor, the **Queen's Inn** *($125; 161 Ontario St., N5A 3H3, ☎271-1400 or 800-461-6450, ≈271-7373)* unfortunately, lacks the charm of its neighbour.

St. Marys

The Westover Inn *($95-$200; ≈, ℜ; 300 Thomas St., N4X 1B1, ☎284-2977 or 800-COTTAGE, ≈284-4043)*, a true haven of peace, lies in a positively breathtaking setting in the heart of the countryside, surrounded by stately trees. If the location isn't enough to win your heart over completely, you're sure to be enchanted by the bright rooms, with their big windows and antique furnishings.

Tour B: Along the Shores of Lake Erie

The parks and villages that follow each other along Lake Erie do not particularly cater to visitors seeking historical inns, but rather to those who appreciate the wilderness and are in search of pleasant campgrounds.

Long Point

Long Point Provincial Park *($15; PO Box 99, N0E 1M0, ☎586-2133)* boasts a very pleasant campground near the lake. Its main asset is that the individual camping sites are separated from each other by large trees.

Port Burwell

Port Burwell Provincial Park *($15; PO Box 9, N0J 1T0, ☎519-874-4691)* has a magnificent campground laid out in the forest right near Lake Erie.

Port Stanley

🦞 You can plan an overnight stay in the cute little village of Port Stanley, since it has one of those delightful inns that are always such a pleasure to find. The **Kettle Creek Inn** *($90, $160 ½b; 216 Joseph St., N5L 1C4, ☎782-3388, ⌐782-4747)* will take you 150 years back in time, for the building dates from 1849 and is made of azure wooden slats graced with white balconies. The place contains very charming and always impeccably kept rooms adorned with pine furniture. Some look onto a small interior courtyard, therefore offering greater peace and quiet.

Tour C: The Far Southwest

Windsor

Windsor has a few medium-quality hotels with fairly reasonable rates, especially during the low season. Most of these are located on Huron Church Drive, a busy street with little to recommend it.

The **Best Western Continental Inn** *($85; ≈, ℜ, ⅄; 3345 Huron Church Dr., N9E 4H5, ☎966-5541 or 800-528-1234, ⌐972-3384)* is one of those places whose large, decently furnished rooms compensate for a nondescript exterior and long, impersonal corridors.

The **Travelodge** *($79; ≈, ℜ; 2330 Huron Church Dr., N9E 3S6, ☎972-1100 or 800-578-7878, ⌐972-6310)* offers the same kind of rooms, but the building is slightly more inviting and contains an indoor swimming pool.

Closer to the downtown area, a stone's throw from the bridge to the United States, the **Holiday Inn** *($110; ⊛, ◯, ⅄;*

1855 Huron Church Dr., N9C 2L6, ☎966-1200, ⌐966-2521) has pretty rooms with all the comforts and offers a wide range of amenities, including a pleasant restaurant and an indoor swimming pool. Good rates are available during the low season if you reserve three days in advance.

If you'd like to have your own kitchenette, try the **Quality Suites** *($154; ⚲, K; 250 Dougall Ave., N9A 7C6, ☎977-9707 or 800-228-5151, ⌐977-6404)*, whose modern rooms are not very cozy but extremely well kept. Not far from the downtown area.

A handsome brick and glass building, the **Hilton** *($110; 277 Riverside Dr. W., N9A 5K4, ☎973-5555 or 800-463-6665, ⌐973-4621)* boasts an excellent location by the riverside, steps away from the casino and downtown Windsor.

Sarnia

Sarnia is a rather uninspiring place with few noteworthy hotels. If you have to stay here, there is always the **Drawbridge Inn** *($67; ≈, ℜ, ◯, ⊛, ⚲; 283 Christine St. N., N7T 5V4, ☎337-7531 or 800-663-0376, ⌐332-8181)*, located downtown, which has attractively decorated rooms.

 RESTAURANTS

Tour A: London and Surroundings

London

Piazza *($; on Dundas, at the corner of Richmond)* is a lunchtime favourite with its many counters, each serving up something different like pasta, bagels and freshly squeezed juices.

Plantation *($; corner of Central Ave. and Richmond St.)* serves a large variety of croissants, muffins, quiches, soups, pasta, teas and coffees, making it an ideal spot for breakfast or lunch. The large bay windows looking out onto the street are wonderful for people-watching.

🦐 In an absolutely adorable Victorian setting, **Abingdon Rose Tea Room** *($-$$; 438 Richmond St.)* will seduce you immediately with its deep armchairs, antiques and low tables that create a comfortable atmosphere. They serve good, simple meals like sandwiches and crêpes.

The modest-looking **Jewel of India** *($$; 390 Richmond, ☎434-9268)* deserves its name, for it truly is a little jewel as far as Indian cuisine is concerned, complete with curries, Tandouris and *nan* bread. Not to mention that you can enjoy a real little feast here without spending a fortune.

🦐 The decor at **Village Café** *($$-$$$; 715 Richmond St., ☎432-2191)* is striking. The walls are brick or painted in warm hues, setting off the colourful benches. You can take your time selecting one of the many appetizing items from the menu in this relaxed atmosphere: salmon tandoori, chicken and asparagus crêpes, and tuna Cajun style are among the tempting choices.

The **Ah So Restaurant** *($$$; 122 Carling St., ☎679-9940)* is both a karaoke bar and a quiet Japanese restaurant where you can dine in a pretty tatami room. Fortunately, the two rooms are well separated. If you come here to eat, you're sure to be satisfied, as the sushi and teriyaki dishes are delicious.

The **Great West Steak House** *($$$; 240 Waterloo, N6B 2N4, ☎438-4149,* ☎438-9569) is known for its succulent steaks.

The **Marienbad** *($$$; 122 Carling St., ☎679-9940)* has managed to keep up a good reputation over the years, attracting guests with its filling but tasty *goulasches* and *schnitzels*.

🦐 **Blue Ginger** *($$$-$$$$; 644 Richmond St., ☎434-5777)* contrasts sharply with the town's other eating establishments. Its decor is minimalist, with a black- and- white colour scheme and stainless steel accents. The menu is also highly original; an eclectic selection of Asian cuisine whose flavours are sure to win you over. Of course, an establishment like this has a distinguished and faithful group of regular customers who appreciate its elegance. In summertime, there is a sidewalk terrace.

Stratford

The long, quaint dining room at **Balzac's** *($; Ontario St.)* takes you back to another era. This is a great place to stop in for coffee or ice cream.

With its wooden benches, wrought-iron tables and artists' drawings on the walls, **Down the Street** *($-$$; Ontario St.)* is more like a friendly cafe where people come to chat than a restaurant. It does have an appetizing menu, however, listing simple, tasty dishes like chicken linguine and Santa Fe Spicy Grilled Cheese.

Fellini's *($$; 107 Ontario St., ☎271-3333)* is a terrific, unpretentious restaurant decorated with checked tablecloths. The menu lists a variety of pasta dishes, offering a good opportunity to sample some succulent Italian specialties.

🦞 **Pazzo** *($$; 70 Ontario St.)* is decorated to resemble a theatre hall, with red curtains, crystal chandeliers and red-and-yellow doors. It seems appropriate in this town. Here, however, you are the actor, and it is up to you to make your own pizza. The selection of toppings for your masterpiece is almost overwhelming. When you have made your decision, your pizza will be cooked in a wood-fired oven. Careful, though: the bill mounts up quickly! On the second floor, **Lindsay's** *($$$; 70 Ontario St., ☎271-4330)* is somewhat trendier. It has a completely different look (large bay windows; bright, spacious dining room) and offers more sophisticated fare. Roast lamb (with beans and mint butter) or goat cheese ravioli are among other promising items on the menu.

Its traditional menu and relaxed atmosphere make the **Olde English Parlour** *($$-$$$; 101 Wellington St., ☎271-2772)* a good place to get together with friends.

🦞 **The Church** *($$$-$$$$; 70 Brunswick St., at the corner of Waterloo, ☎273-3424)*, a century-year-old converted church, has a unique ambiance that is truly irresistible. Add to that its delicious cuisine, and you've got the perfect recipe for a wonderful evening. Friday Saturday and nights are especially good, with jazz music.

St. Marys

Attractive windows next to the sidewalk, an alluring decor and soft music combine to make **Smith & Latham** *($; 145 Church St., ☎284-4469)* the little restaurant for a pleasant lunchtime meal. The fresh food is prepared with quality ingredients (salad with wild mushrooms and goat cheese, ham and Swiss cheese sandwiches). For dessert,

there is a good selection of cakes and pies.

Tour B: Along the Shores of Lake Erie

Port Dover

The terrace at the **Callahan Beach House** *($-$$)* is packed during the fine days of summer with a beach-going crowd that comes for the decent dishes, notably fried fish or fettuccine with seafood.

Port Stanley

At the beachfront **G.T.'s Beach Bar & Grill** *($)*, vacationers can satisfy their hunger while admiring the expanse of Lake Erie's shimmering waters. G.T.'s is more of a snack-bar where you can wolf down a burger before taking another dip.

A few tables are all that make up the dining room at the **Port Café** *($; Joseph St.)*, a delightful place to have a bite to eat at lunchtime. The menu features healthy dishes such as spinach pie and the very nourishing Greek Wrap (a sandwich made with feta cheese and vegetables on pita bread). In the afternoon, it is popular for its deserts, which you can savour with a cup of tea. After you've eaten, check out the small antique shop next to the restaurant.

Inarguably the best restaurant in town, the **Kettle Creek Inn** *($$-$$$; 216 Joseph St., ☎782-3388)* is a real delight. The interior courtyard with several tables sporting parasols provides a pleasant ambiance, which is made even more pleasant by the relaxed holiday atmosphere that prevails here. And what else could one eat here but fresh, carefully prepared fish? Meat dishes and salads are also featured on the menu. On rainy days, guests dine in the charming dining room inside.

Tour C: The Far Southwest

Kingsville

The charming little **Vintage Goose** *($$$; on Lake Erie, 24 Main St. W., ☎733-6900)* is without a doubt the most pleasant restaurant in town, with its appetizing menu and lovely dining room adorned with all sorts of bric-a-brac and statuettes and containing a handful of wooden tables with pretty flowered tablecloths.

Windsor

The **Coffee Exchange** *($; 343 Ouellette St., ☎971-7424)*, located downtown, is *the* place to go for a good cappuccino.

Laura's Place *($$; 322 Pelissier, ☎254-0490)*, a simple but charming little restaurant, serves good Italian cuisine. If pasta doesn't appeal to you, head next door to **Terra Cotta** *($-$$; 318 Pelissier, ☎971-0223)* for a pizza cooked in a wood-burning oven.

The **Old Fish Market** *($$; 156 Chatham W., ☎253-3474)* is decorated in an original manner with fishing nets, buoys, anchors and other such paraphernalia. This nautical atmosphere will help put you in the mood for one of the poached, grilled or fried fish dishes on the menu, which are all served in generous portions.

The façade of the **Plunkette Bistro** *($$-$$$; 28 Chatham St. E., ☎252-3111)*, with its orange-coloured columns, looks somewhat out of place in this part of town. But no matter, the menu features simple but tasty pasta or beef dishes.

If you aren't particularly fond of fish, try **Chatham Street Grill** *($$$; 149 Chatham W., ☎256-2555)*, which has a more traditional, elegant ambiance and serves an appetizing selection of pasta, meat and fish dishes.

Sarnia

Although the Drawbridge Hotel's restaurant, **Desmond** *($$$; 283 Christine St. N., ☎337-7571)* is located in the basement, its tasteful decor makes it a pleasant place to eat. What's more, you'll enjoy an excellent meal here, as the menu lists delicious, expertly prepared meat and fish dishes.

  ENTERTAINMENT

Tour A: London and Surroundings

London

Aeolian Hall hosts year-round concerts by the **London Symphony Orchestra**. For reservations, call ☎679-8778.

The town also has some wonderful playhouses, including the **Grand Theatre** *(471 Richmond St., ☎672-8800)*, where plays are presented year round.

Bars and Nightclubs

There are all sorts of places in town where a good time is guaranteed, whether you're in the mood to dance to popular tunes or sip a drink to the sounds of jazz.

For drinks and some R&B, **Old Chicago** *(153 Carling St.)* is the place to go, while jazz fans can head to the **Underside of 5** *(York St. at the corner of Talbot St.)*. For rock and roll, go to the **Brunswick**.

The **Big Bob** *(York St. at the corner of Wellington St.)* attracts a young crowd of dancing fiends.

Stratford

During the **Stratford Festival**, which takes place every year from May to November, various Shakespeare plays and other classics are presented. The festival is so popular that the town has no fewer than three theatres, the **Festival Theatre** *(55 Queen St.)*, the **Avon Theatre** *(99 Downie)* and the **Tom Patterson Theatre** *(Lakeside Dr.)*.

To reserve seats or obtain information on the festival calendar, call or write to:

Stratford Festival Box Office
55 Queen Street, Stratford, ON, N5A 6V2, ☎271-4040, ☎800-567-1600, ⇒271-2734, www.stratdford_festival.on.ca.

Bars and Nighclubs

Down the Street *(Ontario St.)* is both a pleasant little restaurant and a pub with a good selection of draft beer. Its unpretentious atmosphere makes it a great place to chat.

The pub in the lobby of the **Bentley Hotel** *(Ontario St.)* is a pleasant place to go for afternoon cocktails.

Windsor

Windsor's **Casinos** *(new casino: 377 Riverside Dr. E., N9A 7H7, ☎258-7878 or 800-891-7777, ⇒258-0434, www.casinowindsor.com)* are located on the shores of the Detroit River, opposite the United States, and Americans make up the bulk of their clientele.

SHOPPING

Tour A: London and Surroundings

London

As far as native art is concerned, **Innuit** *(201 Queen Ave., 672-7770)* is definitely one of the loveliest galleries in this part of the province. Inside, you'll find sculptures and lithographs by artists from all over Canada. A feast for the imagination, even if you can't afford to buy anything.

Novacks Travel Bookstore *(211 King St., ☎434-2282)* has the best selection of travel guides and outdoor equipment.

You're sure to spot something that appeals to you while strolling along Richmond Street, which is crowded with charming shops. **Wonders** *(551 Richmond St., ☎439-7288)*, for example, sells African and Asian crafts, as well as comfortable cotton clothing.

Tennis buffs will be delighted to find **Of Courts** *(525 Richmond St., ☎433-3334)*, which sells tennis rackets and clothing.

Red Balloons has attractive children's clothing.

Finally, unless you really plan on savouring some of the chocolate then avoid **Bernard Callebaut's** where its virtually impossible to just browse!

Stratford

Ontario Street, where most of the commercial activity in town is concentrated, is lined with curious little shops. For books, **Fanfare Books** is a must; for home decoration, try **La Cache** or **Bradshaw**.

You'll find some wonderful native art (sculptures and prints) at **Indigena** *(151 Downie St.)*.

Finally, if you're looking for a souvenir of the festival, make sure to stop by the **Theatre Store** *(96 Downie St.)*.

A darling shop for those who like to rummage through all sorts of clothing, **Victoria** *(Ontario St.)* practically guarantees that you will find something you like.

Tour C: The Far Southwest

Windsor

Downtown Windsor is located along Ouellette Avenue, which is lined with all sorts of shops. The Art Gallery of Windsor's shop, **AGW**, has a lovely and original selection of merchandise. There are two branches, one at 500 Ouellette Avenue and the other at the museum *(Tue to Fri 10am to 7pm, Sat 10am to 5pm, Sun noon to 5pm; 3100 Howard Ave., N8X 3Y8, ☎969-4494, ⚏969-3732).*

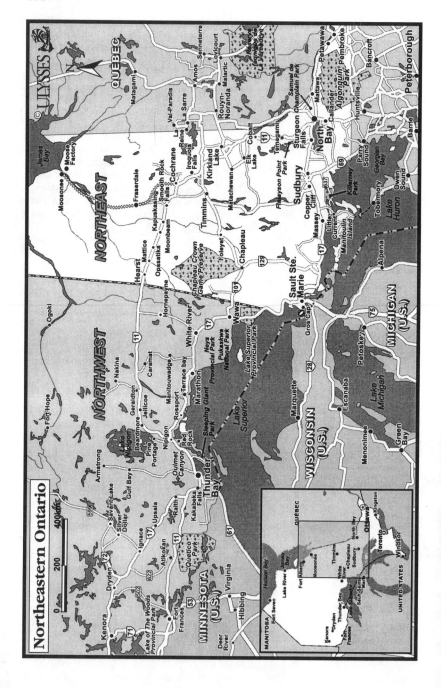

Northeastern Ontario

NORTHEASTERN
ONTARIO

N orth of the 46th parallel lies a vast, untamed stretch of territory dominated by forests, lakes and rivers. It was by exploring these rivers that Europeans first penetrated deep into this wilderness and discovered two virtual inland seas, Lakes Huron and Superior. They also encountered indigenous peoples who lived by hunting and fishing, and soon developed an interest in a luxury product in great demand in the Old World: fur. In the 17th century, the Europeans decided to set up trading posts so that they could do business with the northern natives, who were masters in the art of hunting. It wasn't until the 19th century, however, that these first settlements, which were scattered all over the territory, began to grow into small towns.

The area in this guide defined as Northern Ontario encompasses more than half the province. It is an immense and sparsely populated territory where the landscape is completely dominated by forest. It is not uncommon for villages to be separated by hundreds of kilometres. To enjoy travelling in this wilderness, one must be a lover of solitude, nature and wide expanses. This area is discussed in two separate chapters to help plan your trip. The first chapter, Northeastern Ontario, describes the area from Mattawa to Sault Ste. Marie and the far north. The second chapter, Northwestern Ontario (see p 333), covers the area to the north and west of Lake Superior.

Northeastern Ontario was colonized relatively late. Although the beginning of the twentieth century saw a wave of immigrants (mostly from Québec), the villages remain small, and are few and far between. The colonists settled on arid and infertile land hoping to earn a living from the rich mineral deposits of gold and silver that had been discovered in the area. The forest industry also provided a source of employment.

Villages began springing up here and there, but the number of people willing to take on such a harsh existence has remained small. Today, mining and the pulp and paper industry are the principal activities in this vast territory.

Here are three suggested tours in northeastern Ontario. Tour A: "On the Trail of the First Explorers," includes some of the most important cities in the midnorth. It follows part of the route taken by the earliest explorers in fragile birch bark canoes. Tour B: "Manitoulin Island," takes you to this peaceful place with its country villages. Finally, Tour C: "The Far Northeast," takes you on the discovery of northern villages and vast uninhabited regions. Keep in mind that these tours cover large areas. The distances between towns and villages are often great, so it is important to plan your itinerary in advance.

 FINDING YOUR WAY AROUND

The territory covered in this chapter is vast, and its roads might cover dozens of kilometres before reaching a village. Driving is the best means of transportation here, although many towns and villages are served by buses. A train also goes to North Bay, Sudbury and a number of other towns farther north.

Tour A: On the Trail of the First Explorers

By Car

The 17 is the only highway that stretches all the way across northern Ontario. It starts in Ottawa and runs through North Bay, Sudbury, Sault Ste. Marie, Wawa and Thunder Bay, all the way to Kenora, on the Manitoba border.

If you are coming from Toronto, take the 440 to Barrie and then the 11 to North Bay.

By Bus

You can easily get from one town to another by bus, but it might seem like a long ride, since there are frequent stops along the way.

Bus stations:

Mattawa: Pine St., at the Shell station.

North Bay: 100 Station Rd., ☎(705) 495-4200.

Sudbury: 854 Notre Dame Avenue, ☎(705) 524-9900.

Sault Ste. Marie: 73 Brock St., ☎(705) 949-4711.

By Train

One railway line links Toronto and North Bay, while another runs from Toronto to White River via Sudbury, passing alongside Georgian Bay.

North Bay: 100 Station Rd., ☎(705) 495-4200.

Sudbury: 233 Elgin St., ☎(800) 361-1235
or, if you are arriving from Toronto or western Québec:
2750 Blvd. LaSalle East

Tour B: Manitoulin Island

By Car

If you are coming from the southern part of the province, you can reach Manitoulin Island aboard the ferry

Chi-Cheemaun (car $24, adults $11, children $5.50; ☎800-461-2621), which links Tobermory (at the northern tip of the Bruce Peninsula) to South Baymouth from spring to fall. The crossing takes 1 hour 45 min. Reservations are accepted, but to keep them you must arrive one hour before boarding.

Summer schedule:

Tobermory - South Baymouth
7am; 11:20am; 3:40pm; 8pm

South Baymouth - Tobermory
9:10am; 1:30pm; 5:50pm; 10pm

Spring and fall schedule:

Tobermory - South Baymouth
8:50am; 1:30pm; 6:10pm (Fri only)

South Baymouth - Tobermory
11:10am; 3:50pm; 8:15pm (Fri only)

Visitors arriving from Northern Ontario on Highway 17 can reach the island via Highway 6, which links Espanola to Little Current.

By Bus

There is bus service as far as Little Current. To visit the rest of the island, you'll have to find your own means of transportation (rental car, hitchhiking, bicycle).

Little Current: On Highway 540, ☎(705) 368-2540.

Tour C: The Far Northeast

By Car

This tour starts in North Bay and heads north on Highway 11. This takes you to Iroquois Falls; from there, you have two choices: Highway 101 going through Timmins or, if you prefer, Highway 11, which leads further north to Cochrane and Hearst.

The *Polar Bear Express*, a train that sets out from Cochrane, is the only way to get still farther north, to Moosonee.

By Bus

Buses serve many little communities in Northern Ontario, making it fairly easy to get from one to another.

Bus stations:

Cochrane: Railway St., ☎(705) 272-4228.

Hearst: 1500 Front St., ☎(705) 362-4209.

Timmins: 54 Spruce St., ☎(705) 264-1377.

By Train

There is a train from North Bay to Cochrane; from there the *Polar Bear Express* heads even farther north.

Cochrane: Railway St.

Polar Bear Express: $46; ☎800-268-9281.

To reach Hearst by train, start in Sault Ste. Marie, as there is no service from North Bay.

PRACTICAL INFORMATION

The area code for this chapter is 705.

Tour A: On the Trail of the First Explorers

Almaquin Nipissing Travel Association
at the corner of Seymour Street and
Highway 11
P.O. Box 351
North Bay, P1B 8H5
☎474-6634 or (800) 387-0516

Rainbow Country Travel Association
2726 Whippoorwill
Sudbury, P3G 1E9
☎522-0104 or (800) 465-6655

Algoma Kinniwabi Travel Association
553 Queen Street East, Suite 1
Sault Ste. Marie, P6A 2A3
☎254-4293

Tour B: Manitoulin Island

Rainbow Country Travel Association
2726 Whippoorwill
Sudbury, P3G 1E9
☎522-0104 or (800) 465-6655

Tour C: The Far Northeast

**Cochrane Timiskaming
Travel Association**
P.O. Box 920
Schumacher, P0N 1G0
☎360-1989 or (800) 461-3766

EXPLORING

Tour A: On the Trail of the First Explorers ★★

In 1615, French explorers Samuel de Champlain and Étienne Brûlé along with a crew of Hurons sailed up the Ottawa River to the Mattawa River, crossed Lake Nipissing and continued to Huronia, at the edge of Georgian Bay (Lake Huron). The French remained on friendly terms with the Hurons for the next two decades, during which time they travelled to this region quite frequently, thus familiarizing themselves with the entire area, all the way to Lake Superior. Colonization was, nevertheless, a slow process, and no real settlements — either French or English — were established here for several decades.

This route through the middle of Northern Ontario nonetheless played a major role in the province's early history, for it enabled the *coureurs des bois* (trappers) to develop lucrative trading relations with the natives. This tour follows the trail of these first explorers through the towns of North Bay, Sudbury and Sault Ste. Marie.

From Ottawa, take Highway 17, which leads all the way to Sault-Ste-Marie.

Mattawa

The village of Mattawa lies at the junction of the Ottawa and Mattawa Rivers. Its name actually means "where the rivers meet" in the language of the Algonquin Indians. A peaceful village whose main street is lined with pretty wooden houses, Mattawa has an old-fashioned charm about it. The local residents have made the most of the town's location by laying out a verdant

Deer

park on the banks of the two lovely rivers, providing a perfect place to relax. Mattawa's main attraction, however, is its proximity to Samuel de Champlain park.

Samuel de Champlain Park ★

Samuel de Champlain Park *(Hwy 17, between Mattawa and North Bay, ☎744-2276)* lies along the banks of the Mattawa River, which early colonists used as a fur-trading route to travel deeper into Ontario, toward the Great Lakes. In memory of these explorers, the **Voyageur Museum** houses a small collection of objects related to their way of life, including an interesting replica of the kind of birch-bark canoe they used.

Most sports activities revolve around the Mattawa River, which is the focus of the park. Visitors interested in hiking through the forest will find trails leading to the river and running alongside it for a fair distance, while those who know

a bit about canoeing can paddle to their heart's content, either for a short trip or for a real adventure of several days. Backcountry campsites have been cleared throughout the park, which also has three campgrounds.

Callander

Callander is a modest-looking hamlet that would probably never have attracted much attention if it hadn't been for the Dionne family. The world's first quintuplets were born here in 1934. The event caused quite a stir, and before long people all over the world knew about the five little girls who appeared in numerous advertisements. A few reminders of this time remain around town, though the house where Mrs. Dionne gave birth is now located in North Bay. You can, however, visit the **North Himsworth Museum** *(donation; 107 Lansdowne St., ☎752-2282)*, the former home of Dr. Dafoe, who was in charge of the quintuplets for the first few years of their lives.

North Bay

Upon arriving in North Bay, you will be greeted by long, uninspiring boulevards lined with motels and large shopping centres. These streets, however, are not representative of this northern city, which boasts some lovely homes and a picturesque downtown area (Main Street between Cassell's and Fisher), which is unfortunately fighting a losing battle against the local malls. The beauty of this town lies in its simplicity, its spruce little houses with their well-kept gardens, and above all in its location on magnificent Lake Nipissing. A pleasant **promenade** ★ studded with benches runs along the shoreline. During summer, a peaceful crowd gathers here at the end of the day to savour the last rays of the sun as it slowly disappears into the shimmering waters of the lake. Visitors who so desire can take a cruise from the town dock to French River. Locals also enjoy access to another lovely body of water, Trout Lake, which lies east of town. Not that long ago, this lake was coveted as cottage country by local well-to-do families.

North Bay's growth parallelled that of the Ottawa River valley, since the town's strategic location along both the Great Lakes route and the railway enabled it to develop a prosperous economy linked to the fur trade, and also to serve as a supply centre for northern towns and industries. Up until 1990, North Bay was the hub of the fur trade in Ontario. The hall where the furs were auctioned off had to close due to the drop in sales caused by public opposition to the industry. Auctions are still held from time to time, but on a much smaller scale. The town remains a major stopping point on the route north, however.

Beside the tourist office, you'll see the former home of the Dionne family, a modest log house that was moved here from Callander. It now houses the **Dionne Quintuplet Museum** *(adult $2.75, senior/student $2.25, child $1.50; May, Jun, Sep and Oct, every day 9am to 5pm; Jul and Aug every day 9am to 7pm; Seymour St., P.O. Box 747, P1B 8J8, ☎472-8480),* which displays photographs of Cecile, Emily, Yvonne, Annette and Marie, as well as a number of their personal belongings.

Sudbury ★

Although a few trading posts were set up in this region in the early days of colonization, it wasn't until the arrival of the railroad in 1883 that Sudbury truly began to thrive. When the railroad was being built, the largest nickel deposits in the world were discovered here, along with sizeable deposits of uranium and copper, ushering in a period of major development for the town. The metals came from the Sudbury basin, which was probably created by the impact of a meteorite. To this day, mining plays an important role in the local economy.

The source of Sudbury's prosperity is apparent all over town. Verdant, leafy forests give way to barren, almost lunar landscapes. Over the past few years, all sorts of measures have been taken to restore some of the local greenery, but the traces left by the mining industry seem to be indelible. The town is therefore somewhat lacking in charm. Fortunately, some interesting projects have been launched to compensate for the drab scenery, and attractions such as Science North are well worth a visit.

Science North ★★ *($9.95; Jun to early Sep, 9am to 6pm; May and Oct, 9am to 5pm; Nov to Apr, 10am to 4pm; 100 Ramsey Lake, ☎522-3701)* is an unusual-looking building shaped like a giant snowflake. Its architecture is

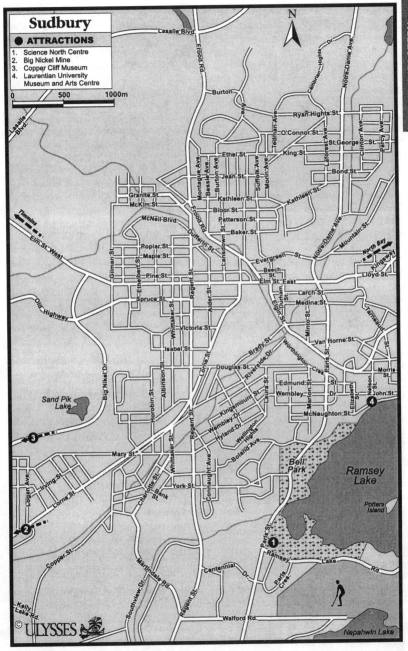

Sudbury

● **ATTRACTIONS**

1. Science North Centre
2. Big Nickel Mine
3. Copper Cliff Museum
4. Laurentian University
   Museum and Arts Centre

0   500   1000m

© ULYSSES

appropriate, since its goal is to familiarize the public with the mysteries of
science and nature. Inside, visitors will
find a whole range of small-scale, the-
matic exhibitions, short films and interactive and educational games intended
to make often complex scientific information easy to understand. Themes
such as the biosphere, the atmosphere
and the geosphere are explored in a
manner that will satisfy the curiosity of
young and old alike. The top floor laboratories are open to all, offering a
unique opportunity to experiment with
a variety of natural and scientific phe-
nomena. The centre also has an **IMAX
theatre** *($8)*, which presents strikingly
realistic films.

To top it all off, Science North boasts a
lovely setting on Lake Ramsey, and a
pleasant park has been laid out along
the shore. Wooden footbridges run
through a swampy area, offering visitors a chance to take a stroll through
tall grasses inhabited by scores of birds
and other little animals. Finally, you can
set out on a lake cruise aboard the
Cortina ($7.95).

> **Please note:** Passes are available for
> Science North, the IMAX theatre,
> the *Cortina* and Big Nickel Mine,
> which have teamed up in order to
> make it more affordable to visit all
> three attractions. The price is $8 for
> one attraction, $13.95 for two,
> $18.95 for three, and $24.95 for a
> day pass to all the attractions.

Big Nickel Mine ★ *(8.95; same schedule as Science North, but closed Oct to
May; take Lorne St. to Big Nickel Rd.,
☎522-3701)*, designed solely for the
tourist industry, contains no ore and
has never been worked. Although this
might seem like something of a let-

down, a tour of the "mine" is nonetheless interesting, as visitors are lead
20 metres underground to explore the
type of installations generally found in
real mines. A minibus provides free
transportation to and from the Science
North complex.

Next to the mine, you'll see a giant
nickel, a reminder that these 5¢ coins
were once made with local nickel.

The **Path of Discovery** *(from Science
North, ☎800-461-4898)*, a guided tour
of the town and its surrounding area,
enables visitors to learn about the geological history of the Sudbury basin. It
also leads to the Inco Mine, one of the
largest producers of nickel in the world.

A few small museums display various
everyday objects from the early
20th century. These places will appeal
to visitors interested in local culture,
but don't expect to find any treasures.
It is always wise to call before stopping
by.

The **Copper Cliff Museum** *(free admission; Jun to Aug, 11am to 4pm; at the
corner of Balsam and Power;
☎682-1332)* displays a wide array of
typical tools found in a miner's shack at
the beginning of the century.

A stop in at the **Flour Mill Heritage
Museum** *(free admission; mid-Jun to
Aug, Tue to Fri 10am to 4pm, Sun 1pm
to 4pm; Saint Charles St., ☎674-2391)*
reveals various 19th-century technology, which offer insight into the daily
life of the area's first inhabitants.

You can also visit the **Laurentian University Museum and Arts Centre** *(donation appreciated; noon to 5pm, closed
Mon; at the corner of Nelson and
John)*, set up inside the former home of
lumber magnate W.J. Bell.

Killarney Park ★★

To get to the little town of Killarney, take Highway 63, which runs alongside lovely **Killarney Park** (*☎287-2800*). This vast stretch of untouched wilderness extends into Georgian Bay and is strewn with scores of crystal-clear rivers and lakes, making it a canoeist's paradise. Exploring the park offers a chance to discover the magical landscapes that characterize the Canadian Shield, where lakes and rivers and birch and pine forests meet the cliffs of the La Cloche Mountains. The park has something for everyone, whether you want to canoe down a river with stretches of turbulent water or prefer to hike or ski along a trail through the woods. The sites at the campground are equipped with electricity, and a number of other spots have been cleared for wilderness camping. You can rent all the necessary equipment for a canoe trip in the little village of Killarney.

Espanola

To reach Maitoulin Island (see p 312), take Highway 6 to Espanola. With some 5,000 residents, this is a fair-sized town for this region. It is dominated by a large pulp and paper company situated at the entrance of the town. In summer, there are guided tours of the factory. Its many businesses and stores make this a good place to buy provisions for your visit to Manitoulin Island.

Massey

Massey lies at the confluence of the Sables and Spanish Rivers, and owes its existence to the lumber industry. You might want to stop by the **Massey Regional Museum** (*$1; every day mid-Jun to early Sep; 160 Sauble St.*),

which focusses on local history, from the first native inhabitants to the beginning of the 20th century.

Blind River

If you did not stop at Massey, Blind River is the next village of any size on Highway 17. Not only does it boast a few tourist attractions, it also has several restaurants. This is a good place to stop and relax before resuming the journey west.

St. Joseph Island

St. Joseph Island lies in the strait separating Lake Huron and Lake Superior. Consisting essentially of vast fields and forests, its appeals lives in its peaceful and bucolic setting. A road circles the island and leads to **Fort St. Joseph National Historic Park** at its southern end. The fort was built in 1796 and was the western-most British military post in Canada. Today the site offers an interpretation centre set up on the ruins of the fort, destroyed by American troops in 1814. Costumed guides offer a glimpse of life at the fort in the early 19th century, with its native peoples, British soldiers and fur traders.

Sault Ste. Marie ★★

The Ojibwa used to call this site Batawing in reference to its location on the banks of St. Mary's River, which forms a series of tumultuous waterfalls between Lake Huron and Lake Superior. The falls (*saults*) also prompted Jacques Marquette, a Jesuit priest, to name the mission he founded here Sainte-Marie du Sault. Its strategic location at the juncture of two of the Great Lakes made it an important supply stop for fur-traders, but up until 1840, it was essentially used to store merchandise. With the opening of the Bruce Mine in the 1850s, the town truly began to flourish.

Today, life in Sault Ste. Marie centres around the iron, steel and wood industries, as well as shipping, since large numbers of vessels pass through the local locks every day. You can watch these immense ships going through the locks from an attractive promenade along the St. Mary's River. This park also attracts a lot of birds, especially barnacle geese. For a closer look at the lock mechanisms, take a tour with **Locks Tour Canada** *($17; Roberta Bondar Dock, ☎253-9850)*.

In 1895, a canal was built around the rapids between Lake Superior and Lake Huron to allow boats to navigate from one Great Lake to the other. With time, the canal became too narrow to allow the passage of modern ships. It has been refurbished to accommodate pleasure boats, and it has an attractive park on the banks of the canal, the **Sault Canal National Historic Site**, with approximately two kilometres of trails.

Sault Ste. Marie, or the Soo, as it is popularly known, is a delightful place. A lovely, peaceful city with long, tree-shaded streets lined with opulent, old-fashioned houses, it has a unique charm and is no doubt one of the most attractive towns in Northern Ontario. Aside from its lovely downtown area and residential neighbourhoods, which you can explore at your leisure, it has a few interesting tourist attractions, and is the starting point for a magnificent excursion to the Agawa Canyon.

The historical retrospective of the **Sault Ste. Marie Museum** *($2; Mon to Sat 9am to 4:30pm, Sun 1pm to 4:30pm; 690 Queen St. E., ☎759-7278)* offers visitors a chance to step back 10,000 years in time. It begins with the first natives to inhabit the region and

leads up to the 20th century. Among other things, visitors will find a reconstructed wigwam and a collection of everyday objects from early colonial times. These articles are not particularly valuable, but the place is nonetheless quite interesting.

The pretty, stone **Ermatinger House ★** *($2; Jun to Sep, every day 10am to 5pm; mid-Apr to May, Mon to Fri 10am to 5pm; Oct and Nov, 1pm to 5pm; 831 Queen St. E., ☎759-5443)* was erected in 1824 by a wealthy fur-trader named Charles Oakes Ermatinger as a gift for his Ojibwa wife. Built before the town developed, it is the oldest house in northwestern Ontario. Upon entering the house, which is furnished with antiques, you will be greeted by guides in period dress, creating the impression that you are reliving a bygone era.

The **Algoma Art Gallery** *(donation appreciated; Mon to Sat 9am to 5pm, Sep to Dec 1pm to 4pm; 10 East St., ☎949-9067)* has two rooms containing works by artists from Canada and elsewhere. The collection is small, but some of the paintings are beautiful. The gallery also presents temporary exhibits.

Roberta Bondar Park was laid out on the shores of St. Mary's River, just a very short distance from downtown, as a tribute to Canada's first female astronaut, a native of Sault Ste. Marie. Its gigantic tent (1,347 m^2) is used for all sorts of events in both summer and winter, including the Winter Carnival.

At the end of Bay Street you can't miss the large hangar that houses the **Canadian Bushplane Heritage Centre** *($5; 9am to 9pm; 50 Pim St., ☎945-6242, www.bushplane.com)*. Many bush planes are on display, including the Beaver, whose sturdiness and reliability permitted the exploration of remote regions in Canada. Bush planes are not

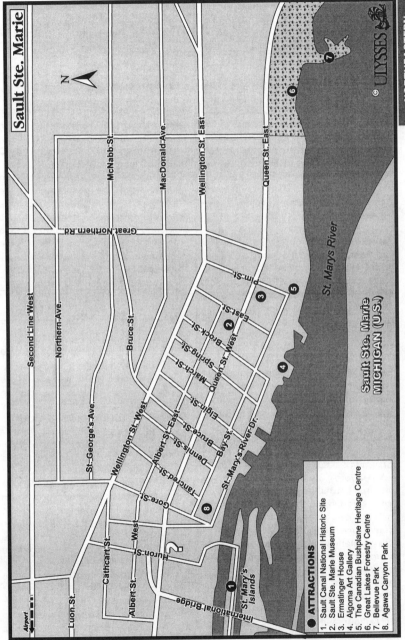

Sault Ste. Marie

N

St. Marys River

Sault Ste. Marie
MICHIGAN (U.S.)

St. Mary's
Islands

International Bridge

Airport

Luon St.
Cathcart St.
Second Line West
St-George's Ave.
Northern Ave.
Great Northern Rd.
McNabb St.
MacDonald Ave.
Wellington St. East
Queen St. East
Bruce St.
Wellington St. West
Albert St. West
Huron St.
Albert St.
Pim St.
East St.
Brock St.
Spring St.
March St.
Elgin St.
Bay St.
Dennis St. East
Bruce St.
Tancred St.
Gore St.
St. Mary's River Dr.
Queen St. West

● ATTRACTIONS

1. Sault Canal National Historic Site
2. Sault Ste. Marie Museum
3. Ermatinger House
4. Algoma Art Gallery
5. The Canadian Bushplane Heritage Centre
6. Great Lakes Forestry Centre
7. Bellevue Park
8. Agawa Canyon Park

the only models featured here. There are also other planes like forest fire fighters. You can climb into the cockpits of some of the planes to get an idea of what it is like to pilot them.

At the **Great Lakes Forestry Centre** *(free admission; Jul Mon-Fri 10am to 4pm; 1219 Queen St. E., ☎759-5740 ext. 2222)*, the largest facility of its kind in the country, researchers study the development of the Canadian forest. Visitors can tour the greenhouses and laboratories where these studies are conducted and learn about some aspects of this natural treasure. Reservations required.

Bellevue Park stretches along St. Mary's River east of town. It is very popular with local residents, who come here to stroll about and look at the bison, deer and other animals in the little **zoo**. The park also attracts large numbers of barnacle geese, who honk up a storm, detracting somewhat from the peacefulness of the setting.

For a memorable outing in the heart of the Northern Ontario wilderness, climb aboard the Algoma train for a visit to the **Agawa Canyon Park** ★★★ *($46; May to Sep, every day 8am, Jan to Mar, Sat and Sun 8am; the station is located in the Station Mall, 129 Bay St., P.O. Box 130, ☎946-7300, ⇒541-2989)*. Comfortably seated in a charming little period train, you will wind through the forest, passing along hillsides and riverbanks and taking in some strikingly beautiful scenery, which changes with the seasons, transforming itself from an intense green in summer to orange and red hues in fall and finally a dazzling white in winter. The train departs early in the morning and travels through the woods for over three hours before reaching its destination in the heart of the forest. Passengers then have two hours to stroll about, visit the falls or climb the hills.

Afterward, you will head back to town with your head full of images of majestic scenery. Reservations are recommended, particularly in the fall.

Gros Cap

Sault Ste. Marie does not lie directly on **Lake Superior**; to see this vast stretch of water, the largest body of fresh water in the world, take Highway 550 to **Gros Cap**. Here, you'll find a pretty, albeit rocky, beach, where you can take a swim. The beach is also the starting point for several hiking trails *(Blue Hiking Trails)*. There is no bus service to Gros Cap. If you don't have a car, your best option is to rent a bike at **Verne's** *(51 Great Northern Rd., ☎254-4901)*.

Tour B: Manitoulin Island ★

Manitoulin Island has been inhabited by native tribes for centuries — nearly 10,000 years, according to archaeological excavations. Their presence here has not been continuous, however; in the 1700s, for reasons that are still unclear, the local natives decided to leave the island and settle farther south. Over a century later, in the 1820s, they were driven back to the island when more and more colonists began settling in southern Ontario. For years, only a handful of natives lived on this huge territory, one of the largest freshwater islands in the world, with an area of 1600 square kilometres. Little by little, however, Manitoulin Island began to attract English colonists, and in the 19th century, the natives had to negotiate with British authorities about sharing their land.

The native presence is quite evident on the island, with Odawa, Potawotami and Ojibwa tribes scattered across the

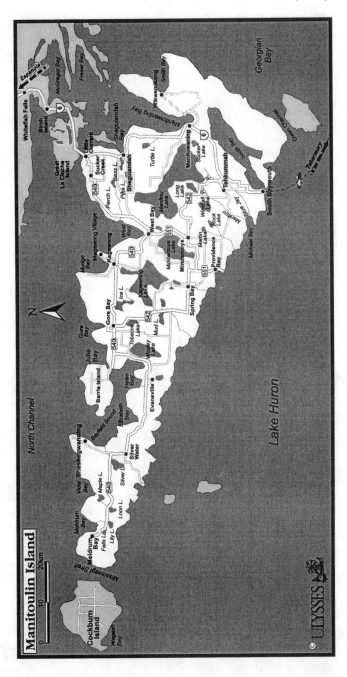

territory. Many villages and lakes also bear native names, such as Sheguiandah, Manitowaning and Mindemoya, which can be traced back to legends that still haunt these areas. The name Manitoulin itself refers to one such legend, according to which the island is the land of the great spirit *Gitchi Manitou*.

A peaceful island with charming little villages, picturesque hamlets and over a hundred lakes, this place will delight visitors looking for rural areas and tranquil natural surroundings, but has little to offer urban souls who are only content in bustling cities. With its long, white sand beaches, hiking trails and waters abounding in fish, it is a veritable playground for fans of the outdoors.

Little Current

Little Current is the first village you will reach if you take Highway 6 to Manitoulin Island. The Hudson's Bay Company built a small trading post here, which gradually developed into the most populous town on the island, with some 1,500 inhabitants. It is nonetheless a peaceful, pretty place.

There is a charming village centre with a few tempting shops and two restaurants. The village ends at a lovely green space along Georgian Bay, which is great for an evening stroll.

Continue along Highway 6.

Sheguiandah

Archaeological excavations carried out near Sheguiandah have revealed traces of human activity in this area dating back nearly 10,000 years. Little is known, however, about these natives, who apparently traded in quartzite.

The **Centennial Museum** *($3; late May to mid-Sep, every day 10am to 4:30pm; mid-Sep to mid-Oct, Sat and Sun; Hwy 6, ☎368-2367)* offers visitors a chance to learn about the island's first settlers through a variety of everyday 19th-century objects and native handicrafts. You can also visit replicas of a smithy and a log house.

Farther south, the road runs along the coast overlooking Manitowaning Bay, offering some beautiful views along the way. The **Ten Mile Point** ★ commands an unimpeded view of the waters of Lake Huron.

Continue on Highway 6 until you reach the road leading to Wikwemikong.

Wikwemikong

Wikwemikong, the only native territory in North America never to have been relinquished to the colonizers, is renowned for its powwows, held on the first weekend in August. Various native families get together for these festivities, which include dances and traditional ceremonies.

Manitowaning

Manitowaning (or more precisely, Manitwaling) is a native word meaning the Lair of Manitou, as the Odawas and Ojibwa of this region used to believe that the great spirit Manitou lived here. Manitou wasn't the only local resident, however; in the early 19th century, this region was granted to the natives, who began settling here in 1836. Two years later, Anglican missionaries came to the area to try to convert the natives to Christianity. **St. Paul's Anglican Church** was erected here in 1845, making it the oldest church in northern Ontario.

Gore Bay Lighthouse

South Baymouth

The *Chi-cheemaun* ferry that links the island to Tobermory lands in South Baymouth, which you'll pass through in the wink of an eye. This tiny hamlet does, however, boast a pleasant location at the mouth of South Bay, on Lake Huron. Several businesses are found along the pier where the *Chi-Cheemaun*, the ferry that crosses to Tobermory on the mainland, is anchored.

Highway 542 heads inland, then leads to Providence Bay.

Providence Bay

Providence Bay is another peaceful little hamlet, whose location near a magnificent sandy **beach** ★ makes it a hit with summer visitors. It also attracts fishing buffs, since salmon can be caught in the waters offshore.

Take Highway 542 to Evansville. From there, take the 540.

Meldrum Bay

On your way west, you will pass through vast stretches of sparsely populated land. Meldrum Bay, the last hamlet on the western part of the island, is a peaceful, isolated little community. A lighthouse dating from the 19th century still stands alongside the Mississagi Strait. It no longer serves its original purpose, but has been converted into the **Mississagi Lighthouse Museum** *($1; late May to Sep every day 9am to 9pm)*, where you can learn about the lives of the lighthouse keepers.

From Meldrum Bay, take Highway 540 to Gore Bay.

Gore Bay ★

The little village of Gore Bay, which is both the administrative centre of the island and a charming little resort area, lies in the heart of the bay of the same name. During summer, it is pleasant to stroll around its bustling marina, where all sorts of boats are moored.

In addition to an attractive marina, Gore Bay has some charming Bed and Breakfasts (see p 326), pretty wood cottages and a lovely promenade beside the water, making it one of the most enchanting villages on the island. If you wish, you can follow the road beside the marina leading out of the village. You will pass several beautiful summer homes facing the lake. At the very end you will see the **Gore Bay Lighthouse** with its red and white beacon. Built around 1870, the lighthouse has an architectural style typical of the era (a stone base surmounted by a square tower built of wooden lathes). Erected to assist in Great Lakes navigation, the lighthouse is privately owned and not open to the public.

Kagawong

A few quaint cottages at the side of the road form the hamlet of Kagawong, which seems frozen in time. At the eastern end of town, a parking lot and a large sign mark the location of the **Bridal Veil Falls**. Take the long wooden staircase down to the short trail that leads to the foot of the falls. From there, you can admire the handiwork of the river that has been sculpting these metres of rock for millennia.

To get to Little Current, take Route 540 east.

Tour C: The Far Northeast

This third tour only covers a tiny part of this immense region. You can drive for hours through this lonely land without seeing a soul. The region's rich natural resources (minerals and wood) have, however, led to the development of a few little communities here and there. Aside from this handful of villages, much of this land is native territory.

Temagami

Temagami's riches are its endless forests, lakes and rivers where canoeists can travel for hours without meeting another living soul, and become one with the serenity of the wilderness. A mere kilometre from the stunning Finlayson Park, Temagami is just the starting point for an adventure to this park. However, there are more comfortable accommodations in this village.

Cobalt

The richness of the Ontario subsoil is one of the main engines of the northern economy. Ever since the beginning of the 20th century when these mineral deposits were discovered, mining communities have sprung up in the area. It was by pure accident that the first rich vein of silver was uncovered here by a lumberjack in 1903. The town of Cobalt was created by the subsequent gold rush of new prospectors to the region. The mining of gold only lasted for a few years, but in 1930, with the discovery of cobalt deposits, the town got a second wind. The downtown **Cobalt North Mining Museum** *($3.25; 26 Silver St., ☎679-8301)* evokes the exciting lives of the miners who came to try their luck in northern Ontario.

Dymond

Past Temagami, Highway 11 heads north. Little by little, the dense mixed forest that characterizes this landscape for many kilometres gives way to a series of little villages. The development of this region dates back to the beginning of the 20th century when the fertile land around Lake Témiscamingue attracted newcomers, mostly from Quebec. They settled here hoping to cultivate the land. However the vast distance from other population centres prevented the produce from getting to the markets. Thus, many turned to the more lucrative fields of mining and forestry. Farming and agriculture remain secondary activities, however. In the area around Dymond, a little town with a few small houses and businesses, there are vast fields. As the road continues north, this rustic scene quickly fades from view as the forest takes over again.

Kirkland Lake

In 1903, the Cobalt area became famous for its rich silver deposits. A few years later, in 1911, a rumour spread about a region somewhat to the north of it: gold had been discovered in Kirkland Lake. For decades, gold mining was the backbone of the local economy. In 1930, no fewer than seven gold mines were in operation in the area, and were the main source of employment for the population.

Many poor settlers flooded to Kirkland Lake to try to make their fortunes. Prospecting was kind to some of them, especially Harry Oakes, whose discovery of gold made him one of the richest men in the world in his time. The **Sir Harry Oakes Chateau** *(Mon to Sat 10am to 4pm; 2 Chateau Dr., ☎568-8800)* recounts the life of this famous prospector. There is also a small geological exhibit.

Iroquois Falls

Another pillar of the local economy, the lumber industry, is very much in evidence here. It is not uncommon to come across a sawmill or to see enormous mountains of logs beside the road. Iroquois Falls is one of the main industrial centres of the northeast. Abitibi-Consolidated (formerly Abitibi-Price) has been exploiting the forest

here for ages and is the main employer in the region. One of its factories stands at the entrance to the village.

At Iroquois Falls, you can either continue north or take Highway 101 west to Timmins.

Timmins

Gold is also the reason for the development of Timmins. It was Harry Preston who discovered gold here in 1909. Two years later, Noah Timmins built housing for the men who had come to work the mines, and a little hamlet began to form. New deposits, discovered over the years, continued to attract people to the region. In 1973 the fusion of several small towns created the city of Timmins. Today, it is the largest urban centre in the region.

Entering the city, you will see a multitude of large commercial centres where most of the town's activity takes place. While lacking in aesthetic value, the main street offers everything a visitor could possibly require during a stay here. Few cities in northeastern Ontario have such a concentration of stores. The town is not completely without charm, though. Spend some time on the side streets and you will come across some of the original houses put up for the families of the early miners. The mining history of the town is very evident, and the residents are very proud of their roots and have made every effort to show it to visitors.

No visit to northeastern Ontario would be complete without taking the **Timmins Underground Gold Mine Tour ★** *($17; late Jun to early Sep, 9:30am, 10:30am, noon, 1:30pm, 3pm; late Apr to late Jun and early Sep to late Oct, 10:30am and 1:30pm; 220 Algonquin Blvd., ☎/≈267-6222)*. Visitors can go down into the mine (no

Moose

longer in operation) to see the works and the methods of extracting the ore. The guides also explain how difficult the working conditions were and the efforts made to improve them, especially with regards to safety. To get a good idea of how the miners lived, visit the museum, "the miner's house," an example of the housing put up by the mine owners at the beginning of the century. You can also watch the process of ore being refined and finally poured into an ingot. If you have time, try panning for gold in the river. Be aware that the temperature in the mine is 3°C, and dress warmly for the descent. For your safety, helmets and footwear are provided.

Visitors can learn about local history at the **Timmins Museum and National Exhibition Centre** *(free admission; Hwy 101 to South Porcupine, 70 Legion Dr.,* ☎*235-5066)*, whose small exhibit includes mining equipment and a prospector's cabin. The place also hosts temporary exhibitions on Ontario's various ethnic communities.

To learn more about how zinc, lead and silver are mined, take the **Kidd Creek Mines Tour** *($3; Jul and Aug 1pm; Hwy 101, 26 km east of town,* ☎*360-1900)*.

Between Timmins and Chapleau is a stretch of forest that is unbroken except for one tiny hamlet. On this stretch of Highway 101, your most likely encounter will be with the occasional moose or deer.

Chapleau

With a sigh of relief, you will arrive at Chapleau, the only real town for many kilometres. It contains only a few simple homes and businesses. However, it is not for the village that people come here; rather, it is the magnificent natural garden beside it, the Chapleau Game Preserve.

Chapleau Crown Game Preserve ★

The Chapleau Crown Game Preserve protects a vast territory teeming with moose, deer and other mammals since hunting has been prohibited since 1925. Only fishing is allowed in this haven of peace and tranquillity. A small section in the southern part of the preserve is accessible by road, while the western section can be reached by train (see "Agawa Canyon Park" on p 312). The train stops at different spots, allowing visitors to access this pristine region more easily.

Cochrane

Cochrane's development was linked to the arrival of the railway near the end of the 19th century. The town has few attractions, save its majestic forest that consists almost entirely of conifers and teems with all sorts of game, making this a veritable paradise for fishing and hunting. The main draw here, however, is the picturesque *Polar Bear Express*, a train that carries passengers northward from Cochrane to Moosonee, on the shores of James Bay.

The *Polar Bear Express* *($46; ☎800-268-9281)* sets out through the forest of conifers around Cochrane. Little by little, the vegetation changes, as trees give way to bushes. The end of the line is Moosonee, the northernmost town in Ontario. You can stay in Moosonee, but if you're short on time, the return trip can be made the same day (8:30am departure from Cochrane and 12:50pm arrival in Moosonee, then 6pm departure from Moosonee and 10pm arrival in Cochrane).

Moosonee

The last northern village served by the train, with no highways connecting it to the rest of the province, Moosonee has been keeping watch over James Bay since the 17th century. A large trading post run by the Hudson's Bay Company once stood just steps away from the present village. The location was a strategic one, since the natives who hunted in these northern climes could go to the trading post and exchange furs for tools. The Europeans, for their part, would come to the post by boat, which they would fill with furs before heading back out to sea, thus avoiding long, perilous and costly trips over land. For many years, life in Moosonee revolved around the fur trade. Although the village doesn't have that much character, it is interesting from an historical point of view.

A large canoe *($10; all summer; Moosonee dock)* carries visitors to and from **Moose Factory Island**, where the Hudson's Bay Company's trading post was located. This little island is still home to several buildings and a smithy dating from the 19th century, as well as a small museum with a collection of objects evoking the early days of colonization in this region (1693). A variety of artifacts related to the fur trade are also on display.

The *Polar Princess Cruise* *($46; Moosonee dock, ☎336-2944)* carries passengers to the mouth of the Moose River, which empties into James Bay. Stopping at Moose Factory Island, it also passes alongside the Ship Sands Island Bird Sanctuary, where you can spot a variety of winged species.

From Cochrane, you can take Highway 11 west, which leads to numerous little villages. This highway runs through the northernmost part of Ontario.

Hearst

Hearst is one of a number of little towns in Northern Ontario with a primarily French-speaking population. For the most part, these communities owe their existence to the railway, which was completed in 1913. Today, people come here mainly for moose hunting.

From Hearst, you can continue meandering west; Highway 11 goes to Thunder Bay.

OUTDOOR ACTIVITIES

Beaches

Tour A: On the Trail of the First Explorers

North Bay is flanked by two magnificent lakes with beautiful sandy beaches. One of the loveliest, and most popular, is **Sunset Beach on Lake Nipissing**, a gorgeous strip of golden sand with a pleasant park beside it. To get there, take Lakeshore Drive to Sunset.

Trout Lake is renowned for its clean, clear, refreshing water. It also has a few pretty beaches. The best by far is **Birchaven Cove**, commonly known as the Cove. To get there, take Lakeside Street all the way to the end.

If you spend a little time in Sudbury, you're bound to see lovely Ramsey Lake. On its shores, you will not only find the Science North centre, but also several parks, including **Bell Park**, whose beach is one of the prettiest in the area, and consequently one of the most crowded as well.

Gros Cap, with its pretty beach lapped by the waters of Lake Superior, lies a short distance from Sault Ste. Marie on Highway 550.

Tour B: Manitoulin Island

There are a few modest hamlets on the southern part of the island, the most noteworthy being **Providence Bay ★**, whose long sandy beach is a swimmer's paradise.

Tour C: The Far Northeast

Finlayson Point Park *(take Hwy. 11 to Temagami, ☎569-3205)* lies on the shores of Lake Temagami and is the starting point for a number of canoe routes and hiking trails across stretches of pristine wilderness. You will find rudimentary but adequate campsites along the way. There are also a number of campgrounds for people who aren't setting off on long expeditions.

Hiking

Tour A: On the Trail of the First Explorers

There are enough hiking trails in Northern Ontario to fill an entire guide, so we can't possibly list them all. We have, however, indicated a few of the most enchanting ones, as well as those most convenient to the major towns in this region.

Samuel de Champlain Park ★ *(Mattawa)* has short, pleasant and well laid-out trails, which lead to the edge of the gorges along the Amable River, where hikers can enjoy some leisurely bird-watching. Frequented by various types of ducks, this place is a real treat for amateur ornithologists.

Located outside of town, but easy to reach, **Canadore College** *(100 College Dr., North Bay, ☎474-1550)* has a few hiking and cross-country trails leading through the forest, as far as the swirling Duchenay Falls.

Killarney Park *(south of Sudbury)* has a few wonderful trails. Some are easy and can be enjoyed by all, while others stretch tens of kilometres and require more preparation. They wind through a lovely forest of birch and pine trees, past some magnificent scenery typical of the Canadian Shield.

The only way to get to **Agawa Canyon Park** is to take the Algoma Train departing from Sault-Ste-Marie (see p 312). The train ride takes you through a wooded region. Once in the park, you have two hours to admire the natural wonders common to this part of Ontario as you hike along any of the numerous paths. Lookout Trail is one of these, and leads to an observatory and a magnificent vista of the canyon. Another option is the River Trail, which runs to the foot of the Black Beavers Falls and Bridal Veil Falls. Many other paths are easily accessible and can be explored within 30 minutes.

Tour B: Manitoulin Island

About 20 kilometres southwest of Little Current, just before West Bay, you will find the **Cup and Saucer Trails ★**, which lead 361 metres up a hill, offering some magnificent views of the island and its surroundings.

On Highway 540, right beside Kagawong, there is a picnic area where you will find a short trail leading to the **Bridal Veil Falls** and then on to Mudge Bay.

Tour C: The Far Northeast

A network of delightful footpaths surrounds the city of **Timmins**. The first of these, the Golden Springs Trail, covers 14 kilometres in a winsome region with many trees and lakes. Other paths also allow you to discover the natural beauty of the region.

 Canoeing

Tour A: On the Trail of the First Explorers

Killarney Park has some outstanding canoe routes through unspoiled wilderness, where the only thing that could possibly disrupt your peace of mind is the twittering of the birds.

Samuel de Champlain Park covers one whole shore of the Mattawa River, whose waters are well-suited to canoeing. Canoes can be rented in North Bay:

Bob's Bait
Trout Lake Rd.
☎472-7479.

Finlayson Point is the starting point for about twenty canoe routes, which lead deep into the heart of the Northern Ontario wilderness. These routes stretch no less than 2,600 kilometres and cover all levels of difficulty.

To rent equipment or participate in a canoeing trip:

Temagami Wilderness Centre
R.R. 1, Temagami, P0H 2H0,
☎569-3733 or 800-881-1189,
≈569-3594,
www.temagami.com.

Lakeland Airways
25 Lakeshore Dr., Temagami,
☎569-3455

Cruises

Tour A: On the Trail of the First Explorers

Sailing the waters of Lake Nipissing is a fun excursion while visiting **North Bay**. A cruise aboard the *The New Chief (federal government dock, Jun to Sep* ☎494-9167, *Sep to May* ☎474-0400, ☎800-387-0516*)* lasts three to six hours and usually has a theme (the first explorers, insect life on the lake, etc.). Passengers have a chance to learn about the history and various inhabitants of this vast stretch of clear water and its surroundings.

The *Cortina ($8)*, which sets out from Science North, takes passengers on a pleasant cruise on the blue waters of Lake Ramsey, offering a chance to take in some splendid scenery.

Sault Ste. Marie has some impressive locks, which many boats pass through every day on their way from Lake Huron to Lake Superior. To see the locks in operation up close while enjoying a pleasant cruise, climb aboard the boat owned by **Locks Tour Canada** *($17; Jun to Oct; Roberta Bondar dock, P.O. Box 325, P6A 5L8,* ☎253-9850, ⚞253-3303*)*, which passes through all the locks.

Rock-climbing

Tour A: On the Trail of the First Explorers

There are all sorts of pleasant surprises in store for rock-climbing buffs, who can scale rock faces here in summer

and icy cliffs in winter. **Lake Nipigon Provincial Park** *(take Hwy 11 from Nipigon,* ☎807-885-3181*)* is a particular favourite with fans of this thrilling sport.

Hunting and Fishing

Tour A: On the Trail of the First Explorers

Salmon, trout, perch and muskie are just a few of the fish you can catch in the lakes and rivers of Northern Ontario. Some places are especially renowned, including Lake Nipissing and Trout Lake, in **North Bay**, and the numerous lakes in **Missinaibi Park** *(north of Chapleau)* which protects the river of the same name.

Tour B: Manitoulin Island

Manitoulin Island is also a popular spot for fishing, and good catches (especially salmon) can be made in the surrounding waters.

Tour C: The Far Northeast

Several parks in Northern Ontario also have something to offer hunting fans. Black bear, deer and moose are among the animals hunters can hope to bag, depending on the region. Some parts of northern Ontario, including the region around **Hearst** are reputed to be good for hunting.

Of course, permits are required for both hunting and fishing. To apply for one, or to obtain information regarding regulations, write to:

Ontario Ministry of Natural Resources
Information Centre
MacDonald Building, Office M1-73
900 Bay Street
Toronto, M7A 2C1
☎416-314-1177 (fishing)
☎416-314-2225 (hunting)

 Downhill Skiing

Tour A: On the Trail of the First Explorers

Mount Antoine *(4 km north of Mattawa on Hwy 533; P.O. Box 822, P1B 8K1, ☎474-9950)*, located north of Mattawa, has gently sloping sides and a vertical drop of about 200 metres, just enough for about ten ski runs. Some hotels in Mattawa, including the **Mattawa Golf & Ski Resort** (see further below), offer skiing packages.

Searchmont *(take Hwy 556, P.O. Box 1029, Sault-Ste-Marie, P6A 5N5, ☎781-2340, www.search mont.com)* lies about ten kilometres north of Sault Ste. Marie. The highest mountain in the region, it has well-maintained runs and modern ski lifts.

 Cross-country Skiing

Tour C: The Far Northeast

Come winter, the **Chapleau Game Preserve** *(☎864-1028)* turns into a snow-covered garden laced with myriad cross-country ski trails. Numerous trails are maintained.

 Dog-sledding

The Far Northeast

The traditional means of transportation for the Inuits, dog-sledding is now a thrilling sport that anyone who's not entirely out of shape can enjoy. The **Temagami Wilderness Centre** (see p 321) organizes two-day dogsledding expeditions during the winter. This way you will get to see the surrounding forest and spend the night in a heated tent in the middle of the woods. An unforgettable experience!

 Snowmobiling

A network of about 33,000 kilometres of snowmobile trails covers the immense territory of Northern Ontario. These interconnected trails enable snowmobilers to travel from town to town, reach small villages and ride through the snow-covered forest, all the while enjoying the majestic scenery around them. To plan a snowmobile trip or to obtain further information, call ☎(800) 263-7533 or ☎(800) 263-2546.

 ACCOMMODATIONS

Tour A: On the Trail
of the First Explorers

Mattawa

Samuel de Champlain Park *(Hwy 17, between Mattawa and North Bay, ☎705-744-2276)*, which protects a vast forest and one bank of the Mattawa River, is a camper's paradise.

The **Valois Motel** *($47; ≈, ℜ, ✕; 701 Valois Drive, P0H 1V0, ☎744-5583)*, on the way into town, is a modest-looking place but has a pleasant riverside location.

If you're looking for an inviting atmosphere, and would like to stay in a charming cottage near a golf course, head to the **Mattawa Golf & Ski Resort** *($80; ≡, K, ℜ, △; Hwy 117 E., P.O.*

Box 609, P0H 1V0, ☎744-5818 or 800-762-2339). Special packages for snowmobilers.

North Bay

You'll have no trouble finding a place to stay in North Bay, which is the largest town in the region and has all sorts of hotels and motels.

For a night in the great outdoors, pitch your tent at **Camp Conewango** *($20; ☒; 18 km northwest of North Bay; take Hwy 63 to Songis Rd and continue for 14 km, ☎776-2320),* an excellent campground located a few kilometres from North Bay.

The **Days Inn** *($85; ≡, △; 255 McIntyre St. W., P1B 2Y9, ☎474-4770)* is one of the few hotels in downtown North Bay. The building looks somewhat austere, but the rooms are perfectly adequate.

The hotels and motels lining Lakeshore Drive are perfect for visitors who have a car and are planning to spend a few days in town. One good choice is the **Venture Inn** *($83 bkfst incl.; ≡, ☒, 㧖; 718 Lakeshore Dr., P1A 2G4, ☎472-7171 or 800-483-6887, ⊶472-8276),* since its well-kept rooms have a certain charm about them and it's located just steps away from the beaches on Lake Nipissing.

The nearby **Sunset Motel Park and Cottages** *($89; ⊛, △, ℛ; 641 Lakeshore Dr., P1A 2E9, ☎472-8370 or 800-463-8370, ⊶476-5647)* has charmingly decorated rooms and little cottages with fireplaces, making for a cozy atmosphere. It is also located just a stone's throw away from Lake Nipissing and Sunset Beach.

You might also try the **Best Western Lakeshore** *($139; ≡, ℛ, △, ⊛, ☒, 㧖; 700 Lakeshore Dr., P1A 2G4,*

☎474-5800 or 800-461-6199, ⊶474-8699) or the **Comfort Inn** *($100; ≡, 㧖; 676 Lakeshore Dr., P1A 2G4, ☎494-9444 or 800-228-5150, ⊶494-8461),* which both have comfortable, modern rooms.

Sudbury

There is no youth hostel or charming B&B in Sudbury, but several international hotel chains are represented here, so comfortable accommodation is readily available. One option is the Sheraton.

If you're looking for a place to pitch your tent, head to the campground in nearby **Fairbank Provincial Park** *($20; take Hwy 144 for 55 km, ☎965-2702).*

During summer, you can rent a room in the student residences at **Laurentian University** *($30/person; Ramesay Lake Rd., ☎675-4814),* which offer basic but nonetheless decent accommodation for the price.

Downtown Sudbury is not a particularly inviting place, but if you have things to do there, the **Ramada Inn** *($81; ≡, ≈, △, ⊛, ℛ, 㧖, ☒; 85 St. Anne Rd., P3E 4S4, ☎675-1123 or 800-854-7854, ⊶675-7727)* should suit your needs.

The various hotels near the Science North complex each seem to be trying to outdo the other by offering as many amenities as possible and attractive modern rooms. The **Travelodge** *($94; ≡, ≈, ⊛, 㧖, ☒; 1401 Paris St., P3E 3B6, ☎522-1100 or 800-578-7878, ⊶522-1668)* offers package deals including accommodation and tickets to Science North. Guests also enjoy the use of an indoor swimming pool.

The nearby **Travelway** *($74; ≡, ℛ; 1200 Paris St., P3E 3A1, ☎522-1122 or 800-461-4883, ⊶522-3877)* has comfortable rooms decorated in a reasonably attractive manner.

Another option is to stay in one of the hotels along Regent Street. You won't find any charming inns here, but some of the places have decent rooms. One of these is the **Venture Inn** *($84; ≡, ℜ; 1956 Regent St., P3E 3Z9, ☎522-7600 or 888-483-6887, ⇌522-7648)*, which is located near the highway, making it a convenient place to stop for the night.

Right nearby stands the **Sheraton** *($100; ≡, ≈, △, ◉, ℜ, ⑂; 1696 Regent St., P3E 3Z8, ☎522-3000 or 800-461-4822, ⇌522-8067)*, a renowned establishment with lovely rooms and all sorts of amenities, including a pool and a sauna.

Sault Ste. Marie

If you head north on Highway 17, you'll come to the **KOA Sault Ste. Marie** *($24.50; 501 Fifth Lane, ☎759-2344)*, which has adequate campsites.

There are a few inexpensive places to stay in town; one of the cheapest is the **Algonquin Hotel** *($33.60 Hostelling International members, $39.20 non-members; 864 Queen St. E., P6A 2B4, ☎253-2311)*, which is that much more of a bargain, since the rooms, albeit modest, are well-kept, and the place is conveniently located near the bus terminal.

⚓ Built at the turn of the century, the very handsome building of the **Brockwell Chambers** *($75 bkfst incl.; 183 Brock St., P6A 3B8, ☎/⇌949-1076)* Bed and Breakfast is certainly the most charming place to stay in Sault-Ste-Marie. Having been renovated with utmost care, it has

three lovely antique-furnished rooms. Each room is spacious and has a private bathroom, making you feel right at home. Breakfast is served in the elegant dining room. This establishment is close to downtown, on a quiet street lined with tall trees.

The nearby **Days Inn** *($73.95; ≡, ≈, ℜ, △, ◉; 332 Bay St., P6A 1X1, ☎759-1400 or 800-329-7466, ⇌759-1266)* offers a similar level of comfort, as well as all sorts of amenities.

The **Bay Front Quality Inn** *($114; ≡, ≈, ℜ, △, ◉; 180 Bay St. E., P6A 6S2, ☎945-9264 or 800-228-5151, ⇌945-9766)* has the dual advantage of being located steps away from downtown Sault Ste. Marie and offering a lovely view of the St. Mary's River. The rooms are a little drab but otherwise perfectly adequate.

⚓ During the summer of 1998, the **Holiday Inn** *($135; ≡, ≈, ℜ, △, ◔, ◉; 208 St. Mary's River Dr., P6A 4V5, ☎705-949-0611 or 800-HOLIDAY, ⇌945-6972)* underwent major renovations to recapture some of the charm it lost over the years and to maintain its reputation as one of the nicer hotels in the city. Notwithstanding its very attractive interior, the hotel's best feature is its prime location on the shores of the St. Mary's river. From the main hallway, you can catch a glimpse of the pool as well as the restaurant and piano bar overlooking the river. Many of the rooms have a view of the river.

With its pretty houses and picturesque waterfront, the downtown district is undoubtedly one of the nicest places to stay in Sault-Ste-Marie. However, if hotels are full or you prefer not staying in the center of town, a series of motels and hotels can be found along the Great Northern Road. As this strip is far from scenic, establishments offer various perks to better accommodate their guests.

The **Water Tower Inn** *($109; ≡, ≈, △, ☺, ℜ; 360 Great Northern Rd., P6A 5N3, ☎705-949-8111 or 800-461-0800, www.watertowerinn. com)* focusses on its warm personal welcome and the latest in sports equipment, while, the **Ramada Inn** *($109; ≡, ≈, △, ⊛, ℜ, ☺; 229 Great Northern Rd., P6B 4Z2, ☎942-2500 ext. 352, 800-563-7262, ≈942-2570)* caters to families and features a bowling alley as well as an enormous pool with a giant slide. Rooms in both establishments are very well-kept.

Tour B: Manitoulin Island

There aren't any big hotel complexes on Manitoulin Island, nor are any major North American chains represented here. You will find a number of B&Bs and campgrounds, however.

Little Current

Ruth's Bed and Breakfast *($50 bkfst incl.; 73 Campbell St. W., POP 1K0, ☎705-368-3891)* is a good place to keep in mind, since it has pretty rooms and a central location in charming Little Current.

The crimson roof of the **Hawberry Motel** *($78; ≡; P.O.Box 123, POP 1K0, ☎705-368-3388, ≈368-3824)* is hard to miss as you enter Little Current. In spite of its exterior, this motel has spacious rooms equipped with a desk, a hair dryer, lots of closet space, and a large bathroom. In short, all the conveniences of home. Although lacking in charm, the rooms are more than adequate.

Sheguiandah

One of several well laid-out campgrounds on the island, **Batman's Cottages, Tent & Trailer Park** *($22; south of Little Current, ☎705-368-2180)* boasts a very pleasant setting.

Spring Bay

The **Rockgarden Terrace Resort** *($180 ½b for 2 people; R.R. 1, POP 2B0, ☎705-377-4652)* offers comfortable rooms in a long building at the top of a cliff overlooking lovely Lake Mindemoya. Pretty, rustic cabins *($190 ½b for 2 people)* are available for those who want a little more space and privacy.

Gore Bay

The Gore Bay marina is a lively place that really gets going at sundown when the boats come in to the harbour. If you enjoy watching the boats on the lake, rent a room at the **Queen's Inn** *($70; 19 Water St., POP 1H0, ☎282-0665)*. This inn is located in a splendid house that faces the bay and dates back to 1880. Although it has been renovated, it has maintained its charm of yesteryear. All five rooms are immaculately clean and elegantly decorated. A more pleasant place is hard to find.

If you prefer the great outdoors, but want to remain within a stone's throw of Gore Bay, the **Evergreen Resort** *($85; ≈, K; R.R.1, POP 1H0, ☎282-2616)* is sure to please, with accommodations ranging from bungalows to small cottages with cozy rooms. Kitchenettes, patio decks with barbecues, fireplaces, and an indoor pool help travellers relax and spend memorable moments.

Tour C: The Far Northeast

Temagami

As you enter the village, you can't miss the rustic wooden buildings of the **Temagami Shores Inn & Resort** *($78; ℛ; Hwy. 11, P.O. Box 68, POH 2H0, ☎569-3200, ⇌569-2752)* by the lake. Surrounded by nature, this inn promises its guests a peaceful sojourn. Some of the nicer rooms have a small balcony where you can sit and watch the lake framed by the endless green of the forest. Open year-round.

Kirkland Lake

The **Comfort Inn** *($85; 455 Government Rd., POK 1A0, ☎567-4909, ⇌567-5022)* is close to downtown on Highway 66. Rooms are more than adequate.

Iroquois Falls

The **Glendale Motel** *($65; Ambridge Rd., 232-4041)* is situated in the heart of this tiny hamlet. Decidedly lacking in charm, with cinder-block walls. However, the rooms are large, clean and reasonably comfortable.

Timmins

Finlayson Point Park *($18.50; take Hwy. 11 to Temagami, ☎705-569-3205)* has numerous campsites.

Everything has been done to make the **Venture Inn** *($80; ≈, ⅅ, ✈; 730 Algonquin Blvd. E., P4N 7G2, ☎268-7171, ⇌264-1991)* as inviting as possible. The big lobby has a fireplace, comfortable sofas and a large wooden staircase that leads to the rooms. Quilts hang on the walls and the guestrooms are beautifully decorated and very comfortable.

If the Venutre Inn is completely booked up, the nearby **Journey's End Motel** *($59; 939 Algonquin Blvd E., P4N 7J5, ☎264-9474 or 800-228-5150, ⇌360-1969)* is a good option, with comfortable rooms.

The **Travelway Inn** *($80 bkfst incl.; ≈, ⅅ, ⊙, ℛ; 1136 Riverside Dr., P4R 1A2, ☎360-1122 or 800-461-9834)* is another good establishment with similarly comfortable rooms, but a little less charm. Located in town, it is close to the shopping centres. Some might prefer this place for the little extras it offers, like irons and ironing boards in the rooms and a gym.

Chapleau

There are some gloomy motels in town, one of which is the **Trois Moulins Motel** *($75; 154 Martel Rd., POM 1K0, ☎864-1313, ⇌864-2772)*. More charming accommodations can be found in the Chapleau game Preserve.

Chapleau Crown Game Preserve

Several outfitters offer comfortable accommodations in the Chapleau Crown Game Preserve. These exceptional establishments in true wilderness surroundings lie on the shores of crystal-clear lakes in this 7,000-kilometre paradise for nature lovers.

You can camp on the peaceful grounds of the **Missinaibi Headwaters Outfitters** *(reservations required, in summer ☎864-2065, in winter ☎444-7780)*, located north of Chapleau. Canoe excursions for beginners and experts are organized.

A stay at the **Wilderness Island Resort** *(P.O. Box 22 057, 44 Great Northern Rd., Sault-Ste-Marie, P6B 6H4, ☎946-2010)* is a truly unforgettable experience. Accessed via the *Algoma Train* or by plane, the place comprises several little round cabins with rustic charm and impeccable comfort. The cabins are scattered across the island, so each provides absolute tranquillity and has a superb view of Wabatongushi Lake. Various outdoor activities like fishing and wildlife observation are organized.

Cochrane

You can camp out in **Greenwater Provincial Park** *($20; ☎272-4365)*. Reservations accepted.

In town, you can try the **Westway Motor Motel** *($59; =; First St., P0L 1C0, ☎272-4285, ≈272-4429)*.

Moosonee

If you're thinking of spending the night in Moosonee, keep in mind that the hotels are quite expensive for what they to offer, and that it's a good idea to make reservations. Try the **Polar Bear Lodge** *($84; ☎705-336-2345)* or the **Osprey Country Inn** *($75; ☎705-336-2226)*.

Hearst

The **Northern Seasons Motel** *($57; =, ≈, △, ⊛; 915 George St., P0I 1N0, ☎705-362-4281, ≈362-4177)*, located near the centre of town, is one of the best options in Hearst.

RESTAURANTS

Tour A: On the Trail of the First Explorers

Mattawa

Drapper's Fine Dining *($$; 510 Valois Dr., ☎744-2323)* is a tastefully decorated and quite charming local restaurant, where you can enjoy a good lunch or dinner. The daytime menu consists of light dishes, while slightly more sophisticated fare is offered in the evening.

North Bay

Aurian's *($; 380 Algonquin, ☎474-CAKE)* pastry shop sells excellent baked goods; the chocolate croissants are particularly tasty.

El Greco *($$; 344 Algonquin, ☎474-3373)* has a simple decor and a clientele of all ages. The menu, made up mainly of spaghetti and lasagna, is hardly original, but the food is consistently good. Part of what makes this place so popular is its friendly, relaxed atmosphere.

East Side Mario's *($$; 285 Lakeshore Dr., ☎497-9555)* has hit on a formula that is sure to please the whole family: generous servings of pasta, a fun decor and a relaxed atmosphere.

Nothing quite beats taking in the tranquil waters of Lake Nipissing while dining aboard the boat *Old Chief ($$; Government Dock, ☎476-7777)*. This vessel has been anchored in North Bay since being replaced by a more modern craft, and was completely renovated and converted into a restaurant that specializes in fish dishes.

If you're looking for something a little dressier, **Churchill's** *($$$; 631 Lakeshore Dr., ☎476-7777)* is just the place. It serves what just may be the best prime rib in town.

Kabuki House *($$$; 349 Main St. W., ☎495-0999)* is a charmingly decorated little place that serves succulent Japanese specialties like *sukiyaki* in an elegant and relaxed atmosphere. A delicious change from the usual burgers and fries.

Sudbury

Cooke House *($; 65 Elm St., ☎673-9274)* has an utterly nondescript decor, but serves good homestyle cuisine.

East Side Mario's *($$; 900A Lasalle Court, ☎524-2200)*, one of a well-known chain of restaurants, is popular because of its friendly, cheerful atmosphere and consistently good pasta dishes.

A modest-looking little house in downtown Sudbury, **Vesta Pasta** *($$; 49 Elgin, ☎674-4010)* is one of those charming places that are such a pleasure to discover. Not only does it have an adorable dining room, but it also serves delectable Italian cuisine. You can't go wrong with the menu; the veal and pasta dishes are all masterfully prepared.

Sault Ste. Marie

A tiny house ingeniously decorated in the style of the 1960s, **Mr. B's** *($; 76 East St., ☎942-9999)* offers a unique atmosphere in which to enjoy a burger or a pizza.

Smart *($; 473 Queen St., ☎949-8484)* is a charming little restaurant with big bay windows. Its interior consists of a few tables and some antique furniture. The warm and friendly atmosphere makes this the perfect place to go for lunch and to try some of the delicious sandwiches and salads made with fresh ingredients.

The **Lone Star Cafe** *($$; 360 Great Northern Rd., ☎949-8111)* is a real landmark in the Soo, with its big plastic cactuses, rubber iguanas and many photos on the walls. This cute restaurant serves Tex-Mex food like quesadillas and fajitas. The friendly ambiance and generous portions make dining here a pleasant experience.

The only reason to dine at the **Holiday Inn** *($-$$ 208 St. Mary's River Dr., ☎949-0611)* is its lovely terrace on the St. Mary's River. The simple menu is limited to pizza, hot dogs, and fruit salads, but the food is quite good.

If you're in the mood for a tender, juicy steak, go to **North 82** *($$-$$$; 82 Great Northern Rd., ☎759-8282)*. With a large dining room, a modern decor and a friendly atmosphere, this is the perfect place for a family dinner or a meal with friends.

The **Thymely Manner** *($$$-$$$$; 531 Albert St., ☎759-3262)* is one of the finest dining establishments in town. Its red brick building is tastefully decorated, and the dining room is perfect for a romantic evening out. The menu will delight the most exacting gourmands, and Italian specialties, like seafood pasta or salmon with herbs, appear on the daily menu. The service is very attentive.

Tour B: Manitoulin Island

Little Current

The **Old English Pantry** *($; Robinson St., ☎368-3341)* is a relaxed, inviting place to linger over a cup of tea and a sandwich. It's also a good place to go for breakfast.

The **Anchor Inn Hotel** *($$; 1 Water St., ☎368-2023)* serves relatively simple cuisine, with an emphasis on fresh fish. While the food is very good, the decor could use a little work. However, there is a pleasant terrace.

Providence Bay

As its name suggests, **The School House** *($$; ☎377-4055)* is located in a charming old country school house. The dining room, which only has about twenty tables, is delightful and the food, delicious, making for a thoroughly enjoyable dining experience. The menu changes with the seasons, and includes a number of fish dishes.

South Baymouth

If you get hungry while waiting for the ferry, you can grab a bite to eat in South Baymouth. Though there are no real restaurants, several little food stands serve hot dogs and sandwiches.

Tour C: The Far Northeast

As you head further north, you will notice that there are fewer restaurants, and that most are dining rooms attached to a hotel or belong to a fast food chain.

Iroquois Falls

A good place to stop along the highway is the restaurant of the **Glendale Motel** *($-$$; ☎232-4041)*, which serves simple food like hamburgers, onion soup, and hot chicken. The place is nothing out of the ordinary, but it's the only restaurant for miles.

Timmins

Casey's *($$; 760 Algonquian Blvd. E., ☎267-6467)* is famous for its grill and relaxed atmosphere. It's hard to miss, since it is located right on the main road, near the Venture Inn. Apart from the large and quite attractive dining room, there is a big terrace that is very pleasant in warm weather.

A touch more sophisticated, **The Fishbowl** *($$; Riverside Dr.)* has a good selection of dishes, including different kinds of fried fish and pasta. Attention has been paid to the decor which is welcoming with its large bay windows, flowers and country-style furniture.

Cochrane

The **JR Ranch BBQ** *($-$$; 63 Third Ave., ☎705-272-4999)* is not exactly elegant, but you can certainly satisfy your hunger here. Roast chicken and ribs make up a good part of the menu.

 ENTERTAINMENT

Tour A: On the Trail of the First Explorers

North Bay

The **Arts Centre** *(at the corner of Main and Wyld)* often hosts entertaining shows.

The **Winter Carnival**, held every year at the beginning of February, is an opportunity to enjoy a variety of sports activities.

The patio of the *Old Chief (Government Dock)* bar is a lovely place to have a drink on warm summer nights, especially in the early evening when you can watch the sun set over the lake.

North Bay even has a nightclub, the **Loft** *(631 Lakeshore Dr., below Churchill's)*, where you can dance the night away in an elegant atmosphere. There is live music on some nights.

Sudbury

The **Sudbury Theatre Centre** *(170 Shaughnessy, ☎674-8381)* presents plays all year round.

Pat and Mario's *(1463 LaSalle, ☎560-2500)* restaurant is known for its Italian cuisine, but its bar also attracts quite a crowd in the evening, and is a good place for a fun night out.

Sault Ste. Marie

The **Bon Soo Winter Carnival**, held every year in late January and early February, livens up the cold winter days with all sorts of sports activities.

For information on the various cultural activities in town, call the **Arts Council of Sault-Sainte-Marie** *(☎945-9756)*. For tickets to various local events, go to **Station Mall** *(293 Bay St., ☎945-5323)*.

In addition to serving good meals, the **Lone Star Cafe** *($$; 360 Great Northern Rd., ☎949-8111)* is a wonderful place to have a beer or spend the evening with friends.

Tour B: Manitoulin Island

Wikwemigong

Every year, for the first few days of August, native families gather at the Wikwemigong reserve for a **Powwow**, during which numerous ceremonies and dances are performed.

 # SHOPPING

Tour A: On the Trail of the First Explorers

North Bay

North Western *(440 Wyld)* sells lovely native handicrafts.

Sudbury

Southridge Mall *(1933 Regent St., Hwy 69, ☎522-5480)* has all sorts of shops for all different tastes. **Rocks** *(☎523-2172)*, to name only one, sells terrific t-shirts and sweatshirts.

Sault Ste. Marie

The train to the Agawa Canyon sets out from the parking lot of the **Station Mall** *(293 Bay St.)*, where you'll find a variety of shops. One of the more interesting ones is **Loon Nest**, which sells handicrafts and souvenirs.

Equipment for cycling, canoeing or skiing can be purchased and rented from the **Old Ski House** *(1156 Great Northern Rd., ☎946-0190)*.

Tour B: Manitoulin Island

Sheguiandah

The **Ten Mile Point Trading Post** *(1651 Southwest 84th Ave.)* has a beautiful selection of native handicrafts. Mocassins, jewellery, sculptures and prints are only some of the many items sold here. If you like this sort of establishment, don't miss this place.

Tour C: The Far Northeast

Timmins

Aside from **Wal-Mart, Business Depot, Zellers** and other stores of this type where you can find just about anything you're looking for, there are some smaller shops along Riverside Drive. **Dumoulin** *(Riverside Dr.)* sells everything you need for a successful fishing expedition.

NORTHWESTERN ONTARIO

Northwestern Ontario is the province's final frontier, stretching west from the shores of Lake Superior, the largest freshwater lake in the world, to Manitoba, and north to Hudson Bay. Two suggested tours cover the length and breadth of this infinite land: Tour A hugs the shoreline of Lake Superior from Gros Cap to Thunder Bay; Tour B explores Sunset Country before heading inland to the Manitoba border.

 FINDING YOUR WAY AROUND

Tour A: Along the Shores of Lake Superior

Bus Stations

Wawa: 29 Mission Rd.,
☎(705) 856-2087.

Thunder Bay: 815 Fort William Rd.,
☎(807) 345-2194.

Tour B: Sunset Country

Kenora: 610 Lakeview Dr.,
☎(807) 468-7172.

 PRACTICAL INFORMATION

Tour A: Along the Shores of Lake Superior

Area Code: 705 or **807**. The former has been indicated in this chapter.

Tourist Information

North of Superior Tourism: 1119 Victoria Avenue, Thunder Bay, P7C 1B7, ☎626-9420 or (800) 265-3951.

Tour B: Sunset Country

Area Code: 807

Ontario's Sunset Country Travel Association: 102 Main Street, Room 201, P.O. Box 647M, Kenora, P9N 3X6, ☎468-5853 or ☎(800) 665-7576.

 EXPLORING

Tour A: Along the Shores of Lake Superior ★★

This whole region is full of wonderful surprises for outdoor enthusiasts, especially if you're interested in going lake and river canoeing or on a hiking or skiing excursion.

Driving west from Sault Ste. Marie on Route 17 takes you through a number of pretty rural towns. However, it is the magnificent backdrop of Lake Superior, a seemingly endless body of fresh water surrounded by dense vegetation and some steep cliffs, that will really take your breath away. Numerous parks protect this unparalleled landscape. It is worth taking the time to stop and explore some of them and drink in their natural beauty.

Thunder Bay is the last stop of the tour. This sizable city was one of first to attract merchants to the region. In fact, a French fort was built here as early as 1673 to protect its lucrative commercial activities. Today, Thunder Bay is the last port of call along the Great Lakes seaway, and is certainly worth a visit.

Wawa

A strip of humdrum motels lines the main road leading into the city. A little

A Unique Landscape

Lake Superior, the cleanest, largest and most westerly of the Great Lakes, boasts some extraordinarily beautiful scenery. Visitors to this vast stretch of untamed wilderness might be surprised to find scraggly spruce trees and even some alpine species. The cold waters of the lake cool the air, occasionally causing abrupt changes in temperature and thus preventing some species from growing.

further along, you will catch sight of a lovely sandy beach at the edge of town.

Lake Superior Provincial Park ★★

Highway 17 runs through **Lake Superior Provincial Park** *(after Sault Ste. Marie on Hwy. 17, ☎705-856-2284)*, which covers some 80 km of Lake Superior shoreline. A vast expanse of greenery, it boasts several magnificent beaches, as well as hiking trails leading deep into the heart of the forest that blankets part of its territory. The park also contains petroglyphs carved by Ojibwa Indians over 9,000 years ago; the best place to see them is Agawa Rock. Many more hiking trails crisscross the park, sometimes unearthing ancient secrets of the Ojibway who have inhabited the land for centuries. Moreover, avid fishers can cast their lines in rivers and lakes at the edges of the park, which abound in trout and pike.

Those wishing to spend a few days in the park can set up camp at the Agawa Bay or Interior campground *(reservations: P.O. Box 267, P0S 1K0, ☎705-856-2284)*.

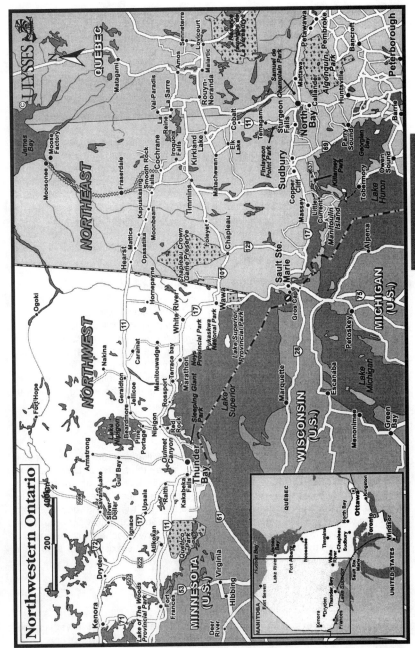

White River

Continuing along Highway 17, the road heads inland, away from the shores of Lake Superior, to the idyllic little village of White River. This place is not known for its charming appearance, however; its real claim to fame is as the home of the bear that inspired A.A. Milne to create the character Winnie-the-Pooh. Harry Colebourn, a captain in the Canadian army, purchased a black bear and named it Winnie after his home town, Winnipeg. When he was called into service in the First World War, he gave the bear to the London Zoo. It was there that Milne saw the bear, which had captured Colebourn's heart. Today, a statue of Winnie-the-Pooh adorns the entrance of the city park. Collectors of stuffed bears flock to White River during the **Winnie's Hometown Festival**, held on the third weekend in August.

You can take a guided tour of the **Hemlo Mine** *(free admission; Mon to Fri at 2pm during high season; children under 10 not admitted; Yellow Brick Rd., ☎238-1121)* to learn about the various steps involved in transforming ore into gold ingots.

Marathon

Marathon is surprisingly busy for a small riverside town. The bustling activity is generated by its prosperous industrial sector; a paper mill and several mines are located nearby. As the gateway to magnificent Pukaskwa National Park (see below), the town is also popular with vacationers.

Pukaskwa National Park ★

Aside from a few extremely beautiful hiking trails, no road leads through **Pukaskwa National Park** *(take the 17 to Rte. 627, a few km before Marathon;* ☎229-0801 ext. 242)*,* which is still more or less untouched. Some of these lead to stunning panoramas, among them the magnificent nearly 60-kilometre-long **Coastal Hiking Trail ★★**. The park covers 1,878 square kilometres and is scored with rivers that are perfect for canoeing and kayaking. The park also protects a vast stretch of boreal forest. The cold temperatures generated by the lake affect the vegetation here; spruce is predominant in some areas, while only alpine species are able to survive in others. For some interesting information on the local vegetation, stop by the **Hattie Cove Interpretive Centre**, which is the starting point for a number of canoe routes. Camping.

Neys Provincial Park

Neys Provincial Park *(take Hwy. 17 a few km past Marathon, then follow the signs for the park,* ☎229-1624) is a small piece of land that looks very ordinary at first sight, but boasts one of the loveliest beaches in northern Ontario and is home to a herd of caribou.

Terrace Bay

Several villages share an exceptional location on the shores of Lake Superior. Terrace Bay is one of these idyllic spots, ensconced in a large bay. The road to town runs along the bay, offering a wonderful view of the lake. Lovely sandy beaches on the outskirts of town will beckon you to stop for a while.

Rossport

To the west, Rossport is yet another picturesque village whose charm is accentuated by the natural beauty of the countryside. Nestled in one of Lake

Caribou

Superior's many bays, Rossport affords a fine view of its sparkling waters. On route to Thunder Bay, it is a nice place to stop.

Nipigon

A trading post was set up here at the mouth of the Nipigon River in 1678, making this the first site on the north shore of Lake Superior to be colonized by the French. Nipigon has the advantage of being located near a fascinating natural attraction, **Red Rock ★**, a series of 200-m-high red cliffs whose colour indicates the presence of hematite.

Ouimet Canyon ★

This breathtaking canyon, which is 107 m deep and about 150 m wide, can be viewed from two thrilling wooden lookouts. Stunted arctic flora is all that can survive in the perpetually cold temperature at the bottom of the canyon and along its steep sides.

Thunder Bay ★★

Natives settled in the Thunder Bay region over 10,000 years ago. When the first Europeans arrived in the area, Ojibwa tribes were still living here. These natives never left this territory, and still make up an large part of the population.

Judging this to be a strategic site, the French founded (Fort) Caministiquoyan here in 1679 to make it easier for merchants to trade in this region. The development of Northern Ontario was a slow process, however, and it wasn't until 1803, with the establishment of the Fort William Company, that people of European descent began settling permanently in this region. The fort soon became the hub of the fur trade, and travellers came here all the way from Montréal to purchase furs from trappers. This naturally had a positive impact on the region's growth, since more and more colonists began taking up residence here. During the 19th century, the two cities Fort William and

Port Arthur developed side by side. They finally joined in 1970 to form Thunder Bay. Because of the way it was founded, the town still has two downtown areas; the southern centre is located around Victoria and Brodie Streets, and the northern centre, between Algoma, Water and Keskus Streets.

Located about a hundred kilometres from Manitoba, Thunder Bay is the last sizeable town in western Ontario. It is a unique place, boasting all the advantages of a modern, dynamic and multicultural city, yet located just a short distance from stretches of wilderness, which you can explore on foot, by canoe or on skis.

Thunder Bay lies on the shores of magnificent Lake Superior, to which it owes some of its prosperity. Its port, the last stop for ships on the St. Lawrence Seaway, is one of the busiest in Canada. If you go to the **port**, you will not only find some gigantic ships, but also 15 grain elevators used for storage, dotting the surrounding area for several kilometres. The biggest one of all is the **Saskatchewan Wheat Pool Terminal**. You can see a small part of the port by strolling along the promenade near the marina, behind the tourist office.

The promenade around the marina is very pretty, but for a closer look at the impressive ships or to view the port from another angle, take a seat aboard the *MV Welcome* ★ *($12.50; 10am departure from the marina; ☎344-2512)*, which takes passengers on a tour of the marina, then follows the Kaministkwia River through town to Fort William. This pleasant excursion takes two hours (one-way), with passengers returning to the marina by bus.

Old Fort William ★★ *($10; mid-May to mid-Oct every day 10am to 5pm;*

Broadway Ave. S., ☎577-2327, ☛473-2327) is a fascinating reconstruction of the original Fort William as it appeared in the early 19th century. The world's largest reconstruction of a fur-trading post, it is an enchanting place to visit. The fort is made up of about forty buildings, where guides in period dress (trappers, merchants and Ojibwa Indians) recreate everyday life in the 1800s, transporting visitors two centuries back in time.

The **Thunder Bay Museum** *($2; 425 East Donata St., ☎623-0801)* displays a wide variety of objects related to local history, including articles used by early settlers, military and medical instruments and a collection of native artifacts. It offers an excellent opportunity to learn more about the daily life of the first native tribes and colonists to inhabit this region.

If you'd like to see some lovely native crafts, stop in at the **Thunder Bay Art Gallery** *($2; closed Mon, Tue to Thu noon to 8pm; Fri and Sat noon to 5pm; on the campus of Confederation College, 1080 Keewatin St., ☎577-6427)*.

At the east edge of town, a **statue of Terry Fox** serves as a tribute to the courage of that young Canadian hero. Suffering from cancer, to which he had already lost a leg, Fox set off on a "Marathon of Hope" across Canada to raise money for research against the disease. He started in Newfoundland and made it across part of Canada, but had to stop here.

Centennial Park is stretched along Boulevard Lake at the northeast edge of town; pretty trails follow the water and run through the woods. This is a pleasant place for the whole family, with picnic areas and a replica of a 1910 logging camp. Canoes and pedalboats can be rented at the lovely beach nearby.

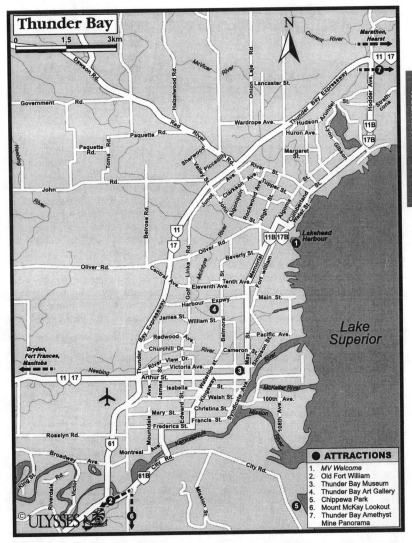

Thunder Bay

0   1,5   3km

N

NORTHWESTWERN ONTARIO

Lake Superior

● ATTRACTIONS

1. *MV Welcome*
2. Old Fort William
3. Thunder Bay Museum
4. Thunder Bay Art Gallery
5. Chippewa Park
6. Mount McKay Lookout
7. Thunder Bay Amethyst Mine Panorama

© ULYSSES

Ferocious Predator Alert

In the Yukon, as almost everywhere else in the northern reaches of Canada, the most fearless, vindictive and invincible predator is not a bear, a wolf or a big cat. It's the black fly. At the end of spring and in early summer, this insect is the uncontested master of the north, chomping out little bits of hide from all mammals within reach of its jaws. You can try to protect yourself with long clothing, a hat, mosquito netting and insect repellent containing up to 95% DEET (a chrysanthemum extract that is particularly distasteful to bugs – and not all that appealing to humans either). If you want to go picnicking somewhere and the little monsters have found you, all you can do is tell yourself that you aren't the only one suffering that fate.

Whole families go to **Chippewa Park** *(south of Hwy. 61B)*, located alongside Lake Superior, for picnics or to ride the carousels in the amusement park. Camping.

The 183 m-high **Mount McKay Lookout** ★, stands next to Thunder Bay, in the heart of the Fort William Ojibwa reserve. From the top, you can enjoy a magnificent view of the town and its surrounding area. Native crafts are sold here as well.

Ontario is rich in **amethysts**, the official stone of the province. The deposits in the Thunder Bay region were formed several million years ago by the intrusion of a boiling, silica-rich liquid into the granite here. As it cooled, the liquid formed crystals of this semi-precious stone, which is a type of quartz. You can tour the **Thunder Bay Amethyst Mine Panorama** *($3; mid-May to Oct 10am to 7pm; 58 km east of Thunder Bay, East Loon Rd.; ☎622-6908)* and even rent tools so that you can chip off a few pieces for yourself.

You can also visit an **agate mine** *(take Hwy. 17 east, then Hwy. 527 north, ☎683-3595)*, the only one of its kind in Canada. You can tour the site and even quarry your own agate.

Sleeping Giant Park ★

Right near Thunder Bay, on Lake Superior, **Sleeping Giant Park** *(take Hwy. 17 then turn onto Rte 587)* protects a rocky peninsula, which was supposedly created by none other than Nanibijou, the "Great Spirit" of the Ojibwa Indians. Legend has it that Nanibijou showed the Ojibwa the location of a rich silver mine in order to reward them for their loyalty. He insisted, however, that the existence of the mine remain a secret from the white man; otherwise he would turn into stone and let them all perish. Unfortunately, the secret leaked out. All the men in the tribe were swallowed up by the waters of Lake Superior, and Nanibijou fell asleep and metamorphosed into a rocky headland, hence the name of the peninsula. Whether you believe the legend or not, there really is a silver mine here. Located about 40 km from Thunder Bay, the park is an excellent place to enjoy the region's striking natural beauty. Its trails lead through enchanting landscapes and offer some splendid views ★★ of the lake. The park also has some extremely pleasant beaches, which are occasionally overrun by the local townspeople on hot summer days. Finally, visitors are welcome to camp here as well. In winter, when the area is blanketed with snow, about 40 km

Black bear

of cross-country trails crisscross this magnificent territory.

Tour B: Sunset Country

This final tour runs to the Manitoba border, passing through a region dotted with small towns and the occasional city. Vast expanses of land populated mainly by caribou, moose and stags stretch to the horizon. Splendid parks protect the area and give visitors the chance to discover local flora and fauna, or to enjoy such sporting activities as fishing and hunting. Most of this immense unchartered territory can only be accessed by hardy adventurers willing to fly to remote areas where no road has ever gone. Careful planning and preparation is essential for this type of undertaking. The tour described here explores the few roads that traverse this part of Ontario. To visit the rest of the region, contact one of the numerous outdoor agencies that organize tours of the hinterland.

Kakabeka Falls

Kakabeka village, the first stop of the tour, has all the tourist facilities (motels, stores, etc.) and is only about 20 kilometres from Thunder Bay. The main reason for stopping here is to see the impressive Kakabeka Falls.

Kakabeka Falls Provincial Park

Kakabeka Falls Provincial Park *(take the 17 from Thunder Bay,* ☎*473-9231 or 800-667-8386)*, located about 20 km west of Thunder Bay, was created in order to protect the impressive Kakabeka Falls, which plunge about 39 m into the Kaministiquia River. As far back as 1688, the *coureurs des bois* (trappers) travelling east to west used to have to pass by these falls, which presented quite an obstacle. The men had to carry their canoes and all their equipment up the rocky escarpment in order to continue their journey. Today, people come here to gaze at this roaring cataract, which is still impressive, although the water is now controlled by hydraulic facilities. In addition to the falls, the park has a number of hiking and cross-country ski trails, picnic areas and campsites.

Quetico Park ★

Quetico Park *(take Hwy 11 from Shabaqua Corners,* ☎*597-2735 or 800-597-4602)* covers a huge expanse

White pelican

of land along the Minnesota border. Its countless lakes and rivers have made it a big favourite with Ontarian canoeists. Motorboats are not permitted on the lakes and rivers that flow through this vast 4,800-square-kilometre territory (special permission has exceptionally been granted to natives of the region), which explains why this park has become somewhat of a haven for canoeists. There are some 1,500 kilometres of calm, navigable waterways. The park also includes a network of hiking trails.

Atikokan

The little village of Atikokan is the gateway to beautiful Quetico Park. Its convenient location attracts many visitors, although it has no attractions as such.

Fort Frances

A busy border station, Fort Frances lies on the Minnesota (U.S.A) border, in a prosperous region with a thriving pulp and paper industry. People come here mainly for hunting and fishing.

The **Fort Frances Museum** *(259 Scott St.)* has a series of exhibitions on the fur trade and the lifestyle of the region's first native inhabitants.

Lake of the Woods Provincial Park ★

Lake of the Woods Provincial Park *(take the 71 from Bergland, south of Kenora, then pick up the 600, ☎488-5531)* encompasses the magnificent lake after which it was named. This vast stretch of water has 105,000 km of shoreline and attracts some remarkable bird species. With a little luck, you might spot a group of white pelicans or a majestic bald eagle. You can also take a walk on one of the many hiking trails along the shore or set out on the water to see a few of the 15,000 islands that stud the lake.

Kenora

Kenora is located at the western edge of Ontario, a few kilometres from the Manitoba border. In the 19th century, both provinces tried to lay claim to this part of the territory. Ontario won out, and was officially granted the land in 1892. Kenora wasn't actually founded until 1905, with the union of three small municipalities, Keewatin, Norman and Rat Portage. Its name was formed by combining the first two letters of these three names (Ke-No-Ra).

The Kenora region is rich in natural resources, especially wood. The pulp and paper industry thus plays a major role in the local economy. The local lakes and forests have also led to the development of another prosperous industry, tourism, since this is a true paradise for fishing and hunting, not to mention lovely outings in the great outdoors, on the shores of Lake of the Woods.

Dryden

Dryden is a medium-sized city located on Route 17, between Thunder Bay and Kenora. Though it can hardly be considered charming, the city does have some stores and a few comfortable motels. Beside the tourist information office you can see Maximillian, a six-metre-high statue of a moose, the city's emblem.

Upsala

Like many of the hamlets in the region, Upsala is attuned to its natural surroundings and blends well into the landscape that engulfs it. Its proximity to the Thousand Lakes lake, a clear body of freshwater teeming with fish, makes it a favourite amongst fishermen anxious for a good catch. Enjoy the peaceful setting at one of the outdoor recreational centres on the shores of the lake.

Armstrong

North of Thunder Bay, a single road leads to Armstrong. This village would go unnoticed if it weren't for nearby Wabakimi Park (see below), a giant terrain that is only accessible by canoe or by plane. The village is a good starting point for excursions into the park, since many outdoor recreational centres are located here.

Wabakimi Park

Wabakimi Park was enlarged in 1995 and now preserves over one million hectares of forests, lakes and rivers. As no road enters this enormous park, the only way to get there is by canoe or by plane. Except for a train that carries visitors into the park, no signs of civilization disturb the serenity of the area. The park is home to a large herd of caribou, as well as moose, wolves and other animals. This nature-lovers' paradise will satisfy the most intrepid visitor hoping to set foot on land that remains unblemished by modern-day living. Hunting and fishing excursions are available.

 OUTDOOR ACTIVITIES

Northwestern Ontario, a forest kingdom ruled by majestic evergreens, is a wonderful place to enjoy the outdoors — not only for intrepid explorers ready to set off for days into the heart of this imposing vegetation, but also for more timid nature-lovers looking for some easy trails to follow. Whether you're interested in hiking or cross-country trails or would rather ride down tumultuous rivers in a canoe like the region's first explorers, the parks in this region have something for everyone with a taste for fresh air and vast expanses of wilderness.

NORTHWESTWERN ONTARIO

Hiking

Tour A: Along the Shores of Lake Superior

A new hiking trail just opened along Lake Superior from **Wawa** to **Rossport** via the **White River**. This trail stretches over 200 km through exceptional wilderness. Hiking it takes several days and is therefore not for everyone; make sure to be well prepared before setting out.

You can't go into **Pukaskwa Park** by car, but you can explore this uninhabited territory on scores of hiking trails, including the outstanding **Coastal Hiking Trail**, which runs alongside the lake, affording some magnificent views. It stretches 57 km, but does not make a loop, so you have to retrace your steps to get back to where you started.

The **Agawa Rock** trail, in **Lake Superior Provincial Park**, is a relatively easy walk through a wooded area to the lakeshore. To see the Ojibway pictograms drawn in red ochre, follow the cliff on your left to Agawa Rock. Be careful as the path might be slippery. More experienced hikers seeking a challenge can take on the Coastal Trail, a 55-kilometre footpath that contours the lake by climbing steep cliffs and crossing beaches. The trail can be accessed at several points in the park, so you can follow it for a shorter stretch if you like. Those interested in hiking the entire trail should be aware that it is difficult in certain areas. Nine campgrounds are located at different spots along the trail. Each of the 11 paths traversing the park reveal magnificent scenery, bits of local history, and sometimes even secrets of the aboriginal people who have made this their homeland for centuries.

 # Canoeing

Tour A: Along the Shores of Lake Superior

Pukaskwa Park is crisscrossed by scores of rivers. The **Hattie Cove Interpretive Centre** serves as the starting point for a number of canoe routes, some of which are short and easy enough for those who only want to paddle about for a few hours. Another option is to start out from Marathon and follow the shores of Lake Superior along the park to Michipicoten Harbour. This trip covers about 180 km, so you'll need to arrange transportation back to Marathon. It is easy to camp along the lakeshore (backcountry sites).

Organized canoe trips of the waters around Thunder Bay are available for those who don't want to head out on their own.

Wild Waters Nature Tours
☎767-2022

Superior Wilderness Adventure
☎768-4343

If you wish to explore Lake Superior Provincial Park by canoe or kayak, but not alone, you can take part in one of the excursions organized by **Naturally Superior Adventures** *(R.R. 1, Wawa, ☎/≈705-856-2939)*. This agency also rents boats and gives courses.

Experience North Adventure *(☎888-463-5979, www.exnorth.com)* in Sault Ste. Marie organizes thrilling canoe and kayak trips into the park or elsewhere in the region.

Tour B: Sunset Country

Quetico Park, with its rivers and tranquil lakes, far from all modern development, is a true paradise for those seeking a peaceful natural setting in which to enjoy some leisurely canoeing. Some people claim that this is one of the best places in North America to go paddling. While this may be an exaggeration, the park nevertheless has something to offer canoeists of all different levels.

Canoes can be rented at:

Quetico North Tourist Services
P.O. Box 100, Atikokan, P0T 1C0,
☎929-3561.

Canoe Canada also proposes memorable canoe trips in Quetico Park. Trips may last several days and are thus geared at hardy adventurers. In addition to navigating magnificent waterways, certain excursions include fishing and wildlife observation.

Canoe Canada
P.O. Box 1810, Atikokan, P0T 1C0,
☎597-6418, ⊷597-5804.

 Cruises

Tour A: Along the Shores of Lake Superior

The **Thunder Bay** harbour is one of the most spectacular places in town, with its huge grain elevators, some of which can hold up to 362,650 tonnes of grain, and the enormous ships loading up with goods to be distributed all over the world. The *MV Welcome (marina 10am; ☎344-2512)* runs up and down the port, which is one of the largest in Canada.

Tour B: Sunset Country

Nature-lovers will be both enchanted and surprised by scenery at **Lake of the Woods**, which has no fewer than 15,000 little islands and is home to some remarkable animal life. The *M.S. Kenora (late Jun to Aug, every day; Harbourfront, Kenora, ☎468-9124)* offers passengers a chance to get acquainted with the landscape of this region while enjoying a relaxing excursion on the shimmering waters of the lake.

 Rock-climbing

Tour A: Along the Shores of Lake Superior

There is a rock- and ice-climbing school in **Thunder Bay** *(Outward Bound Wilderness School, ☎982-2212 or 888-OUTWARD)*.

 Hunting and Fishing

Northwestern Ontario is a fishing and hunting paradise. This immense territory is so rich in lakes and rivers that it is difficult to single out any one spot for fishing. The multitude of parks and reserves are perfect fishing grounds. This large sector is also favoured by hunters. Again many parks are known for their game, most notably the Kenora region, **Kettle Lakes Provincial Park** *(32 km northwest of Timmins, Hwy. 101, ☎705-363-3511)* and **Wabakimi Provincial Park**

Downhill Skiing

**Tour A: Along the Shores of
Lake Superior**

The Thunder Bay area has no fewer than four sizeable mountains where you can go downhill skiing: **Mount Loch Lomond**, the **Candy Mountain Ski Resort**, **Mount Baldy** and **Big Thunder Mountain**. For skiing conditions, call ☎800-667-8386.

 Cross-country Skiing

**Tour A: Along the Shores of
Lake Superior**

Come winter, when the parks are blanketed in white, most of the hiking trails are transformed into cross-country trails, enabling skiers to head deep into the heart of a silent forest, where only the conifers are still green. The landscapes are just as fascinating as in summer, and you can soak up all the peace and quiet of the sleeping wilderness around you. Many parks, including **Sleeping Giant** and **Kakabeka Falls** have ski trails.

Outdoor Centres

The sheer magnitude and remoteness of northwestern Ontario make it impossible to visit in its entirety. Fortunately, many agencies organize hunting and fishing expeditions, canoe trips and wildlife observation in secluded areas of this extensive territory. To get there, you usually have to take somewhat unusual means of transportation – like bushplanes, or canoeing along unspectacular waterways that lead into the heart of the wilderness. The following list of agencies offer thrilling adventure tours around Ontario's more isolated regions. Excursions include food and lodging.

Thunder Bay
WildWaters Nature Tours, R.R.14, Dog Lake Road, P7B 5E5, ☎767-2022, ≈768-8149. Canoeing, wildlife observation, fishing.

Kakabeka Falls
Blue Loon Adventures, R.R.1
☎888-846-0066
www.foxnet.net/~blueloon/
Wildlife observation.

Whitefish Lake
Artesian Wells Resort, R.R.2 , Nolalu P0T 2K0, ☎/≈933-5000
artwell@norlink.net
Fishing, dog sledding.

Atikokan
Brown's Clearwater West Lodge, P.O. Box 1766 A, P0T 1C0, ☎/≈597-2884. Fishing, canoeing, snowmobiling.

Sioux Narrows
Totem Lodge - Yellowbird, P.O. Box 180, P0X 1N0, ☎226-5275, ≈226-5187, totemlodge@aol.com
Fishing, hunting.

 ACCOMMODATIONS

Tour A: Along the Shores of Lake Superior

Wawa

Three kilometres north of town, you'll find the **Wawa RV Resort and Campground** *(Hwy. 17, ☎705-856-4368)* equipped with all sorts of amenities, including a heated swimming pool and a sauna. Sites with and without hookups available.

At the **Kinniwabi Pines Motel and Chalet** *($45; Hwy. 17 S., ☎705-856-7302,*

~856-2772), located near the beach, guests can choose between a room or one of three small cottages *($65)*.

Thunder Bay

The last major town in northern Ontario, Thunder Bay is a lovely place with a wide range of accommodations.

Located in a delightfully peaceful setting, the **Longhouse Village** *($16; R.R. 13, 1594 Lakeshore Dr., P7B 5E4, ☎983-2042)* is actually a youth hostel with dormitories — the perfect place for visitors looking for a friendly atmosphere. If you have a tent, you can opt for one of the campsites *($16)* instead.

During summer, visitors can stay in the residence halls at **Lakehead University** *($20/person, $30 for 2 people; 955 Oliver Rd., P7B 5E1, ☎343-8612)*.

On Arthur Street, you will find a good selection of modern hotels and motels, whose fully equipped rooms are perfect for anyone planning to spend a few days in town. We especially recommend the **Victoria Inn** *($83.95; 555 Arthur St. W., ☎577-8481 or 800-387-3331, ~475-8961)*, whose relatively new rooms are well kept, and the **Best Western Crossroad Motor Inn** *($78; 655 Arthur St. W., P7E 5R6, ☎577-4241 or 800-265-3253, ~475-7059)*, which has simple, but decent rooms.

The **Best Western Nor'Westers** *($89; R.R. 4, 2080 Hwy. 61, P7C 4Z2, ☎473-9123)* is another good option for visitors looking for modern comfort, since it offers a whole slew of amenities, including a workout room, a swimming pool and rooms equipped with a fireplace.

The **White Fox Inn** *($129; 1345 Mountain Rd., ☎577-FOXX or 800-603-FOXX, www.whitebox.com)* is one of those B&Bs that you will remember for a long time. A relaxing atmosphere pervades the rooms, each of which is tastefully decorated with a different theme.

One of the nicer places to stay in Thunder Bay is the **Valhalla Inn** *($125; 1 Valhalla Inn Rd., P7E 6J1, ☎577-1121 or 800-964-1121, ~475-4723, www.valhallainn.com)*. Rooms are large and pleasant, and have recently been refurbished. In addition to its nice decor, the inn has a fitness centre.

Tour B: Sunset Country

Kenora

One safe bet is the **Journey's End Motel** *($81; 1230 Hwy. 17, P9N 3W8, ☎468-8845)*, whose rooms are quite comfortable for the price.

RESTAURANTS

Tour A: Along the Shores of Lake Superior

Thunder Bay

You can enjoy a good meal in a relaxed atmosphere at the **Port Arthur Brasserie and Brew Pub** *($; 901 Red River Rd., ☎767-4415)*.

The **Prospector Restaurant** *($$$; 27 South Cumberland, ☎345-5833)* is a popular choice for steak or seafood.

The atmosphere at some restaurants is so romantic that you can't help but have a lovely evening. This is true of

Armando Fine Italian Cuisine *($$$; 28 North Cumberland)*, the perfect place to savour excellent Italian cuisine to the soothing strains of violin music.

 The **Hoito Restaurant** *($$; 288 Bay St., ☎344-2922)* is well-known in Thunder Bay for its delicious, innovative cuisine. What makes the menu unique is an ingenious blend of Finnish and Canadian culinary traditions. The crêpes on the breakfast menu are truly delectable.

Harrington Court *($$$; 170 North Algoma St., ☎345-2600)* is set up inside a carefully restored old house, which offers an unparalleled atmosphere for fine dining.

The restaurant at the **White Fox Inn** *($$$-$$$$; take Hwy. 61 to 1345 Mountain Rd., ☎577-FOXX)*, located just outside town, is worth the detour. Guests enjoy excellent food and a refined atmosphere, and the wine list will satisfy even the most demanding connoisseurs.

 ENTERTAINMENT

Tour A: Along the Shores of Lake Superior

Thunder Bay

Quality shows are presented at the **Thunder Bay Community Auditorium** *(450 Beverly St., ☎684-4444 or 800-463-8817)*.

Bars and Nightclubs

The **Port Arthur Brasserie and Brew Pub** *(901 Red River Rd., ☎767-4415)* is a pleasant place with an interesting selection of imported beer. Things pick up considerably during the summer when everyone heads outside on to the pretty terrace.

The **Outpost** *(955 Oliver Rd., ☎343-8110)*, with its big dance floor and pool tables, is always packed with fun-seeking students.

Merlin's Bistro and Boutiques *(127 May St., ☎622-3445)* is an engaging spot for a quiet evening out and a drink or two.

For a little line-dancing and two-stepping, head to the **Golden Nugget** *(555 Arthur St. W., ☎475-6977)*, which showcases live country music on certain evenings.

INDEX

INDEX

INDEX

INDEX

INDEX

INDEX

Travel Notes

OTHER ULYSSES GUIDES

ATLANTIC CANADA, 2nd edition
This guide covers Newfoundland and Labrador, as well as New Brunswick, Nova Scotia and Prince Edward Island. Picturesque fishing villages, the famous Cabot Trail, national parks, beaches, the brand new Confederation Bridge; it's all here!
Benoit Prieur
272 pages, 23 maps, 8 pages of colour photos
$24.95 CAN $17.95 US   £12.99   2-89464-113-3

BED & BREAKFASTS IN QUÉBEC 1999-2000
Four types of accommodations to help you discover the intimate side of Québec: rooms in private homes with breakfast included, small country inns, farm-stays, and country houses which can be rented for a longer stay.
Fédération des Agricotours
300 pages, 19 maps, 14 pages of colour photos
$13.95 CAN $10.95 US   £6.50   2-89464-199-0
current edition 2-89464-096-X

CANADA 1999-2000
Every province and territory has been covered in depth in order to produce the most complete travel guide. Major cities, small hamlets and exhilarating outdoor adventures from coast to coast!
Collective
656 pages, 85 maps, 8 pages of colour photos
$29.95 CAN $21.95 US   £14.99   2-89464-198-2

MONTRÉAL, 4th edtion
This guide reveals more than 300 sights in this Québec metropolis along 20 walking, bicycling and driving tours. There are detailed maps for each tour, plans of the galleries of the Museum of Fine Arts and maps of the underground city. Practical addresses for every budget. A comprehensive revision by real Montrealers ensures that the latest hip spots are included.
François Rémillard et al.
4⅛ x 7, 416 pages, 26 maps, 8 pages of colour photos, French-English glossary
$19.95 CAN $14.95   £9.99   2-89464-190-7

OTTAWA
The first complete practical and cultural guide to the Canadian capital. The fine museums, Parliament Hill, the best restaurants, and the festivals that enliven the streets in the summer and the Rideau Canal in the winter.
Pascale Couture
160 pages, 13 maps
$16.95 CAN $12.95 US   £8.99   2-89464-170-2

QUÉBEC 1999-2000
More sights and thousands of practical addresses for every region. Travellers will also find an augmented outdoor activities section, more maps, brilliant colour photos and illustrations.
François Rémillard et al.
576 pages, 81 maps, 22 pages of colour photos, French-English glossary, index.
$29.95 CAN $21.95 US   £14.99   2-89464-202-4
current edition 2-921444-78-X

TORONTO, 2nd edition
Discover another side of Canada's biggest metropolis, from the bustle of downtown Yonge Street to the picturesque shores of Lake Ontario. Walking tours through its multicultural neighborhoods; restaurants and bars for all tastes and budgets.
Jennifer McMorran, Alain Rondeau
304 pages, 20 maps, 8 pages of colour photos
$18.95 CAN $13.95 US £9.99 2-89464-121-4
current edition 2-89464-015-3

WESTERN CANADA, 2nd edition
The only travel guide to cover both Alberta and British Columbia. The Rocky Mountains, with their ski resorts and national parks, as well as the metropolis of Vancouver, the burgeoning city of Calgary and stop in Victoria, for a cup of tea!
Collective
496 pages, 45 maps, 8 pages of colour photos
$29.95 CAN $21.95 US £14.99 2-89464-086-2

ULYSSES GREEN ESCAPES

CYCLING IN ONTARIO
This unique guidebook is designed to provide the traveller with all the information required to plan worry-free cycling holidays in the different regions of Ontario. It includes 35 tours, a multitude of safety-tips, plus details on accommodations, ground conditions, access to interesting trails, and more.
John Lynes
256 pages, 45 maps
$22.95 CAN $16.95 US £9.99 2-89464-191-5

HIKING IN QUÉBEC, 2nd edition
The only hiking guide devoted exclusively to the regions of Québec! This guide presents descriptions of close to 100 hikes in every corner of Québec, classified according to their level of difficulty.
Yves Séguin
368 pages, 22 maps
$22.95 CAN $16.95 US £11.50 2-89464-013-7

ULYSSES CONVERSATION GUIDES

FRENCH FOR BETTER TRAVEL
Thousands of words and expressions to make your next trip *à la française* a success. Colour illustrations, phonetic pronunciation and a two-way index help you get your message across.
Collective
192 pages, 6 double-pages in colour
$9.95 CAN $6.95 US £4.50 2-89464-181-8

ULYSSES TRAVEL JOURNALS

ULYSSES TRAVEL JOURNAL 80 DAYS
Here is the newest arrival in the Ulysses' Travel Journal series. In a larger format with more pages (224), it is ideal for Phileas Fogg-type travellers who take long trips and detailed notes about their adventures.
paperback, spiral bound 2-89464-247-4
5¼ x 8¼, 224 pages
$14.95 CAN $9.95 US

ORDER FORM

ULYSSES TRAVEL GUIDES

☐ Atlantic Canada	$24.95 CAN $17.95 US	☐ Lisbon	$18.95 CAN $13.95 US
☐ Bahamas	$24.95 CAN $17.95 US	☐ Louisiana	$29.95 CAN $21.95 US
☐ Beaches of Maine	$12.95 CAN $9.95 US	☐ Martinique	$24.95 CAN $17.95 US
☐ Bed & Breakfasts in Québec	$13.95 CAN $10.95 US	☐ Montréal	$19.95 CAN $14.95 US
☐ Belize	$16.95 CAN $12.95 US	☐ New Orleans	$17.95 CAN $12.95 US
☐ Calgary	$17.95 CAN $12.95 US	☐ New York City	$19.95 CAN $14.95 US
☐ Canada	$29.95 CAN $21.95 US	☐ Nicaragua	$24.95 CAN $16.95 US
☐ Chicago	$19.95 CAN $14.95 US	☐ Ontario	$27.95 CAN $19.95US
☐ Chile	$27.95 CAN $17.95 US	☐ Ottawa	$17.95 CAN $12.95 US
☐ Colombia	$29.95 CAN $21.95 US	☐ Panamá	$24.95 CAN $17.95 US
☐ Costa Rica	$27.95 CAN $19.95 US	☐ Peru	$27.95 CAN $19.95 US
☐ Cuba	$24.95 CAN $17.95 US	☐ Portugal	$24.95 CAN $16.95 US
☐ Dominican Republic	$24.95 CAN $17.95 US	☐ Provence - Côte d'Azur	$29.95 CAN $21.95US
☐ Ecuador and Galapagos Islands	$24.95 CAN $17.95 US	☐ Québec	$29.95 CAN $21.95 US
☐ El Salvador	$22.95 CAN $14.95 US	☐ Québec and Ontario with Via	$9.95 CAN $7.95 US
☐ Guadeloupe	$24.95 CAN $17.95 US	☐ Toronto	$18.95 CAN $13.95 US
☐ Guatemala	$24.95 CAN $17.95 US	☐ Vancouver	$17.95 CAN $12.95 US
☐ Honduras	$24.95 CAN $17.95 US	☐ Washington D.C.	$18.95 CAN $13.95 US
☐ Jamaica	$24.95 CAN $17.95 US	☐ Western Canada	$29.95 CAN $21.95 US

ULYSSES DUE SOUTH

☐ Acapulco	$14.95 CAN $9.95 US	☐ Cartagena (Colombia)	$12.95 CAN $9.95 US
☐ Belize	$16.95 CAN $12.95 US	☐ Cancun Cozumel	$17.95 CAN $12.95 US

ULYSSES DUE SOUTH

☐ Puerto Vallarta	$14.95 CAN $9.95 US	☐ St. Martin and St. Barts	$16.95 CAN $12.95 US

ULYSSES GREEN ESCAPES

☐ Cycling in France .... $22.95 CAN
$16.95 US

☐ Cycling in Ontario .... $22.95 CAN
$16.95 US

☐ Hiking in the .... $19.95 CAN
Northeastern U.S. $13.95 US

☐ Hiking in Québec .... $19.95 CAN
$13.95 US

ULYSSES CONVERSATION GUIDES

☐ French for Better Travel ..... $9.95 CAN
$6.95 US

☐ Spanish for Better Travel .... $9.95 CAN
$6.95 US

ULYSSES TRAVEL JOURNAL

☐ Ulysses Travel Journal ... $9.95 CAN
(Blue, Red, Green, Yellow, Sextant)
$7.95 US

☐ Ulysses Travel Journal ... $14.95 CAN
80 Days $9.95 US

TITLE	QUANTITY	PRICE	TOTAL

Name _____	Sub-total
Address _____	Postage & Handling : $8.00*
_____	Sub-total
_____	
Payment : ☐ Money Order ☐ Visa ☐ MasterCard	G.S.T. in Canada 7%
Card Number _____	
Signature _____	TOTAL

ULYSSES TRAVEL PUBLICATIONS
4176 St-Denis,
Montréal, Québec, H2W 2M5
(514) 843-9447 fax (514) 843-9448
www.ulysses.ca
*$15 for overseas orders

U.S. ORDERS: **GLOBE PEQUOT PRESS**
P.O. Box 833, 6 Business Park Road,
Old Saybrook, CT 06475-0833
1-800-243-0495 fax 1-800-820-2329
www.globe-pequot.com